Excel Timesaving Techniques™ For Dummies®

Cheat Sheet

Greg's Favorite Timesave...

Here's a list of my favorite timesavers and where you can go to find ou... the book.

To Save Time	See Technique
Customizing the Excel screen display	1
Saving your worksheets where you can find them	4
Making the most efficient cell selections	10
Naming ranges so that you can select them and go to them in an instant	26
Creating formulas that trap error values so that they don't spread in the worksheet	29
Creating formulas that perform date and time calculations	30
Quickly finding the workbook you need to edit	31
Freezing panes in the worksheet display so that row and column headings are always visible	32
Preventing unwanted changes in the spreadsheet	38
Creating instant lists in Excel 2003	53

Setting Up Custom Views on Your Worksheet

Excel's Custom View feature can be a great timesaver in spreadsheets that you edit on a regular basis and that require you to frequently change the display settings of the Excel window in order to get these edits done.

You can use Excel's Custom View feature to save any of these types of changes to the worksheet display as a custom view. This way, instead of taking the time to manually set up the worksheet display that you want, you can have Excel re-create it for you simply by selecting the custom view. When you create a custom view, Excel can save any of the following settings:

- ✔ Current cell selection
- ✔ Print settings (including different page setups)
- ✔ Column widths and row heights (including hidden columns)
- ✔ Display settings on the View tab of the Options dialog box (Tools⇨Options)
- ✔ Current position and size of the spreadsheet window
- ✔ Window pane arrangement (including frozen panes)

See Technique 32 for details on how to set up custom views for a spreadsheet and use them to get the screen display just the way you need it in an instant.

For Dummies: Bestselling Book Series for Beginners

Excel Timesaving Techniques™ For Dummies®

Cheat Sheet

Function Key Shortcuts

Knowing and using the function keys in Excel can save you a great deal of time.

Function Key	Purpose
F1	Opens the Excel Help task pane.
Ctrl+F1	Displays and hides the current Excel task pane.
Alt+F1	Charts the selected range on a new chart sheet (same as F11).
F2	Edits the current cell and positions the insertion point at the end of its entry.
Shift+F2	Inserts a new comment into the current cell.
F3	Displays the Paste Name dialog box enabling you to paste a range name into the formula you're building.
Shift+F3	Displays the Insert Function dialog box (same as clicking the Insert Function button on the Formula bar).
F4	Cycles through the absolute cell reference, both kinds of mixed cell references (absolute row, relative column, and relative row and absolute column), and back to relative cell references when building or editing a formula.
Ctrl+F4	Closes the active workbook in Excel.
F5	Opens the Go To dialog box.
Ctrl+F5	Restores the window size of the active workbook window.
F6	Switches the cell pointer to the next pane in an Excel worksheet that's been split into panes.
Shift+F6	Switches the cell pointer to the previous pane in an Excel window that's been split into panes.
Ctrl+F6	Switches the cell pointer to the next window when more than one workbook window is open. Switches the cell pointer to the next pane clockwise when the worksheet is split into four panes.

Function Key	Purpose
F7	Opens the Spelling dialog box to spell check the worksheet when the worksheet contains unknown words or spelling errors.
F8	Turns EXT mode on and off. (EXT mode enables you to add to a cell selection with the cursor keys.)
Shift+F8	Turns ADD mode on and off. (ADD mode enables you to move the cell pointer without adding to a cell selection when defining a nonadjacent selection with the cursor keys.)
Alt+F8	Opens the Macro dialog box so you can run a macro you've defined.
F9	Recalculates all the worksheets in all open workbooks.
Shift+F9	Recalculates the current worksheet in the active workbook.
Ctrl+F9	Minimizes the selected workbook to an icon in the Excel window.
F10	Selects the Excel menu bar.
Shift+F10	Opens the shortcut menu for a selected item.
Ctrl+F10	Maximizes or restores the active minimized workbook.
F11	Charts the selected range on a new chart sheet (same as Alt+F1).
Shift+F11	Inserts a new worksheet in the workbook (same as Shift+F1).
Alt+F11	Opens Visual Basic Editor where you can edit the contents of a macro or custom function defined for the current workbook.
F12	Opens the Save As dialog box so that you can save your changes in a new workbook file.

Copyright © 2005 Wiley Publishing, Inc. All rights reserved.

Item 7427-2.

For more information about Wiley Publishing, call 1-800-762-2974.

For Dummies: Bestselling Book Series for Beginners

Excel Timesaving Techniques™

FOR DUMMIES®

Excel Timesaving Techniques™

FOR DUMMIES®

by Greg Harvey

WILEY

Wiley Publishing, Inc.

Excel Timesaving Techniques™ For Dummies®

Published by
Wiley Publishing, Inc.
909 Third Avenue
New York, NY 10022
www.wiley.com

For general information on our other products and services or to obtain technical support, please contact our Customer Care Department within the U.S. at 800-762-2974, outside the U.S. at 317-572-3993, or fax 317-572-4002.

Wiley also publishes its books in a variety of electronic formats. Some content that appears in print may not be available in electronic books.

Library of Congress Control Number: 2004112340

ISBN: 0-7645-7427-2

Manufactured in the United States of America

10 9 8 7 6 5 4 3 2 1

1V/SQ/RQ/QU/IN

WILEY

About the Author

Greg Harvey has authored tons of computer books, the most recent being *Adobe Acrobat 6 PDF For Dummies* and *Roxio Easy Media Creator For Dummies*. He started out training business users on how to use IBM personal computers and their attendant computer software in the rough and tumble days of DOS, WordStar, and Lotus 1-2-3 in the mid-80s of the last century. After working for a number of independent training firms, he went on to teach semester-long courses in spreadsheet and database management software at Golden Gate University in San Francisco.

His love of teaching has translated into an equal love of writing. For the last ten years or more, *For Dummies* books have been his favorites to write because they enable him to address his favorite audience, the beginner. They also enable him to use humor (a key element to success in the training room) and, most delightful of all, to express an opinion or two about the subject matter at hand.

Dedication

To all the people connected with the *For Dummies* phenomenon with whom I've had to the pleasure to work over the last decade, be they in the editing, management, production, or marketing end of the business, starting with IDG Books and extending to Hungry Minds and all the way up to Wiley Publishing: Thanks for the great memories and many good times!

Author's Acknowledgments

I am always so grateful to the many people who work so hard to bring my book projects into being, and this one is no exception. If anything, I am even more thankful for the talents given the special task-oriented nature of the *Timesaving Techniques* series.

This time, special thanks are in order to Andy Cummings and Tiffany Franklin for giving me this opportunity to write and write and write about Excel in this new *Timesaving Techniques* format. Next, I want to express great thanks to my project editor, Paul Levesque, for all his ready help and seasoned answers to my questions on the nature of this series and, to my partner in crime, Christopher Aiken (I really appreciate all your encouragement on this one). Thanks also go to Kim Darosett for the great copy edit, Doug Sahlin for the great technical edit, Courtney MacIntyre and Erin Smith for coordinating its production, and everybody at Wiley Publishing and TECHBOOKS Production Services for proofreading and indexing.

Publisher's Acknowledgments

We're proud of this book; please send us your comments through our online registration form located at www.dummies.com/register/.

Some of the people who helped bring this book to market include the following:

Acquisitions, Editorial, and Media Development

Project Editor: Paul Levesque

Acquisitions Editor: Tiffany Franklin

Senior Copy Editor: Kim Darosett

Technical Editor: Doug Sahlin

Editorial Manager: Kevin Kirschner

Media Development Manager: Laura VanWinkle

Media Development Supervisor: Richard Graves

Editorial Assistant: Amanda Foxworth

Cartoons: Rich Tennant (www.the5thwave.com)

Production

Project Coordinators: Courtney MacIntyre, Erin Smith

Layout and Graphics: Lauren Goddard, Stephanie D. Jumper, Michael Kruzil, Jacque Roth

Proofreaders: Jennifer Connolly, Carl Pierce, Dwight Ramsey, Brian H. Walls

Indexer: Joan Griffitts

Publishing and Editorial for Technology Dummies

Richard Swadley, Vice President and Executive Group Publisher

Andy Cummings, Vice President and Publisher

Mary Bednarek, Executive Acquisitions Director

Mary C. Corder, Editorial Director

Publishing for Consumer Dummies

Diane Graves Steele, Vice President and Publisher

Joyce Pepple, Acquisitions Director

Composition Services

Gerry Fahey, Vice President of Production Services

Debbie Stailey, Director of Composition Services

Contents at a Glance

Introduction   **1**

Part I: Making Excel Work Your Way   **5**

Technique 1: Customizing the Excel Screen Display   7

Technique 2: Customizing the Excel Menus and Toolbars   13

Technique 3: Perfecting Your Spreadsheet Workspace   19

Technique 4: Saving Your Worksheets So You Can Find Them   22

Technique 5: Tailoring Excel's Error Checking to Your Needs   27

Technique 6: Utilizing Excel's Editing Settings   31

Technique 7: Streamlining Excel Program Startup   36

Technique 8: Saving Time with Excel Add-ins   40

Part II: Quick Worksheet Creation Tricks   **45**

Technique 9: Navigating the Worksheet in a Snap   47

Technique 10: Making the Most Efficient Cell Selections   53

Technique 11: Speeding Through Long Data Entries with AutoCorrect   58

Technique 12: Data Entry Tricks   62

Technique 13: Speeding Up Data Entry with AutoFill   67

Technique 14: Ensuring Accurate Data Entries with Data Validation   72

Technique 15: All Aboard the Numerical Entry Express!   78

Technique 16: Verifying Entries with Text to Speech   82

Part III: Handy Ways to Format and Present Worksheet Data   **85**

Technique 17: Instant Range Formatting   87

Technique 18: Style Formatting Magic   92

Technique 19: Controlling When Certain Formats Are Used   97

Technique 20: Customizing Number Formats   102

Technique 21: Dazzling Alignments for Data Entries   111

Technique 22: Charting Data in a Snap   117

Technique 23: Chart Customization Tricks   123

Part IV: Worksheet Formula Timesavers   **129**

Technique 24: Efficient Formula Copying   131

Technique 25: Speeding Up Table Creation with Array Formulas   137

Technique 26: Using Range Names   141

Technique 27: Smarter Formula Construction   148

Technique 28: Trapping Those Terrible Errors   154

Technique 29: Eliminating Errors with Error Tracing   158

Technique 30: Creating Efficient Date and Time Formulas   164

Part V: Worksheet Editing Timesavers   **169**

Technique 31: Quickly Finding the Workbook You Want to Edit   171

Technique 32: Controlling the Worksheet Window Display   177

Technique 33: Managing Worksheet Windows   182

Technique 34: Quick and Easy Insertion and Deletion   187

Technique 35: Outline and Subtotal Magic   191

Technique 36: Consolidating Data from
Different Worksheets   195

Technique 37: Editing with Search & Replace
and Spell Check   199

**Part VI: Tips for Printing, Sharing,
and Reviewing Workbooks   205**

Technique 38: Spreadsheet Security   207

Technique 39: Printing Tricks for
Flawless Reports   219

Technique 40: Sharing Data with Other
Office Programs   230

Technique 41: Sharing Workbooks
on a Network   238

Technique 42: Sending Workbooks Out
for Review   247

**Part VII: Streamlining Data Listing
and Data Analysis   253**

Technique 43: Adding and Editing Data Lists
with the Data Form   255

Technique 44: Sorting Worksheet Data   261

Technique 45: Quick and Easy Basic Data
List Filtering   267

Technique 46: More Data List Filtering
plus Statistical Analysis   272

Technique 47: Doing What-if Analysis
in a Snap with Data Tables   280

Technique 48: Easy What-if Analysis through
Scenarios and Goal Seeking   284

Technique 49: Summarizing Data with
Pivot Tables and Pivot Charts   291

Part VIII: Internet-Related Timesavers   301

Technique 50: Saving Worksheets
as Web Pages   303

Technique 51: Importing Web Data
into the Worksheet   310

Technique 52: Using Hyperlinks to
Make Jumps in Workbooks   317

Part IX: The Scary (Or Fun) Stuff   323

Technique 53: Instant Lists in Excel 2003   325

Technique 54: Sharing Excel Workbooks
and Lists with a SharePoint Web Site   330

Technique 55: Entering Data and
Issuing Commands by Voice   337

Technique 56: Sprucing Up Your
Spreadsheets with Graphics   342

Technique 57: Doing Automated
Table Lookups   349

Technique 58: Using Text Formulas
for Fun and Profit   355

Technique 59: Creating Queries to Import
Data from an External Database   358

Technique 60: Automating Repetitive Tasks
with Macros   365

Technique 61: Creating Custom Functions
to Use in Your Worksheets   374

Index   379

Table of Contents

Introduction **1**

Saving Time with This Book 1

Foolish Assumptions 2

What's In This Book 2

Part I: Making Excel Work Your Way 2

Part II: Quick Worksheet Creation Tricks 2

Part III: Handy Ways to Format and Present Worksheet Data 2

Part IV: Worksheet Formula Timesavers 3

Part V: Worksheet Editing Timesavers 3

Part VI: Tips for Printing, Sharing, and Reviewing Workbooks 3

Part VII: Streamlining Data Listing and Data Analysis 3

Part VIII: Internet-Related Timesavers 3

Part IX: The Scary (Or Fun) Stuff 3

Icons Used in This Book 4

Where to Go from Here 4

Part 1: Making Excel Work Your Way **5**

Technique 1: Customizing the Excel Screen Display **7**

Standard Display Settings 8

Switching to Full Screen 8

Customizing the Worksheet Display 9

Setting a new standard column width 9

Setting a new standard row height 10

Modifying the number of sheets in a workbook 10

Customizing the worksheet gridlines 11

Saving Custom Display Settings 11

Creating a template 11

Using a template 12

Technique 2: Customizing the Excel Menus and Toolbars **13**

Showing the Toolbars and Menus in All Their Glory 13

Toolbars and Menus Made to Order 14

A Toolbar and Menu of Your Own 16

Adding Macros and Links to Toolbars and Menus 17

Technique 3: Perfecting Your Spreadsheet Workspace **19**

Saving Your Workspace 19

Opening a Workspace Whenever Excel Launches 20

Technique 4: Saving Your Worksheets So You Can Find Them **22**

Modifying the Default File Location 23

Saving New Files with Summary Information 24

Changing the AutoRecover Settings 25

Technique 5: Tailoring Excel's Error Checking to Your Needs **27**

Modifying the Error Checking Settings 28

Suppressing All Error Indicators 29

Hiding Error Values On-Screen and in Print 29

Technique 6: Utilizing Excel's Editing Settings **31**

Putting the Cell Pointer in the Right Direction 32

Completely Turned Off to AutoComplete 32

Doing the Drag-and-Drop Thing 33

Please make room for me 33

When drag-and-drop flops 33

Doing Direct Cell Editing 34

Technique 7: Streamlining Excel Program Startup **36**

Excel Desktop Shortcut 36

Adding Excel to the Quick Launch Toolbar 37

Pinning Excel to the Start Menu 38

Launching Excel on Windows Startup 39

Technique 8: Saving Time with Excel Add-ins **40**

Installing Add-ins 40

Using the Built-in Add-ins 41

Getting Online Add-ins 42

Part II: Quick Worksheet Creation Tricks   45

Technique 9: Navigating the Worksheet in a Snap   47
Saving the Cell Pointer's Position   47
Going Direct   48
    Leaping through data ranges and hopping over blanks   *48*
    Going right to the last cell in a sheet   *49*
    Zipping through the sheets   *50*
A Little Go To Magic   51
Zooming Out to Get the Big Picture   52

Technique 10: Making the Most Efficient Cell Selections   53
AutoSelect at Your Service   54
Go To It and Select It   55
Going for the Big Selections   56

Technique 11: Speeding Through Long Data Entries with AutoCorrect   58
Setting the Correct AutoCorrect Settings   58
Losing the Links   59
Taming the Smart Tags   60

Technique 12: Data Entry Tricks   62
Making the Same Entry in Many Places   62
Putting the Wraps on the Data Entry   63
Let's Do It as a Group!   65

Technique 13: Speeding Up Data Entry with AutoFill   67
Getting Your Fill of AutoFill   67
    Using AutoFill to generate a sequentially numbered series   *69*
    Copying an entry instead of filling in a series   *69*
Incrementally Speaking   70
Fill Lists Made to Order   71

Technique 14: Ensuring Accurate Data Entries with Data Validation   72
Only the Valid Need Apply   72
    Data entries from a list   *73*
    Copying data validation settings   *74*
    Finding cells using data validation   *75*

Information Please!   75
Warnings to Make Them Wary   76

Technique 15: All Aboard the Numerical Entry Express!   78
Taking Advantage of the Numeric Keypad   78
Putting the Decimal Places at Your Service   79
Number Please!   80

Technique 16: Verifying Entries with Text to Speech   82
"Can You Hear Me Now?"   82
    Speak on Enter   *83*
    Reading by columns and rows   *83*
Modifying the Text to Speech Settings   84

Part III: Handy Ways to Format and Present Worksheet Data   85

Technique 17: Instant Range Formatting   87
Head-to-Toe Table Formatting with AutoFormat   87
Getting Artistic with the Format Painter   89
Cutting and Pasting Formats Only   90

Technique 18: Style Formatting Magic   92
Styling   93
    Applying predefined styles in a spreadsheet   *93*
    Customizing predefined styles   *94*
Creating Styles of Your Own   94
Merging Styles from One Book into Another   95

Technique 19: Controlling When Certain Formats Are Used   97
Formats to Suit Every Condition   97
    When two conditions are better than one   *99*
    Finding cells with conditional formatting   *100*
Making Your Outstanding Errors Stand Out   100

Technique 20: Customizing Number Formats   102
Creating Custom Number Formats   102
    Custom formats that conditionally format entries   *105*
    Custom formats that hide certain entries   *106*

Assigning Custom Number Formats to Styles
and Toolbars 107

Applying Euro Currency Formats 109

Technique 21: Dazzling Alignments for Data Entries 111

Line Me Up 111
Indenting data entries 112
Using nonstandard vertical alignment 113
Rotating text entries 113
Getting Your Text under Control 114
Making text wrap within a cell 114
Shrinking the text to fit within a cell 115
Centering a heading across columns 116

Technique 22: Charting Data in a Snap 117

Instant Charts 117
Chart Wizard Magic 119

Technique 23: Chart Customization Tricks 123

Getting the Chart Titles and Headings
in Balance 123
Scaling and Formatting the Chart Axes 125
Tricks for Making the Plotted Data Easier
to Decipher 127

Part IV: Worksheet Formula Timesavers 129

Technique 24: Efficient Formula Copying 131

Going from Relative to Absolute 131
When It's Copy Time 133
*Making one-dimensional copies down
or across* 134
*Making two-dimensional copies both down
and across* 135

Technique 25: Speeding Up Table Creation with Array Formulas 137

A Quick Look at Array Ranges 137
Hurray for Array Formulas! 138
Editing Array Formulas 140

Technique 26: Using Range Names 141

Name That Range! 141
*Creating names from row and
column headings* 142
*Assigning range names that span
different sheets* 143
Assigning Range Names to Constants 144
Using Your Range Names in Formulas 144
Using range names in new formulas 145
Assigning range names to existing formulas 145

Technique 27: Smarter Formula Construction 148

Pointing Out Cell References in Formulas 148
Putting the Insert Function Feature
at Your Service 150
Using Labels Instead of Cell References
in Formulas 152

Technique 28: Trapping Those Terrible Errors 154

If I Were a Logical Function 154
Trapping Division by Zero Errors 155
Trapping All Types of Error Values 156

Technique 29: Eliminating Errors with Error Tracing 158

Formula Auditing 101 158
Tracing Formula Precedents 160
Tracing Formula Dependents 161
Finding the Original Error and Fixing Its
Formula 162

Technique 30: Creating Efficient Date and Time Formulas 164

The Deal with Dates and Times 164
You Do the Date Math! 165
When Your Time Is Up 166

Part V: Worksheet Editing Timesavers 169

Technique 31: Quickly Finding the Workbook You Want to Edit 171
Opening Recently Used Files 171
Making the Most of the File Search Task Pane 172
   Doing a basic file search 172
   Conducting the file search and using the results 173
   Doing an advanced file search 174
Searching for Files in the Open Dialog Box 175

Technique 32: Controlling the Worksheet Window Display 177
Zooming In for the Edits 177
Frozen Panes in My Windows 179
A Worksheet with a Custom View 180

Technique 33: Managing Worksheet Windows 182
Opening Panes in the Worksheet Window 182
Comparing Sheets in the Same Workbook 184
Comparing Sheets in Separate Workbooks 185

Technique 34: Quick and Easy Insertion and Deletion 187
Inserting and Deleting Cells in an Existing Range 187
Inserting and Deleting Rows and Columns 188
Inserting and Deleting Worksheets 190

Technique 35: Outline and Subtotal Magic 191
Adding Outline Levels to a Table or List 191
Subtotaling a Table or List 193

Technique 36: Consolidating Data from Different Worksheets 195
Consolidating Data by Position 195
Consolidating Data by Category 197
Linking Consolidated Data 197

Technique 37: Editing with Search & Replace and Spell Check 199
Using Find and Replace 199
Eliminating Typing Errors with Spell Check 201
   Customizing the Spell Check settings 202
   Adding words to a custom dictionary 203

Part VI: Tips for Printing, Sharing, and Reviewing Workbooks 205

Technique 38: Spreadsheet Security 207
Assigning a Password for Opening a Workbook 207
   Opening a password-protected workbook 209
   Changing or deleting passwords 210
Protecting the Worksheet Against Unwanted Changes 211
   Unlocking cells for data entry 211
   Turning on worksheet protection 212
   Removing protection from a worksheet 213
   Enabling cell range editing by certain users 214
   Protecting the structure of the workbook file 216
Hiding Sensitive Worksheet Data 217

Technique 39: Printing Tricks for Flawless Reports 219
Making Last-Minute Adjustments with Print Preview 219
   Manipulating the margins and column widths 221
   Manipulating the page settings 221
Controlling Bad Page Breaks 222
   Using the Page Break Preview feature 223
   Changing the scale of the printing 224
Adding Headings to Your Report 225
   Headers and footers made to order 225
   Print titles on every page 226
Printing the Formulas in the Report 227
Printing the Charts in the Report 228

Technique 40: Sharing Data with Other Office Programs 230
Swapping Data via the Clipboard 230
Importing Text Files into Excel 232
Embedding Excel Data in Other Office Documents 235
   Embedded worksheet data 235
   Linking worksheet data 237

Technique 41: Sharing Workbooks on a Network 238
Let's All Learn to Share 238
   Editing changes not available to a shared workbook 239
   Sharing a workbook 239

Setting your sharing options	*240*
Turning on change tracking	*241*
Merging Changes from Different Users	243
Conflict resolution worksheet style	*243*
Accepting or rejecting highlighted changes	*244*
Turning off file sharing	*245*
Merging Different Copies of a Shared Workbook	245
Distributing the copies	*245*
Merging the changes	*246*

Technique 42: Sending Workbooks Out for Review — **247**

Getting a Workbook Ready for Review	247
Getting your two cents in	*248*
Comments: Now you see them, now you don't	*248*
Editing and formatting comments	*248*
Deleting comments in a worksheet	*249*
Sending Out a Workbook for Review	250
Replying with changes	*250*
Merging changes into the original workbook	*250*

Part VII: Streamlining Data Listing and Data Analysis — *253*

Technique 43: Adding and Editing Data Lists with the Data Form — **255**

Creating a New Data List and Data Form	255
Adding new records with the data form	*257*
Finding records with the data form	*258*
Editing records in the data form	*259*
Removing records from the data list with the data form	*260*

Technique 44: Sorting Worksheet Data — **261**

Don't Be Out of Sorts	261
Sorting records in a data list	*262*
Sorting on a record number field to restore a list to its original order	*264*
Sorting a list on more than three key fields	*264*
Sorting the Field Names in a Data List	265

Technique 45: Quick and Easy Basic Data List Filtering — **267**

AutoFilter Basics	267
Making it into the top-ten list	*268*
Saving subsets of a data list as custom views	*269*
Customizing the AutoFilter Settings	270

Technique 46: More Data List Filtering plus Statistical Analysis — **272**

Putting the Advanced Filter in Service	272
Specifying filtering criteria	*274*
Setting up AND and OR filtering criteria	*274*
Setting up calculated filtering criteria	*276*
Getting Data List Statistics	277

Technique 47: Doing What-if Analysis in a Snap with Data Tables — **280**

Creating a One-Variable Data Table	280
Creating a Two-Variable Data Table	282

Technique 48: Easy What-if Analysis through Scenarios and Goal Seeking — **284**

Exploring Different Scenarios	284
Reaching a Target with Goal Seeking	288
Performing goal seeking	*288*
Goal seeking graph style	*289*

Technique 49: Summarizing Data with Pivot Tables and Pivot Charts — **291**

Creating Pivot Tables	291
Pivoting the fields in the table	*294*
Formatting the values in the pivot table	*295*
Selecting new summary functions	*296*
Creating a calculated field for the pivot table	*297*
Creating a Pivot Chart	298

Part VIII: Internet-Related Timesavers — *301*

Technique 50: Saving Worksheets as Web Pages — **303**

Saving Worksheets as Web Pages	303
Opening your new Web page at the time you save it	*305*
Saving all the worksheets in a workbook	*305*
Saving just part of a worksheet	*306*
Adding data to an existing Web page	*306*
Creating Interactive Web Pages	307

Technique 51: Importing Web Data into the Worksheet   **310**

Capturing Information for the Spreadsheet with Web Queries   310

Importing XML Data into a Worksheet   313

Technique 52: Using Hyperlinks to Make Jumps in Workbooks   **317**

Adding Hyperlinks to a Worksheet   317

Following Links in a Worksheet   320

Editing Links in a Worksheet   321

Creating Hyperlinks for Custom Menus and Toolbars   321

Part IX: The Scary (Or Fun) Stuff   **323**

Technique 53: Instant Lists in Excel 2003   **325**

Creating an Excel 2003 List   325

Converting an existing list into an Excel list   *326*

Creating an Excel list from scratch   *327*

Sorting and Filtering the List   327

Toggling the List's Total Row On and Off   328

Easy List Editing   328

Inserting or deleting rows and columns   *329*

Converting a list back into a regular cell range   *329*

Deleting a list   *329*

Technique 54: Sharing Excel Workbooks and Lists with a SharePoint Web Site   **330**

Adding Excel Spreadsheets to the SharePoint Site   330

Opening the spreadsheets on the SharePoint site   *332*

Adding a list of your spreadsheets to SharePoint site home page   *333*

Publishing Lists to the SharePoint Site   334

Publishing an Excel list on a SharePoint site   *334*

Synchronizing list data   *336*

Technique 55: Entering Data and Issuing Commands by Voice   **337**

Hands-Free Data Entry   337

Just Tell Me What to Do   339

Choosing menu items, dialog box options, and toolbar buttons   *340*

Telling the cell pointer "where to go"   *340*

Technique 56: Sprucing Up Your Spreadsheets with Graphics   **342**

Jazz It Up with Clip Art   342

Adding Images from Graphics Files   343

Drawing Objects for the Spreadsheet   344

Drawing various shapes   *345*

Using text boxes as callouts   *346*

Making a statement with WordArt   *346*

Drawing diagrams and organization charts   *347*

Technique 57: Doing Automated Table Lookups   **349**

Looking Up a Single Table Value   349

Performing a vertical table lookup   *350*

Performing a horizontal lookup   *351*

Doing a Two-Way Lookup in a Data Table   352

Technique 58: Using Text Formulas for Fun and Profit   **355**

Getting Right on the Case   355

Joining Separate Text Entries Together   356

Replacing Text Formulas with Their Results   357

Technique 59: Creating Queries to Import Data from an External Database   **358**

Setting Up the Data Source Definition   358

Creating the Database Query   360

Technique 60: Automating Repetitive Tasks with Macros   **365**

Recording and Playing Back Macros   365

Recording the macro   *366*

Playing back the macro   *368*

Editing Macros in the Visual Basic Editor   369

Modifying the settings for VBA properties   *370*

Getting user input by adding a custom dialog box   *371*

Technique 61: Creating Custom Functions to Use in Your Worksheets   **374**

Creating Custom Functions   374

Saving Custom Functions in an Excel Add-in   376

Index   **379**

Introduction

F ew things are more disappointing to me as a software trainer than to see people who have just enough basic knowledge to work in a sophisticated program such as Excel waste inordinate amounts of time doing their work "the hard way" because they don't really know how to go about harnessing the program's features. This book is a vehicle for taking that next step into efficient use of Microsoft Excel, a program about which I have written a great deal and am naturally very partial. It is my sincere hope that it helps you become not only more competent in Excel but also much more confident in your ability to use rather than be used by it.

Saving Time with This Book

The *Timesaving Techniques For Dummies* books focus on high-payoff techniques that save you time, either on the spot or somewhere down the road. These books get to the point in a hurry, with step-by-step instructions to pace you through the tasks you need to do, without any of the fluff you don't want. I've identified more than 60 techniques that Excel users need to know to make the most of their time. In addition, each technique includes lots of figures that make following along a breeze. Decide for yourself how to use this book: Read it from cover to cover if you like or skip right to the technique that interests you the most.

In *Excel Timesaving Techniques For Dummies,* you can find out how to

- ✔ **Tame time-consuming tasks:** Because I demystify the inner workings of Excel for you, letting you in on more than 60 tips and tricks along the way, you can spend more time on creating great results and less time on fiddling with a feature so that it works correctly.

- ✔ **Take your skills up a notch:** You're already familiar with the basics of using Excel. Now this book takes you to the next level, helping you become an even savvier Excel user.

✔ **Customize Excel to meet your needs:** Spending some upfront time customizing Excel so that it works faster, more reliably, and more like how you work on a daily basis can save you time (and aggravation) later.

✔ **Automate repetitive tasks:** This book shows you how to lighten your work load by taking fewer steps to do everyday tasks, especially those involving data entry and formatting in the worksheet.

Foolish Assumptions

I'm only going to make one foolish assumption about you and that is that you use Microsoft Excel in your work or studies at the basic level. If pushed, I further guess that you aren't particularly interested in knowing Excel at an expert level but are terribly motivated to find out how to do the stuff you need to get done more efficiently. If that's the case, then this is definitely the book for you. Fortunately, even if you happen to be one of those users who's highly motivated to become the company's resident spreadsheet guru, you've still come to the right place.

As far as your hardware and software go, I'm assuming that you already have a version of Excel between Excel 97 and 2003 (the latest) installed on your computer and that you're using a standard installation running on a version of Windows between Windows 95 and Windows XP or Windows 2000. Although the figures in this book all show Excel 2003 happily running on Windows XP, it makes no difference to most of the written instructions if you're using an earlier version of Excel on an earlier version of Windows.

What's In This Book

Excel Timesaving Techniques For Dummies is divided into nine parts that contain loosely related techniques for working smarter and faster. That way,

you can go after the procedures in the particular part of the book that really interest you at the time, putting all the rest of the tips and tricks aside until you need to have a look at them. In case you're the least bit curious, here's the lowdown on each part and the types of techniques you can expect to find there.

Part I: Making Excel Work Your Way

These techniques enable you to cut through the Excel screen clutter and get the program to work and look the way you want it. Find out how to customize everything from the Excel screen display to the pull-down menus and toolbars. You also find out how to streamline program startup and save time by knowing exactly where you saved the spreadsheet you worked on the day before.

Part II: Quick Worksheet Creation Tricks

The techniques in this part are dedicated to showing you more efficient ways not only to build your spreadsheets but also to make them more accurate. Here you find out how to quickly navigate the worksheet, make proficient cell selections, and do data entry like the pros. In addition, you find out how to ensure accurate entries with Excel's data validation and Text to Speech features.

Part III: Handy Ways to Format and Present Worksheet Data

This part contains the techniques that you need to easily and quickly make the data in your worksheet its most presentable. Here you find out how to instantly format tables of data through a combination of tips and tricks. You also find out how to create and apply custom number formats and select the alignment features best suited to the particular data you're working with. Finally, you find out how to quickly conjure up charts and graphs that can demonstrate trends and analyses otherwise hidden in the data itself.

Part IV: Worksheet Formula Timesavers

The techniques in this part are devoted to enabling you to create efficient and well-formed formulas in your Excel spreadsheets. Here you find out how to accurately copy formulas using all types of cell references, greatly speed up table creation through the use of array formulas, and document formulas through the sagacious use of range names. As if this weren't enough, you also find out how to create formulas that trap Excel error values and prevent them from spreading far and wide throughout the spreadsheet and, in the event that they do succeed in getting out, how to trace their source and eliminate them on the spot.

Part V: Worksheet Editing Timesavers

The techniques in this part center on how to make efficient editing changes in a completed spreadsheet. Knowing these techniques can save you oodles of time if you're among the more common worksheet users who spend a majority of the time adding to and updating existing company workbooks. Here you find out how to quickly find the workbook you want to edit, control the Excel screen display so you can see what you're editing at all times, use the editing tips and tricks of the pros, as well as consolidate data from several worksheets and subtotal their data without even breaking a sweat.

Part VI: Tips for Printing, Sharing, and Reviewing Workbooks

Tops among the techniques in this part is the first one on spreadsheet security and how to protect your sensitive data from unwarranted opening or edits without ending up being locked out of the file yourself. Here you also find out how to produce flawless printed reports, share Excel data with the other programs you run, share your workbook files on a local network, and send your files out to coworkers and clients for a formal review.

Part VII: Streamlining Data Listing and Data Analysis

This part is dedicated to skillful means for turning great quantities of raw data into usable information. Here you find techniques for organizing, searching, sorting, and filtering the data you keep. You are also introduced to what-if analysis and data summation in all its glory in the form of data tables, scenarios, goal seeking, and those wonderful pivot tables and pivot charts.

Part VIII: Internet-Related Timesavers

The techniques in this part give you the inside track on sharing Excel data on the World Wide Web. Here you find out how to instantly convert your Excel worksheet data and charts into HTML documents ready to publish to your Web pages either on the Internet or your company's intranet. You also find out how to easily import data from Web pages directly into Excel where you can manipulate the data to your heart's content and how to add hyperlinks to your worksheets to make any kind of jump you need, from one worksheet to another in the same workbook all the way to any address on the Internet.

Part IX: The Scary (Or Fun) Stuff

This last part contains a potpourri of techniques, some of which are thrown in for the fun of it and others that you may at first perceive to be somewhat of a stretch. (I don't actually include techniques here that you really need to apprehensive of.) Among the fun techniques, you find out how to use Excel 2003 lists (which are a real delight and are so easy they almost create themselves), how to do worksheet data entry and issue Excel commands with the power of your voice, and how to spruce up the look of your spreadsheets with art images (both those you draw and others you import).

Among the less instantly comfortable techniques in this part are creating lookup formulas that return data from schedules and other data tables, creating text formulas that manipulate text entries that were entered in the wrong case or which you need to combine, setting up queries to the corporate database that return data to the Excel worksheet, using macros to automate all those repetitive tasks, and creating custom functions for instantly performing specialized calculations not covered by any of Excel's built-in functions.

Icons Used in this Book

I have strategically placed the following icons throughout all 61 techniques in this book. Their purpose is to get you to pay close attention to something I'm saying, and each has its own way of doing that.

 This icon denotes some really cool information (in my humble opinion) that, if you pay particular attention to, will pay off by making your work more enjoyable or productive (or both).

 This icon denotes a tidbit that you ought to pay extra attention to; otherwise, you may end up taking a detour that wastes valuable time.

 This icon denotes a tidbit that you ought to pay extra attention to; otherwise, you'll be sorry. I reserve this icon for those times when you can lose data and otherwise mess up your spreadsheet.

 This icon denotes some extra tip or trick tidbit that can end up saving you even more time, especially when used in tandem with the general points being made in the current technique.

Where to Go from Here

The question of where to go from here couldn't be simpler: Head off to read the great Rich Tennant cartoons at the beginning of each of the nine parts, of course. Which part and technique you jump into after that is a matter of personal interest and need. Just don't forget to have fun while discovering how to work smarter and faster in Excel.

Part I

Making Excel Work Your Way

The 5th Wave   By Rich Tennant

"Our automated response policy to a large
company-wide data crash is to notify
management, back up existing data, and
sell 90% of my shares in the company."

Technique

Customizing the Excel Screen Display

Save Time By

✓ Switching in and out of Full Screen view

✓ Customizing sheet and workbook settings

✓ Saving your custom settings in a workbook template

What can I say? The Excel program window (shown in Figure 1-1) is a busy place. Filled with all kinds of buttons and bars, it's a wonder that there's any place left for entering your precious spreadsheet data. Therefore, the first technique that any dedicated Excel user needs to know is how to control the look and feel of the Excel display screen.

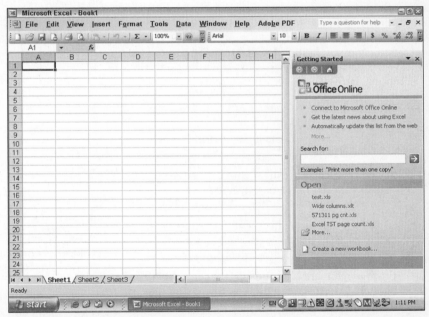

• **Figure 1-1: Is it Grand Central Station? No, just the Excel program screen.**

Here you find out how to max out the worksheet display so that you access as many cells and as much of your spreadsheet data as possible, thus saving you from having to waste a lot of your precious time just scrolling up and down and back and forth to view the cells you need to work with. You also find out how to customize the display so that it represents more the type of spreadsheets you create and then how to save these custom display settings in worksheet templates that enable you to immediately utilize all these settings in new workbooks you generate from them.

Standard Display Settings

Controlling the Excel display screen includes not only hiding unwanted toolbars that surround the worksheet but also modifying the sheet's look and feel. Each time you launch Excel, the program opens a new workbook whose sheets use a whole bunch of standard display settings.

These standard settings consist of the following:

✔ Three blank worksheets each identified by their own sheet tabs.

✔ 256 columns in each sheet with a standard width of 8.43 characters (64 pixels) and labeled with a column header using letters (A through IV).

✔ 65,536 rows in each sheet with a standard row height of 12.75 points (17 pixels) and labeled with a row header (1 through 65536).

✔ Gridlines demarcating the edge of each sheet's columns and rows and thereby displaying the outline of each worksheet cell.

Switching to Full Screen

The fastest and simplest way to remove the screen clutter caused by the Excel toolbars and thereby

maximize the number of cells displayed on your screen is by switching to Full Screen view (View⇨ Full Screen). As soon as you choose this command, Excel temporarily hides any open toolbars. The program also gets rid of the Formula bar at the top and the sheet tabs, the horizontal scroll bar, and the program's Status bar at the bottom, leaving only the Worksheet menu bar, column and row headers, vertical scroll bar, and Windows taskbar surrounding the blank worksheet cells (see Figure 1-2).

In Full Screen view, Excel displays a floating Full Screen toolbar in the lower-right corner of the screen. To switch back into normal screen view, simply click the toolbar's Close Full Screen button. Excel closes the Full Screen toolbar and restores all the missing toolbars.

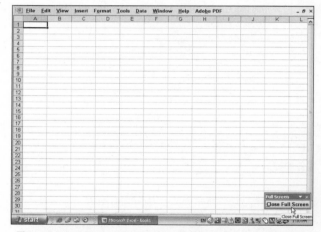

• **Figure 1-2: Maximizing the worksheet real estate in Full Screen view.**

Working without the benefit of the Formula bar is fine as long as all you're doing is entering scads of spreadsheet data or checking up on your data entries. If, however, you're doing more than this kind of simple data entry and editing, you'll probably need to have the Formula bar displayed on the screen. To display the Formula bar while Excel is in Full Screen view, follow these steps:

1. **Choose Tool⇨Options.**

2. **Select the View tab in the Options dialog box.**

3. **Select the Formula Bar check box and then click OK to close the Options dialog box.**

After displaying the Formula bar when the program is in Full Screen view, it continues to appear on the screen as you switch in and out of Full Screen view. If you decide that you don't need the Formula bar on the screen in Full Screen view, deselect the Formula Bar check box in Step 3 of the preceding steps.

 Auto-hiding the Windows taskbar gives you a little more worksheet real estate. Just right-click the Start button and choose Properties to open the Taskbar and Start Menu Properties dialog box. Click the Taskbar button in this dialog box and then select the Auto-Hide the Taskbar check box and click OK. After that, Windows keeps the taskbar hidden until you position the mouse pointer somewhere along the bottom of the screen. As soon as you move the mouse pointer out of this area, Windows hides the taskbar again.

Customizing the Worksheet Display

Excel offers all sorts of ways to customize the appearance of the worksheet display. Here's a sampling of what you can do:

✔ Modify the width of some or all the columns and rows in any of the three worksheets.

✔ Change the number of sheets in the workbook.

✔ Control whether the worksheet gridlines that define the boundaries of each cell are hidden or displayed and determine the color used when they are shown on-screen.

Setting a new standard column width

If you're working on a spreadsheet that almost universally requires a different standard column width (usually one wider than the 8.43 characters or 64 pixels standard), you can easily set a default width for every column in the worksheet:

1. **Choose Format⇨Column⇨Standard Width.**

Excel opens the Standard Width dialog box, shown in Figure 1-3.

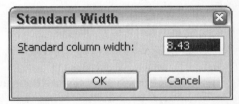

• **Figure 1-3:** Designating a new standard width for the columns in a worksheet.

2. **Enter the new width in characters (between 0 and 255) in the Standard Column Width text box.**

 Setting a column width to 0 is the equivalent of hiding the column in the worksheet by choosing Format⇨Column⇨Hide. You can use this technique to hide columns you use in calculating certain worksheet formulas but don't necessarily want printed as part of the final spreadsheet. However, if you enter 0 here as the new standard width, you hide all the columns in the worksheet, making it impossible to add, edit, or print data in any of its cells!

3. **Click OK to close the Standard Width dialog box.**

Changing the value in the Standard Width dialog box changes the default column width for all the columns in only the active worksheet. Using this command has no effect on the width of columns that you manually resized or resized with the AutoFit feature.

 If you want to change the default column width for all the worksheets in your workbook, select all the sheets (by Ctrl+clicking their sheet tabs or right-clicking the tab of the active sheet and then clicking Select All Sheets on the shortcut menu) before you open the Standard Width dialog box and set a new default value.

Setting a new standard row height

Note that Excel doesn't provide an equivalent command for setting a new default height for all the rows in a worksheet. This is probably because the program automatically adjusts the height of the row to accommodate the data that you enter in its columns. If you're creating a spreadsheet where you would benefit by having a new standard row height (presumably, a taller one), you can set all the rows in the worksheet to a new height by using this work-around:

1. **Click a letter in the Column header.**

Clicking a column letter in the Column header selects all the rows in that column in the worksheet.

2. **Choose Format➪Row➪Height.**

Excel opens the Row Height dialog box, shown in Figure 1-4.

• **Figure 1-4: Designating a new row height for all the selected rows in a worksheet.**

3. **Enter the new row height in characters (between 0 and 255) in the Row Height text box.**

 Setting the row height to 0 is the equivalent of hiding the row in the worksheet by choosing Format➪Row➪Hide. You can use this technique to hide rows you use in calculating worksheet formulas but don't necessarily want to appear in the printout. However, if you enter 0 here when all the rows of the worksheet are selected, standard width, you hide all the rows in the entire worksheet, making it impossible to add, edit, or print data in any of its cells!

4. **Click the OK button to close the Row Height dialog box.**

Excel changes the height of all the rows in the worksheet.

To remove the cell selection from all the rows in the column whose heading you clicked, click any single cell with the mouse pointer.

Modifying the number of sheets in a workbook

In the olden days of Excel, when the program first started supporting the use of more than one worksheet in a single spreadsheet file, the program automatically provided each new workbook that you opened in the program with 17 blank worksheets. In the more recent versions of Excel (all those in the 2000 series), the program default has been lowered to a much more modest three sheets in every new workbook. For some users, 17 was far too many sheets for their modest spreadsheet needs, and for others, three sheets are far too few for the types of complex spreadsheets they routinely create.

Although Excel makes it easy to insert new worksheets in a workbook (you simply choose Insert➪Worksheet to pop a new one in), if you find yourself having to manually add new sheets to many of the new workbooks you start, you should probably modify the default number of sheets that Excel adds to all new workbooks:

1. Choose Tools⇨Options to open the Options dialog box.

2. Select the General tab in the Options dialog box.

3. Enter a new value between 1 and 255 in the Sheets in a New Workbook text box or select this value with the box's spinner buttons; then click OK.

After changing the value in the Sheets in a New Workbook text box, Excel adds that number of sheets to any new workbook you create.

Customizing the worksheet gridlines

When creating a standard spreadsheet application such as the standard profit and loss statement and balance sheet, the worksheet gridlines that are automatically displayed in all new worksheets provide a much needed background with which to visually align the data. In other, more nonstandard applications such as online forms and presentations with embedded charts, gridlines not only are often confusing to the eye but actually interfere with the presentation of the information the sheet contains.

To give the heave-ho to a worksheet's gridlines in the current worksheet, follow these steps:

1. Choose Tools⇨Options to open the Options dialog box.

2. Select the View tab in the Options dialog box.

3. Deselect the Gridlines check box and then click OK.

Turning off gridlines in a worksheet display has no effect on whether or not the gridlines appear on paper when the sheet is printed. To prevent Excel from adding gridlines to a printed report, the Gridlines check box on the Sheet tab in the Page Setup dialog box (File⇨ Page Setup) must not be selected before you send the sheet to the printer. You check this in print preview.

When you display the column and row gridlines on the screen, Excel uses your Windows desktop settings to determine what color to assign the gridlines (usually, they appear in light blue). If you want to assign a new, perhaps bolder, color to the gridlines, follow these steps:

1. Choose Tools⇨Options to open the Options dialog box.

2. Select the View tab in the Options dialog box.

3. Select the Gridlines Color drop-down list box, select the new color in the pop-up color palette, and click OK.

When you select a new color for the gridlines, it doesn't just affect how the gridlines appear on your screen. Excel also uses this color in printing the gridlines in a worksheet when the Gridlines check box is selected on the Sheet tab in the Page Setup dialog box.

Saving Custom Display Settings

While it's all well and good that Excel gives you plenty of choices for customizing its screen display, it sure would be a waste of time if you had to manually modify all the various screen settings each time you started working on a new workbook. Fortunately, you can save your custom display settings as an Excel template, and then any time you need to generate a new spreadsheet that uses those settings, you can do so simply by opening the template.

Creating a template

To create an Excel template with your custom display settings, follow these steps:

1. Launch Excel and then manually make all the changes to the display settings that you want saved in the new template.

When making changes to display settings for a template, select the settings that you find yourself manually changing over and over again (such as inserting an additional worksheet, removing the gridlines, and selecting a new standard column width). When entering display values (such a new default column width or row height), select the value.

2. Choose File⇨Save or click the Save button on the Standard toolbar to open the Save As dialog box.

3. From the Save as Type drop-down list, choose Template (*.xlt), as shown in Figure 1-5.

• **Figure 1-5:** Selecting Template (·.xlt) as the file type for saving a new worksheet template.

4. Highlight the temporary filename (Book1, Book2, and so on) in the File Name combo box (be sure you don't select the .xlt filename extension) and then type in a descriptive name for the new template.

When replacing the temporary filename with one of your own, pick a brief name that describes the new settings, such as 15 Wide Col, No Gridlines, or 4-Sht Book. Be aware that when you generate a workbook from the template you're creating, Excel uses the main

filename in the workbook's temporary filename as in 15 Wide Col1, No Gridlines2, and 4-Sht Book3.

5. Click Save to close the Save As dialog box and save your settings in the new template file.

Using a template

To use your template to generate a new workbook with your custom display settings, follow these steps:

1. If the template is currently open, close it by choosing File⇨Close on the menu bar or by pressing Ctrl+W.

   You must close a new template file before you can generate files from it.

2. Choose File⇨New to open the New Workbook task pane.

To use your new template, don't click the **New** button on the Standard toolbar or press the keystroke shortcut Ctrl+N. Doing so automatically opens a new workbook using the Excel out-of-the-box settings, giving you no opportunity to generate the new book from any other template. Choose File⇨New on the menu bar instead.

3. Select the On My Computer link under the Templates section of the New Workbook task pane.

   The Templates dialog box opens.

4. Double-click the name of the template you want to use, or click its name and then click OK.

Excel opens up a new blank workbook from the template file, using all the custom display settings that you saved as part of it.

Technique 2

Customizing the Excel Menus and Toolbars

Save Time By

- ✔ Displaying full toolbars and menus
- ✔ Customizing toolbars and menus
- ✔ Creating your own menus
- ✔ Adding macros and links to toolbars and menus

This technique centers on customizing the Excel toolbars and pull-down menus. Taking the time to get the Excel toolbars (especially the Standard and Formatting toolbars that Excel automatically displays whenever you launch the program) and the pull-down menus the way you want them saves you valuable time when creating and editing your spreadsheets. (Just think about how many times you access their buttons and menu items in a single work session, and you'll understand why.)

Excel makes it easy to customize the position, behavior, and even content of its many toolbars and pull-down menus. This customization includes placing the Standard and Formatting toolbars on two separate rows, always displaying full pull-down menus, and customizing the buttons and command options found on the built-in bars and menus as well as those found on the bars and menus you build on your own.

Showing the Toolbars and Menus in All Their Glory

Excel tries to save valuable screen space by automatically placing the Standard and Formatting toolbars on the same row at the top of the screen. This is fine except for when you're using one a smaller monitor in a relatively low screen resolution (such as 800 x 600 or 1024 x 768) where it's impossible to have all the buttons on either toolbar display at the same time and where you're often forced to waste time in clicking the Toolbar Options button to have access to options that are currently hidden.

To ensure that all the buttons on both the Standard and Formatting toolbars are always displayed, follow these steps:

1. **Choose View⇨Toolbars⇨Customize to open the Customize dialog box.**

2. **Select the Options tab in the Customize dialog box, as shown in Figure 2-1.**

3. **Select the Show Standard and Formatting Toolbars on Two Rows check box and then click the Close button.**

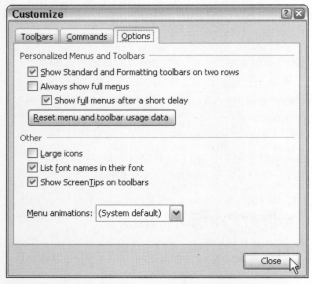

• **Figure 2-1:** Forcing Excel to display the Standard and Formatting toolbars on two rows.

 To get Excel to display all of a menu's options the moment you open it, select the Always Show Full Menus check box on the Options tab of the Customize dialog box. This stops the program from shortchanging you on how many options you see when you first open a particular menu. (Menus don't show all their options until the menus are open for several moments — moments that often seem like a lifetime.)

Toolbars and Menus Made to Order

When the software engineers at Microsoft put together the Excel toolbars and menus, they tried to select the buttons and options that most users need most of the time. Of course, you may very well not be "most users" when it comes to using Excel and wish that they had included command options that currently aren't there and left out others that you rarely use.

The good news is that you can easily make the program more efficient by customizing any of the existing toolbars and pull-down menus so that they consist of just the options you use in the order in which you'd like to see them.

To customize a built-in Excel toolbar, you follow these steps:

1. **Choose View⇨Toolbars⇨Customize to open the Customize dialog box.**

2. **If the toolbar you want to customize is not already displayed on the screen, select the Toolbars tab in the Customize dialog box and then select that toolbar's check box.**

3. **To add a new button to the toolbar now displayed, select the Commands tab in the Customize dialog box and then select the desired command category in the Categories list box. Scroll to the command's icon in the Commands list box and then drag the icon from the Customize dialog box to its new place on the toolbar.**

   You can release the mouse button as soon as the box with the + (plus) appears on the mouse pointer. Excel indicates where the new button will be inserted on the toolbar by displaying the bold I-beam-type indicator on the toolbar.

4. To delete a button from the toolbar, drag its button from the toolbar, and then when the box with the X in it appears at the mouse pointer, release the mouse button.

5. To rearrange the buttons on the toolbar, drag the button icon to its new position on the bar (indicated by the bold I-beam-type indicator).

6. To add a vertical separator bar that groups the buttons, locate the button in front of which the separator will be inserted and then drag that button slightly to the right. As soon as you release the mouse button, the separator bar appears.

To remove a vertical separator, drag the button that the separator is directly in front of to the left until the bar disappears.

7. After you finish customizing the toolbar, click the Close button to close the dialog box and return the functionality to the toolbars and menus.

The steps for customizing one of Excel's pull-down menus are the same as those for customizing a toolbar, except that after opening the Customize dialog box and selecting the Commands tab, you must choose the name of the menu you want to customize. The steps for adding commands, deleting menu items, and rearranging them on a particular menu are the same as those for doing these things to a toolbar: just keep in mind that the bold, I-beam-type indicator shows you where the command you add will be inserted on the pull-down menu.

 You can use the controls in the Rearrange Commands dialog box (see Figure 2-2) to quickly add, delete, or modify the order of the buttons on any Excel toolbar or items on any of its pull-down menus. To open this dialog box, click the Rearrange Commands button on the Commands tab of the Customize dialog box.

• **Figure 2-2: The Rearrange Commands dialog box makes it easy to add, delete, or reorder the options on Excel toolbars and menus.**

To customize a menu or toolbar in the Rearrange Commands dialog box, follow these steps:

1. If you're customizing a pull-down menu, click the Menu Bar option button and then select the pull-down menu name in its drop-down list box. If you're customizing a toolbar, click the Toolbar option button and then select the toolbar name in its drop-down list box.

Excel displays all the menu items or toolbar buttons for the menu or toolbar you selected in their current order.

2. To add an item or button, click the menu item or button in front of which you want to insert the new button and then click the Add button. In the Add Command dialog box that appears, select the option you want added and click OK.

3. To delete an item or button, select it in the Rearrange Commands dialog box and then click the Delete button.

4. To modify the position of an item or button, select it in the Rearrange Commands dialog box and then click the Move Up or Move Down button until the item or button appears in the desired position.

5. After you finish customizing your menu or toolbar, click the Close button in the Rearrange Commands dialog box and then click the Close button in the Customize dialog box.

A Toolbar and Menu of Your Own

Sometimes it makes more sense to create your own toolbar or pull-down menu rather than fool around customizing the ones that come with Excel. By building your own custom toolbar or menu, you can bring together just the commands that you normally rely on. For example, you can concoct a Calculation toolbar or pull-down menu that contains only the options that you frequently use in building your spreadsheet formulas.

To create a custom toolbar, follow these steps:

1. Choose View⇨Toolbars⇨Customize to open the Customize dialog box.

2. Click the Toolbars tab and then click the New button to open the New Toolbar dialog box, shown in Figure 2-3.

• **Figure 2-3: You name your new custom toolbar in the New Toolbar dialog box.**

3. Enter your name for the custom toolbar in the Toolbar Name text box and then click OK.

Excel adds the custom toolbar's name to the Toolbars list box in the Customize dialog box and displays a blank floating toolbar that shows only the first few letters of its name.

4. To add a tool to the new toolbar, select the Commands tab in the Customize dialog box, click the desired command category in the Categories list box, scroll to the command's icon in the Commands list box, and then drag the command's icon from the Customize dialog box to the new toolbar.

Excel automatically expands the toolbar to accommodate the buttons you add.

5. Repeat Step 4 until you have added all the tools you want to appear on your new toolbar.

6. If you want to group the buttons on the new toolbar, locate the buttons in front of which you want the separators to appear and then drag the buttons slightly to the right.

 You can also reposition the buttons you add to a new toolbar simply by dragging them to their places.

7. When you have the new toolbar exactly the way you want it, click the Close button to close the Customize dialog box.

After creating a custom toolbar, be sure to test out its buttons by clicking them at the appropriate moments in building or editing your spreadsheet (not all Excel commands can be executed on a blank worksheet).

The process for creating a custom menu is the same as for a toolbar except that to start the custom menu, you select the New Menu item at the bottom of the Commands tab of the Customize dialog box. Then you drag this New Menu item from the Customize dialog box to the place where you want it to appear on the Excel menu bar. To rename the menu to something besides New Menu, right-click New Menu on the Excel menu bar and choose Name from the shortcut menu. Then replace New Menu with the new name you've chosen.

17

 If you want to assign a hot key to the name you give your new custom menu, type an ampersand (&) immediately in front of the letter in the menu name. (Just make sure that it isn't already assigned to one of the other items on the same menu.)

To add an item to your new menu, drag the command from the Customize dialog box to the tab under the menu. (Don't release the mouse button until the bold, I-beam-type indicator appears on the tab and the box with the plus sign (+) appears next to the mouse pointer.) Removing and repositioning items on your custom menu is no different from making these types of modifications to a standard pull-down menu.

Adding Macros and Links to Toolbars and Menus

Built-in commands are not the only things you can add to the toolbars and pull-down menus you customize or create from scratch. You can also add macros you've recorded and hyperlinks to particular documents, folders, and even favorite Web sites. To do this, you attach the macro or link to a custom button that you add to a toolbar or to a custom menu item that you add to a pull-down menu.

To attach a macro or hyperlink to a custom button that you add to a toolbar, follow these steps:

1. Choose View➪Toolbars➪Customize to open the Customize dialog box.

2. If the toolbar to which you want to add the custom button is not already open, select the Toolbars tab and then select the toolbar's check box to display it in the Excel screen.

3. Select the Commands tab and then select Macros near the bottom of the Categories list box, as shown in Figure 2-4.

When you select the Macros category, the Commands list box gives you a choice between a Custom Menu Item and a Custom Button.

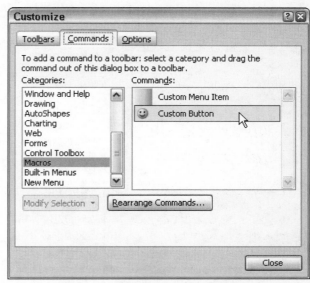

• **Figure 2-4: The Macros category contains two choices: Custom Menu Item and Custom Button.**

4. Drag the Custom Button (with the Happy Face icon) and drop it into position on the toolbar from which you want to be able to run the macro or select the hyperlink.

5. Right-click the Custom Button you just added to the toolbar and then click either the Assign Hyperlink➪Open item (to attach a hyperlink to it) or the Assign Macro item (to attach a macro to it) on the shortcut menu, shown in Figure 2-5.

If you choose Assign Hyperlink➪Open, Excel opens the standard Assign Hyperlink dialog box where you can select an existing file or Web page or e-mail address to link to. If you choose Assign Macro, the program opens the Assign Macro dialog box where you can select the macro to run when the button is clicked.

6. Select the link to the hyperlink's destination in the Assign Hyperlink dialog box or the macro to run in the Assign Macro dialog box; then click OK.

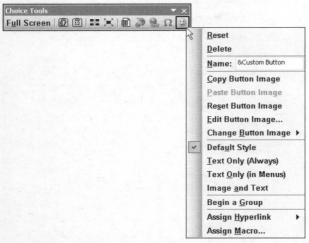

• **Figure 2-5:** Select the Assign Hyperlink or Assign Macro item to attach a link or macro to the new button.

7. To select a new icon for the button, right-click the custom button and choose Change Button Image. From the icon pop-up palette that appears, choose the new icon you want to use.

 You can use the Button Editor — which you can open by selecting Edit Button Image on the button's shortcut menu — to modify the icon that you choose on the Change Button Image's icon palette. This editor lets you make pixel-by-pixel changes to the image, either by erasing pixels or by painting with new colors.

8. Click the Close button in the Customize dialog box.

The process for assigning a hyperlink or macro to a menu item is almost the same, except that you select Custom Menu Item in the Macros category on the Commands tab of the Customize dialog box. Then you drag this Custom Menu Item to the place on the pull-down menu where you want it to appear. Next, you assign either a hyperlink or macro to it by right-clicking the Custom Menu Item on its pull-down menu and then choosing either Assign Hyperlink⇨ Open or Assign Macro on its shortcut menu.

After assigning the link or macro, you will want to rename the menu item. To do this, right-click Custom Menu Item on its pull-down menu and then click the Name option and replace Custom Menu Item with a name of your own. If you want to assign a hotkey to one of the characters in the new name, be sure to type an ampersand (&) immediately in front of the character in the custom menu name that you want to so designate.

Technique 3

Perfecting Your Spreadsheet Workspace

Save Time By

- Creating a workspace with all the spreadsheets you're working on
- Opening the workspace when Excel launches

An Excel workspace (sometimes known as an *arranged workspace*) is really just a special file that keeps a record of all the workbooks open at the time you save the workspace, as well as all the workbooks' screen attributes — things like window sizes and arrangement, screen magnification, and any other display settings in use at the time. (See Technique 1 for details.) Workspaces are real timesavers because they enable you to immediately resume work the next day on whatever workbooks you had open the day before. All you have to do is open the workspace file, and Excel does all the heavy lifting: opening the individual workbooks and arranging their windows and setting up the screen attributes so they're in the same condition you left them in.

When you're involved with a particularly complex spreadsheet project that requires you to work with the same workbook files over the course of several work sessions, you can save even more time by having Excel automatically open the workspace file when you launch the program. That way, you have all the spreadsheets open and arranged so that you're ready to go the moment you start working with Excel.

Saving Your Workspace

Creating a workspace is literally as simple as choosing File⇨ Save Workspace, naming the workspace file, and selecting a place in which to save the new workspace file (which is automatically given the filename extension .xlw) in the Save Workspace dialog box, shown in Figure 3-1. The hard part is actually opening the workbooks you want to work with in the workspace and arranging their windows and display settings the way you want them prior to saving this workspace file. But then, this is the stuff that you have to do anyway to be able to work with more than one Excel workbook at a time.

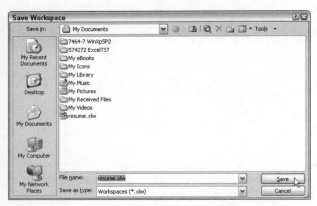

• **Figure 3-1:** Saving the information about the current work environment in a new workspace file.

To re-create the workspace environment, all you have to do is open the workspace file. When looking for the workspace file in the Open dialog box (File⇨ Open), remember that workspace files use the .xlw (for Excel workspace) file extension rather than the normal .xls filename extension.

To have the workspace in your next Excel work session exactly the way you left it at the close of business, don't save the workspace file until after you have saved all your changes to the open Excel workbooks and are ready to exit Excel.

If you've already created the workspace file in a previous work session and want to save any display changes to it under the same filename, choose File⇨Save Workspace and then click Save in the Save Workspace dialog box. When Excel displays an alert dialog box warning you that you're about to replace the existing file, just click Yes to save your changes to the same workspace file.

Opening a Workspace Whenever Excel Launches

When you know that you'll be using a particular workspace for some time in your Excel work, you can speed up the process of setting up your work environment by having Excel automatically open the workspace file when you launch the program. The process for doing this is twofold: You need to designate a folder on your computer as the alternate startup folder, and then you have to save the workspace file in that folder.

Any Excel file that you save in the XLSTART folder provided by Microsoft (and saved in the `C:\Program Files\Microsoft Office\Office11` folder when you're using Excel 2003) automatically opens when you launch the program.

Excel enables you to designate an alternate folder (which you must create with Windows Explorer) for automatic startup. I recommend saving the workspace file you want automatically opened in the alternate startup folder that you specify because no matter where you put this folder it just has to be easier to find than Microsoft's XLSTART folder!

To designate a folder (which you've already created on your system with Windows Explorer) as the alternate startup folder, follow these few steps:

1. Choose Tools⇨Options and then select the General tab in the Options dialog box.

2. Select the At Startup, Open All Files In text box and then enter the path to the folder where you're going to save your workspace file.

Unfortunately, Excel doesn't provide a Browse button here that enables you to locate this folder visually, so you have to tough it out and type the folder's pathname in this text box. Remember that the pathname consists of the drive letter followed by a colon and the names of all the subfolders separated by backslashes, as in `C:\XL Alt Start` shown in Figure 3-2.

3. **Click OK to close the Options dialog box.**

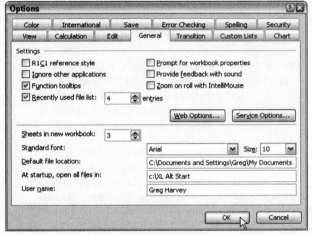

• **Figure 3-2:** Designating the alternate startup folder in the Options dialog box.

After you designate your alternate startup folder, follow these steps to save the workspace file that you want Excel to automatically open on startup:

1. **Choose File⇨Save Workspace to open the Save Workspace dialog box.**

2. **From the Save In drop-down list box, select the folder you designated as the alternate startup folder, as shown in Figure 3-3.**

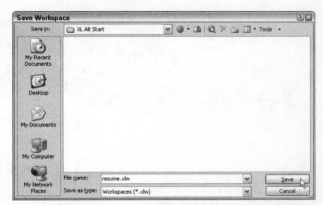

• **Figure 3-3:** Saving the workspace file in the alternate startup folder in the Save Workspace dialog box.

3. **Click Save to close the Save Workspace dialog box.**

After you save the workspace file in your Excel alternate startup folder, each time you start Excel the program opens the file and uses its information to load your workbook files, arrange their windows, and invoke their display settings.

When you finish your work with the workbooks opened in the workspace and no longer want to see them every time you launch Excel, you need to move the workspace file out of the alternate startup folder into another folder on your hard disk, or, if you're really sure that you have no need for the workspace, you can delete it by moving it into the Windows Recycle Bin.

Technique 4

Saving Your Worksheets So You Can Find Them

Nothing is as frustrating as knowing that you've saved a workbook file only to discover later that you haven't the foggiest idea where on your great big humongous hard disk you saved it. Excel tries to guard against this type of aggravation by automatically saving every new workbook in the My Documents folder. Many times, however, saving all the different types of workbooks you create in the same generic My Documents folder on your local disk just isn't practical. This is especially true in a network environment where spreadsheets are not normally saved locally.

This technique concentrates on ways you can minimize the annoyance of not knowing where you saved a new workbook file. These include changing the default folder from the generic My Documents to a more specific folder and setting up the Save command so that you're automatically prompted to fill in summary information on the new workbook file. Although the latter procedure does not itself guard against saving a new workbook in the wrong folder, it does help you more quickly and easily find the file if you forget where you saved it.

The final procedure in this technique covers the use of the AutoRecover feature to guard against losing unsaved data if Excel becomes unresponsive and needs to be shut down or your computer experiences a sudden shutdown that prevents you from manually saving your edits. By setting AutoRecover to a comfortable interval, you can be assured of losing as few worksheet edits as possible in such an event. You can also set the folder location where Excel saves your recovered workbook.

Modifying the Default File Location

If your Excel work habits are anything like mine, you tend to find yourself at certain times having to build several workbooks of the same type (time cards, financial statements, expense reports, and so on) that all need to be saved in the same folder. For those times, you can streamline this process and guard against saving the new workbook in the wrong location by changing the default file location. That way, when you first save the workbook, you don't have to bother with changing the folder, and you don't have to worry about saving the workbook in an unintended place.

To change the default file folder location to a folder that you've already created with Windows Explorer, follow these steps:

1. **Choose Tool⇨Options to open the Options dialog box.**

2. **Select the General tab in the Options folder.**

3. **In the Default File Location text box, enter the pathname to the folder you want as the default, as shown in Figure 4-1.**

   This assumes that you've planned ahead and already used Windows Explorer to create such a folder.

 The pathname consists of the drive letter followed by a colon and the names of all subfolders separated by backslashes, as in `C:\Accounting\Expenses`.

4. **Click OK to close the Options dialog box.**

After changing the default file location in the Options dialog box, the next time you open the Save As dialog box (shown in Figure 4-2) to save a new workbook (by choosing File⇨Save, clicking the Save button on the Standard toolbar, or pressing Ctrl+S), the name

of the folder at the end of the new pathname appears in the Save In drop-down list box. (If you want to check that the path to this folder is correct, select the Save In drop-down list to display it.) Then all you have to do to complete the save operation is to edit the temporary filename and click Save.

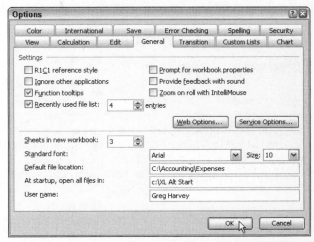

• **Figure 4-1: To change where Excel automatically saves its files, enter the pathname in the Default File Location text box.**

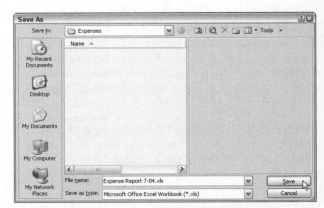

• **Figure 4-2: After designating a new default file location, Excel automatically selects that folder for all new files you save.**

Don't forget to change the Default File Location on the General tab of the Options dialog box when you finish creating all the files that should be saved in that location. Otherwise, you'll end up saving files that don't belong there, defeating the purpose of modifying this location in the first place.

Saving New Files with Summary Information

Even if you never mess up and save a new workbook in the wrong folder, you might as well admit that eventually you'll end up forgetting where you intentionally put some of them. This next procedure can go a long way in helping you quickly find and open any workbook that you've temporarily misplaced, regardless of the reason.

Microsoft programs such as Word and Excel 2003 enable you to save summary information on every document you create as part of the document's file properties (see Figure 4-3). (You can display the properties by choosing File➪Properties.) This summary information can include data such as the document's title, subject, author, company, category, keywords, and comments. The great thing about this summary information is that it's searchable from the Excel File Search task pane (File➪File Search), so you can use whatever summary data you know about a lost workbook to find and open it. (See Technique 31 for details.)

The bad thing is that Excel doesn't automatically prompt you to enter this summary information when you first save the file, so more likely than not, you don't end up entering the facts and keywords that may some day prove vital to your being able to locate and reopen the file. Fortunately, you can change this situation so that Excel automatically displays the Properties dialog box and selects its Summary tab every time you save a new workbook file. (This dialog box appears after you designate the folder and filename and click the Save button in the Save As dialog box.)

• **Figure 4-3:** You can use the data entered on the Summary tab of the File Properties dialog box in searching for misplaced workbooks.

To get this going, you follow these simple steps:

1. **Choose Tools➪Options to open the Option dialog box.**

2. **Select the General tab and then select the Prompt for Workbook Properties check box, as shown in Figure 4-4.**

3. **Click OK to close the Options dialog box.**

 When entering summary data for new workbooks, get in the habit of assigning standard general data to the Subject or Category fields (such as Invoice or Expense Report) along with information specific to the spreadsheet in the Title and Keywords fields. That way, you can narrow down the field to files of a certain type even if you don't have specifics on the file.

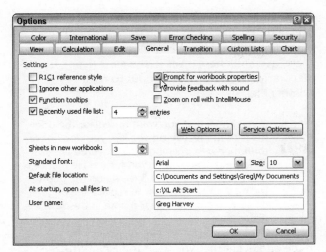

• **Figure 4-4:** Setting up Excel to automatically display the Summary tab of the Options dialog box when you first save a file.

Changing the AutoRecover Settings

The AutoRecover feature is turned on when you install Excel so that every ten minutes the program automatically saves any editing changes made since the workbook was last saved. The program saves all the edits you've made since the last AutoRecover save in a special document-recovery backup file located in the folder designated as the AutoRecover save location. Then if your computer experiences some sort of power failure or Excel unexpectedly goes comatose on you (a very rare occurrence but not completely unheard of) before you can save the workbook yourself, you can open this recovery backup file and use it instead of the original file.

 AutoRecover doesn't operate on a new workbook that you've never manually saved with File➪Save, so be sure to save your new workbook before you enter a bunch of formulas and data in it, or you could end up losing it all.

If you're not comfortable with the ten-minute AutoRecover save interval, you can shorten or lengthen it. For some users, this interval is too long because they would never want to have to reenter ten minutes worth of data. For others, it's too short because it seems like Excel's always interrupting their work by saving their data changes. To modify the AutoRecover settings, follow these steps:

1. Choose Tools➪Options to open the Options dialog box.

2. Select the Save tab to display the AutoRecover settings for the program, as shown in Figure 4-5.

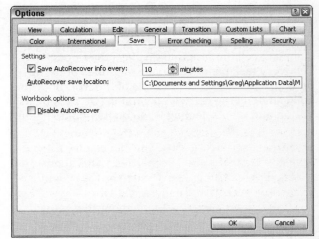

• **Figure 4-5:** Access the Save tab of the Options dialog box to modify the program's AutoRecover settings.

3. To modify the AutoRecover save interval, enter the new time value (between 1 and 120) in the Minutes text box or use the spinner buttons to select it.

4. To select a new folder into which to save recovery backup files, select the AutoRecover Save Location text box and then enter the pathname for this new folder.

Normally, you don't have to worry about this folder location because the Document Recovery task pane (discussed later in this section) finds the backup file for you and enables you to compare the recovered file to the original and, if you so desire, replace the original with the recovered version.

5. **Click OK to close the Options dialog box and put your new settings into effect.**

 Select the Disable AutoRecover check box on the Save tab of the Options dialog box at your own peril. In disabling this feature, you run the risk of losing all your data should you have a software or hardware mishap before you take the time to manually save the file.

If your software freezes up or your computer crashes when the AutoRecover feature is enabled and in use during a work session, the next time you launch Excel, the program displays the Document Recovery task pane. This pane identifies both the original and recovered versions of the workbook file. You can open the recovered version (by clicking its button and then selecting Open on its pop-up menu)

to see how much of the data was recovered. If you decide that you want to retain the recovered version of the file and replace the original version, choose File⇨Save and choose Yes in the alert dialog box that warns you that you're about to replace the existing file.

 If you know that you want to replace the original with the recovered version, you don't have to bother with opening the recovered file. Just click the drop-down button for the file marked [Recovered] and select Save As on the pop-up menu. If you don't want to replace the original, be sure to enter a new filename in the Save As dialog box.

In the odd event that you want to discard the recovered version and retain only the original (and presumably less complete) version of the file, simply click the Close button in Document Recovery task pane and then select the No (Remove These Files. I Have Saved the Files I Need) option button in the alert dialog box that appears.

Technique 5

Tailoring Excel's Error Checking to Your Needs

Save Time By

- Modifying the Error Checking settings
- Hiding error indicators in cells
- Hiding error values in cells

Anyone with any experience building Excel worksheets knows that formula errors, the bane of all spreadsheets, are inevitable. Whenever Excel cannot successfully calculate one of your formulas according to its internal rules, the program returns an error value to its cell, indicated by the error name in all caps punctuated by a number sign at the beginning (#) and an exclamation point (!) or question mark (?) at the end, as in #VALUE!, #NAME?, and #DIV/0!, to name but a few.

Not only are these error values ugly as sin, but they also tend to propagate themselves all over the worksheet, spreading to all formulas that refer to the cells that contain them. (See Techniques 31 and 32 for tips on how to stop error values from spreading all over the place and eliminate them from the worksheet.)

In an attempt to help you identify what in the blazes has caused your formula to go haywire and return an error value rather than the result you wanted, Excel now adds error indicators to cells. These indicators appear as tiny green triangles in the upper-left corner of the cells containing the error values, as shown in Figure 5-1. When you position the mouse pointer over an error indicator, a Smart Tab icon (the exclamation point in a diamond) appears with a ToolTip containing an explanation of the problem.

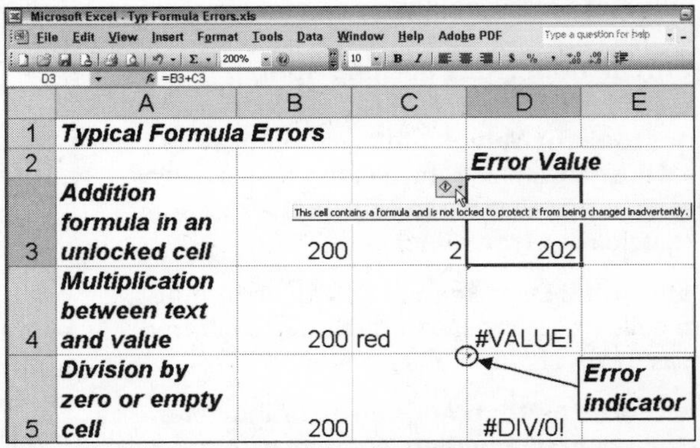

• **Figure 5-1: Errors, errors everywhere and indicators telling you what's wrong to boot!**

When you're new to Excel, the ToolTips connected to the error indicators are a godsend because they reinforce the rules and start to make sense of those largely inexplicable error values. As you become a more experienced user, they lose their luster and can become downright annoying (obscuring data you want to see and otherwise getting in your way as you inadvertently pass the mouse pointer over them).

Fortunately, Excel makes it easy to control when error indicators appear in cells containing error values. You can also temporarily suppress the display of all error indicators in the worksheet. As part of this technique on cleaning up the error indicators in your worksheet, I give you tips on temporarily suppressing the display of those unsightly error values both on-screen and in your printouts.

Modifying the Error Checking Settings

The Error Checking tab of the Options dialog box (Tools⇨Options), shown in Figure 5-2, contains a list of check-box options that correspond to conditions in which Excel adds an error indicator to a cell. Note that in this list, only the first check box option has to do with actual error values in the cells. All the other options have to do with conditions that might be problematic to the spreadsheet even though they don't result in blatant error values.

Here is the entire list of Error Checking options:

- ✔ **Evaluates to Error Value:** Adds error indicators to cells whose formulas return error values and includes ToolTips that try to explain the reason for the particular error value.

- ✔ **Text Date with 2 Digit Years:** Adds an error indicator to cells that contain two-digit dates entered as text, as in '89 or '76.

- ✔ **Number Stored as Text:** Adds an error indicator to cells that contain numbers entered as text, as in '1123 or '45.67.

- ✔ **Inconsistent Formula in Region:** Adds an error indicator to any cells containing formulas whose structures don't match the prevailing pattern in the rest of those in a particular table.

- ✔ **Formula Omits Cells in Region:** Adds an error indicator to any cells containing formulas that don't refer to cells within a particular table when most of the others do.

- ✔ **Unlocked Cells Containing Formulas:** Adds an error indicator to any unlocked cells containing formulas (you can unlock cells by pressing Ctrl+1, clicking the Protection tab, and deselecting the Locked check box).

- ✔ **Formulas Referring to Empty Cells:** Adds an error indicator to any cells containing formulas referring to empty cells. (This is the only Error Checking option not selected by default.)

- ✔ **List Data Validation Error:** Adds an error indicator to cells that contains entries that don't follow the data validation condition applied to them.

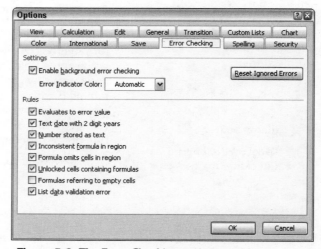

• **Figure 5-2:** The Error Checking options enable you to modify when error indicators appear.

As you can see from the list of Error Checking options, error indicators often don't represent an error per se but simply an anomaly in the prevailing pattern. If you're not particularly concerned about inconsistencies in your spreadsheets, you can simply deselect their check box options to prevent Excel from cluttering the worksheet with these types of indicators.

 Don't disable the Evaluates to Error Value option unless you're a real spreadsheet ace who can immediately tell what's causing a formula to return an error value. You'll be cheating yourself out of the ToolTip info telling you what's wrong so you can quickly eliminate the error.

 You can make the error indicators more or less prominent in the worksheet by selecting a new color for their triangles on the Error Indicator Color pop-up palette.

Suppressing All Error Indicators

When you're dealing with a worksheet that for whatever reason is riddled with error values and their attendant error indicators, you can get rid of the indicators in one fell swoop by following these simple steps:

1. **Choose Tools⇨Options.**

2. **Select the Error Checking tab in the Options dialog box.**

3. **Deselect the Enable Background Error Checking box and then click OK.**

As soon as you close the Options dialog box, Excel temporarily removes all the error indicators from the entire worksheet. To restore them, all you have to do is open the Error Checking tab of the Options dialog box and then select the Enable Background Error Checking box again.

 Suppressing the display of the error indicators has no effect on the display of error values in the worksheet. To do that, you either have to fix the problem or use one of the techniques in the following section for hiding their display.

Hiding Error Values On-Screen and in Print

Sometimes, you'll want to suppress the display of those nasty-looking error values in a worksheet until you get all the data entered that you need to make all the error values really disappear. (Error values running throughout the worksheet can tend to make the client a little nervous.) When it comes to suppressing their display, you have a couple choices:

✔ You can nip them in the bud so to speak by building formulas that suppress the display and trap any possible errors before they spread anywhere else in the worksheet (see Technique 28 for details).

✔ You use the Conditional Formatting feature to blank them out.

Follow these steps to use the Conditional Formatting feature:

1. **Select the cell or range of cells containing the error values you want to blank out.**

2. **Choose Format⇨Conditional Formatting.**

3. **Click the drop-down button in the box that reads Cell Value Is and select Formula Is from its pop-up menu.**

4. **Type =ISERROR(in the text box to the right.**

5. **Reselect the cell or range of cells containing the error values you want blanked out or type their addresses.**

 If you want to drag through the cells to select this range but the Conditional Formatting dialog box gets in the way, minimize the dialog box by clicking its Condense button (the one with the tiny worksheet icon).

6. **Type) to close the parentheses for the ISERROR function.**

7. Click the Format button to open the Format Cells dialog box.

8. On the Font tab, click the Color drop-down button and then select the white square on the pop-up palette that appears. (The white square is at the intersection of the very last column and row of the upper palette.) Then click OK.

When you close the Format Cells dialog box, the Conditional Formatting dialog box resembles the one shown in Figure 5-3.

9. Click OK to close the Conditional Formatting dialog box.

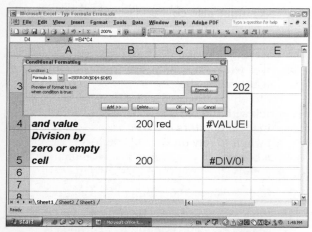

• **Figure 5-3:** Setting up a conditional format to blank out the display of error values in a range.

As soon as you click OK, Excel replaces all the error values in the cell or cell range you selected with white, effectively blanking out their error value results without disturbing their formulas.

If all you want to do is suppress the display of error values in a printout of the worksheet, you don't have to go to all that trouble of first blanking out their display by setting up a conditional format. All you have

to do is follow these simple steps prior to sending the worksheet to the printer:

1. Choose File⇨Page Setup to open the Page Setup dialog box.

2. On the Sheet tab, click the Cell Errors As drop-down button to open its drop-down list, shown in Figure 5-4.

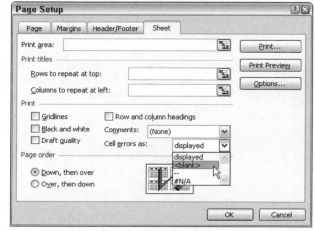

• **Figure 5-4:** Replacing the error values in the printout of a worksheet with blanks, N/A, or dashes.

3. From the drop-down list, select <blank>, – (dashes), or #N/A (the Not Available value) to replace the default value displayed in the Cell Errors As box.

4. Click OK to close the Page Setup dialog box or click Print if you're ready to print your worksheet.

 Click the Print Preview button rather than the Print button if you want to make sure that all the error values are really gone from the printout before you send the job to the printer.

Technique 6

Utilizing Excel's Editing Settings

Save Time By
- ✔ Selecting new cell pointer directions
- ✔ Dumping AutoComplete
- ✔ Using cell drag-and-drop
- ✔ Direct editing in cells

Excel's Edit settings, found on the Edit tab of the Options dialog box (shown in Figure 6-1), offer a wide array of editing options, most of which are selected by default and seldom, if ever, need changing. Therefore, instead of focusing solely on how to change these options to suit your work habits, this technique also covers how to more efficiently use of a few them when modifying your spreadsheets.

This technique begins by covering how and when to change the direction in which the cell pointer moves when you press Enter and then gives you the lowdown on why you might want to disable the AutoComplete feature. You then discover how to efficiently use Excel's drag-and-drop editing (and when it's best to stick with the old cut-and-paste standby). The technique concludes by giving you pointers on when to edit a cell's contents directly in the cell and when to rely on the old tried-and-true cell editing on the Excel Formula bar.

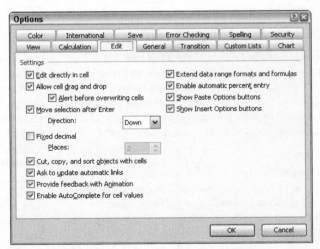

• **Figure 6-1: The Edit settings offer a wide array of editing options that seldom need changing.**

Putting the Cell Pointer in the Right Direction

As you're probably well aware, Excel attempts to make the drudgery of data entry in the worksheet's cells as efficient as possible by setting it up so that the program automatically moves the cell pointer down one cell in the same column when you finish what you're doing and press Enter. (Of course, you can always click the Enter button on the Formula bar to complete an entry or edit rather than press the Enter key.)

What you may not be aware of is that you can easily alter the behavior of the Enter key so that it moves the cell pointer in another direction or doesn't move the cell pointer at all. To change the direction that the cell pointer moves when you press Enter, open the Edit tab of the Options dialog box and select any of the following options in the Direction drop-down list box to replace the default Down option:

- **Right** to move the cell pointer to the cell in the next column to the right in the same row

- **Up** to move the cell pointer to the cell in the row immediately above in the same column

- **Left** to move the cell pointer to the cell in the previous column to the left in the same row

To prevent Excel from moving the cell pointer out of the current cell when you press Enter, deselect the Move Selection After Enter check box on the Edit tab.

The best reason for changing the direction that the cell pointer moves upon pressing Enter is when you find yourself editing a data list or table of spreadsheet data in that particular direction. Here are a few examples:

- If you find that you're editing the entries across the rows of a table from left to right (the direction we read), you would select Right as the Direction option.

- If you're doing the editing across the rows of a table from right to left (a direction I tend to favor due to my left-handedness), you would select Left as the Direction option.

- If you were editing the columns of an Excel data list (also known by the misnomer, database) from the last record (at times, the most recent record) at the bottom upwards towards the first record, it would make perfect sense for you to select Up as the Direction option.

The only reason I ever disable the Move Selection After Enter check box is to keep the cell pointer stationary is when I need to enter master formulas in blank cells that I intend to copy down the column or across the row with the AutoFill feature. In that situation, I don't want Excel to move the cell pointer off of the master formula when I press Enter to complete its entry, and I also don't want to interrupt the entry sequence by having to click the Enter button on the Formula bar.

Completely Turned Off to AutoComplete

I'm sure that the Microsoft engineers who invented the AutoComplete feature for the Office suite of programs must have thought they had come up with the slickest thing since sliced bread. However, I find this feature particularly noxious when entering spreadsheet data because I seldom need to enter the same entry several times in the same column or row of a table. (And if I do run into this situation, I have enough sense to use the AutoFill feature to copy the repeated entry down the column or across the row.)

As a result, I find it much better for my health (especially my blood pressure) to disable the Enable AutoComplete for Cell Values option immediately after installing Excel. Therefore, I suggest that you live a little longer as well and stop reading this book long enough to disable this editing option on your copy of Excel as well. (It's easy to do: Just deselect its check box on the Edit tab of the Options dialog box.)

Doing the Drag-and-Drop Thing

Drag-and-drop editing in the worksheet is great as long as you never disable the Alert before Overwriting Cells option — which appears immediately beneath the Allow Cell Drag and Drop option on the Edit tab of the Options dialog box. Otherwise, you can too easily obliterate parts of your spreadsheet by replacing data you don't want disturbed with the data you're moving. At least when the Alert before Overwriting Cells option is enabled, you get a warning that you're about to mess up and replace data that you might need. Of course, if you do mess up and end up replacing entries with the data you're moving or copying (see the warning on copying with drag-and-drop that follows), you can always puts things back to right by using the Undo feature (Ctrl+Z).

 When you hold down the Ctrl key to copy (rather than move) the cell selection with drag-and-drop, Excel doesn't display the Replace Contents alert box — the one that still gives you the chance to abort the procedure even after you release the mouse button.

Please make room for me

Drag-and-drop spreadsheet editing is most effective when you not only need to move or copy a range of cells to a new (blank) place in the worksheet but also want to insert the cells into an existing table of data. To do this kind of insert moving or copying, you must hold down the Shift key as you drag the cell selection to its new position. Excel indicates where the selected data will be inserted at the time you drop it by displaying an I-beam-type indicator in front of the mouse pointer:

- ✔ When the I-beam pointer runs horizontally between rows, you know that the selection will be inserted as a new row in the existing table of data.

- ✔ When it runs vertically between columns, you know that the selection will be inserted as new column in the table.

Figures 6-2 and 6-3 illustrate this kind of insertion when moving a cell range with drag-and-drop. In Figure 6-2, I selected the cell range A12:R12 (note that many columns are hidden) in preparation for moving it up a row so that it comes in between the Rock and Jazz rows without overwriting any existing data. This figure shows the heavy insertion I-beam indicating where the selected range will be inserted when I release the mouse button.

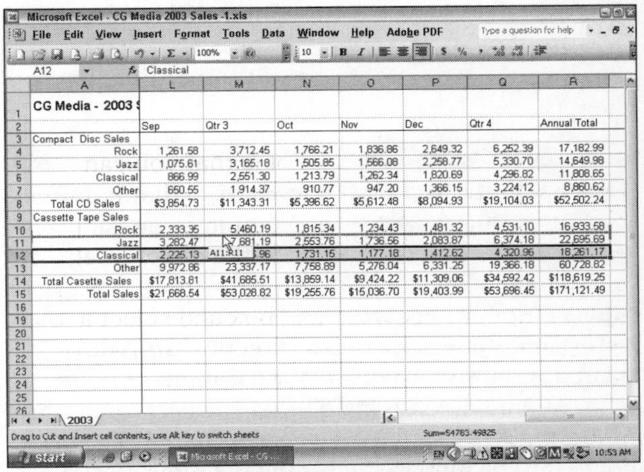

• **Figure 6-2: Getting ready to move data in between existing rows of a table.**

Figure 6-3 shows the worksheet after releasing the mouse button. As you can see, Excel inserts the selected range into row 11 while at the same time moving the Jazz cassette sales data down to row 12.

When drag-and-drop flops

Drag-and-drop provides a simple, easy, and, above all, direct way of editing the contents of a worksheet. It does, however, have a big limitation: It's only good when you have direct screen access to both the source range and destination range. This doesn't mean that you have to be able to see both ranges at the same time on the screen (although that's always nice). It does mean that you have to be able to go between the two ranges — either by scrolling to them on the same worksheet or by moving between two windows that you've created on the screen.

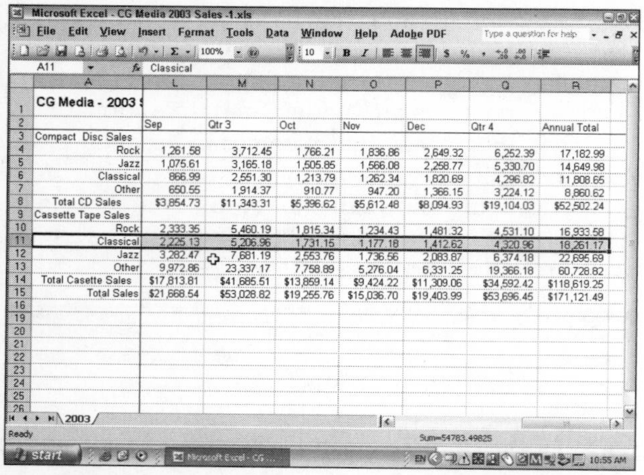

• **Figure 6-3:** The worksheet after moving the selected data in the table.

For example, you can't use drag-and-drop to move or copy a range of cells from one worksheet to another in the same workbook unless you've taken the time to set up separate windows for the sheets beforehand. And unless you have other reasons for setting up the windows, using drag-and-drop to make the move or copy just wastes valuable time.

In such a case, using the standard cut-and-paste method to make the move or copy is much more efficient. After cutting or copying the cell selection to the Clipboard (Ctrl+X or Ctrl+C, respectively), click the new sheet and select the first cell in the range in which you want the data moved or copied, and then press Enter to complete the procedure. (You can also press Ctrl+V to do this.)

Doing Direct Cell Editing

Direct cell editing offers you an alternative to editing the data or formula you've entered into a cell on the Formula bar above the sheet's work area. To directly edit the contents of a cell, you double-click the cell — or press F2 — to place the Insertion point in its contents, and then you edit its characters as you would on the Formula bar (or in a Word document). When you finish modifying the cell's contents, you complete

the edit by pressing the Enter key or by clicking the Enter button on the Formula bar (the button with the green check mark). To bail on the edit and restore the original contents, press Esc.

> Pressing F2 to direct edit always positions the Insertion point at the very end of the cell entry. When you double-click the cell, Excel places the Insertion point as close as possible to the position of the white cross in that cell.

The question inevitably arises as to when it's more efficient to edit a cell entry directly versus editing it on the Formula bar. For me, this decision depends upon the length of the cell entry and its position in the spreadsheet. When dealing with really long and complex formulas in a cell (like the one shown in Figure 6-4), editing them directly in the cell can end up obscuring the cells in the surrounding region to the right and below the cell, which is okay unless you need to refer to these cells in your edit. In such a case, you would find it much more beneficial to edit the cell's formula on the Formula bar. This leaves most of the worksheet unconcealed except at the very top where the multiple lines for the Formula bar obscure the column header and the first rows of the sheet, as shown in Figure 6-5.

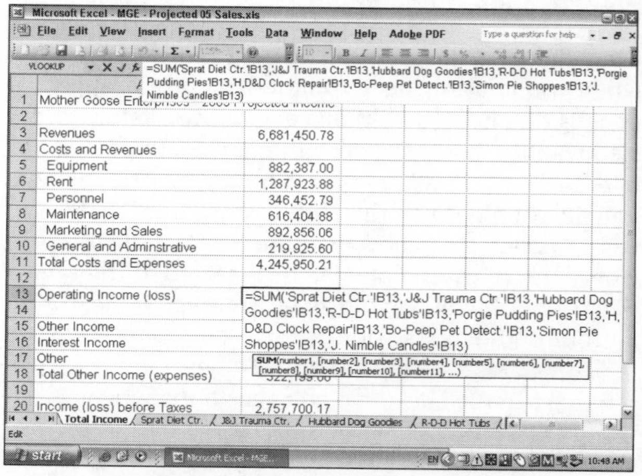

• **Figure 6-4:** Editing a really long formula like this one in its cell obscures any data in cells in the region to its right.

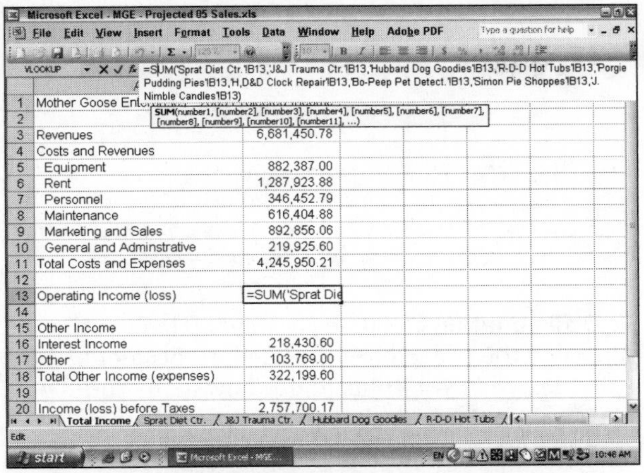

• **Figure 6-5:** Editing a really long formula on the Formula bar leaves most of the worksheet unconcealed.

Technique

7

Streamlining Excel Program Startup

Save Time By

✓ Adding an Excel desktop shortcut

✓ Adding Excel to the Quick Launch toolbar

✓ Pinning Excel to the Start menu

✓ Launching Excel on Windows startup

Lucky Technique 7 is all about quick-and-easy ways to launch the Excel program. Although the procedures outlined in this technique may seem really simple, when you think about how many times you launch Excel even in a week's time, let alone a month's, I think you'll agree that they're worth their weight in gold.

In this technique, all the ways for streamlining the Excel startup are designed so that you never have to go through that clumsy Start⇨ All Program Files⇨Microsoft Office⇨Microsoft Office Excel 2003 routine (the Microsoft engineer that came up with that one should be ashamed of himself)! The most obvious way to completely avoid this utterly Byzantine command sequence is to put the Excel program icon at your fingertips, either by placing it on the desktop as a shortcut or as an icon on the Windows taskbar or Start menu. And if all you ever seem to do on your computer is run Excel, you can even go the final step of having Windows automatically launch the program as part of the computer startup procedure.

Excel Desktop Shortcut

The most basic procedure for putting the Excel startup at your fingertips is to put an Excel shortcut icon pointing to the Excel program's executable file on your computer's desktop. To do this, follow these steps:

1. **Click the Start button on the Windows taskbar and then select Search on the Start menu.**

2. **Select the All Files and Folders link in the Search Companion task pane.**

3. **Type excel.exe in the All or Part of the File Name text box and then click the Search button.**

4. **Right-click EXCEL.EXE in the main pane of the Search Results dialog box and then choose Send To⇨Desktop (Create Shortcut) from the file's shortcut menu, as shown in Figure 7-1.**

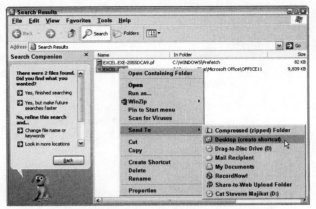

• **Figure 7-1: Creating a desktop shortcut for the Excel program file in the Search Results dialog box.**

5. **Click the Close button in the upper-right corner of the Search Results dialog box to close it.**

As soon as you close the Search Results dialog box, you will see that Windows has added a Microsoft Office Excel 2003 desktop shortcut. (See Figure 7-2.) You can, if you wish, rename this icon to something more manageable — such as Excel 2003 — by right-clicking the icon and then deleting the redundant Microsoft Officepart.

• **Figure 7-2: The Microsoft Excel 2003 shortcut icon.**

To launch Excel from your computer's desktop, simply double-click the (Microsoft Office) Excel 2003 desktop shortcut icon.

Adding Excel to the Quick Launch Toolbar

The only problem with launching Excel from a desktop shortcut is that you have to have access to the Windows desktop in order to use it. This means that you can't use it to launch Excel when, for example, you're working in another application full screen such as Microsoft Word or PowerPoint.

To be able to launch Excel without accessing the Windows desktop, you can add your Excel desktop shortcut to the Windows Quick Launch toolbar. This toolbar resides to the immediate right of the Start button on the Windows taskbar and is readily available at all times.

 If the Quick Launch toolbar doesn't appear after the Start button on your Windows taskbar, its display is turned off. To turn it back on, right-click the taskbar, select Properties and then select the Show Quick Launch check box on the Taskbar tab of the Taskbar and Start Menu Properties dialog box before you click OK.

To add your Excel desktop shortcut to the Quick Launch toolbar, follow these few steps:

1. **Display the Windows desktop by clicking the Show Desktop button on the Quick Launch toolbar (if the desktop is not already displayed).**

If the Quick Launch toolbar isn't displayed on your computer's taskbar, display it by right-clicking on a blank area on the taskbar and then choosing Toolbars⇨Quick Launch.

2. **Drag the Excel desktop shortcut icon to the place on the Quick Launch toolbar where you want it to appear.**

Excel indicates the place where the Excel icon will be inserted by displaying a heavy, I-beam-type pointer in between the existing buttons on the Quick Launch toolbar.

3. Release the mouse button to create a new Excel button on the Quick Launch toolbar, as shown in Figure 7-3.

• **Figure 7-3:** The Quick Launch toolbar after adding the Excel desktop shortcut to it.

 You don't have to double-click the Excel button that you add to the Quick Launch toolbar to launch Excel. You only need to click it once, just as you would any of the buttons on the numerous Excel toolbars.

 You may have to enlarge the Quick Launch toolbar to display all its icons. To do this, position the mouse pointer on the right edge of the bar (marked by a double line of dots) and drag the double-headed arrow pointer until all the icons are shown. If the double-headed arrow pointer doesn't appear, the taskbar is locked. Right-click the taskbar and then clear the Lock the Taskbar item on the pop-up menu to unlock it. After enlarging the Quick Launch toolbar to display all its icons, you can once again lock the taskbar by selecting this item.

Pinning Excel to the Start Menu

What if you're one of those users who never display the Quick Launch toolbar on the Windows taskbar because you don't want to waste all that precious taskbar real estate on a few crummy launch buttons? Well, for you, I suggest making Excel a permanent part of the Start menu. That way, you can always launch Excel by clicking the Start button (something you can't remove from the Windows taskbar) or by pressing Ctrl+Esc and then selecting the Microsoft Office Excel 2003 menu item on the Start menu.

To make Microsoft Office Excel 2003 a permanent item on your computer's Start menu, follow these steps:

1. Launch Excel and then immediately close its program window.

You must manually start Excel in order to add its menu item to the Recently Opened section of the Start menu. To launch Excel, double-click the Excel desktop shortcut or click the Excel button on the Quick Launch toolbar. If you have neither, you have to do this by choosing Start⇨All Programs⇨Microsoft Office⇨Microsoft Office Excel 2003. (Doing that should give you a real incentive to complete the rest of these steps!)

2. Click the Start button on the Windows taskbar or press Ctrl+Esc to open the Start menu.

3. Right-click the Microsoft Excel 2003 item on the Start menu and then choose the Pin to Start Menu option, as shown in Figure 7-4.

4. Click anywhere outside the Start menu or press Esc to close the menu.

 If a Microsoft Excel 2003 item doesn't appear on your Start menu after following these steps, the Number of Programs on Start Menu option has been set to 0. Right-click the taskbar and then select Properties. Next, select the Start Menu tab in the Taskbar and Start Menu Properties dialog box and then click the Customize button. Finally, enter a value greater than 0 (and not more than 30) in the Number of Programs on the Start menu text box before you select OK.

After pinning Microsoft Excel 2003 to the Start menu, you can always launch Excel by clicking the Start button on the taskbar (or by pressing Ctrl+Esc) and then selecting this menu. This menu item now appears in the permanent programs section of the Start menu (which is the top-left portion of the menu) along with the other permanent programs, including your Internet and e-mail applications.

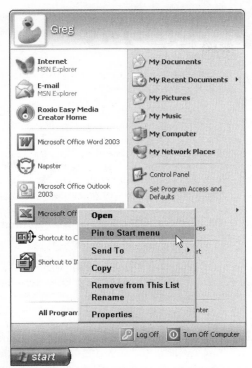

• **Figure 7-4:** Pinning the Microsoft Excel 2003 menu item to the Start menu.

Launching Excel on Windows Startup

For you real hardcore Excel users, the only real solution to the Excel launch problem is to have Windows automatically launch Excel for you every time you start your computer! The procedure is easy: All you have to do is drag the Microsoft Office Excel 2003 menu item from the Microsoft Office submenu to the Startup submenu:

1. Click the Start button on Windows taskbar or press Ctrl+Esc to open the Start menu.

2. Choose All Programs⇨Microsoft Office to open the submenu.

3. Drag the Microsoft Office Excel 2003 menu item from this submenu to the Startup menu on the All Programs menu.

4. Drop the Microsoft Office Excel 2003 menu item anywhere on the Startup submenu, as shown in Figure 7-5.

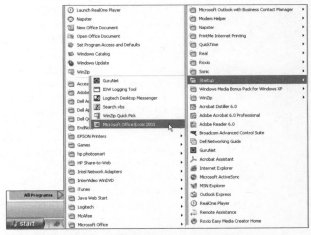

• **Figure 7-5:** Dragging Microsoft Excel 2003 to the Windows Startup menu.

After moving Microsoft Office Excel 2003 to the Windows Startup menu, Windows launches the program every time you start or restart Windows.

 To stop having Excel launch every time you start your computer, drag the Microsoft Office Excel 2003 item back to its original home on the Microsoft Office submenu.

Saving Time with Excel Add-ins

Technique 8

Save Time By
- ✔ Installing add-ins
- ✔ Using the add-ins included with Excel
- ✔ Finding add-ins online

Excel add-in programs provide a quick-and-easy way to extend the basic features of Excel. Most of the add-in programs created for Excel offer you some kind of specialized function or group of functions that extend Excel's computational abilities. For example, Excel includes an Analysis ToolPak that gives you immediate access to some fifteen additional sophisticated statistical functions, including such things as Anova, Covariance, F-Test: Two-Sample for Variances, Fourier Analysis, Histogram, Rank and Percentile, t-Test, and z-Test, among others. It also includes a Conditional Sum Wizard, Lookup Wizard, and Solver Add-in that you can use to perform other types of analysis.

As part of the Excel program, Microsoft offers you a group of spreadsheet-type add-ins that you can start using right away. In addition, you can search the Microsoft Web site for additional add-ins that you can download for free as well as a number of other third-party Web sites where you can purchase the Excel add-ins for download.

Installing Add-ins

Before you can use any add-in program, the add-in must be installed in the proper folder on your hard drive, and then you must select the add-in in the Excel Add-Ins dialog box. Excel add-in programs are saved in a special file format identified with the .XLA (for Excel Add-in) filename extension. These XLA files are normally saved inside the Library folder (sometimes in their own subfolders) that is located in the Office11 folder. The path to this folder on most computers is C:\Program Files\Microsoft Office\Office11\Library.

After an add-in program is installed in the Library folder, its name then appears in the Add-Ins dialog box, which you open by choosing Tools➪ Add-Ins. To activate an add-in program (and thereby put it into the computer's memory), select the check box in front of its name in the Add-Ins dialog box (see Figure 8-1), and then click OK.

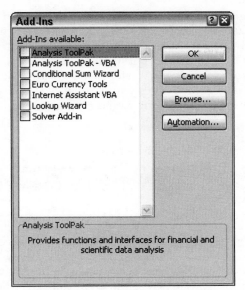

• **Figure 8-1: Activating add-in programs that have already been installed on your computer.**

If you ever copy an XLA add-in program to a folder other than the Library folder in the Office11 folder, its name won't appear in the Add-Ins dialog box. You can, however, activate the add-in by clicking the Browse button in the Add-Ins dialog box to navigate to the add-in file and then clicking OK.

Using the Built-in Add-ins

You can start enhancing the power of Excel right away by making use of the add-in programs Microsoft provides as part of Excel. The add-ins that Microsoft make available for your use include

✔ **Analysis ToolPak:** Adds extra financial, statistical, and engineering functions to Excel's pool of built-in functions. To access these functions (and get help on using them), choose Tools⇨ Data Analysis after activating this add-in.

✔ **Analysis ToolPak VBA:** Enables VBA programmers to publish their own financial, statistical, and engineering functions for Excel.

✔ **Conditional Sum Wizard:** Helps you set up formulas that sum data only when the data meets the criteria you specify. To use this wizard, choose Tools⇨Conditional Sum after activating this add-in.

✔ **Euro Currency Tools:** Enables you to format worksheet values as euro currency and adds a EUROCONVERT function for converting other currencies into euros. To access these tools, choose Tools⇨Euro Conversion after activating this add-in.

✔ **Internet Assistant VBA:** Enables VBA programmers to publish Excel data to the Web.

✔ **Lookup Wizard:** Helps you set up formulas that return data from an Excel list by using known data in that list. (See Technique 57 for details.)

✔ **Solver Add-In:** Calculates solutions to what-if scenarios based on cells that both adjust and constrain the range of values.

The first time you activate any of the add-ins included with Excel, the program immediately displays an alert dialog box telling you that the add-in is not currently installed and asking you if you want to install it. All the add-ins included as part of Excel show up in the list box in the Add-Ins dialog box but don't actually take up disk space until you're ready to use them. Select Yes in this alert dialog box to install the add-ins selected in this list. Keep in mind that Excel needs to access your Office CD-ROM or its files on your network in order to install any of these included add-in programs.

To save computer memory (RAM) that may be needed for doing calculations in the workbook you're editing, you can deactivate any of the add-in programs that you're not currently using. Just open the Add-Ins dialog box, deselect the check box in front of the add-in program's name, and click OK.

Deactivating an add-in does not uninstall the program; it only removes the add-in from the computer's RAM memory. If you deactivate add-ins to save memory, remember to open the Add-Ins dialog box and activate them when you again need access to their functions.

Getting Online Add-ins

The add-ins that Microsoft includes as part of the Excel program aren't the only ones that you can lay your hands on. You can find additional free Excel add-ins on the Microsoft Office Web site, and many third-party vendors sell Excel add-ins that you can often purchase online and then immediately download onto your hard drive.

To locate free Excel add-ins from Microsoft, go online to the Office Web site at

    office.microsoft.com

 You can get to this Web page quickly from within Excel by choosing Help⇨ Microsoft Office Online.

Once there, click the Excel link, enter add-ins as the search text in the Search text box, and click Go. Doing this brings up a Web page similar to Figure 8-2, listing pages of free add-ins that you can download and use with your version of Excel. (Note that add-ins are very version-specific, so be sure that you only download those that are compatible with the version of Excel that you're using.)

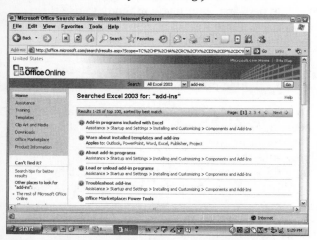

• **Figure 8-2:** Looking for freebie Excel add-ins on the Microsoft Office Web site.

To find third-party vendors and get information on their add-ins, launch your Web browser and then do a search for Excel add-ins. This brings up a Web page full of links to various outfits that make and sell all types of Excel add-ins, as shown in Figure 8-3. Note that many of these sites offer specialized templates and Excel training along with their add-ins.

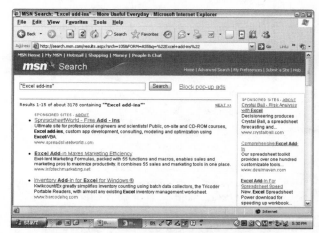

• **Figure 8-3:** Searching for freebie Excel add-ins on the World Wide Web.

Even before you do this Web search, you may want to pay a visit to the Macro Systems Web site at www.add-ins.com (see Figure 8-4). Macro Systems offers a wide variety of Excel add-ins, sold both in collections and as single items. The Macro Systems add-ins are divided into categories that include Time Saving Add-ins, Charting Add-ins, Data Related Add-ins, Financial Add-ins, and so on.

 When visiting the Macro Systems Web site, be sure to download its free add-in, Time Saving Microsoft Excel Solutions. This online book is in the Microsoft help file format and is chocked full of hints on how to work smarter and faster. To get this book, scroll down the Add-ins.com home page until you see the Free Add-ins section and then click the Free Downloadable Book link.

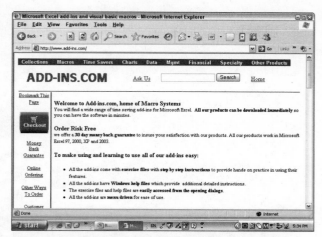

• **Figure 8-4:** It's a veritable add-in heaven for Excel users at Macro Systems' Add-ins.com.

Part II

Quick Worksheet Creation Tricks

Technique **9**

Navigating the Worksheet in a Snap

Save Time By

✔ Saving the cell pointer where you need to work next

✔ Zipping to the end of a table, sheet, or workbook

✔ Using Go To

✔ Zooming out on the worksheet

Nothing is quite as time-consuming and tedious as having to scroll through column after column or row after row of data and blank cells to find the place in your spreadsheet where you need to continue entering data or make some editing changes. In my Excel training classes, I make it a real point to thoroughly cover the most efficient ways to navigate the spreadsheet. Here, in this technique, I give the same tips and tricks for getting where you need to go as quickly as possible.

 This technique on effectively navigating the spreadsheet and Technique 10 on making the most efficient cell selections are probably the most important timesavers in this part of the book; so, listen up!

Saving the Cell Pointer's Position

Many Excel users forget the simple fact that the program always saves the cell pointer's current position in the workbook as part of the file. This means that when you're working on a spreadsheet over a period of several days, you want to make sure that at the end of your work session you set yourself up in the workbook so you're immediately ready to go the next time you open the workbook file.

To do this, I always make a conscious effort to position the cell pointer in the cell at the beginning of the range where I will continue working the next time I open the spreadsheet. Then I save the workbook file one last time before exiting the Excel program. That way, the next time I work on the spreadsheet, I'm ready to resume entering the remaining data or to continue making my edits without having to waste any time scrolling or finding that position.

Going Direct

As even the most novice of Excel users is well aware, a worksheet covers an awfully big area of which only the smallest bit is ever displayed on-screen at any one time. Many times when making editing changes to a particularly large worksheet or in an especially complex workbook (that is, whose data is flung across several worksheets), you have to move directly to the place you need to go. This can involve moving from one end of a table or list of data to the other, from one cell range to the next, or even from one sheet to the next. Scrolling through the columns and rows of any given sheet or clicking sheet tab after sheet tab to find your place in these kinds of spreadsheets is just plain inefficient.

Leaping through data ranges and hopping over blanks

This first procedure enables you to

- Leap from end to end in a long table or list of data.
- Hop from the end of one occupied cell range to the next over all the blanks in between.

How this works is that if the cell pointer is located on a blank cell and you hold down Ctrl as you press an arrow key, the cell pointer jumps to the next cell in the direction of the arrow key that contains any type of entry. (You can also do this by pressing the End key and an arrow key — the only difference here is that you have to release the End key before you press Enter.) Alternately, if the cell pointer is located on a cell that has some sort of entry and you press Ctrl plus an arrow key (or End, arrow key), the cell pointer jumps in the direction of the arrow to the last cell containing an entry followed by a blank cell.

Figures 9-1 through 9-4 illustrate this kind of blank-to-occupied, occupied-to-occupied leapfrogging. In Figure 9-1, the cell pointer is in cell A2, a blank cell. When I press Ctrl+↓, the cell pointer just jumps down three rows to cell A5, the first occupied cell below it (see Figure 9-2).

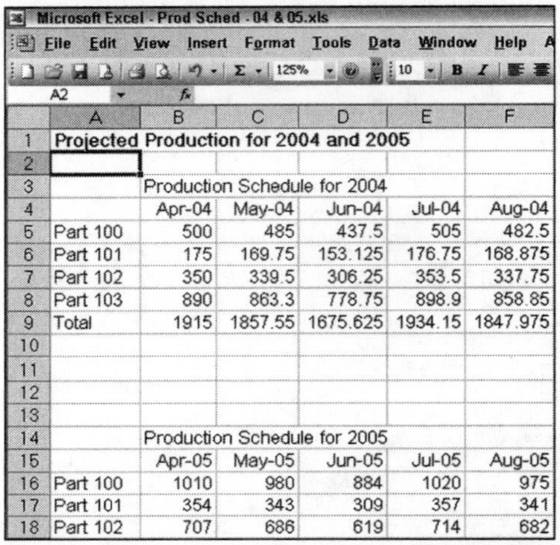
Microsoft Excel - Prod Sched - 04 & 05.xls
File Edit View Insert Format Tools Data Window Help
A2

	A	B	C	D	E	F
1	Projected Production for 2004 and 2005					
2						
3		Production Schedule for 2004				
4		Apr-04	May-04	Jun-04	Jul-04	Aug-04
5	Part 100	500	485	437.5	505	482.5
6	Part 101	175	169.75	153.125	176.75	168.875
7	Part 102	350	339.5	306.25	353.5	337.75
8	Part 103	890	863.3	778.75	898.9	858.85
9	Total	1915	1857.55	1675.625	1934.15	1847.975
10						
11						
12						
13						
14		Production Schedule for 2005				
15		Apr-05	May-05	Jun-05	Jul-05	Aug-05
16	Part 100	1010	980	884	1020	975
17	Part 101	354	343	309	357	341
18	Part 102	707	686	619	714	682

• **Figure 9-1: Starting in the cell pointer in blank cell A2 and moving downward by pressing Ctrl+↓.**

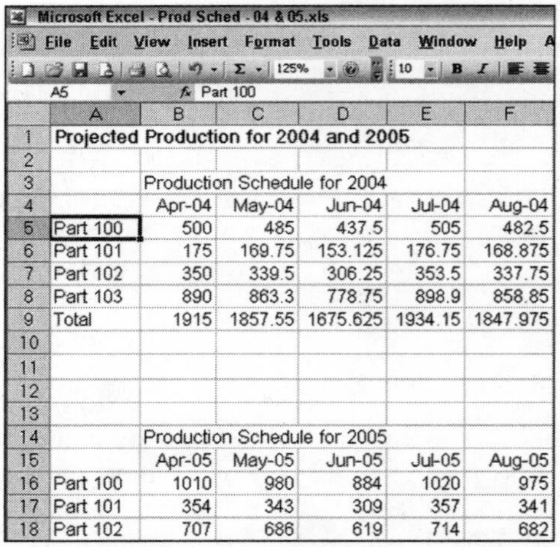
Microsoft Excel - Prod Sched - 04 & 05.xls
File Edit View Insert Format Tools Data Window Help
A5 Part 100

	A	B	C	D	E	F
1	Projected Production for 2004 and 2005					
2						
3		Production Schedule for 2004				
4		Apr-04	May-04	Jun-04	Jul-04	Aug-04
5	Part 100	500	485	437.5	505	482.5
6	Part 101	175	169.75	153.125	176.75	168.875
7	Part 102	350	339.5	306.25	353.5	337.75
8	Part 103	890	863.3	778.75	898.9	858.85
9	Total	1915	1857.55	1675.625	1934.15	1847.975
10						
11						
12						
13						
14		Production Schedule for 2005				
15		Apr-05	May-05	Jun-05	Jul-05	Aug-05
16	Part 100	1010	980	884	1020	975
17	Part 101	354	343	309	357	341
18	Part 102	707	686	619	714	682

• **Figure 9-2: The cell pointer jumps down to A5 — the first occupied cell after the blanks in that column.**

However, when I press Ctrl+↓ a second time (see Figure 9-3), the program jumps the cell pointer down to cell A9 because this is the last occupied cell before the blank cell in A10. When I press Ctrl+↓ again, Excel jumps the cell pointer down to cell A16 (see Figure 9-4), the first occupied cell after the blanks in that column.

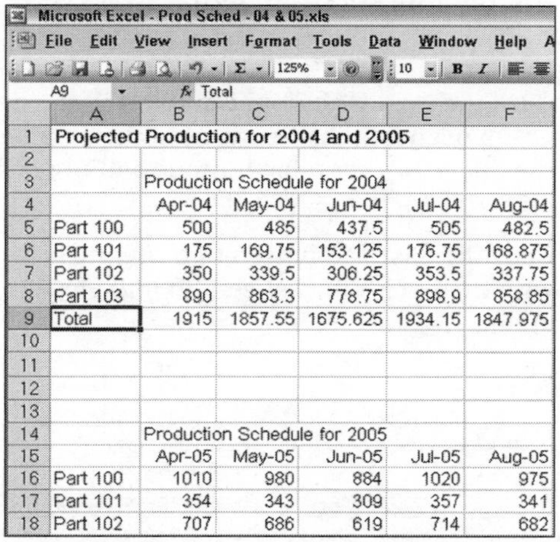

	A	B	C	D	E	F
1	Projected Production for 2004 and 2005					
2						
3		Production Schedule for 2004				
4		Apr-04	May-04	Jun-04	Jul-04	Aug-04
5	Part 100	500	485	437.5	505	482.5
6	Part 101	175	169.75	153.125	176.75	168.875
7	Part 102	350	339.5	306.25	353.5	337.75
8	Part 103	890	863.3	778.75	898.9	858.85
9	Total	1915	1857.55	1675.625	1934.15	1847.975
10						
11						
12						
13						
14		Production Schedule for 2005				
15		Apr-05	May-05	Jun-05	Jul-05	Aug-05
16	Part 100	1010	980	884	1020	975
17	Part 101	354	343	309	357	341
18	Part 102	707	686	619	714	682

• **Figure 9-3: Pressing Ctrl+↓ again moves the cell pointer down to A9 — the first occupied cell before a blank.**

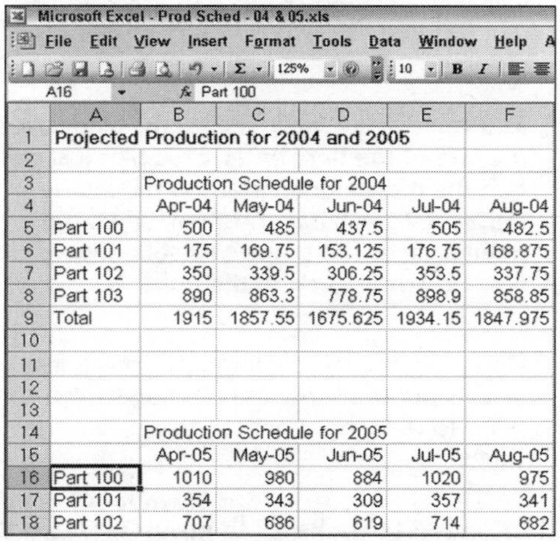

	A	B	C	D	E	F
1	Projected Production for 2004 and 2005					
2						
3		Production Schedule for 2004				
4		Apr-04	May-04	Jun-04	Jul-04	Aug-04
5	Part 100	500	485	437.5	505	482.5
6	Part 101	175	169.75	153.125	176.75	168.875
7	Part 102	350	339.5	306.25	353.5	337.75
8	Part 103	890	863.3	778.75	898.9	858.85
9	Total	1915	1857.55	1675.625	1934.15	1847.975
10						
11						
12						
13						
14		Production Schedule for 2005				
15		Apr-05	May-05	Jun-05	Jul-05	Aug-05
16	Part 100	1010	980	884	1020	975
17	Part 101	354	343	309	357	341
18	Part 102	707	686	619	714	682

• **Figure 9-4: Pressing Ctrl+↓ again moves the cell pointer down to A16 — the first occupied cell after the blanks.**

In navigating the sample worksheet shown in Figures 9-1 through 9-4, I could go on in this manner — leaping from one occupied cell to the next and hopping over all the blanks in between.

Of course, if you happen to be in the very last occupied cell in a particular column or row and then use the Ctrl+arrow key combination again, Excel jumps to the very last worksheet cell in that direction in that column or row (that is, column IV when you press Ctrl+→, column A when you press Ctrl+←, row 65536 when you press Ctrl+↓, and row 1 when you press Ctrl+↑).

Before inserting new rows or columns in a worksheet with which you're not totally familiar, press Ctrl plus the appropriate arrow key to make sure that no hidden data ranges will be split by your insertion. If the cell pointer shoots to the very first or last column or row of the sheet, you know the way is clear.

Going right to the last cell in a sheet

When you're building a new spreadsheet that has only one table in it, you can use the keystroke shortcut Ctrl+End to zip right to the last cell in the sheet. This keystroke shortcut jumps you right to the end of the occupied regions in your worksheet, enabling you to identify open areas in the sheet where you can build new tables and lists of data.

Understand, however, that the last cell of a worksheet can be, and often is, itself blank. This is because Excel defines the last cell in any given worksheet as the one that lies at the intersection of the last occupied row and column and considers a row or column to be occupied if any of its cells have data in them.

As Figure 9-5 illustrates, the last cell of the sheet is blank whenever you've made any entries in the last occupied column even when your data entries don't yet extend down to the last occupied row. The last cell also is blank if you've made any entries in the last occupied row of the sheet but haven't made it all across to the last occupied column.

 Whereas the last cell that Excel takes you to when you press Ctrl+End constantly changes when you expand the data ranges in the sheet, the first cell the program takes you to when you press Ctrl+Home is always A1 of whatever sheet is active.

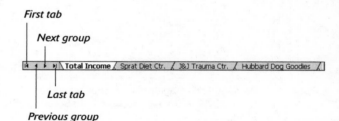

• **Figure 9-5:** Pressing Ctrl+End takes you directly to the last cell in the sheet.

Zipping through the sheets

It's bad enough trying to find your place in a spreadsheet containing data spread all over a single worksheet, but it's even worse when you're dealing with a spreadsheet whose data is parsed out over several worksheets. (Dealing with more than two worksheets can be a real nightmare.) Nevertheless, many spreadsheets benefit greatly from a multisheet layout — especially those that consolidate data from many time periods or that contain schedules of data that are used as lookup tables referred to by formulas in the main sheet.

To help you get quickly to the sheet you need in a spreadsheet that utilizes many sheets (more than the default three), you can rely on the Sheet Tab scrolling buttons (see Figure 9-6) to bring the worksheet you want to work with into view so you can activate it:

✔ Click the Next Group button to bring the next group of sheet tabs into view in the area between the Sheet Tab scrolling buttons and the horizontal scroll bar.

✔ Click the Last Tab button to bring the last group with the book's final sheet tab into view in this area.

First tab

Next group

Last tab

Previous group

• **Figure 9-6:** Using the Sheet Tab scrolling buttons to scroll through the sheets of a workbook.

 You can display more sheet tabs by decreasing the size of the horizontal scroll bar; just position the mouse pointer at the beginning of the horizontal scroll bar and then, when the pointer takes the shape of a split double-headed arrow, drag to the right.

Don't forget that scrolling a sheet tab into view is not the same as selecting it: You still need to click the sheet tab to activate the sheet.

If you don't need to make a big jump between the sheets in your workbook, you can move quickly from sheet to sheet by pressing the Ctrl+Page Down and Ctrl+Page Up keystroke shortcuts. Press Ctrl+Page

Down to activate the next sheet in the workbook, and press Ctrl+Page Up to activate the previous one. The great thing about these keystroke combinations is that they not only bring the sheet tab into view but also automatically activate the sheet at the same time!

A Little Go To Magic

I find that a lot of users forget that the Excel Go To feature is a great way to go directly to a particular cell range in the spreadsheet. This is probably because many users don't bother to assign names to their cell ranges — see Technique 26 for details — which is really what makes using Go To worthwhile.

To use the Go To dialog box, follow these steps:

1. **Press F5 or Ctrl+G (or choose Edit⇨Go To).**

Excel opens a Go To dialog box similar to the one shown in Figure 9-7.

2. **Enter the address of the cell you want to go to (such as E150 or AB20) in the Reference text box, or if your spreadsheet contains range names, select the name of the range in the Go To list box. Then click OK.**

If you enter a cell address, Excel positions the cell pointer in that cell. If you select a range name, the program selects all the cells in the range, making the first cell in that range the active one.

After you use the Go To feature to jump to a particular cell or cell range, the Reference text box shows the address of the active cell from which you jumped. This means that if you decide that you want to return to the cell you originally came from, all you have to do is press F5 (or Ctrl+G) and then immediately press Enter — you don't even need to take time to examine the contents of the Go To dialog box.

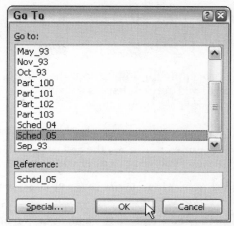

• **Figure 9-7:** Using the Go To dialog box to jump directly to a new cell in the worksheet.

After you use the Go To feature to return to the cell that marked your original starting point, the Reference text box shows the address of the cell or range that you originally jumped to. This means that, if you change your mind yet again and decide that you want to revisit the cell or range you originally jumped to, you can do so by pressing F5 (or Ctrl+G) and then immediately pressing Enter.

You can, in fact, bounce back and forth from source to destination and then from destination back to source with F5, Enter, F5, Enter, as long as you need to compare and go back and forth between the two regions of the spreadsheet. And whenever you need to head over to a new region, just enter a new cell address in the Reference text box or select a new range name for it.

 The great thing about using Go To with cell range names is that Excel whisks you back and forth not only between separate regions in the same worksheet but also between regions on separate worksheets.

Zooming Out to Get the Big Picture

The last procedure for finding your desired place in a worksheet and getting there is a visual one. Here are the general steps you follow:

1. Use the Zoom feature to zoom out on the worksheet until you can see the cell range or embedded chart you want to work with.

2. Click somewhere in the range or chart to set the cell pointer in it.

3. Use the Zoom feature to zoom in on the new region so you can read and work with its data.

Figures 9-8 and 9-9 illustrate how you can make this work. First, I zoomed out on the work by setting the magnification to 15% of normal (by entering 15 into Zoom button's text box on the Standard toolbar). As you see in Figure 9-8, doing this made all the data in the table in the initial cell range A1:R15 completely illegible while at the same time revealing the location of two additional items on the worksheet — an embedded chart in the cell range J92:P112 and another table of data in the cell range R92:AJ104.

To get directly to the table in the range R92:AJ104 and be able to edit its data, I clicked the cell pointer on cell U104 while the sheet was still in 15% magnification. Then I increased the magnification back to normal (by selecting 100% in the Zoom button's pop-up menu on the Standard toolbar), as shown in Figure 9-9.

 After hunting a cell range in this manner, I immediately assign a name to the range (see Technique 26) so that afterwards I can return to the range with the Go To feature (see "A Little Go To Magic," earlier in this technique, for details).

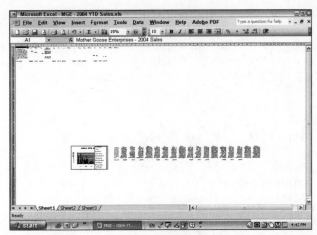

• **Figure 9-8:** Zooming out to 15% magnification reveals the location of a second table of data and an embedded chart.

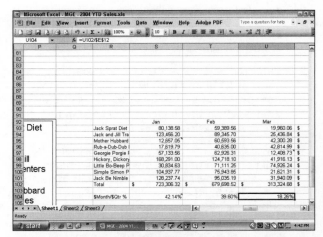

• **Figure 9-9:** Resetting the cell pointer and zooming back to 100% magnification.

Technique 10

Making the Most Efficient Cell Selections

Save Time By

- Selecting ranges with AutoSelect
- Selecting ranges with Go To
- Selecting entire columns, rows, or sheets

Because cell selection is one of the most basic and regularly performed worksheet task, knowing how to efficiently select ranges of cells in the spreadsheet can go a long way toward making you a truly effective worker. Cell selection, while rudimentary, is still very important to taking a lot of the drudgery out of spreadsheet work. After all, selecting cells is the thing you have to do before you can assign new formatting and alignment; move, copy, or reorient the data; and print specific parts of the spreadsheet.

Before going over some of the fancier and more grandiose procedures for selecting cells in a worksheet, you might want to review the two basic procedures for using a mouse to select single cell ranges in the worksheet:

- Click the first cell in the range and then drag the thick, white-cross pointer to the last cell.

- Click the first cell in the range, and then hold down the Shift key as you click the last cell you want to select (a procedure known as Shift+clicking).

To select multiple, nonadjacent cell selections at a time (also known as a noncontiguous cell selection), you follow these steps:

1. **Select the first cell range with your mouse as usual.**

2. **Hold down the Ctrl key as you use your mouse to select the second range.**

   When you hold down the Ctrl key as you start to select the second range, Excel does not deselect the first range — as it normally would — so this first range continues to be highlighted (shaded) in the worksheet, as shown in Figure 10-1.

3. **Repeat Step 2 as needed to select all additional ranges that need to be included in the noncontiguous cell selection and then release both the Ctrl key and the mouse button at the same time.**

Microsoft Excel - Book1

File   Edit   View   Insert   Format   Tools   Data   Window   Help   Adobe Pl

D3   ƒx 4947.1172928

	A	B	C	D	E	F	G	H
1								
2								
3		34.56		4947.117	1632.549	3265.097		
4		107.136		321.5626	106.1157	212.2313		
5		332.1216		20.90157	6.897518	13.79504		
6		1029.577		1.358602	0.448339	0.896677		
7		3191.689		0.088309	0.029142	0.058284		
8		9894.235		0.00574	0.001894	0.003788		
9								
10								
11								
12								

• **Figure 10-1: Selecting two cell ranges as part of a noncontiguous cell selection.**

Keep in mind that you can also use the keyboard to select cell ranges. After moving the cell pointer to the first cell in the range, hold down the Shift key as you press the appropriate cursor key (an arrow key or Page Up or Page Down). Holding down the Shift key anchors the cell range on the first cell and enables the program to extend the range when you press a cursor key. If you find holding down the Shift key too tiring, you can anchor the cell range on the current cell by pressing F8 — that puts the program into EXT (Extend) mode.

 When selecting a range of cells that contain sequential data via the keyboard, you can really save time by combining the Ctrl+arrow key trick to hop from one end of a table of data to the other with the Shift key. By pressing Ctrl+Shift+arrow key, Excel selects from the current cell all the way to the last occupied cell in the arrow's direction in one fell swoop.

To select a noncontiguous range with the keyboard, you follow these steps:

1. Position the cell pointer in the first cell of the first range to select, press F8 to put the program in EXT mode, and then select the range with the cursor keys.

2. Press Shift+F8 to switch the program into ADD mode and then move the cell pointer to the first cell of the second range you want to select.

3. Press F8 again to switch back into EXT mode and then select this second range with the cursor keys.

4. Repeat Steps 2 and 3 until you select all the ranges you want included in the noncontiguous cell selection.

AutoSelect at Your Service

AutoSelect is a great timesaving feature that enables you to select an entire table of data as a single cell selection in a couple of double-clicks of the mouse. To use AutoSelect to select your table, follow these few steps:

1. Position the mouse pointer in the first cell in the table of data you want to select.

Note that for this procedure to work, the columns and rows of the table must not contain blanks.

2. Position the mouse pointer somewhere along the bottom border of the cell pointer and then, when the mouse pointer changes to an arrowhead pointing to crisscrossed double-headed arrows (as shown in Figure 10-2), hold down the Shift key and double-click the mouse.

Microsoft Excel - Cell Selections.xls

File   Edit   View   Insert   Format   Tools   Data   Window

B3   ƒx 34.56

	A	B	C	D	E	F
1						
2						
3		34.56	4,947.12	1,632.55	3,265.10	
4		107.14	321.56	106.12	212.23	
5		332.12	20.90	6.90	13.80	
6		1,029.58	1.36	0.45	0.90	
7		3,191.69	0.09	0.03	0.06	
8		9,894.23	0.01	0.00	0.00	
9						
10						
11						
12						

• **Figure 10-2: Getting ready to select the first column of the table.**

If you forget to hold down the Shift key before you double-click, the cell pointer just jumps to the last occupied cell in the column without extending the cell selection.

3. **Position the mouse pointer somewhere along the right edge of the current cell selection and then, when the mouse pointer changes to an arrowhead pointing to crisscrossed double-headed arrows — as shown in Figure 10-3 — hold down the Shift key and double-click the mouse a second time.**

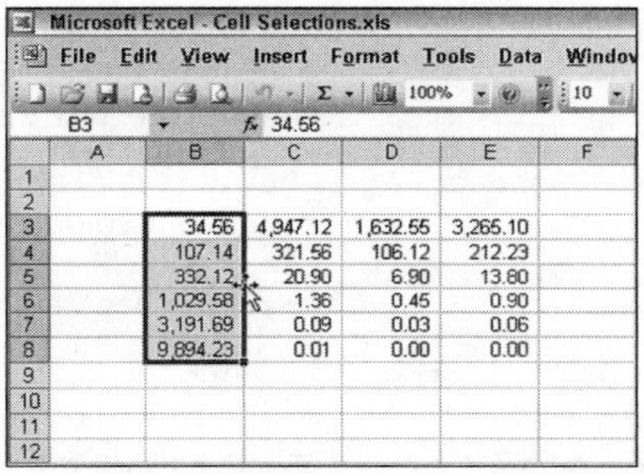

• **Figure 10-3: Extending the cell selection down the first column of the table with AutoSelect.**

After you double-click the right edge of the first cell selection (while holding down the Shift key to extend it), Excel extends the cell selection to include all the columns of data in the table, stopping automatically at the first blank row in the worksheet (see Figure 10-4).

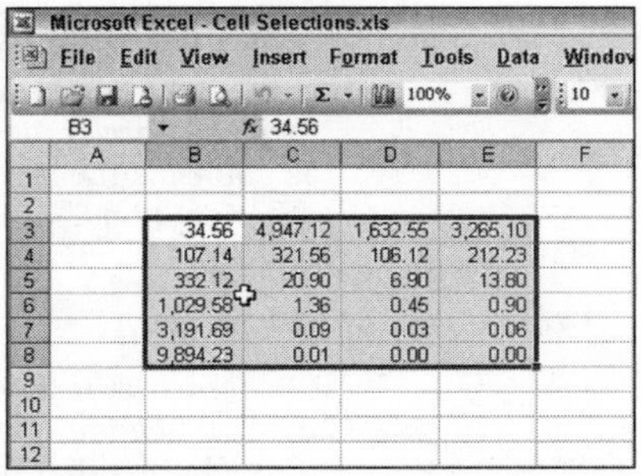

• **Figure 10-4: Extending the cell selection across the table with AutoSelect.**

Go To 1t and Select 1t

In Technique 9, I outline how you can use Excel's Go To feature to jump instantly to anywhere in the current worksheet. At that time, I also suggest that you go out of your way and give names to the cell ranges (as outlined in Technique 26) that you routinely use in a spreadsheet.

One reason why I keep harping about this is because giving names to cell ranges enables you to use the Go To feature to instantly select the entire range whenever you need to refer to it. (This little tidbit is worth its weight in gold when it comes to a cell range in a spreadsheet that you routinely need to print out.) For example, in the table of data shown in the cell range B3:E8 shown in Figure 10-5, I assigned five range names:

- ✔ **data_table** to the cell range B3:E8 to select the entire table of data

- ✔ **first_col** to the cell range B3:B8 to select only the first column of data

- ✔ **second_col** to the cell range C3:C8 to select just the second column of data

- ✔ **third_col** to the cell range D3:D8 to select just the third column of data

- ✔ **fourth_col** to the cell range E3:E8 to select only the last column of data

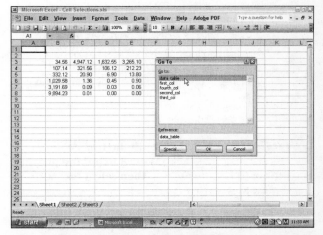

• **Figure 10-5: Selecting a cell range by choosing its range name in the Go To dialog box.**

After assigning the range names, selecting the entire table of data (for printing or for formatting) from anywhere in the workbook (I don't have to be on the same worksheet), takes only two steps:

1. **Press F5 or Ctrl+G to open the Go To dialog box.**

2. **Select the range name you want (data_table, for example) in the Go To list box and then click OK.**

Note that although using the Go To feature to select named cell ranges is by far the easiest way to do it, you can use this feature to select a range of cells by entering the address of the first and last cell in the range in the Go To dialog box as follows:

1. **Press F5 or Ctrl+G, and then enter the address of the first cell in the range to be selected in the Reference text box and click OK.**

2. **Press F8 to switch Excel into EXT (Extend) mode.**

3. **Press F5 or Ctrl+G, and then enter the address of the last cell in the range to be selected in the Reference text box and click OK.**

4. **Press F8 to switch Excel out of EXT mode and back into Ready mode.**

 Don't forget the last step of this Go To procedure, or you'll really think Excel has gone haywire when any move you make in the worksheet continues to highlight intervening cells.

Going for the Big Selections

In addition to being able to select single and multiple cell ranges in a worksheet, you also need to be aware of some tricks for quickly making big selections, including selecting entire columns, rows, and, yes, even the entire worksheet. Table 10-1 gives you an overview of this very handy information.

TABLE 10-1: SELECTING COMPLETE COLUMNS, ROWS, AND SHEETS

To Select This	Do This
Current worksheet	Press Ctrl+A or click the square formed by the intersection of the column and row headers.
All worksheets in the workbook	Right-click the tab of the active worksheet and then choose Select All Sheets.
Sequential worksheets	Click the tab of the first sheet and then hold down the Shift key as you click the tab of the last worksheet to select.
Nonsequential worksheets	Click the tab of the first sheet and then hold down the Ctrl key as you click the tabs of the other worksheets to select.
Single column	Click the letter of the column in the column header.
Sequential columns	Click the first column's letter in the column header. Then drag through the letters of the other columns to the left or right, or press Shift+→ or Shift+←.
Nonsequential columns	Click the first column's letter in the column header and then hold down the Ctrl key as you click the letters of the other columns.
Single row	Click the row's number in the row header.
Sequential rows	Click the first row's number in the row header. Then drag through the other numbers of the other rows up or down, or press Shift+↓ or Shift+↑.
Nonsequential rows	Click the first row's number in the row header and then hold down the Ctrl key as you click the numbers of the other rows.

When you select multiple worksheets, Excel goes into Group mode (indicated by [Group] after the filename on the title bar). In Group mode, all the data entry, formatting, and editing you do in the active sheet is simultaneously performed in the other selected sheets as well.

Technique 11

Speeding Through Long Data Entries with AutoCorrect

AutoCorrect is Excel's attempt to save you time when doing data entry in a spreadsheet. It anticipates what you enter and, if necessary, corrects it or converts it into special types of data such as live hyperlinks and *smart tags* — data recognized as being of a particular kind, such as Wall Street financial symbols and personal names. The AutoCorrect feature in Excel encompasses three areas:

✔ **AutoCorrect:** Automatically corrects common spelling errors whenever you make them in cell entries

✔ **AutoFormat As You Type:** Automatically turns Web addresses and network paths into live hyperlinks and expands data lists when you add a new record to them

✔ **Smart Tags:** Enables you to control all the smart tag settings, including checking the workbook for data that Excel identifies as a type of smart tag, controlling the appearance of the Smart Tag indicator in the worksheet cells, looking online for more smart tag applications, and making the smart tags identified in your spreadsheet a permanent part of the workbook file by embedding them in it

Setting the Correct AutoCorrect Settings

The AutoCorrect options can save you a great deal of spell-checking time, especially if you go to the trouble of adding your own common typos to the ones that the feature is already set to take care of. When you first open the AutoCorrect dialog box (Tools⇨AutoCorrect Options) and select its AutoCorrect tab (see Figure 11-1), Excel activates all the check box settings that dispose of many common typing errors such as typing with the Caps Lock key on or failing to capitalize the days of the week or the beginning of a sentence.

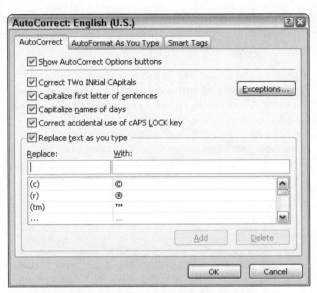

• **Figure 11-1: Entering new replacements for the AutoCorrect feature.**

The program also selects the Replace Text As You Type check box that activates all the automatic corrections contained in the list box below. If you don't want to use one of these readymade corrections (such as automatically turning three periods in a row into a real live ellipsis), simply select the entry in the list box and then click the Delete button to get rid of it.

If you have a tendency to make a certain typo that's not already included on the list, you can add it by entering the typo in the Replace text box and the automatic replacement in the With text box and then clicking Add.

 If you have certain abbreviations that shouldn't be capitalized or special terms with more than one capital letter at the beginning that you routinely use in your spreadsheets, instead of deactivating the AutoCorrect settings that otherwise change them, use the Exceptions button to add the particular abbreviations or terms to either the lists of First Letter or INitial CAps exceptions that the program then leaves alone.

Losing the Links

Excel has this nasty tendency to automatically turn any cell entry that looks like a Web address, an e-mail address, or a path to a network folder into a live hyperlink. If you then click this link (even by accident), Excel attempts to open the Web page, e-mail message program, or Windows Explorer with the network folder. Now, this is not good, because you can end up online (especially if your computer is connected to the Internet as part of its network or uses some sort of wireless connection) when all you intended to do was click a cell to select it!

Fortunately, you can stop Excel from making all these addresses hot by taking these steps:

1. Choose Tools➪AutoCorrect Options to open the AutoCorrect dialog box.

2. Select the AutoFormat As You Type tab.

3. Deselect the Internet and Network Paths with Hyperlinks check box (as shown in Figure 11-2) and then click OK.

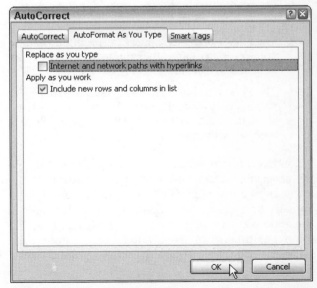

• **Figure 11-2: Turning off the automatic hyperlinks setting.**

If you have a worksheet that already contains hot links and you want to deactivate them, you need to right-click each link and choose Remove Hyperlink from the menu that appears.

Taming the Smart Tags

Depending upon the type of work you do with Excel, the Smart Tags feature may appear to you to be either one of the most brilliant or one of the most useless program features. The way smart tags work in Microsoft Office applications such as Word and Excel is that the programs scan their documents looking for particular types of entries (called *recognizers*) to which it can affix a specific type of smart tag program. For example, Excel comes with three smart tag programs, one for dealing with dates, another for dealing with financial symbols used by Wall Street, and a third for dealing with personal names:

✔ The Date smart tag program enables you to open your Microsoft Outlook calendar right to the date contained in the cell (assuming the date is one that the calendar program covers).

✔ The Financial Symbol smart tag program enables you to get an online stock quote for the company in question from MSN Money.

✔ The Person Name smart tag program enables you to add people to your Outlook Contacts list, send an e-mail message to them, or schedule a meeting with them.

When Excel identifies an entry for a particular smart tag program, it inserts a Smart Tag indicator in the lower-right corner of its cell — the indicator initially appears as a small purple triangle. To select one of the actions offered by a particular smart tag program, position the mouse pointer over its smart tag indicator and then position the mouse pointer over

the Smart Tag Actions button (the one with the i enclosed in a circle) that appears to the right of the indicator and click its drop-down button.

If smart tags sound like something that would only complicate your life unnecessarily, you simply need to make sure that the smart tags option is turned off. To do this, select the Smart Tags tab in the AutoCorrect dialog box (Tools⇨AutoCorrect Options), and then make sure that the Label Data with Smart Tags check box is deselected before you click OK.

If, however, smart tags seem like something that might well enhance your work, you do just the opposite:

1. **On the Smart Tags tab of the AutoCorrect dialog box, select the Label Data with Smart Tags check box, and then in the Recognizers list box, select the check boxes for the smart tag programs you want to activate. (See Figure 11-3.)**

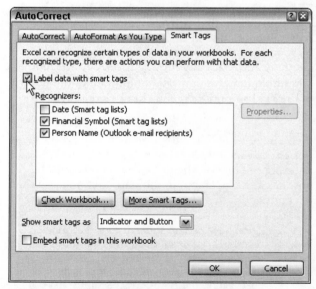

• **Figure 11-3: Modifying the smart tag settings.**

2. If you want to suppress the appearance of the smart tag indicators in the recognized cells, choose None or Button Only from the Show Smart Tags As drop-down list.

3. If you want to be able to save smart tags as part of the workbook file, select the Embed Smart Tags in This Workbook check box.

4. When you're finished making your selections, click OK.

Technique 12

Data Entry Tricks

Save Time By

- Entering the same value in multiple cells
- Constraining entries to a single range
- Working in Group mode

Let's face it: Data entry, while one of the most important spreadsheet tasks you do, is also often one of the most tedious. The tips in this technique (especially when coupled with those in Techniques 13, 14, and 15) are designed to take some of the drudgery out of doing data entry by helping you work more efficiently and, at the same time, more accurately.

These tips include

- Taking advantage of Excel's ability to enter the same entry in multiple cells or cell ranges in one operation.

- Constraining data entry to a preselected cell range. (This one applies only when you're creating a standard table of data and you know beforehand how many columns and rows it takes up.)

- Doing simultaneous data entry in multiple worksheets of the same workbook by working in Group mode. (This one applies only to spreadsheets that use multiple worksheets, all of which share a common layout and data.)

Making the Same Entry in Many Places

Many spreadsheets use the same column or row headings — even the same values — over and over again. When you know ahead of time that you need to enter the same label or value in many cells in the same worksheet, you can do this by following these simple steps:

1. Select all the cells and cell ranges that require the same entry as a noncontiguous cell selection. (See Technique 10 if you need help doing this.)

2. Type the label or value into the active cell of the noncontiguous cell selection.

Pause for a second after entering the data in the active cell and resist the natural temptation to complete this entry by pressing the Enter key or clicking the Enter box on the Formula bar.

 The third and last step in this procedure is critical to entering the data in all the selected cells rather than in just the active one.

3. **Press Ctrl+Enter to complete the data entry, entering it in every cell in the noncontiguous cell selection.**

Figures 12-1 and 12-2 illustrate how this procedure works. In Figure 12-1, I need to enter Rock as the first music category for both CDs and Cassettes in cells A4 and A10. To make this entry at the same time in both cells, I first select them as a noncontiguous cell selection and then type Rock into the active cell A10.

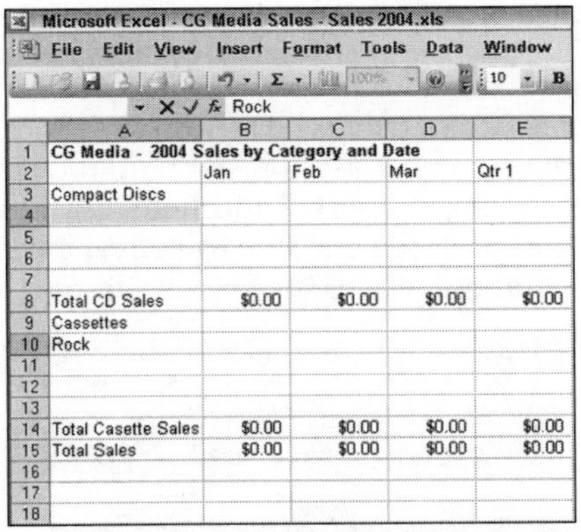

• **Figure 12-1: Getting ready to make the same entry in the two selected cells by pressing Ctrl+Enter.**

To complete the data entry in both cells A4 and A10, I must remember to press Ctrl+Enter rather than just press the Enter key alone or click the Enter button on the Formula bar. Figure 12-2 shows the worksheet after I press Ctrl+Enter to insert Rock in both cells A4 and A10.

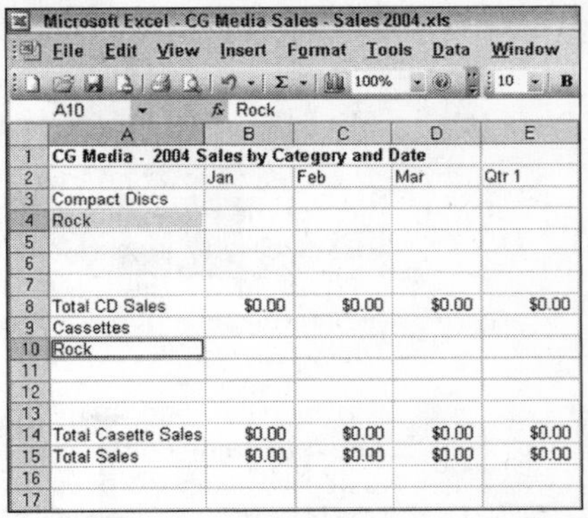

• **Figure 12-2: The worksheet after entering the same category entry in both selected cells in one operation.**

Before collapsing the cell selection containing the same entry, apply any formatting common to the entries. In my example, I indented both Rock category entries by clicking the Increase Indent button on the Formatting toolbar before dispensing with the noncontiguous cell selection.

Putting the Wraps on the Data Entry

One of the most efficient ways to enter data into a new table in your spreadsheet is to preselect the range with the blank cells where you need to enter the data before you start doing any data entry. The reason that preselecting the blank cell range works so well is that in so doing, you constrain the cell pointer to that range — provided you press *only* the keystrokes shown in Table 12-1 to complete the data entries and to move the cell pointer within the range. This frees you from having to pay any attention to repositioning the cell pointer when entering the table data. That way, you can keep all your attention where it should be on the printed copy from which you're taking the data.

TABLE 12-1: KEYSTROKES FOR MOVING WITHIN A SELECTED CELL RANGE

When You Press This	The Cell Pointer Moves Here
Enter	Down each row and then right across the remaining columns of the selected range. (Moves one column to the right, same as Tab when the selection consists of a single row.)
Shift+Enter	Up each row and then left across the remaining columns of the selected range. (Moves one column to the left when the selection consists of a single row.)
Tab	To the next column right and then to the beginning of the next row down in the selected range. (Moves down one row when the selection consists of a single column, same as Enter.)
Shift+Tab	To the next column left and then to the beginning of the row above in the selected range. (Moves up one row when the selection consists of a single column, same as Shift+Enter.)
Ctrl+period (.)	From one corner to the next corner of the selected range, in a clockwise direction.

When entering data in a preselected range, you must not press an arrow key to complete any of the entries, or you'll end up collapsing the cell selection at the same time you put the new entry in the current cell.

Figures 12-3 and 12-4 illustrate how doing data entry in a preselected cell range works. In these figures, I'm constructing a simple table that will list the sales prices for furniture in the upcoming spring sale.

In Figure 12-3, I have reached the end of the data entry for the second row of the table — the one containing the column headings — and I'm just about to

enter the last column heading `Sales Price` in cell E3. To get to this point, I've already entered the table heading in A2 (the first cell of the selected cell range) by pressing the Enter key. Doing so repositioned the pointer down one row in cell A3. I then completed each column heading entry in cells A3, B3, C3, and D4 across row 3 by pressing the Tab key, which automatically advances the cell pointer one column to the right upon data entry completion.

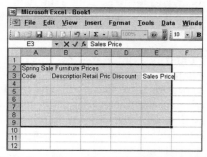

• **Figure 12-3:** Entering column headings across the row with Tab in the preselected cell range A2:E9.

When I press Tab again to insert the Sales Price column heading in cell E3 — the last column of the selected cell range — Excel automatically advances the cell pointer down one row to cell A4 (see Figure 12-4), the first column of the selected range.

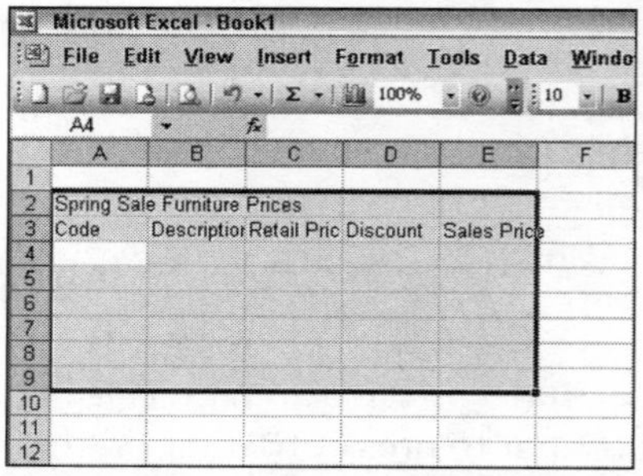

• **Figure 12-4:** Sales table after entering the last column heading in E3 and pressing Tab.

At this point, I want to switch the direction of my data entry, preferring to enter the Code numbers down each column by pressing Enter (instead of

Tab) to complete their entries. When I reach cell A9 in the last row of the cell selection and press Enter to complete its entry, Excel automatically advances the cell pointer to B2 — the top row of the next column. After pressing the Enter key twice to move down this row to the blank cell in B4, I'm all set to enter the description of the piece given the Code Number 12-305 (it's a 36-inch round table).

I continue along in this manner entering the furniture descriptions down the rest of column B, the retail prices down column C, and the discount percentages down column D. After that, to complete the table, I click E4 (which collapses the cell selection to just that cell) and enter the master formula that calculates the spring sale price (using the table's retail price and discount amount), which I then copy down the rest of the column using AutoFill. (See Technique 13.)

Let's Do It as a Group!

When you select more than one worksheet at a time (see Technique 10), Excel goes into what is called Group mode (indicated by the appearance of [Group] after the filename on the title bar of the Excel window). When the program is in Group mode, any entry you make in the active worksheet is also made in all the other selected sheets.

You can put this Group feature to good use when building spreadsheets that naturally use multiple worksheets and which require the same entries in the same cells of each sheet. For example, suppose you're creating a spreadsheet that tracks sales over the 12 months of the current fiscal year and you want to put each of the 12 monthly sales tables on a separate worksheet (because this makes it so much easier to consolidate their data when you want to create a table showing the total annual sales). Each table requires the same row and column headings and will occupy the same region of cells on its sheet.

Rather than enter all the column and row headings for the initial sales table on the first worksheet and then copy these headings to the other 11 worksheets, a quicker way is to select all 12 worksheets, and then just by entering the headings in the active worksheet, you're also entering them in all the other selected sheets.

Figure 12-5 illustrates how this works. To begin this new workbook, I added nine additional worksheets to the default three. Next, I selected all 12 sheets (by right-clicking the tab of Sheet1, the active sheet, and then selecting Select All Sheets on its shortcut menu). This puts the program into Group mode so that the common worksheet title and all row headings that you see in this figure are not only entered into cell B1 and the range A3:A14 in Sheet1 but in all the other 11 selected sheets as well.

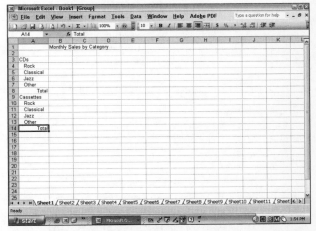

• **Figure 12-5:** Entering the same column and row headings in each of the selected sheets in Group mode.

Figure 12-6 confirms the fact that Group editing really works. (I swear no special effects were used in the taking of this screen shot.) For this figure, I clicked the tab for Sheet10. Doing this not only immediately deselected all the other sheets and switched the program out of Group mode but instantly revealed that this worksheet contains exactly the same headings that I entered in Sheet1. (Refer to Figure 12-5.) The only difference between the two screen shots is that, before taking Figure 12-6, I had the good sense to stop and save the workbook so that there was no danger that I could lose this data and have to go through this Group editing procedure again.

 Selecting another worksheet while in Group mode immediately deselects all but the new active worksheet and switches you back into normal, single-sheet editing mode. Therefore, don't stop to check the entries on another sheet until you've completed all the common data entry, at which time you can ungroup the sheets (by right-clicking a sheet tab in the group and selecting Ungroup Sheets). Then select the individual sheets to display their data by selecting their sheet tabs.

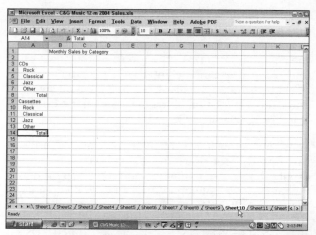

• **Figure 12-6:** Sheet 10 now contains the same entries that I made in Sheet1 (refer to Figure 12-5) thanks to Group editing.

Technique 13

Speeding Up Data Entry with AutoFill

Save Time By

- Filling in commonly used series
- Filling with different increments
- Creating custom fill lists

Once in a blue moon, a software feature comes along that's so handy that you wonder how you ever got along without it. Excel's AutoFill feature is that kind of spreadsheet innovation for me. Here, for once, is some Microsoft Intelli-sense that actually does make some sense because it is a real timesaver.

With AutoFill, you can fill out a sequential series of entries (such as months of the year or days of the week) across a row or up or down a column simply by entering the first entry in the series and then dragging the cell pointer by its Fill handle — the tiny black square that appears in the lower-right corner of the active cell. In addition, you can have Excel increment the entries in the series by values other than just one (be it one day, one month, or one number). And as if that isn't enough, Excel also enables you to create your own custom fill lists that tell Excel how to fill in a list whenever you enter one of its unique members and then go for the Fill handle.

All three of these procedures are covered in this technique on AutoFill, which is undoubtedly one of my favorite Excel features.

 You also use this same AutoFill feature to extend formulas in the tables in your spreadsheet. When using AutoFill to copy formulas, the feature naturally adjusts its cell references instead of generating a sequential series — see Technique 24 for details.

Getting Your Fill of AutoFill

Straight out of the box, AutoFill is about as versatile and easy to use as any Excel feature can be. Table 13-1 shows the kinds of initial entries you can make — with examples of the kind of series that they generate — when you drag the Fill handle across or down new cells. As you can see from the examples shown in this table, Excel can create a fairly wide array of sequential date and time series as well as some highly individual ones (for item and code numbers), all of which don't require you to customize the feature whatsoever.

TABLE 13-1: SAMPLES OF SERIES YOU CAN GENERATE WITH AUTOFILL

Initial Value	Series Created by AutoFill in the Next Three Cells
September	October, November, December
Sep	Oct, Nov, Dec
Monday	Tuesday, Wednesday, Thursday
Fri	Sat, Sun, Mon
3/13/1999	3/14/1999, 3/15/1999, 3/16/1999
4-Jan	5-Jan, 6-Jan, 7-Jan
Dec-04	Jan-05, Feb-05, Mar-05
8:00 AM	9:00 AM, 10:00 AM, 11:00 AM
11:03	12:03, 13:03, 14:03
Quarter 1	Quarter 2, Quarter 3, Quarter 4
Qtr 4	Qtr 1, Qtr 2, Qtr 3
Q2	Q3, Q4, Q1
40 Mill Road	41 Mill Road, 42 Mill Road, 43 Mill Road
'00945	'00946, '00947, '00948
L17-800	L17-801, L17-802, L17-803

 When you drag the Fill handle over the next cell, you can tell right away what kind of sequential series your initial entry will generate. The ToolTip trailing the mouse pointer shows you right away the next item in the sequence that Excel is creating.

Figures 13-1 and 13-2 illustrate the use of the AutoFill feature to generate a sequential series from an initial entry. In Figure 13-1, I entered January into cell A2 and then dragged the Fill handle down column A until I reached cell A13. Note that Excel displays a ToolTip next to the black cross pointer, which indicates that dragging down to cell A13 takes me from January through July and September all the way to the month of December.

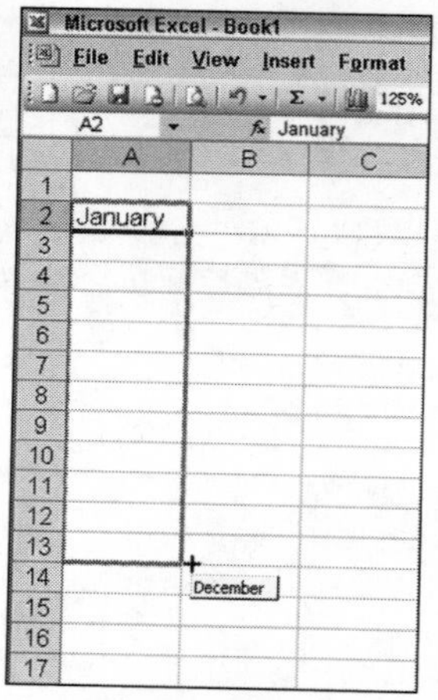

• **Figure 13-1:** Using AutoFill to generate the series of months from an initial January entry in cell A2.

Figure 13-2 shows the new worksheet with the 12-month series after I released the mouse button. Notice the appearance of the AutoFill Options button to the right of the Fill handle.

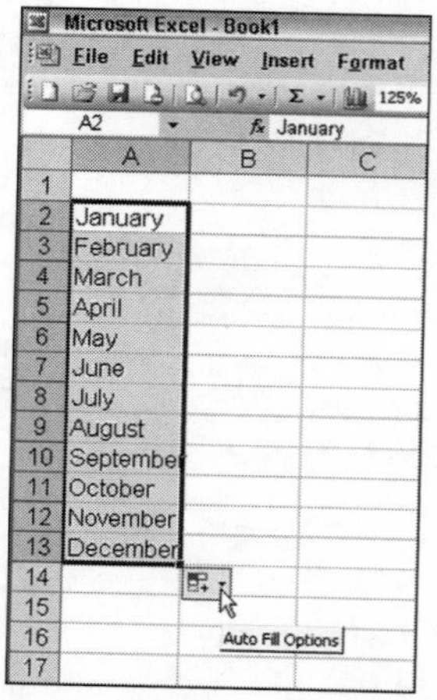

• **Figure 13-2:** Series of months created after dragging the Fill handle down to cell A13 and releasing the mouse button.

The AutoFill Options button gives you access to menu options that enable you to convert a series in the fill range into copies of the initial value (and vice versa to convert copies into a filled series) as well as to fill the range with formatting only or to fill the series without copying the formatting of the initial cell. To suppress the display of this button, deselect the Show Paste Options check box on the Edit tab of the Options dialog box (Tools⇨Options).

Using AutoFill to generate a sequentially numbered series

As you may have noticed in the last two examples in Table 13-1, in initial entries that mix numbers and text — as in 40 Mill Road — or entries whose numbers are entered as labels rather than values — as in '00945 or L17-800 — Excel is really good at identifying what number to increment.

As a result, you'd probably expect Excel to be an ace when it comes to generating a sequentially numbered series such as 1, 2, 3, 4, and the like (useful in numbering your data list records so that you can refer to them and sort them by record number). Unfortunately, AutoFill falls flat on its face (can a software feature have a face?) when it comes to doing this. To prove it, all you have to do is enter the number 1 in any blank cell and then drag the Fill handle over just a few blank cells in columns to the right or below to prove this point: Instead of generating the simplest of sequentially numbered series (1, 2, 3, 4 . . .), Excel just stupidly copies the number 1 to all the cells you drag through.

Fortunately, Excel does provide a way to force AutoFill (however reluctantly) to create a sequential series from an initial value rather than just copying it everyplace you drag the Fill handle. The only problem is that it requires the use of the Ctrl key, which is used in other mouse operations (cell drag-and-drop, for instance) to switch to making a copy of the selected cells or objects. In this case, however, depressing the Ctrl key as you drag the Fill handle prevents Excel from copying the number and forces it to generate a true sequentially numbered series.

 If you, like me, routinely forget to hold down the Ctrl key and therefore end up with the same number copied into a range of cells, select Fill Series on the pop-up menu attached to the AutoFill Options button (which automatically appears on the cell pointer's Fill handle as soon as you release the mouse button) to convert the copies into a bona-fide numeric sequence, as shown in Figure 13-3.

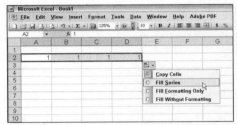

• **Figure 13-3: Converting a range filled with copies of the same number into a sequential series.**

Copying an entry instead of filling in a series

You can also use the Ctrl key to force Excel to copy an initial entry in the cell range you drag through in those situations where Excel would otherwise use the entry as the starting point for generating a sequential series. Here, the association of the Ctrl key with copying in drag-and-drop operations makes perfect sense (reinforced by the appearance of a tiny plus sign that appears above and to the right of the black cross mouse pointer).

Figure 13-4 illustrates how you can force Excel to copy an initial entry in a cell range rather than use it to generate a new series. In this new worksheet, I entered the column heading Module 5 in cell A2. To copy this heading across row 2 to the cell range B2:D2 (rather than generate the series Module 5, Module 6, Module 7, and Module 8), I hold down the

Ctrl key as I drag the Fill handle through this range. Note the presence of the plus sign above the black cross mouse pointer, here correctly indicating that Excel will make a copy rather than generate a series.

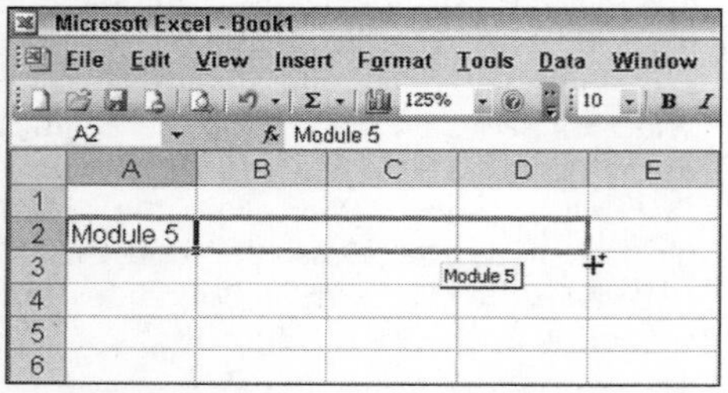

• **Figure 13-4:** Pressing Ctrl while dragging the Fill handle to force Excel to make copies rather than generate a series.

You don't have to press the Ctrl key before you drag the range of cells. You can convert a filled range into copies of the initial cell value by pressing Ctrl after you've selected the fill range as long as it's before you release the mouse button. After that, you have to click the AutoFill Options button and select Copy Cells on its pop-up menu to make this conversion.

Incrementally Speaking

As you may have noticed, whenever Excel generates a series from an initial entry, it automatically increases the series by an increment of one (be it by one day, one month, one hour, one minute, one widget, you name it). Fortunately, the AutoFill feature is very teachable so that you aren't stuck with always generating a series that increases the base value by one. As long as you provide at least two entries that exemplify how many units Excel is to increase (or decrease) the entries in the series, you can generate series with almost any kind of increments.

Figure 13-5 illustrates how you generate a series that uses an increment other than one unit. In this example, the increment is three, so Excel generates a series that enters every third monthbeginnig with June. To do this, I have to enter two samples: Jun in cell A2 and Sep in cell B2. (This gives Excel the idea

to increment the months by three units rather than one.) With that out of the way, I select both cells A2 and B2 and then drag the Fill handle to the right to cell D2. As you can see from the ToolTip that appears to the left of the black cross pointer in this figure, Excel will enter Mar in cell D2. If I release the mouse button at this point, Excel will generate the series Jun, Sep, Dec, Mar in the cell range A2:D2.

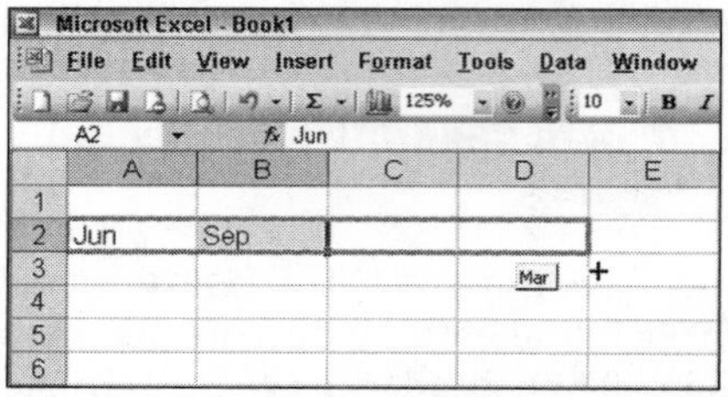

• **Figure 13-5:** Generating a series that uses every third month as its increment.

Well, what about a sequential series that decreases rather than increases (in other words, one that uses a negative increment)? To generate this kind of series with AutoFill, all you have to do is enter the larger value in the first cell of the range to be filled, the smaller value (the one that exemplifies the negative increment) in the next cell (either in the cell in the column to the right if you want to generate the series across the row or in the row below if you want to generate it down the column). Select both cells — the one with the entry showing the starting value and the next one showing the amount of decrease — and then drag the Fill handle to extend the series as far as you want to go.

For example, suppose I want to create a numerical series going down column A — starting in cell A2 with a value of 1000 — that decreases by 100 units in each cell below. To generate this decreasing series, you enter 1000 in cell A2 and 900 in cell A3. Then select the range A2:A3 before you drag the Fill handle down the rows of the column. Excel then enters 800 in cell A4, 700 in cell A5, 600 in cell A6, and so on. (Note that when you select the cells that demonstrate the increment to use, Excel knows right away that you want to generate a series, even when your entries are purely numerical.)

Fill Lists Made to Order

Excel is quite capable of generating a new series on its own when the initial entry in the series (or first two entries, when using an increment besides one) contains a numerical component that it can increase or decrease. However, to have the program generate a series containing no numerical elements (such as the days of the week: Monday, Tuesday, Wednesday, and so on), Excel needs to know beforehand all the items in the series and their order.

To do this, you create a custom list. When creating a custom list, you can have Excel generate it from a cell range in a worksheet that already contains the items, or you can enter the items manually. I suggest that you have Excel create a new list from existing entries in the spreadsheet whenever possible. That way, you have a chance to proof the entries in the worksheet before you turn them into a custom list.

To create a custom list from existing worksheet entries, follow these steps:

1. **Enter the entries for the custom list in their proper sequence down a column or across a row of the active worksheet.**

2. **Select the cell range containing the entries for the custom list.**

3. **Choose Tools⇨Options to open the Options dialog box and then select the Custom Lists tab.**

   When you open the Custom Lists tab after selecting the cell range with these entries, this cell range (in absolute values) appears in the Import List from Cells text box. If this range is not correct or you forgot to select it before opening the Options dialog box, click in this text box and then select the range in the worksheet. (Excel automatically collapses the Options dialog box as you drag through the cells.)

4. **Click the Import button.**

   As soon as you click Import, Excel adds the list to the Custom Lists pane on the left and displays all its entries in the List Entries pane on the

right, as shown in Figure 13-6. You can then edit the individual entries in the List Entries box if necessary. (This is where you would type the entries for a new list that you create from scratch before clicking the Add button.)

5. **Click OK to close the Options dialog box.**

After creating a custom list, you can then generate the list across any row or up or down any column simply by entering the initial entry in a cell and then dragging the Fill handle in one of the four directions. Figure 13-7 illustrates how this works. Here, I generated the custom list of cities created earlier from a range of cell entries (refer to Figure 13-6) in a new worksheet by entering the first city (Seattle) in cell A2 and then dragging the Fill handle to cell F2.

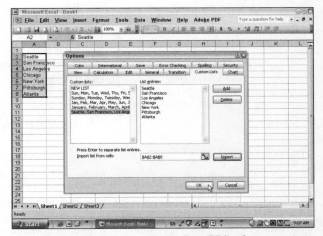

• **Figure 13-6:** Creating a custom AutoFill list from a range of existing entries.

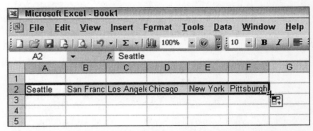

• **Figure 13-7:** Generating the series of cities across row 2.

Technique 14

Ensuring Accurate Data Entries with Data Validation

Save Time By

- Setting up data validation criteria
- Creating input messages
- Using error alerts

This technique acquaints you with a very versatile and, in the long run, great timesaving feature that Excel calls *data validation*. You use this nifty feature to prevent the users of your spreadsheets from ever getting a chance to enter the wrong type of data entry or a type that's not on your list (when dealing with labels) or within a tolerable range (when dealing with numbers) in critical cells of its worksheets.

Not only can you restrict the types of data entries that you or any other spreadsheet user can make, you can also add input messages to your validated cells that indicate what types of entries are permissible there. As if this weren't enough, you can also tag the validated cells with error alerts that flash an alert symbol along with a custom message indicating the data entry rules for the current cell!

Only the Valid Need Apply

The heart and soul of the data validation feature is the Settings tab of the Data Validation dialog box (Data⇨Validation). The Settings tab, shown in Figure 14-1, is where you specify the criteria under which Excel considers any data entry made in the current cell to be kosher.

The first control on the Settings tab is the Allow drop-down list box. By default, this box is set to Any Value to allow you to do any type of data entry in the current cell. To change all that anything-goes stuff by making only a certain type of entry permissible, select one of the other Allow options:

- **Whole Number** restricts data entry to a whole number that is equal to, greater than, less than, or within a range of numbers that you then specify.

- **Decimal** restricts data entry to a decimal number that is equal to, greater than, less than, or within a range of values that you then specify.

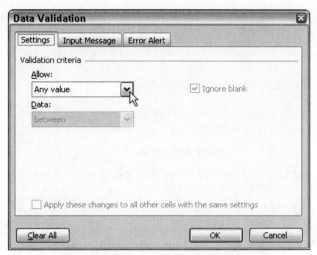

• **Figure 14-1: The Settings tab of the Data Validation dialog box is where you set the validation criteria.**

✔ **List** restricts data entry to one of the items on a list (whose items must already have been entered in a range of cells in the worksheet). When using this Allow option, Excel enables you to create an in-cell drop-down list (with its very own tiny drop-down button) from which you or your users can select the entry.

✔ **Date** restricts data entry to a date that is equal to, before, after, or within a range of dates that you then specify.

✔ **Time** restricts data entry to a time that is equal to, before, after, or within a range of times that you then specify.

✔ **Text Length** restricts data entry to a number of characters that is equal to, greater than, less than, or within a range of numbers that you then specify.

✔ **Custom** restricts data entry to the parameters specified by a Logical formula (one that evaluates to TRUE for allowable entries or FALSE for invalid ones) that's already been entered into a

cell of the worksheet to which you then refer. (See Technique 15 for an example of data validation using the Custom setting.)

 By default, all data validation settings regard blank cells as valid. If you want to prevent users from leaving a cell blank, while at the same time making their entries conform to your other data validation criteria, clear the Ignore Blank check box on the Settings tab.

Data entries from a list

Enabling users to do data entry by selecting the data from an in-cell drop-down list is one of the most popular uses for the data validation feature. Not only does this type of data validation prevent users from selecting an invalid entry, but it also enables them to make a correct entry without having to do any typing.

Figures 14-2 and 14-3 illustrate how you would use the data validation List setting to create an in-cell drop-down list. In Figure 14-2, I started a new worksheet by entering a list of cities in cell range J2:J7 (with the help of the AutoFill feature — see Technique 13). This list represents the only valid entries for the City column of my new Account Rep Assignments table.

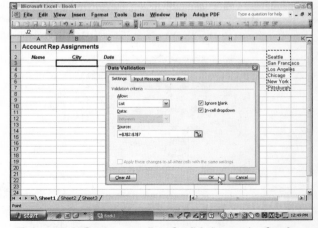

• **Figure 14-2: Setting up a list of valid city entries for the new table of account rep assignments.**

To use the data validation List setting to restrict the data entry in this new table to any of the cities on this list, I then followed these steps:

1. **Position the cell pointer in the first blank cell to use this data validation setting (B3 in this example).**

2. **Choose Data⇨Validation to open the Data Validation dialog box with the Settings tab selected.**

3. **Select List in the Allow drop-down list box.**

4. **Put the Insertion point in the Source text box and then drag through the range of cells containing the list of valid entries (J3:J7 in this case).**

   Because Excel automatically selects the In-cell Dropdown check box, the program will add a drop-down button that reveals this list of cities whenever the user selects the cell.

   To force users to select one of the cities — making it invalid to leave the cell blank — clear the Ignore Blank check box.

5. **Click OK to close the Data Validation dialog box.**

After the Data Validation dialog box closes, Excel adds a drop-down button to the right side of the current cell. To select one of the cities on the list from its menu, click this button and then click the name of the city to enter in cell B3, as shown in Figure 14-3.

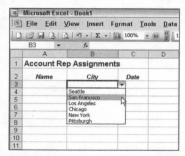

• **Figure 14-3: Selecting a city from the cell's new drop-down list.**

Copying data validation settings

After assigning your data validation criteria to a particular cell, you can then copy these criteria to all the cells in the vicinity that need to use the same restrictions. To do this, you follow these steps:

1. **Copy the cell with the data validation to the Clipboard.**

   (Choose Edit⇨Copy or press Ctrl+C.)

2. **Select the cell range into which to copy the data validation criteria.**

3. **Choose Edit⇨Paste Special or to open the Paste Special dialog box.**

4. **Click the Validation option button (see Figure 14-4) and click OK.**

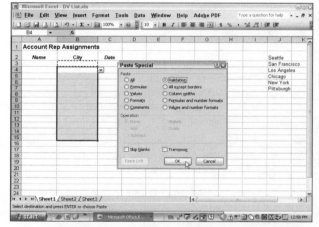

• **Figure 14-4: Copying the data validation criteria down the column with Paste Special.**

For example, to copy the data validation criteria that cause the cell to display the cities drop-down list box from the original cell B3 down the column to the range B4:B15, I copied the contents of B3 to the Clipboard and then selected the range B4:B15. Next, I opened the Paste Special dialog box, clicked the Validation option button, and clicked OK. As a result, all the cells from B3 down B15 use the same data validation criteria. When you put the cell pointer in any of those cells, a drop-down button appears on the right side of the cell. When clicked, this button reveals the city drop-down list.

Finding cells using data validation

Most data validation settings that you assign to cells are invisible. (Okay, the List setting may be the exception here, but even the List setting is invisible when the cell pointer isn't in the cell.) To help you locate the cells in the active worksheet that use some sort of data validation criteria, you can use the Go To feature to find (and select) them:

1. **Press F5 or Ctrl+G to open the Go To dialog box.**

2. **Click the Special button to open the Go To Special dialog box.**

3. **Click the Data Validation option button and click OK, as shown in Figure 14-5.**

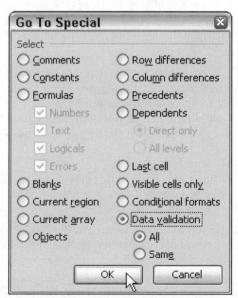

• **Figure 14-5:** Finding all the cells in the worksheet that use data validation.

Because the All option button underneath the Data Validation option is automatically selected by default, Excel selects all the cells and cell ranges in the worksheet that have some type of data validation criteria assigned to them.

4. **Use the Enter or Tab key to move the cell pointer around the selection from cell to cell and from cell range to cell range.**

5. **To find out what type of data validation a particular cell in the selected range uses, choose Data⇨Validation and check out its criteria on the Settings tab.**

 In a spreadsheet that uses many different types of data validation settings, you can find all the cells that use the same criteria. To do so, position the cell pointer in a cell that you know uses the criteria you want to find, open the Go To Special dialog box, click both the Data Validation and Same option buttons, and click OK.

Information Please!

The only problem with data validation is that because it's invisible to spreadsheet users, many times the only way they know they've hit a cell that uses it is when they try to make what the cell now considers an invalid entry. When anybody tries to complete an entry with text or a value that is verboten in the cell, Excel beeps at them and then displays an alert dialog box with the following unhelpful message:

```
The value you entered is not valid.
A user has restricted the value that can
   be entered into this cell.
```

The user can then click the Retry button and try to put something in the cell that Excel does find acceptable, or he or she can click the Cancel button and forget the whole thing.

To give users a fighting chance at rectifying their error by making an acceptable entry in the cell, I heavily suggest (actually, I'm begging you on bended knee) that you assign an input message to the cell explaining to the poor user what kind of entry is now valid. To do this, open the Data Validation dialog box (Data➪Validation) and then click the Input Message tab.

There, you can enter a title for the message in the Title text box (this appears in bold at the top of the text box displaying the input message) as well as the explanatory message text you want displayed in the Input Message list box, as shown in Figure 14-6.

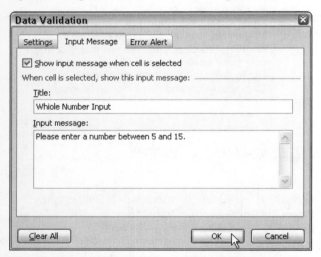

• **Figure 14-6:** Adding an input message explaining to the user the data validation settings in effect in cell A2.

Figure 14-7 shows you how the input message explaining the data validation settings in cell A2 (see Figure 14-6) appears when the cell pointer is in this cell. Now, there's no excuse for the user not knowing what entries are allowed in this cell.

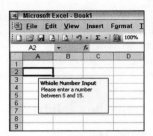

• **Figure 14-7:** Text box with input message that appears when the user selects cell A2.

Warnings to Make Them Wary

As the old saying goes, "You can lead a horse to water, but you can't make him drink." Sometimes, flashing an input message just isn't enough to keep users on the right path. (The numb nuts go ahead and still try to enter forbidden data.) If you're in danger of this happening, it's time to bring out the heavy artillery by adding an error alert message as well. (You can always forgo the input message and just add the error alert message letting users know exactly what kind of behavior will and won't be tolerated in that cell.)

To add an error alert message that appears whenever the user tries to make an entry that violates the cell's data validation criteria, open the Data Validation dialog box and select the Error Alert tab, shown in Figure 14-8. The settings on this tab enable you to

✔ Select a type of indicator to display in the alert dialog box (Stop, Warning, or Information) from the Styles drop-down list box.

✔ Enter a title for the warning in the Title text box (which appears in bold in the title bar of the custom alert dialog box).

✔ Type the text of the message in the Error Message list box (which appears in the body of the alert dialog box).

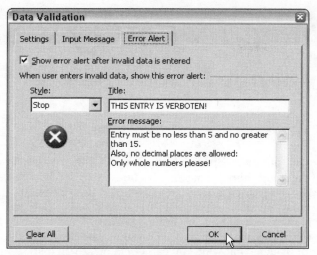

• **Figure 14-8:** Adding a warning message that appears in place of the standard alert dialog box.

 Don't select the Warning or Information type of error alert message unless you want it to be possible for your users to sidestep the validation settings and enter invalid data in the cell. (The Warning type allows this with its Yes button and the Information type with its OK button.) Only the default Stop type prevents users from going ahead and making invalid entries in the cell.

After adding an error alert message, whenever the user tries to enter something outside the bounds set by the cell's data validation settings, Excels beeps at them and then displays your custom error alert dialog box. Figure 14-9 shows you how the custom error alert dialog box (defined in Figure 14-8) appears when you try to enter an invalid number (in this case, any whole number less than 5 or greater than 15 or any decimal number at all). When this Stop type of error alert appears, your users have two choices:

✔ Click Retry to have another go at entering the data (in hopes that the user can get it right this time).

✔ Click Cancel to clear the aberrant entry from the cell (and thus forget about the whole thing).

• **Figure 14-9:** Custom alert dialog box that appears when the user attempts to make an invalid entry.

Technique 15

All Aboard the Numerical Entry Express!

Save Time By

- Using the numerical keypad
- Fixing your decimal places
- Restricting data entry to numbers only

Numbers, numbers, numbers. Spreadsheets are full of them, and because they don't get there by magic, it behooves you to know all the tricks of the trade for entering them as efficiently as possible. The first trick is the most obvious — use your computer's 10-key pad (or the equivalent thereof) to make all your numerical entries. The second trick is to let Excel set the decimal places in your numerical entries that all use a set number of places (that way, you can concentrate on just entering the correct digits). The third trick is not to allow any errant text entries into a cell range that should only contain numbers.

Taking Advantage of the Numeric Keypad

Seeing that pressing the Enter key automatically advances the cell pointer to a new cell in the next row down — conveniently getting you in place for your next entry — I don't see that you have any excuse for not entering ranges of numerical entries from your keyboard's numeric keypad. (After all, your keypad does have an Enter key nearby even if it's embedded in the standard keyboard, as is the case on almost all laptops.) When it comes to entering spreadsheet numbers with any speed, using the number keys along the top row of the standard QWERTY keyboard just doesn't cut it.

Unfortunately, the numeric keypad on your computer is not really the equivalent of the old adding machine's 10-key number pad. On the computer keyboard, the keypad mostly does double-duty with other keys (cursor keys when the pad stands apart from the standard keyboard, and other letter and punctuation keys when it's embedded within the keyboard itself).

As a result of this double functioning, you have to engage the numeric keypad in Excel by pressing the Num Lock key before you can use the pad to enter your spreadsheet numbers. This locks in the number function and simultaneously locks out the secondary cursor or letter-key function. (Excel lets you know when the number function is engaged by displaying the NUM indicator on the status bar.)

Always look for the NUM indicator on the status bar before using the numeric keypad. That way, you save yourself from a lot of wasted time and unnecessary aggravation that comes from entering errant letters and punctuation in it or from having the cell pointer move off the cell.

If you're using a laptop computer, you may have to do more than just engage Num Lock to produce numbers from your embedded numeric keypad. Some laptops also make you hold down a special Fn (Function) key to activate the numeric pad.

Putting the Decimal Places at Your Service

Remember to use the Fixed Decimal setting when you need to do heavy-duty numerical data entry in a spreadsheet. When you turn on this setting, Excel automatically enters a decimal point using the number of decimal spaces you specify for numeric entries. This speeds up your numeric data entry enormously (especially when you're doing the data entry from the keyboard's numeric keypad) because you no longer have to take time to type the period for the decimal point (you just type digits and press Enter).

To toggle on the Fixed Decimal setting, follow these steps:

1. **Choose Tools⇨Options to open the Options dialog box.**

2. **On the Edit tab, select the Fixed Decimal check box, as shown in Figure 15-1.**

The moment you activate the Fixed Decimal check box, the Places text box below and to its right becomes available.

3. **Specify the number of decimal places that you want Excel to fix in all the numbers you enter.**

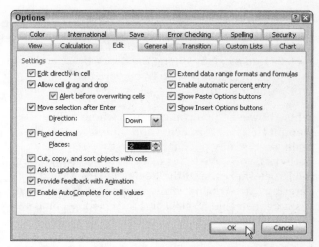

• **Figure 15-1: Fixing the number of decimal places in all numerical entries.**

By default, the Places text box selects 2 as the number of decimal places to fix in your numbers (which makes sense given that much numeric data entry represents financial figures in dollars and cents). To modify the number of decimal places, enter a new value in the Places text box (between –300 and 300) or use its spinner buttons to select it.

4. **Click OK to close the Options dialog box.**

Enter a negative number in the Places text box to have Excel pad the digits you type with trailing zeros equal to this number's absolute value. For example, enter –2 in the Places text box to have all your entries automatically increased by a factor of 100. (For example, if you type 789, Excel enters 78900 in the cell.)

Excel lets you know when the Fixed Decimal setting is turned on by displaying FIX on the far right of the Status bar. While this setting is active, the only time you have to be concerned with decimal points is when the numbers you're entering don't conform to the number of decimal places you set. For example, if you use the two-decimal-place default for entering financial figures in the worksheet, you enter all standard dollar-and-cents numbers simply by typing their digits. (For example, you enter the value $150.24 into a cell by typing the digits 15024 and then pressing Enter — don't you dare take time to type a dollar sign.)

When, however, you come upon a whole dollar amount that has zero cents and therefore doesn't really require any decimal places (they're purely optional), you have to make a choice. Either you can tell Excel where to put the decimal place or end up entering extra trailing zeros. Suppose that you need to enter the value $200.00 and the Fixed Decimal setting with the default two decimal places in turned on. If you type 200 in the current cell, Excel reduces it to 2 when you press Enter. To get the program to put 200 in the cell, either you have to type 200 and then press the period (.) key before Enter, or you have to type 20000 (which looks nothing like the value $200.00).

Don't forget to turn off the Fixed Decimal setting (by clearing its check box on the Edit tab of the Options dialog box) as soon as you finish with your numeric data entry marathon. Otherwise, you or a coworker may be completely thrown off when Excel stubbornly refuses to enter your numbers as you type them!

Number Please!

When it comes to numerical data entry, efficiency is key — but not if it comes at the expense of accuracy. This procedure covers a way that you can use the data validation feature (see Technique 14 for details) to make it impossible for users to enter anything but numerical entries in a cell range. The downside of adding this type of data entry safeguard is that it can possibly stop the flow of your data entry cold. The upside is that you don't have to worry about errant punctuation and letter keystrokes converting cell entries into text that later spawns error values in formulas that reference those cells.

To ensure numerical data entry, you need to use Excel's ISNUMBER function in a formula as part of a Custom type of data validation setting. ISNUMBER is an Information-type function that returns a logical TRUE value when its argument is numerical and a logical FALSE value when it's not numerical. This function uses the following syntax:

`=ISNUMBER(value)`

Whenever the ISNUMBER function returns a TRUE value as a part of a Custom-type data validation setting, Excel finds the data entry to be valid and allows the data entry. However, whenever the function returns a FALSE value, the program finds the entry to be invalid and rejects the data entry.

Figures 15-2 through 15-4 illustrate how you set up this type of numerical data validation for a cell range in your spreadsheet. For this example, I want to inoculate the cell range C4:E9 with this type of protection. This range contains all the numerical values in my little sales table.

I start this process by selecting cell C4, the first cell of the range to be protected. It's here that I define the numerical data validation that I then copy with Paste Special to the rest of the range:

1. **Choose Data⇨Validation to open the Data Validation dialog box.**

2. **On the Settings tab, select Custom in the Allow drop-down list.**

3. **In the Formula text box, type =ISNUMBER (and then click cell C4 to enter it as the argument before typing a close parenthesis [)] to close off the function. (See Figure 15-2.)**

    For this data validation setting, you don't need to add an input message. (Here, you already know what kind of entry you intend to make.) All you need to add is a custom error alert message that helps the user identify the nature of his or her error.

4. **Select the Error Alert tab.**

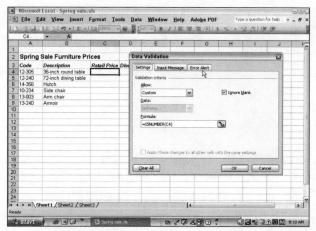

• **Figure 15-2: Setting up a custom validation formula that rejects anything but numerical entries.**

5. Leave the default Stop style selected, enter a heading for the message's title in the Title text box, and enter the text for the message in the Error Message list box. (See Figure 15-3.)

6. Click OK to close the Data Validation dialog box.

Before copying the Custom data validation setting to other cells in the range, you need to test it out and make sure that it's truly bulletproof when it comes to text entries. Figure 15-4 shows you what happened when I tried to enter my name in cell C4. When testing the cell, be sure to try entering all manner of numerical entries (whole numbers, decimal numbers, negative numbers, and zero). Also try to sneak a value in as text in the cell (as you might do when entering zip codes and the like) by prefacing the digits with an apostrophe (').

When you're convinced that your data validation setting is airtight, you can copy the setting to all the other cells in the range where you intend to do

numerical data entry. To do this, you first copy the cell with the original data validation setting to the Clipboard (Ctrl+C) and then select the cell range (C4:E9 in my example). Finally, you click the Validation option button in the Paste Special dialog box (Edit⇨Paste Special) and then click OK.

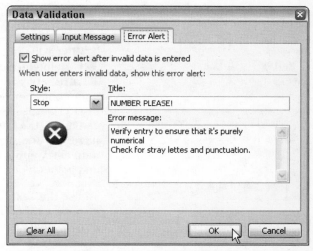

• **Figure 15-3: Adding an error alert to the numeric custom data validation setting.**

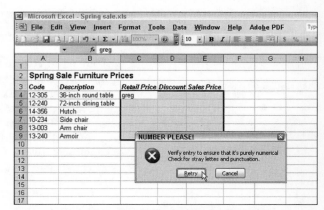

• **Figure 15-4: Illegal text entry foiled by the numeric custom data validation settings.**

Technique 16

Verifying Entries with Text to Speech

Save Time By

- ✔ Using Speak on Enter as you make data entries
- ✔ Having the computer read back entries in a cell range
- ✔ Selecting the perfect voice and speed

Excel includes a powerful feature known as Text to Speech that can help you through the drudgery of checking and verifying the accuracy of your data entries. By using Text to Speech, you can have your computer read out loud your data entries either as you make them or afterwards. As you listen to the computer read the data entries, you can check the hard copy from which they came to ensure that you haven't made any typos. If you notice a discrepancy between a spoken data entry and what's on the paper copy, you can stop Text to Speech and make the necessary corrections before continuing with the reading.

To use the Text to Speech feature, your computer must be equipped with a sound card and have access to speakers or headphones (minimal requirements that I'll bet every computer that can run Excel 2003 can easily meet). Note that you can use Text to Speech without having installed and set up Excel's Speech Recognition feature for entering data entries by voice and issuing voice commands.

"Can You Hear Me Now?"

To use the Text to Speech feature, choose Tools⇨Speech⇨Show Text to Speech Toolbar. If the Text to Speech feature isn't already installed on your computer, Excel asks if you want to install this feature. You then follow the prompts to install this feature. (Make sure that you have the Office 11 CD-ROM handy when you do this or make sure that you can provide the Windows Installer with the path to the Office program files on your network.) When Text to Speech is installed, Excel displays the Text to Speech toolbar, shown in Figure 16-1.

Speak Cells   *By Rows*   *Speak On Enter*

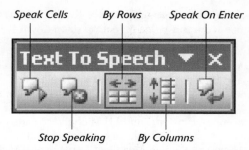

Stop Speaking   *By Columns*

• **Figure 16-1:** Use the tools on the Text to Speech toolbar to verify the data entries you make.

Speak on Enter

One of the most effective ways to use Text to Speech is its Speak on Enter mode. When you click the Speak on Enter button on the Text to Speech toolbar, the Text to Speech feature reads every data entry you make back to you. (The program actually says the words, "Cells will now be spoken on Enter," the moment you click this button.)

When the program is in this speaking mode, the Text to Speech feature speaks every data entry you complete. Note that, in the world of Excel, "complete" in this case means you've either pressed the Enter key or pressed a cursor-movement key such as an arrow key, Tab, or Page Down. The feature does not speak the entry if you complete it by clicking the Enter button on the Formula bar.

Note that the Speak on Enter button is a toggle; you turn off this speaking mode by clicking the button a second time. When you click the button to turn Speak on Enter mode off, Text to Speech says, "Turn off Speak on Enter."

Reading by columns and rows

Text to Speech is not just useful when entering new data in your spreadsheet. You can also use it to verify the accuracy of ranges that have already been entered into a worksheet. To have the program read back the entries in a cell range, follow these steps:

1. Position the cell pointer in the first cell of the range whose values you want to verify with Text to Speech.

2. If the Text to Speech toolbar is not displayed in Excel, choose Tools⇨Speech⇨Show Text to Speech Toolbar.

3. Click the Speak Cells button (the first one) in the Text to Speech toolbar.

   As soon as you click this button, Excel automatically selects all the cells it can identify as a single range in the region around the cell pointer. It then starts reading the entries out loud across the rows of the range as it moves down the columns.

4. (Optional) To change Text to Speech's direction from across rows to up and down columns, click the By Columns button.

If you catch a mistake, click the Speak Cells button to temporarily halt the reading of the rest of the range and then move the cell pointer to the appropriate cell and edit its contents. To resume reading the remaining cells in the range, click the Speak Cells button again.

 Don't use the arrow keys to move the cell pointer, or you'll collapse the cell selection, reducing it from the current range down to the current cell. Instead use Tab, Shift+Tab, Enter, or Shift+Enter to move the cell pointer and to complete the cell edit. (Refer to Table 12-1 for more on using Tab, Shift+Tab, Enter, or Shift+Enter to move the cell pointer.)

When Excel reaches the last cell in the selected range and reads its contents, Text to Speech automatically stops and takes the program out of Speak Cells mode. If you want to turn off Text to Speech before it reaches the last cell, click the Stop Speaking button.

Modifying the Text to Speech Settings

When using Text to Speech, you can modify the speaking voice used as well as the speed at which the program reads your data entries. To change these Text to Speech settings, follow these steps:

1. **Click the Start button on the Windows taskbar and then select Control Panel.**

2. **If you're in Category view, click the Sounds, Speech, and Audio Devices link and then click the Speech link. Otherwise, in Classic view, double-click the Speech icon.**

3. **Select the Text to Speech tab in the Speech Properties dialog box. (See Figure 16-2.)**

• **Figure 16-2:** Selecting the voice and specifying the speed for Text to Speech.

4. **Select the name of the voice that you want to use from the Voice Selection drop-down list.**

You can select LH Michael, LH Michelle, or Microsoft Sam as the voice. LH stands for Lerned and Hauspie (the creator of Michael's and Michelle's voices). To me, LH Michael sounds like the voice used by the eminent physicist, Stephen Hawking, and LH Michelle sounds like the female equivalent of that voice. And Microsoft Sam sounds like the voice of HAL 9000 in Stanley Kubrick's *2001: A Space Odyssey,* when Dave was disconnecting his memory circuits!

5. **Select the Use the Following Text to Preview the Voice text box and then edit the text that you want the voice to say to you.**

For example, when previewing the Microsoft Sam voice, you can enter the text whether "I'm afraid Dave. Dave, I'm afraid," to see whether you think this voice sounds like HAL 9000 as well.

6. **Click the Preview Voice button to have the voice that you selected read back the text shown in the Use the Following Text to Preview the Voice text box.**

7. **If you want to adjust the voice speed, drag the Voice Speed slider toward Slow or Fast to either slow down the speaking or speed it up.**

After adjusting the speed, be sure to click the Preview Voice button again to make sure that you haven't slowed or sped up the rate of speaking too much.

If you drag the slider toward Slow when the Microsoft Sam voice is selected, you definitely have a dead ringer for HAL 9000 in his famous disconnection scene.

8. **Click OK to close the Speech Properties dialog box and then click the Close button in the Sounds, Speech, and Audio Devices window to close it.**

Part III

Handy Ways to Format and Present Worksheet Data

The 5th Wave   By Rich Tennant

Mr. Grady had a way of getting more out of an on-line project than other teachers.

Ms. Stubb's 7th Grade Class

CLOGGING 'n Squash Carving

Mr Grady's 6th Grade Class

GLOBAL ECONOMIC STABILITY

Right after data entry comes formatting. As I hope you know, when building a new spreadsheet, you don't stop to take the time to assign formats to the data entries you make (by typing dollar signs, commas, and the like). Instead, you enter all the raw data and then assign the required formatting to the various cell ranges.

When formatting cells in a standard table of data, you can usually rely on the AutoFormat feature to apply the various types of formatting to all the different elements in one fast-and-easy operation. When formatting individual ranges of cells that aren't part of a standard table of data, you can use Excel's handy-dandy Format Painter to quickly copy an existing format to unformatted ranges that need it. Finally, you can preformat a blank cell range by copying just the formatting assigned to any formatted cell and pasting that formatting into the cell range.

Head-to-Toe Table Formatting with AutoFormat

Using Excel's AutoFormat feature to format a table of data is a real no-brainer. Simply position the cell pointer in any cell of the table and choose Format⇨AutoFormat to open the AutoFormat dialog box, shown in Figure 17-1. Excel then automatically selects all the cells in the table (including the one with the table's title). All you have to do is select the table format in the AutoFormat dialog box that you want to apply to the selected range and then click OK.

The list box in the AutoFormat dialog box offers 16 distinct table formats from which you can choose. Excel gives descriptive names to these table formats, which are arranged by category in two columns in this list box. At the very bottom of the list box, you find a None table format that you can select to remove any previously selected table formatting from the selected range.

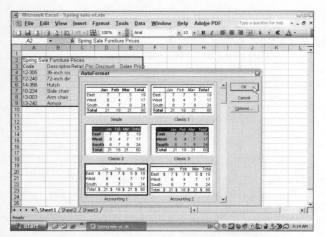

• **Figure 17-1: Selecting the table format to apply to the selected table of data.**

When choosing the table format to apply to the cell range containing your data, use the thumbnails of the different formats as a guide. These thumbnails attempt to show what alignment, attributes (such as bold or italics), number formatting, borders, and patterns will be applied to the selected cell range. Also, all the table formats (except for None) automatically widen the columns and heighten the rows of the table as needed to display all the data after applying these various attributes to their cells.

The None table format removes all formatting from the cells of the table, including any attributes manually assigned to individual cells or cell ranges prior to applying table formats with AutoFormat. Selecting None does not, however, restore column widths that Excel changed as part of previously selecting one of the other table formats.

Figure 17-2 shows how the furniture sales price table (shown selected in Figure 17-1) appears after applying the Accounting 1 table format to its cells. As you can see in this figure, when Excel applies this formatting

to the table in the cell range A2:E9, it formats the table and column headings and the financial data in columns C, D, and E, as well as widens columns B through E using its AutoFit feature. Unfortunately, the program misapplied the Currency and Comma Style number formats to the Discount data in the range D4:D9. Because AutoFormat couldn't tell that these numbers represent percentages and not dollars and cents, I still need to apply the Percent Style number format to this range.

	A	B	C	D	E	F
1						
2	Spring Sale Furniture Prices					
3	Code	Description	Retail Price	Discount	Sales Price	
4	12-305	36-inch round table	$ 1,250.00	$ 0.25	$ 937.50	
5	12-240	72-inch dining table	1,400.00	0.25	1,050.00	
6	14-356	Hutch	2,500.00	0.25	1,875.00	
7	10-234	Side chair	350.00	0.15	297.50	
8	13-003	Arm chair	500.00	0.15	425.00	
9	13-240	Armoir	1,750.00	0.25	1,312.50	
10						
11						

• **Figure 17-2: Furniture sales price table automatically formatted with the Accounting 1 table format.**

Excel makes it easy to customize any of its 16 built-in table formats:

1. **Click the Options button in the AutoFormat dialog box.**

The dialog box expands to display individual check box format options in the Formats to Apply area along the bottom.

2. **To customize a particular table format, select its thumbnail in the AutoFormat list box and then clear all the individual format check boxes in the Formats to Apply area that you don't want to use.**

For example, in Figure 17-3 I selected Classic 3 table format and then removed its borders by clearing the Border check box in the Formats to Apply area.

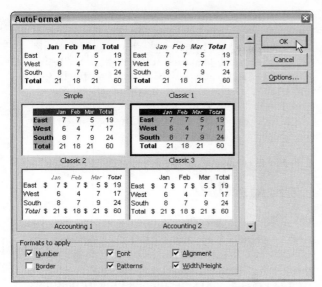

• **Figure 17-3:** Customizing a table format by limiting which formats it applies.

Getting Artistic with the Format Painter

AutoFormat is perfect for those times when you have a discrete table of data that needs formatting and you want to use one of its prefab table formats throughout. For the other times when you just need to apply a few different attributes to a cell range or two, seriously consider using the Format Painter to get the job done. As the name implies, the Format Painter enables you to copy the formatting from one prototypical cell to all the others that you drag through — in essence painting them with all its attributes.

Oh that all painting were as easy as painting with the Format Painter! The steps for copying a cell's formatting are as simple as can be:

1. **Select the cell that already contains the formatting that you want to copy.**

This cell can be manually formatted with several different attributes such a new cell alignment, font attribute, and number format.

2. **Click the Format Painter button on the Standard toolbar (the one with the paintbrush icon).**

After you click the Format Painter button, Excel displays a marquee in the cell pointer in the current cell, and a paintbrush icon appears next to the white cross mouse pointer, as shown in Figure 17-4.

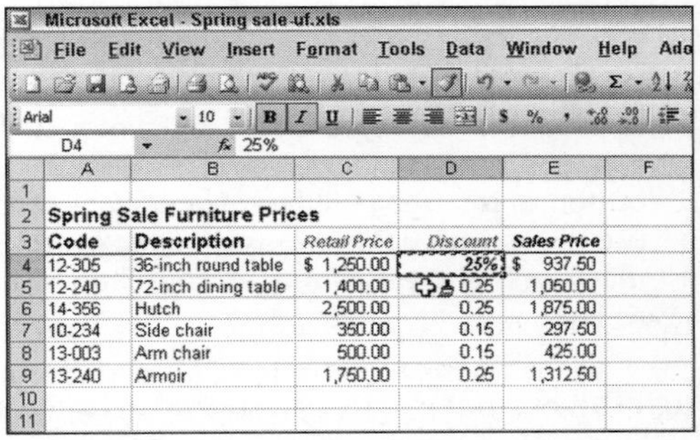

• **Figure 17-4:** Using the Format Painter to copy all the formatting applied to a cell.

3. **Drag through the cells to which you want to apply the same formatting as in the current cell.**

When you release the mouse button, Excel applies all the formatting in the prototype cell to the range you selected with the Format Painter mouse pointer. Figure 17-5 illustrates this: Here, I copied the Percent Style number format plus the bold and italics attributes applied to cell D4 to this range by dragging through the cell range D5:D9 with the Format Painter mouse pointer.

Microsoft Excel - Spring sale-uf.xls

File   Edit   View   Insert   Format   Tools   Data   Window   Help   Add

Arial   10   B I U ≡ ≡ ≡ ≡ $ % , ⁰⁄₀ ⁰⁄₀ 綠

D5   f 25%

	A	B	C	D	E	F
1						
2	Spring Sale Furniture Prices					
3	Code	Description	Retail Price	Discount	Sales Price	
4	12-305	36-inch round table	$ 1,250.00	25%	$ 937.50	
5	12-240	72-inch dining table	1,400.00	25%	1,050.00	
6	14-356	Hutch	2,500.00	25%	1,875.00	
7	10-234	Side chair	350.00	15%	297.50	
8	13-003	Arm chair	500.00	15%	425.00	
9	13-240	Armoir	1,750.00	25%	1,312.50	
10						
11						

• **Figure 17-5:** Cell range D5:D9 after using the Format Painter to copy all the formatting applied to cell D4.

To format more than one range, double-click the Format Painter button instead of single-clicking it. That way, the Format Painter stays engaged until you next click the Format Painter button to disengage it. In between, you can use the mouse pointer to paint through as many cells and cell ranges as your little heart desires.

Although the Format Painter makes copying from one cell to another range a real breeze, copying formats is not its only claim to fame. You can also use the Format Painter to copy column widths in a worksheet. To do this, you click the letter of the column whose width you want to copy in the column header and then double-click the Format Painter button to engage it. Finally, click or drag through the letters of the columns that need to be the same width and then click the Format Painter to disengage it.

As if this weren't enough, you can also use the Format Painter to copy the attributes of one graphic object (such as a piece of WordArt, an AutoShape, a Clip Art image, or a graphics file inserted into the worksheet — see Technique 56) to other objects of the same type.

For example, suppose that you insert a photo into a worksheet and then edit that photo with the More Contrast and Less Brightness buttons in the Picture toolbar. After a bit, you add another photo to the sheet with the same exposure problems. You can then use the Format Painter to copy the contrast and brightness settings applied to the first photo onto the second one. All you do is click the edited photo to select it, click the Format Painter button, and then click the second unedited photo. Excel then immediately copies the same contrast and brightness exposure settings to it.

Cutting and Pasting Formats Only

As I'm sure you're aware, whenever you move or copy formatted cells from one part of the worksheet to another, Excel automatically copies the formatting along with the cell contents. What you may not be aware of is that you can copy just the formatting applied to a cell or cell range and — leaving behind the contents — paste that formatting into a new range.

The range into which you copy the formatting can be blank or can contain cell entries. If the range is blank, all cell entries that you make there take on the copied formatting. If the range already contains cell entries, the copied formatting is immediately applied to them, replacing any existing formatting.

To copy just the formatting from a cell or cell range to a new place in the worksheet, follow these steps:

1. **Select the cell or range that contains the formatting you want to copy.**

2. **Choose Edit⇨Copy or press Ctrl+C to copy the cells to the Clipboard.**

   Excel copies both the cell contents and the formatting in the selected cell(s) to the Windows Clipboard.

3. **Select the cell or cell range into which you want to copy the formatting now residing on the Windows Clipboard.**

4. Choose Edit⇨Paste Special to open the Paste Special dialog box.

 Be sure you don't choose Edit⇨Paste instead of Edit⇨Paste Special. Otherwise, Excel will plunk down not only the formatting but the contents of the cells as well. And if you're pasting into a cell range with entries, these entries will be replaced. If you mess up, press Ctrl+Z until you put everything right in the range.

5. Click the Formats option button in the Paste area of the Paste Special dialog box (shown in Figure 17-6) and then click OK button.

Excel closes the Paste Special dialog box and immediately applies all the formatting applied to the original cell or cell range and copied to the Clipboard to the cell range that's currently selected in the worksheet.

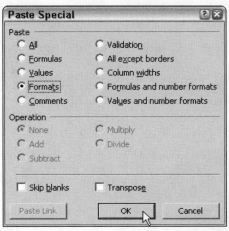

• **Figure 17-6:** Using the Formats option in the Paste Special dialog box to paste only the formatting on the Clipboard.

Style Formatting Magic

Save Time By

- Using the built-in styles
- Creating and using custom styles
- Copying custom styles from one workbook to the next

When it comes to looks, everyone wants to be in style. When it comes to getting your worksheets to look their best, you can facilitate their formatting by using Excel's styles. Styles are perfect for applying standard formatting to many cell ranges across the spreadsheet. What makes them so great is that should you need to tweak their formatting a bit, you simply make the changes to the style itself and those changes are instantly updated in every cell to which that style is applied.

Excel styles can regulate any of the following formatting attributes in a cell:

- **Number** to determine which number format is used. (If the cell contains a text entry, the Number aspect of the style is ignored.)

- **Alignment** to determine what kind of horizontal and vertical text alignment, text control (wrap text or shrink to fit), or text direction is used.

- **Font** to determine what font, font style, font size, attributes (underline, strikethrough, superscript, or subscript), or font color is used.

- **Border** to determine what kind of border (including line style and color), if any, is used.

- **Patterns** to determine what kind of cell shading, if any, is used.

- **Protection** to determine the status (on or off) of the Locked and Hidden cell protection attributes.

This technique gives you vital information on how to use and customize the six predefined styles that are immediately available to you in any workbook you open as well as how to create your own custom styles. Finally, you find out how to copy your favorite custom styles from one workbook to another so that you don't have to waste time reinventing a style.

Styling

Each Excel workbook you open comes with six predefined styles. The Normal style is the default style applied to every cell of every new workbook. Figure 18-1 shows you the Style dialog box (Format⇨Style) displaying the different formatting attributes that the Normal style uses. Keep in mind that anytime you manually apply new formatting attributes to a cell, either with the buttons on the Formatting toolbar or the options in the Format Cells dialog box (Ctrl+1), these attributes are applied to the basic settings in effect from the cell's current style. If any of these manually selected attributes conflict with attributes set by the current style, they override and replace them.

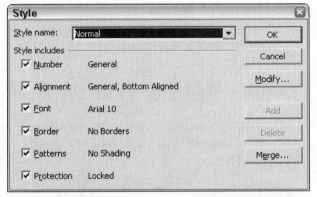

• **Figure 18-1: The Normal style is automatically applied to all the cells in a new workbook.**

The other predefined styles — Comma, Comma (0), Currency, Currency (0), and Percent — are all used to format cells containing numeric values with the most common number formats. As such, their particular styles define only a new Number setting — these styles don't change the Alignment, Font, Border, Patterns, or Protection settings. When you apply any of these styles, they replace the General number format set by the Normal style with that of their own.

Applying predefined styles in a spreadsheet

You can always apply any of the predefined styles to a cell selection by opening the Style dialog box (Format⇨Style), selecting the name of the style to apply in the Style Name drop-down list box, and then clicking OK. But Excel offers a much more direct procedure when applying the Comma, Comma (0), Currency, Currency (0), and Percent styles.

To apply these styles, select the cells to be formatted and then click the appropriate button(s) on the Formatting toolbar, shown in Figure 18-2. In the case of the Comma, Currency, and Percent styles, all you have to do is click the corresponding toolbar buttons. In the case of the Currency (0), which doesn't display any decimal places, you need to first click the Currency Style button (which displays two decimal places) and then click the Decrease Decimal buttontwo times (which takes the decimal places away). Likewise, when you want to apply the Comma (0) style to a cell selection, you click the Comma Style button and then click the Decrease Decimal button twice to remove its two decimal places.

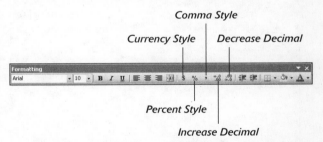

• **Figure 18-2: Applying the Currency, Percent, and Comma styles from the Formatting toolbar.**

 To be able to select any style from a drop-down list on the Formatting toolbar (see Figure 18-3), customize this toolbar by adding the command that displays a Style drop-down list box. This command is located in the Format categories on the Commands tab. (See Technique 2 for details on customizing toolbars.)

• **Figure 18-3:** The Formatting toolbar after customizing it by adding a Style drop-down list box.

Customizing predefined styles

Excel makes it a snap to customize any of its six predefined styles. Of the six, most users end up customizing the Normal style in order to quickly and easily make basic formatting changes to all the cells of a new workbook. For example, suppose your company prefers to use Times New Roman 12 point as the default font and font size for all its spreadsheets. To accomplish this in a new workbook, you would modify the Normal style using the following steps:

1. **Open a new workbook and then Choose Format⇨Style to open the Style dialog box.**

2. **Select Modify to open the Format Cells dialog box, shown in Figure 18-4.**

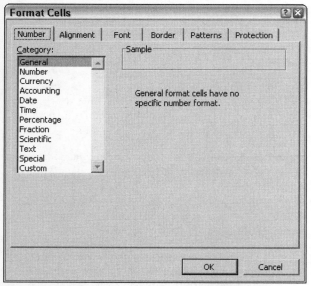

• **Figure 18-4:** Customize the style by making changes to its attributes in the Format Cells dialog box.

3. **On the Font tab, select Times New Roman in the Font list box and 12 in the Size list box and then click OK.**

4. **Click OK in the Style dialog box to close this dialog box and put the new attributes in effect.**

After changing the font and font size for the Normal font, all the cells in the blank workbook now use Times New Roman 12-point type instead of the usual Arial 10 point.

 Modifications that you make to a predefined style such as Normal are saved as part of the current workbook file. However, these changes don't carry over to new workbook files; they continue to open with the original, unmodified styles. To make use of your customized styles, you need to copy them into the new workbook. (For more on copying styles, see the "Merging Styles from One Book into Another" section, later in this technique.)

Creating Styles of Your Own

Excel makes it extremely easy to create new styles for your spreadsheet. When creating a new style, you can either

✔ **Build it by modifying the attributes of one of the predefined styles.** You select the basic style in the Style dialog box and then make all the necessary changes to the number format, font, alignment, borders, shading, and protection attributes in the Format Cells dialog box (see the preceding section, "Customizing predefined styles") required by the new style.

✔ **Create it from an example cell.** To create a style by example, you choose a sample cell (which should contain a typical data entry) and then format it with all the attributes (number format, font, alignment, borders, shading, and protection) that you want used in the new style.

I personally favor the second method because it enables me to see how the new attributes for the new style actually affect the appearance of typical data in the sample cell before I create it. To see how this works, follow along with the steps for creating a new Title Style for instantly formatting the headings for tables of data in a new spreadsheet:

1. **Select a cell to use as the sample cell in a new workbook, make a typical data entry in it, and then manually format the cell with all the attributes you want the new style to assign.**

   To format the cell with the desired attributes, use the buttons on the Formatting toolbar or the controls in the Format Cells dialog box (Ctrl+1).

2. **Choose Format⇨Style to open the Style dialog box.**

3. **Select the Style Name text box and replace Normal with the unique name you want to give the new style, as shown in Figure 18-5.**

   As soon as you begin typing in the new style name, the Style Includes area in the Style dialog box changes to a Style Includes (By Example) area that lists all the attributes that your new style will use.

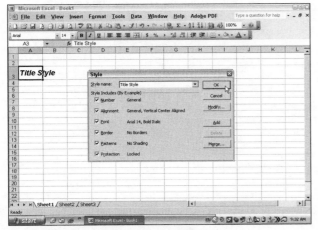

• **Figure 18-5:** Creating a new style from a sample formatted cell.

4. **Click OK to close the Style dialog box and complete the creation of your new style.**

After creating a new style, you can apply its formatting to a cell selection (single range or noncontiguous selection) in the worksheet by opening the Style dialog box (Format⇨Style), selecting the name of the style in the Style Name drop-down list box, and clicking OK. Of course, you can make applying a style a heck of a lot easier by adding a Style drop-down list box to the Formatting toolbar. (See Technique 2 for details on customizing Excel toolbars.)

 If you create a custom style that you rely on all the time, consider assigning it to a button that you add either to the Formatting toolbar or to some custom toolbar. That way, you can format a cell selection with the style by clicking its button. To do this, create a keystroke macro that selects the custom style (see Technique 60) and then assign this macro to a Custom button and add this button to one of the toolbars (see Technique 2).

Merging Styles from One Book into Another

The only problem with styles as far I can see is that they are available only in the workbook in which you create them. To get around this, you need to know how to copy custom styles (as well as any predefined styles that you've customized) into a new workbook file. To accomplish this type of style merge, follow these straightforward steps:

1. **If the new spreadsheet into which you want to copy existing styles has not yet been saved, make a data entry in one of its cells.**

   Doing this prevents Excel from closing the unsaved workbook the moment you open the workbook with the styles you want to merge.

2. **Open the existing workbook (Ctrl+O) containing the styles you want to use in your new spreadsheet.**

3. **Switch back to the blank workbook making this spreadsheet active.**

You can do this either by clicking its button on the Windows taskbar or by selecting it at the bottom of the Window pull-down menu.

4. **Choose Format⇨Style to open the Style dialog box.**

5. **Click the Merge button near the bottom of the Style dialog box to open the Merge Styles dialog box.**

6. **Select the name of the open workbook file that contains the styles you want copied into your new workbook, as shown in Figure 18-6.**

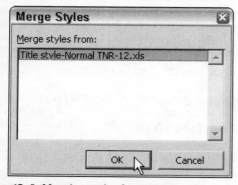

• **Figure 18-6:** Merging styles from another open workbook.

If the open workbook you selected contains modifications to the predefined styles (which also exist in the new workbook), an alert dialog box appears asking you to confirm the merging of styles that have the same names.

7. **If the confirmation alert dialog box appears, click Yes to have the predefined styles in the active workbook overwritten or No to prevent them from being copied into the new workbook. If this confirmation dialog box does not appear, click OK in the Merge Styles dialog box to close it.**

8. **Click OK in the Style dialog box to close it and return to the active spreadsheet.**

9. **Switch back to the workbook whose styles you just merged and then close it (Ctrl+W).**

After merging styles from an open workbook, you have immediate access to all the styles that you copied in your new spreadsheet.

 If you have a bunch of custom styles that you want available in all workbooks of a certain type (such as invoices or balance sheets), merge those styles into a new workbook and then save the workbook as an Excel template file. (See Technique 1.) When you generate new spreadsheets from this template, they will automatically contain your custom styles.

Technique 19

Controlling When Certain Formats Are Used

Excel includes a nifty little feature called *conditional formatting* that tells the program to format a cell range in one way when the range contains one type of data entry and in a completely different manner when it doesn't. Conditional formatting can go a long way in helping you keep tabs on very significant or potentially disastrous conditions that crop up in your spreadsheet.

Most of the time, you apply conditional formatting to cells that contain formulas whose evaluated values are key in the spreadsheet (such as subtotals or grand totals). Applying conditional formatting to these cells can help you flag any potential errors that result from goof-ups made in the input cells referenced in the formulas. You can also use conditional formatting to flag unexpected formula results, such as totals that exceed your wildest expectations as well as totals that are way below your most pessimistic projections.

This technique looks at ways you can use conditional formatting to alert yourself when certain key values change in your spreadsheet (for better or worse). It begins by looking at how you can use conditional formatting to select one type of cell format when normal conditions exist in the cell and another special formatting when some sort of abnormal condition crops up. You also find out how to use conditional formatting to warn you when certain kinds of errors have crept into the spreadsheet.

Formats to Suit Every Condition

Conditional formatting enables you to set up two types of criteria that determine when the program applies the conditional formatting you designate:

✔ **Cell Value Is:** Compares the value (constant) you specify in the Conditional Formatting dialog box against the value entered in the cell. When Excel compares this constant to the cell value and the criteria you specify for them is met (is between, equal to, greater than, less than, greater than or equal to, or less than or equal to), Excel applies the conditional formatting to the cell. When the condition is not met, Excel uses the regular formatting applied to the cell.

✔ **Formula Is:** Evaluates the logical formula you enter in the Conditional Formatting dialog box. When this formula evaluates to TRUE, Excel applies the conditional formatting you define to the cell. When the formula evaluates to FALSE, Excel applies the regular formatting to the cell.

When you want to be warned when a cell contains a particular value or exceeds or falls below a certain number, the Cell Value Is type of conditional formatting is the way to go. To get an idea of how you would use this type of conditional formatting, follow along with the steps for displaying the entry in a cell in red with bold and strikethrough whenever it contains a negative value:

1. **Position the cell pointer in the cell where you want to apply conditional formatting.**

2. **Choose Format⇨Conditional Formatting to open the Conditional Formatting dialog box, shown in Figure 19-1.**

   When Excel opens this dialog box, the Cell Value Is option is automatically selected along with Between as the comparison operator.

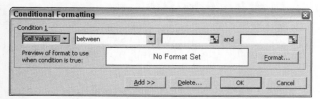

• **Figure 19-1:** The Conditional Formatting dialog box when you first open it.

3. **Select Less Than in the second drop-down list box (the one that now contains Between).**

4. **Press Tab to select the last text box and then type** 0, **as shown in Figure 19-2.**

   After setting up the condition for the special formatting, you must specify what formatting attributes to use. The Font attributes that you can set for conditional formatting are limited to font style, underlining, strikethrough, and color. For this example, I turn on strikethrough and bold and select red as the font color.

• **Figure 19-2:** The Conditional Formatting dialog box after specifying the first condition.

5. **Click the Format button in the Conditional Formatting dialog box to open the Format Cells dialog box.**

6. **On the Font, Border, and Patterns tabs, select the attributes to be used when the condition is true. When you're finished selecting your attributes, click OK. (See Figure 19-3.)**

   When you close the Format Cells dialog box, the Conditional Formatting dialog box shows your first condition along with a preview of the formatting that Excel will apply when the condition is true. At this point, you can either add another condition (see the next section, "When two conditions are better than one"), or if you need only the one condition — as is the case here — you can close the dialog box.

7. **Click OK to close the Conditional Formatting dialog box and put the conditional formatting into effect in the current cell.**

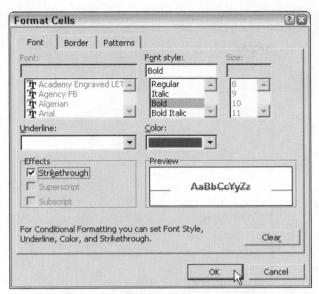

• **Figure 19-3: Selecting the attributes for the first condition in the Format Cells dialog box.**

Figure 19-4 shows how the conditional formatting assigned to cell C4 at the top of the Retail Price column of the Spring Sales table appears when it kicks in. For this figure, I intentionally entered -1200 in the cell rather than the correct 1200 figure (negative values make no sense in this price column). Because this cell now contains a value less than zero (that is, a negative value), the conditional formatting kicks in (because the basic condition is true), and as a result, the red, boldface, and strikethrough attributes are added to the regular cell formatting.

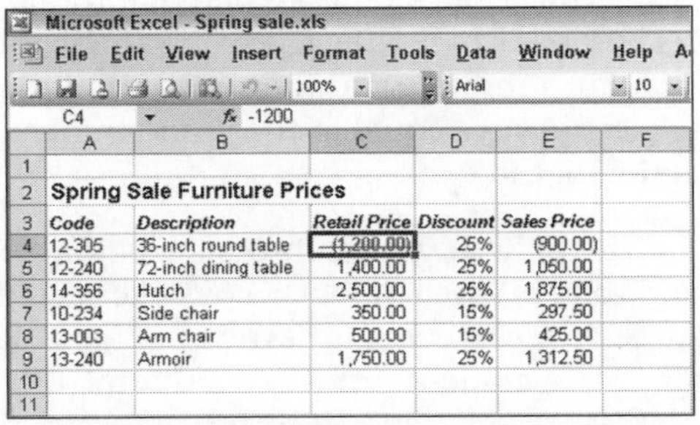

• **Figure 19-4: Table displaying the conditional formatting when a negative value is entered in the cell.**

To copy the conditional formatting you see applied to cell C4 down to the other cells in the Retail Price column (you don't want to have to pay to have customers take any of your furniture), follow these steps:

1. **Copy cell C4 to the Clipboard (Ctrl+C) and then select the cell range C5:C9.**

2. **Choose Edit⇨Paste Special to open the Paste Special dialog box.**

3. **Select the Formats option button and then click OK.**

Excel then pastes the conditional formatting for cell C4 to all the other Retail Price cells, so they will also alert you with the same kind of in-your-face formatting should any errant negative entries come their way.

When two conditions are better than one

When setting up conditional formatting for a cell, you're not limited to a single condition. You can set up several conditions, each with its own unique attributes that are used when its particular condition is true. Most of the time, you find that two conditions are completely adequate to cover all the possible contingencies.

To set up a second condition in the Conditional Formatting dialog box (Format⇨Conditional Formatting), you click the Add button after defining the first condition and the formatting to use when this condition is true. Clicking this button expands the Conditional Formatting dialog box by adding a Condition 2 area with identical controls for defining the second condition and the formatting that it applies.

Figure 19-5 illustrates how this works. For this figure, I added a second condition to cell C4 in the Spring Sales table. It adds bold to the font and garish yellow shading to the cell if it ever contains a value above 1,250. Now, Excel not only alerts me with red, bold, and strikethrough type if the value in cell C4 is negative but also alerts me with bold type and bright yellow shading if the value exceeds 1,250.

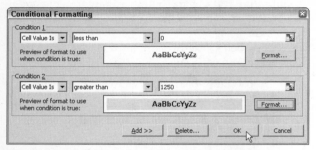

• **Figure 19-5:** Adding a second condition that applies a different formatting when the value is above 1,250.

Finding cells with conditional formatting

Excel makes it easy to locate and select the cells in your worksheet that use conditional formatting. This makes it quick work of finding particular conditional formatting that you want to reuse by copying to other parts of the spreadsheet.

Open the Go To dialog box (F5 or Ctrl+G) and then click the Special button. Excel opens the Go To Special dialog box (see Figure 19-6) where you select the Conditional Formats option button and then click OK.

Excel then selects all the cells in the worksheet that contain some type of conditional formatting. You can use the Enter or Tab key or Shift+Enter or Shift+Tab keys to move from one selected cell to another throughout all the ranges.

 To save time and select only the cells that contain a certain type of conditional formatting, position the cell pointer in a cell that uses the type you want to locate. Then open the Go To Special dialog box, select both the Conditional Formatting option button and the Same option button, and click OK. (See Figure 19-6.)

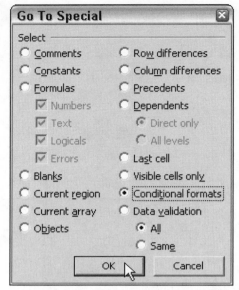

• **Figure 19-6:** Selecting the cells in the worksheet that use conditional formatting.

Making Your Outstanding Errors Stand Out

Although conditional formatting is most useful for alerting you to anomalies that crop up in your spreadsheet data, you can also use it to warn you when certain types of errors crop up that aren't related to errors in the formulas themselves. For example, you can use conditional formatting to flag errors in a typical sales table — one that totals the columns and rows of figures to ensure that the sum of the column subtotals and the sum of the row subtotals are always equal to the grand total at the intersection of the two.

Note that the only way the subtotals wouldn't equal the grand total is when you or a coworker accidentally deletes or replaces one of the SUM formulas that calculate a column's or row's subtotal. If you don't protect your formulas against this type of unintentional editing (as I suggest in Technique 38), you can at least set up this type of conditional formatting to notify you if such an error occurs.

Figure 19-7 illustrates a situation where you could apply this type of conditional formatting. Here, you have a typical table of data that calculates the subtotals and grand total of the quarterly sales for a bunch of different stores. E12 contains the formula that returns the grand total (by summing the row subtotals in the cell range E3:E11).

To alert me if this sum of the row subtotals ever becomes unequal to the sum of the column totals (in the cell range B12:D12), I set up conditional formatting for this grand-total cell E12. In the Conditional Formatting dialog box, I select Formula Is as the type and then enter the following formula in the accompanying text box:

```
=SUM($B$12:$D$12)<>SUM($E$3:$E$11)
```

As for the formatting to be applied when the inequality set up by this formula is true, I go with bold and red as the font attributes and bright yellow shading for the cell background. That way, if cell E12 ever lights up like a Christmas tree with this garish formatting, I know right away that some knucklehead (probably me) has gone and messed up one of the SUM formulas that calculates the column and row subtotals.

Figure 19-8 shows you how this conditional formatting appears in cell E12 when just such a thing occurs. For this figure, I intentionally replaced the

SUM formula in cell C12 with 0. As a result, the total for cell range B12:D12 no longer is equal to that of the cell range E3:E11, and the conditional formatting is immediately applied to cell E12.

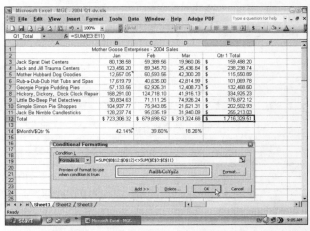

• **Figure 19-7:** Table where the sum of the column subtotals should always equal the sum of the row subtotals.

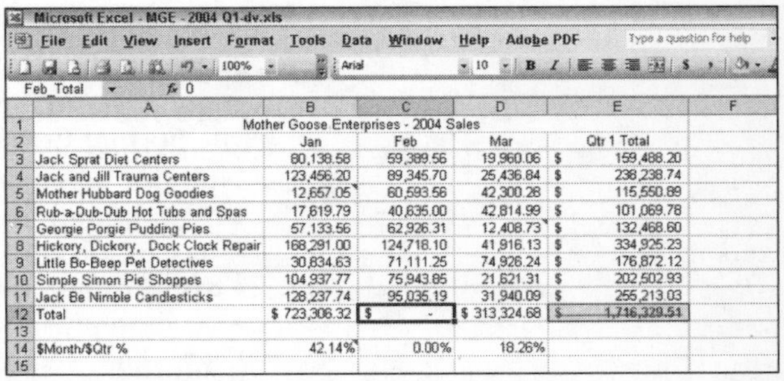

• **Figure 19-8:** Conditional formatting applied to the grand total cell when the inequality condition is true.

Technique 20

Customizing Number Formats

Excel includes a wide variety of number formats designed to make the values in your spreadsheets easy to decipher for anyone who uses them. For those times when the program doesn't hand you a ready-made number format that fits the bill, you can quickly customize one of the existing formats to suit your needs.

This technique covers how to create custom number formats for your spreadsheets and how to assign them to Excel custom styles and toolbars for easy access. This technique also covers how to use the Euro Currency add-in to format currency expressed in euros.

Creating Custom Number Formats

The easiest way to create a custom number format is to format a sample number with the built-in number format whose attributes most closely match the ones you want in the new custom format. Continue by opening the Format Cells dialog box (Ctrl+1), selecting the Custom category on the Number tab to display the built-in format's codes, and then building the custom number format by editing its number format codes, as necessary.

Excel's number formats can consist of up to four sections:

✔ First section specifies how to format positive numbers

✔ Second section specifies how to format negative numbers

✔ Third section specifies how to format zeros

✔ Fourth section specifies how to format text

Each part of the format is separated by semicolons (;). If a particular format doesn't specify formatting for negative numbers or zeros, Excel formats them like it does positive numbers. If the format doesn't specify what to do with text, text is formatted as it normally is with the default, Normal format. Table 20-1 shows the codes you'd use in the various sections of the custom number format you're creating.

TABLE 20-1: NUMBER FORMAT CODES

Code	What It Signifies
#	Digit placeholder that displays only significant digits and does not display insignificant zeros so that ####.# displays 2450.48 as 2450.5 in the cell.
0 (zero)	Digit placeholder that displays insignificant zeros if a number has fewer digits than the number of places in the format so that the code #.00 displays 4.5 as 4.50 in the cell.
?	Digit placeholder that adds spaces for insignificant zeros on either side of the decimal point to align numbers on the decimal point so the code 0.?? ensures that 10.5 and 12.75 line up because the program pads 10.5 with an extra space.
\ (backslash)	Displays the character that immediately follows as text.
* (asterisk)	Repeats the character that immediately follows to fill the column width.
"text"	Displays whatever *text* you enclose in the double quotes as text. Note that the following characters do not have to be enclosed in quotes: $, -, +, /, (,), :, !, ^, &, ' (open single quote), ' (close single quote), ~, {, }, =, <, >, and a space.
@	Text placeholder. By itself, it converts whatever number is entered in the cell into a text entry. When followed by text enclosed in quotation marks, it appends that text onto the number so that the format code @" estimate" appends the word *estimate* to each number.
%	Percentage that adds a percent sign at the end of the number to indicate that its value is a multiple of a hundred.
. (period)	Decimal point.
, (comma)	Thousands separator.
( )	Enclosing the code for the negative numbers in the second section of the format displays negative numbers in parentheses as (4.50) instead of -4.50. Add a hyphen (-) to negative fo rmat code to have a negative number preceded by a minus sign.
E-, E+, e-, e+	Converts number into scientific notation.
_ (underscore)	Inserts space equal in width to the character that immediately follows, as in _) to pad values with a space equal to the close parenthesis.
m	When not following the h or hh code, inserts the month as a number without leading zeros, as in 7-4-05.
mm	Inserts the month as a number with leading zeros, as in 07-4-05.
mmm	Inserts the month as a three-letter abbreviation, as in Jan, Feb, Mar, and so on.
mmmm	Inserts the full name of the month, as in January, February, March, and so on.
d	Inserts the date as a number without leading zeros, as in 4-1-04.
dd	Inserts the date as a number with leading zeros, as in 4-02-04.
ddd	Inserts the day of the week with a three-letter abbreviation, as in Mon, Tue, or Wed.
dddd	Inserts the full day of the week, as in Monday, Tuesday, or Wednesday.
yy	Inserts the last two digits of the year, as in 2-15-05.
yyyy	Inserts all four digits of the year, as in 2-15-2005.

(continued)

TABLE 20-1 *(continued)*

Code	What It Signifies
h	Inserts the number of the hour without leading zeros, as in 9:15.
hh	Inserts the number of the hour with leading zeros, as in 09:15.
m	When immediately following the h or hh code, inserts the number of minutes without leading zeros (0-59), as in 5:5.
mm	Inserts the number of the minutes with leading zeros (00-59), as in 5:05.
s	Inserts the number of seconds without leading zeros (0-59), as in 5:05:7.
ss	Inserts the number of seconds with leading zeros (00-59), as in 5:05:07. For fractions of a second, use a format that includes fractions such as h:mm:ss.00.
[ ]	Displays hours greater than 24 and minutes or seconds greater than 60.
AM/PM	Inserts AM or PM after time numbers depending upon whether the time is before or after noon, as in 10:15 PM. (Otherwise Excel formats the time using a 24-hour clock as in 22:15.)
[Color]	Specifies the font color for the section of the format as specified by the color name, as in [BLACK], [BLUE], [CYAN], [GREEN], [MAGENTA], [RED], [WHITE], or [YELLOW]. Note that [Color] must precede the other codes in the section, as in [RED](#,##0) in the negative section, to have negative values displayed in red and enclosed in parentheses.
[Color*n*]	Specifies a font color for the section of the format as specified by a number (*n*) between 1 and 56. Note that this [Color*n*] code must precede all other code in the section.

When defining custom formats for currency, you enter the currency signifier, as in $ for dollars, £ (Alt+0163) for pounds, ¥ (Alt+0165) for yen, and € (Alt+0128) for euros. Use a comma (,) to indicate the presence of the thousands separator and a period (.) to indicate the decimal point. When defining custom date formats, you can separate the parts of the date with either a hyphen (-) or a slash (/). When defining time formats, you separate each part with a colon (:).

 To find out the keystroke numeric code that inserts special characters such as the cent symbol or degree symbol into a custom format, open the Character Map program (Start⇨All Programs⇨Accessories⇨System Tools⇨Character Map) and then select the characters. Windows displays the Alt+keystroke combination, if one exists, in the lower right of the Character Map dialog box. To use this numeric code, enter the code from the numeric keypad while holding down the Alt key.

To get an idea of how you create your own custom number format, follow these steps for building a format that displays your financial values in the spreadsheet like you do when writing a check, as in 1,234 and 56/100 dollars:

1. **Enter 1234.56 in a blank cell of the current worksheet to create a sample amount and make sure that this cell is current.**

2. **Choose Format⇨Cells (Ctrl+1) to open the Format Cells dialog box, shown in Figure 20-1.**

3. **On the Number tab, select Fraction in the Category list box and then scroll down the Type list and select As Hundredths (30/100).**

The Sample area now shows the number in the current cell as 1234 56/100.

4. **Select Custom in the Category list box.**

The Type text box now contains the code # ??/00, your starting point for creating your custom format.

5. **Position the Insertion point at the very beginning of the Type list box and then type #,##.**

The Type text box now contains the code #,### ??/00, and the sample reads 1,234 56/100. Now, all you have to do is add the stock text and between the whole and fractional digits and the dollars text at the end.

6. **Position the Insertion point after the last pound sign (#) and then type " (open quote), press the spacebar, type and, and then type " (close quote).**

The Type text box now contains the code #,###" and"??/00, and the sample reads 1,234 and 56/100.

7. **Position the Insertion point at the very end of the code (after the last 0) and type " (open quote), press the spacebar to insert a space, type dollars, and then type " (close quote).**

The Type text box now contains the code #,###" and"??/00" dollars", and the sample reads 1,234 and 56/100 dollars, as shown in Figure 20-2.

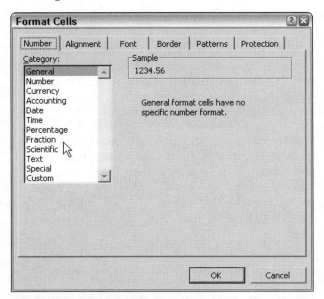

• **Figure 20-1:** Selecting the Fraction category to apply a close format to the base number.

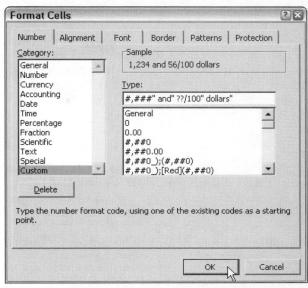

• **Figure 20-2:** The Number tab of the Format Cells dialog box showing the custom number format codes.

8. **Click OK to close the Format Cells dialog box and apply the new custom format to the current cell in the worksheet.**

When you close the Format Cells dialog box, Excel applies the custom format to the 1234.56 sample number in the current cell. To apply this custom format to other cells in the worksheet, you need to select the cells, open the Number tab of the Format Cells dialog box, select Custom in the Category list box, select the #,###" and"??/00" dollars" code at the very bottom of the Type list box, and click OK.

Custom formats that conditionally format entries

You can use Excel's number format codes to create custom number formats that do conditional formatting (much like the conditional formatting feature discussed in Technique 19). To create a conditional format, you set up the condition inside square brackets using the same comparative operators (=, >, <, >=, <=, and <>) as you do in simple formulas.

For example, you can create a conditional custom format that displays a cent sign (¢) after all values that are less than a dollar and displays a normal dollar sign and two decimal places for all values over or equal to one dollar. To do so, open the Number tab of the Format Cells dialog box, select the Custom number category on the Number tab, and enter the following code in the Type text box:

```
[<1].00¢;$0.00
```

In this conditional format, when the number in the cell is less than 1, the program adds the cent sign (¢) to the decimal number showing two places. Otherwise, when the number is 1 or any number greater, the program uses the second part of the conditional format (after the semicolon), which adds the dollar sign ($) and two decimal places to the number.

When creating conditional custom formats, you're not limited to two formats: the one used when the condition is true and the other when it's false. You can, in fact, create up to three formats: one format used when the first condition is true, a second format when the second is true, and a third format for all other cases.

For example, say that you want to create a conditional format that applies the General number format using a red font when a number is less than 1, blue when its value is greater than 100, and default black when its value is anywhere in between. To do so, open the Format Cells dialog box, select the Custom number category on the Number tab, and enter the following number codes in the Type text box:

```
[RED][<1]General;[BLUE][>100]General;General
```

In this conditional custom number format, the font color red is assigned to any values below 1, and blue is assigned to any values higher than 100. The default, black color is assigned to all other values (that is, any number between 1 and 100).

Custom formats that hide certain entries

Because Excel number formats consist of four sections (one each for positive numbers, negative numbers,

zeros, and text) that determine how specific types of entries are formatted, you can easily create custom formats that hide a particular type of entry by leaving its section blank.

For example, to create a number format that hides the contents of a cell only when it contains text, open the Format Cells dialog box, select the Custom number category on the Number tab, and enter the following number codes in the Type text box:

```
_(* #,##0.00_);_(* (#,##0.00);0;
```

In this custom number format, Excel applies the standard Comma style formatting to positive and negative numbers, while at the same time displays 0 for cells that contain zero. However, because I failed to add a number format code in the fourth section (after the third semicolon), Excel hides any text entry.

To create a custom format that does just the opposite — that is, hides all numbers and displays only text — you simply enter two semicolons with no number format codes whatsoever:

```
;;
```

In this custom number format, the two semicolons delineate three of the possible four sections: the positive number before the first semicolon, the negative number immediately following the first semicolon, and the zero section of the format immediately following the second semicolon. However, because all three sections are empty, Excel hides the display of positive, negative, and zero values, displaying only text entries. If you want to create a custom format that hides the display of all entries in a cell, just add the third semicolon to these other two with no codes (and no spaces) as in:

```
;;;
```

Because all four sections of the number format are now delineated and empty, Excel suppresses the display of all types of entries in the cells to which this custom number format is applied.

Assigning Custom Number Formats to Styles and Toolbars

Frankly, the only problem with custom number formats is that they're just not that easy to use. To apply them to a cell selection, you have to open the Number tab of the Format Cells (Ctrl+1) dialog box, select Custom in the Category list box, and then find the darned number format codes in the Type list box containing that long listing of codes.

To make your custom number formats much more accessible, I suggest that, at the very least, you assign the custom number formats to styles that you can then select from the Style dialog box (or Style drop-down list if you follow my advice and add this little gem to the Formatting toolbar or one of your own design — refer to Figure 18-3 in Technique 18).

To hitch one of your custom number formats to a new style, follow these steps:

1. **Apply the custom number format you want to assign to a style to a sample entry in your worksheet.**

To do this, select the cell, open the Number tab of the Format Cells dialog box (Ctrl+1), select Custom in the Category list box, select the format's codes in the Type list box, and click OK.

2. **Choose Format➪Style to open the Style dialog box.**

3. **Enter the new name for your style in the Style Name text box.**

When you type the new style name, the Style dialog box displays the number codes for the custom number format in the Style Includes (By Example) area, as shown in Figure 20-3.

4. **Click OK to close the Style dialog box.**

 Be sure to save your worksheet after assigning your custom number formats to new styles. Keep in mind that styles are saved only as part of the current workbook. To use these styles and their custom number formats in other workbooks you build, you have to merge the styles into them. (See Technique 18 for more on merging styles.)

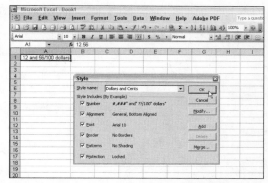

• **Figure 20-3: Assigning a custom number format to a new style.**

If you start using a custom number format on a frequent basis, you may want to do more than just assign the format to a style that you can apply from the Style dialog box or drop-down list box that you add to a toolbar. You can add the style to a button that you add to the Formatting toolbar or a toolbar of your own design.

To add a style that applies a number format to a button, follow these three steps:

1. **Assign the custom number format to a custom style (as described in the preceding steps).**

2. **Record a keystroke macro (see Technique 60) that selects that style.**

3. **Assign the keystroke macro to a custom button on one of your toolbars. (See Technique 2.)**

To see how easy this is, follow along with the steps for assigning a custom number format — one that hides all types of entries in a cell — to a new button on my Custom Formats toolbar (a toolbar of my own design):

1. Create the custom number format that hides all types of entries. To do so, open the Number tab of the Format Cells dialog box, select Custom in the Category list box, enter ;;; in the Type text box, and click OK. (See Figure 20-4.)

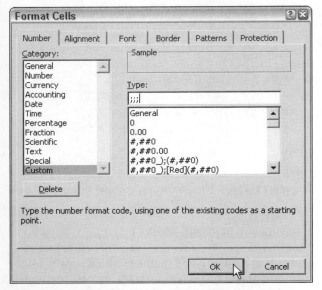

• **Figure 20-4:** Creating the custom number format that hides all types of cell entries.

2. Assign the new custom format to a new style by choosing Format⇨Style, entering All Hidden in the Style Name text box, and clicking OK. (See Figure 20-5.)

3. Begin recording a keystroke macro that selects this new All Hidden style. To do so, choose Tools⇨Macro⇨Record New Macro, enter All_hidden in the Macro Name text box, select Personal Macro Workbook in the Store Macro In drop-down list box, and click OK. (See Figure 20-6.)

4. To finish recording the macro, choose Format⇨Style, select All Hidden in the Style Name drop-down list box, click OK, and then click the Stop button in the Stop Recording toolbar.

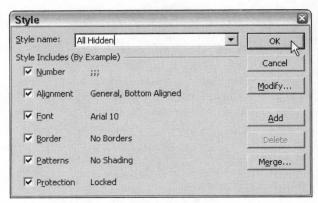

• **Figure 20-5:** Assigning the custom number format to a new style called All Hidden.

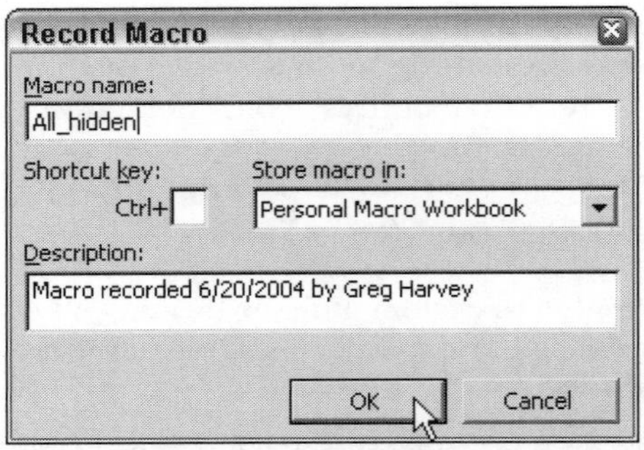

• **Figure 20-6:** Recording a keystroke macro All_hidden that selects the All Hidden style.

5. Choose View⇨Toolbars⇨Customize to open the Customize dialog box. If the toolbar to which you want to add the custom button isn't already visible, click the Toolbars tab and select this toolbar's check box.

6. Click the Commands tab, select the Macros in Categories list box, and then drag the custom button from the Customize dialog box to the desired position on the toolbar, as shown in Figure 20-7.

7. Assign the keystroke macro to the custom button by right-clicking on the button and then selecting Assign Macro on its shortcut menu.

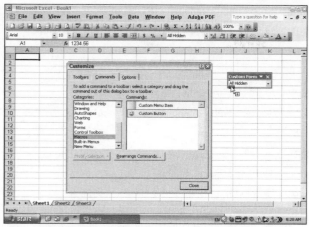

• **Figure 20-7:** Adding a custom button to the Custom Formats toolbar to which to assign the All_hidden macro.

8. Select the All_hidden macro in the Macro Name list box and click OK, as shown in Figure 20-8.

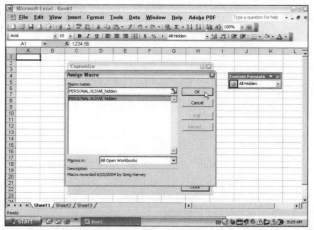

• **Figure 20-8:** Assigning the All_hidden macro to the custom button.

9. (Optional) Change the button image and button name (see Technique 2) and then click the Close button in the Customize dialog box.

After you close the Customize dialog box, you can test your new button. Select a cell that contains some sort of data entry and then click the All Hidden button on your toolbar. The entry should immediately disappear from the cell (while still being visible on the Formula bar). To redisplay the cell entry, apply another format, such as General, to it.

> The All Hidden button will work in any worksheet that you build provided that you merge the All Hidden style into the new workbook *before* clicking the button. If you don't do the merge, you'll get a Run-time error '450' when you click the button; Excel is caught running a macro that tries to apply a style that doesn't yet exist in the new file!

Applying Euro Currency Formats

Before leaving the subject of custom number formats, there's one more custom number format that I want you to be aware of. This is the Euro Currency number format that is supplied as part of the Euro Currency Tools add-in program that comes with Excel. This add-in is heaven sent if you deal with currency from the countries in the European Union that have recently adopted the euro as their basic currency.

When you activate this add-in (see Technique 8), Excel adds a Euro button to the Formatting toolbar that automatically formats your cell selection with the euro currency symbol (€) and two decimal places. In addition to this formatting button, the add-in also provides you with a EuroValue toolbar (see Figure 20-9) that you can use to convert the euro currency values to the former currency of a particular member country and a member's former currency into euros. To make this type of conversion, all you have to do is click the appropriate conversion on its drop-down list.

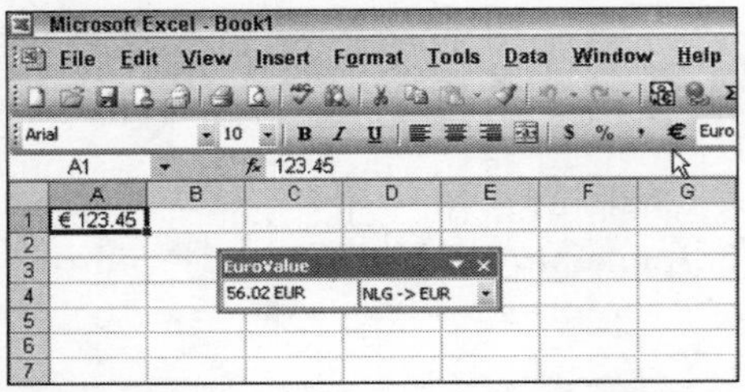

• **Figure 20-9:** Use the EuroValue toolbar to convert euro currency to and from a member's pre-euro currency.

The conversion options on this drop-down list make extensive use of the three-letter ISO codes that refer to particular countries and their former currencies within the union. (Refer to Table 20-2 to decode these abbreviations.)

In addition to the EuroValue toolbar, the Euro Currency Tools add-in attaches a Euro Conversion command to the Tools pull-down menu. Selecting this command opens a Euro Conversion dialog box that also enables you to convert from one euro member currency to another.

TABLE 20-2: EURO CONVERSION ISO CODES

ISO Code	Country/Region	Unit of Currency
ATS	Austria	Schilling
BEF	Belgium	Franc
EUR	Euro member state	Euro
FIM	Finland	Markka
FRF	France	Franc
DEM	Germany	Deutsche mark
GRD	Greece	Drachma
IEP	Ireland	Pound
ITL	Italy	Lira
LUF	Luxembourg	Franc
NLG	Netherlands	Guilder
PTE	Portugal	Escudo
ESP	Spain	Peseta

Technique 21

Dazzling Alignments for Data Entries

Save Time By

✔ Using unusual horizontal and vertical alignments

✔ Indenting data entries

✔ Wrapping text within cells

✔ Centering an entry across cells

Most of the time, the Formatting toolbar's Align Left, Center, Align Right, and Merge and Center buttons are all you need to put your spreadsheet's data entries into good order. You should, however, keep in mind that Excel has much more to offer than these four standard formatting buttons when it comes to properly aligning and orienting your data.

Using these other less standard alignment options can often go a long way towards making the tables in your spreadsheet read better by enabling you to keep their data more compact in their columns. More importantly, they can save you from later having to waste time dealing with paging problems caused by tables that unnecessarily split across more than one page of the report.

This technique looks at several of these less standard alignment options that you can apply to both text and numeric entries in the tables in your spreadsheets. It also covers text options that enable you to efficiently format long text entries such as the titles and column and row headings for your tables.

Line Me Up

The Alignment tab of the Format Cells dialog box (opened by pressing Ctrl+1 — see Figure 21-1) contains four sections with options that enable you to control the positioning of the data entries in their cells:

✔ **Text Alignment** to change the horizontal and vertical alignment of the entries in their cells. In addition to the normal left, center, and right horizontal alignment, you have a choice between using left or right indent, filling the cell with the characters in the entry, justifying the characters to fill the width of the cell, and centering the entry across a selection of cells.

Vertical alignment options include aligning the entries with the top edge of the cells, bottom edge, or centered between the two edges. Or you can wrap the entry on different lines that are either justified between the top and bottom cell edges or evenly distributed between the two.

✔ **Orientation** to reorient the data entries by rotating up or down the angle of the baseline that their characters rest on or by setting the entries so the characters appear one over the other in a single thin column.

✔ **Text Control** to wrap the text in the entries on as many lines as needed to stay within the current column width (thereby automatically increasing the row heights), reduce the font size of the entries so that they fit on one line within their current column widths, or to merge the current cell selection into one large cell within which the entry on the leftmost cell is aligned.

✔ **Right-to-Left** to change the normal left-to-right reading order of the characters to right to left, as required when using a language such as Hebrew or Arabic whose characters are read in that order.

Indenting data entries

Normally when it comes to horizontal alignment, Excel either automatically sets the first character of the entry flush with the left edge of the cell (the left alignment default for all text entries) or the last character of the entry flush with the right edge (the right alignment default for all numeric entries). If you center a data entry (by clicking the Center button on the Formatting toolbar), Excel attempts to make the space between the left edge and the first character in the entry equal to the space between the last character and the right edge.

Instead of relying on centering to set off particular entries in a worksheet, many times you can just indent the entries from the left edge to set them off from the others. For example, Figure 21-2 shows a sales table that contains sales figures for three kinds of recording media: CDs, cassette tapes, and LPs. Each of these three groups has it own subheadings that list the same four music categories (Rock, Jazz, Classical, and Other). You can improve the legibility of the row headings for this table by indenting these category subheadings.

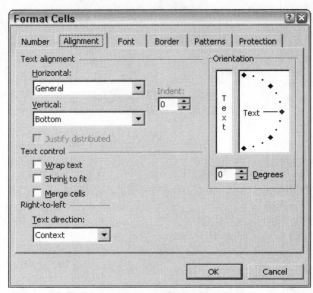

• **Figure 21-1: Use the options on the Alignment tab of the Format Cells dialog box to select unusual alignments.**

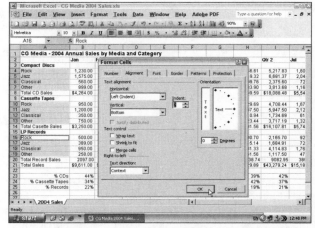

• **Figure 21-2: Sales table showing the breakdown of sales by media and category.**

To do this, you could just select all the ranges with the subheadings as a single cell selection and then click the Increase Indent button on the Formatting toolbar. However, if you want to indent the headings more than a single character (which is the default when you click the Increase Indent button), you're better off doing this from the Alignment tab of the Format Cells dialog box.

Figure 21-2 shows you how. Select the Alignment tab in the Format Cells dialog box (Ctrl+1). Select Left (Indent) in the Horizontal drop-down list, select 2 in the Indent text box (either by typing 2 or selecting it with the spinner buttons), and click OK. Figure 21-3 shows you the results. Here, I have indented the cell ranges A4:A7, A10:A13, and A:16:A:19 two characters in one operation.

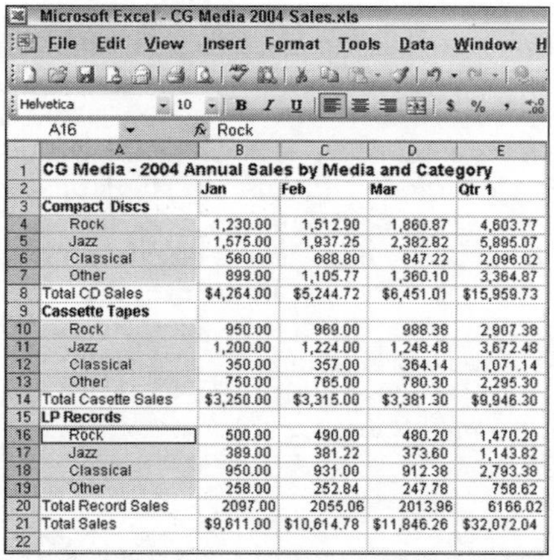

	A	B	C	D	E
1	CG Media - 2004 Annual Sales by Media and Category				
2		Jan	Feb	Mar	Qtr 1
3	Compact Discs				
4	Rock	1,230.00	1,512.90	1,860.87	4,603.77
5	Jazz	1,575.00	1,937.25	2,382.82	5,895.07
6	Classical	560.00	688.80	847.22	2,096.02
7	Other	899.00	1,105.77	1,360.10	3,364.87
8	Total CD Sales	$4,264.00	$5,244.72	$6,451.01	$15,959.73
9	Cassette Tapes				
10	Rock	950.00	969.00	988.38	2,907.38
11	Jazz	1,200.00	1,224.00	1,248.48	3,672.48
12	Classical	350.00	357.00	364.14	1,071.14
13	Other	750.00	765.00	780.30	2,295.30
14	Total Casette Sales	$3,250.00	$3,315.00	$3,381.30	$9,946.30
15	LP Records				
16	Rock	500.00	490.00	480.20	1,470.20
17	Jazz	389.00	381.22	373.60	1,143.82
18	Classical	950.00	931.00	912.38	2,793.38
19	Other	258.00	252.84	247.78	758.62
20	Total Record Sales	2097.00	2055.06	2013.96	6166.02
21	Total Sales	$9,611.00	$10,614.78	$11,846.26	$32,072.04
22					

• Figure 21-3: Sales table after indenting each row category subheadings two characters.

Using nonstandard vertical alignment

By default, Excel vertically aligns the baseline of all your data entries with the bottom edges of their cells. In certain cases, you can improve the look of the spreadsheet by increasing the height of rows by using other vertical alignment options. When you select the Top or Center vertical alignment options, you often have to manually increase the height of the rows before you can see the effect that these options have on the vertical positioning of the data entries. When you select the Justify option or the Distributed vertical alignment option, Excel automatically increases the height of the rows as needed to wrap the text onto several different lines in order to maintain the current column widths.

Figure 21-4 illustrates this situation. For this figure, I applied the Justify Vertical alignment option to cell A1 — the cell containing the spreadsheet title. (Refer to Figure 21-3 to see how this title originally looked when its long text entry spilled over into the blank columns B, C, and D to the right.) After applying this vertical alignment option, Excel wraps the title onto four separate lines. The program does this by automatically increasing the height of line 1 from 15.75 characters (21 pixels) to 63 characters (84 pixels) while at the same time leaving the width of column at 20.14 characters (146 pixels).

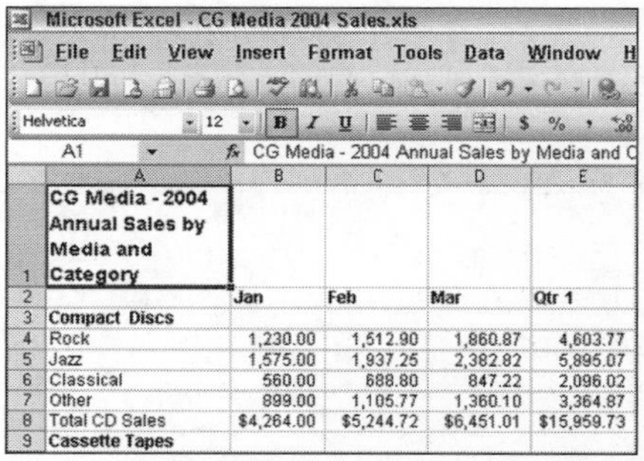

	A	B	C	D	E
1	CG Media - 2004 Annual Sales by Media and Category				
2		Jan	Feb	Mar	Qtr 1
3	Compact Discs				
4	Rock	1,230.00	1,512.90	1,860.87	4,603.77
5	Jazz	1,575.00	1,937.25	2,382.82	5,895.07
6	Classical	560.00	688.80	847.22	2,096.02
7	Other	899.00	1,105.77	1,360.10	3,364.87
8	Total CD Sales	$4,264.00	$5,244.72	$6,451.01	$15,959.73
9	Cassette Tapes				

• Figure 21-4: Applying the Justify Vertical alignment option to cell A1 with the long spreadsheet title.

Instead of using a blank row to separate your table titles from the first row of data, apply the Top or Center Vertical alignment option to the cells with the titles and then manually increase the height of their rows. If you don't want to change the vertical alignment of the titles, you create a sense of vertical space simply by increasing the height of the first row of data.

Rotating text entries

Long column headings tend to inflate the width of the individual columns in order to display all their characters. These are the leading culprits in making tables of data much wider than they need to be — often preventing an otherwise manageable table from fitting on the page when printed. Instead of widening the columns just to display long headings, you can often keep those column widths down to a reasonable size simply by rotating their column headings. You'd be surprised how much real estate you can save by rotating column headings up even as little as 45 degrees.

Figures 21-5 and 21-6 illustrate how this rotating-column-headings trick can save on overall table width. In Figure 21-5, you see the column headings for the production schedule right before rotating their baselines up (technically counterclockwise) by 60 degrees. As you can partially see in columns H, I, and J, displaying the headings for these columns makes them much wider than they really need to be.

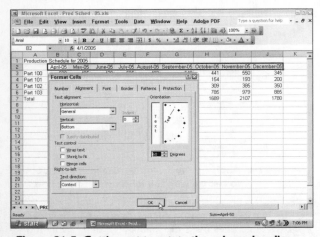

• **Figure 21-5:** Getting set to rotate the column headings 45 degrees counterclockwise.

To make this project schedule more compact without having to shorten the text for the column headings, I simply use the Orientation control on the Alignment tab of the Format Cells dialog box to rotate the headings up 60 degrees. Figure 21-6 shows the same schedule after rotating the column headings and then choosing Format⇨Column⇨AutoFit Selection. As you can see in this figure, rotating these headings up and then narrowing the column widths really compact this table.

• **Figure 21-6:** Schedule after rotating the column headings up to narrow their columns.

To squeeze columns down to one character wide for forms that just use check boxes, rotate the column headings 90 degrees counterclockwise or select the orientation wherein the characters appear one over the other. (To do the latter, select the Alignment tab of the Format Cells dialog box and click the sample that shows the word Text with the characters aligned this way.)

Getting Your Text under Control

The Alignment tab on the Format Cells dialog box provides you with three methods for managing the text entries in your spreadsheet. The first two controls are specifically designed to manage extra-long text entries so that they fit within a column width that's considerably narrower than would otherwise be required to display all the text. The last method enables you to center a text heading over several columns as you might want to do with a title for a table of data.

Making text wrap within a cell

When you want to maintain a set column width by wrapping long text entries in a cell selection onto several lines, select the Wrap Text check box in the Text Control section of the Alignment tab. You can use this control to break up a long table heading that would normally spill over several blank columns so that all its text fits within the current column width set for the data in rows below. You can also use it to effectively control long column headings that would otherwise force you to widen the columns of data much more than is necessary to just display their numerical entries.

Figures 21-7 and 21-8 illustrate this kind of situation and solution. Figure 21-7 shows a sales table whose column headings are extra long. They're so long in fact that it would require widening their columns way beyond what is necessary just to display the financial data.

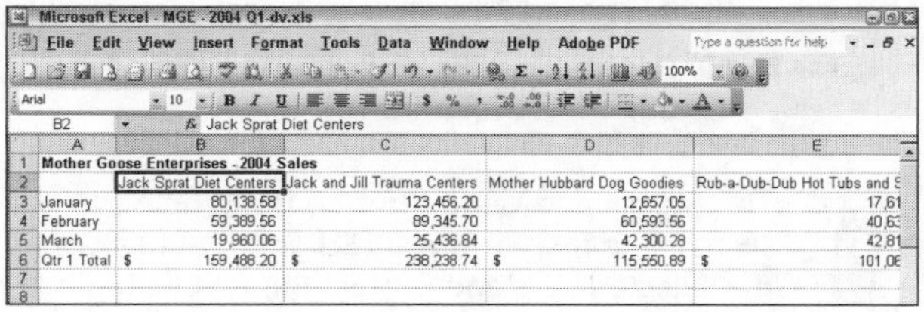

• **Figure 21-7:** Sales table with really long column headings whose text needs to be wrapped.

To remedy this situation and make this table much more compact, follow these steps:

1. **Select the columns that contain the long column headings.**

In this example, I selected the letters B through J in the column header.

2. **Manually narrow the selected columns to the width necessary for displaying the data entries.**

For this example, with the help of the Width ScreenTip, I narrowed the selected columns to a width of 12.86 characters (95 pixels) by dragging the right border of one of the selected columns. (Here, narrowing one column automatically narrows all the other selected columns.) Doing this,

of course, truncates the long column headings in the second row.

3. **Select the range of cells with the long column headings that you want wrapped to the new narrower column widths.**

For this example, I selected the cell range B2:J2.

4. **Open the Format Cells dialog box (Ctrl+1), select the Alignment tab, select the Wrap Text check box, and click OK.**

Figure 21-8 shows the results of this operation. Excel automatically wraps the column headings so that they're entirely displayed within the current column widths. At the same time, the program automatically increases the height of row 2 to accommodate these wrapped lines of text.

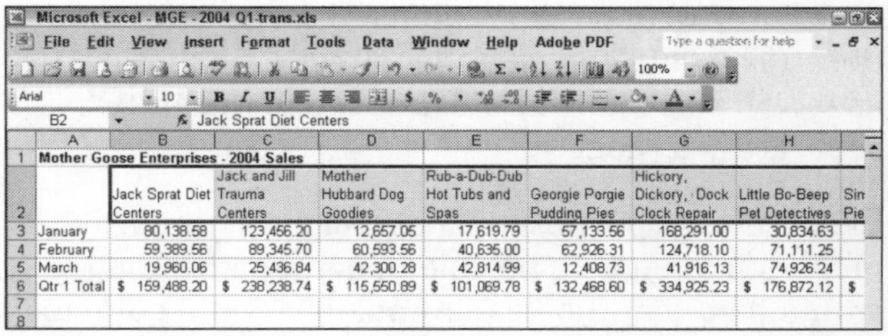

• **Figure 21-8:** Sales table after wrapping the column headings to display on several lines in the narrower columns.

Shrinking the text to fit within a cell

The second way of getting long text entries to fit within a certain cell width is to shrink their text down to size with the Shrink to Fit check box option. This option is a lot less successful than Wrap Text because Excel often ends up shrinking your text entries so much that they're illegible without the use of a magnifying glass. (See Figure 21-9 for a prime example of this.)

Reserve the Shrink to Fit option to those text entries that almost fit within the current column width to guard against reducing them so much that they're no longer legible.

• **Figure 21-9: Sales table after making the column headings illegible by shrinking them to fit the various column widths.**

Centering a heading across columns

The Merged Cells check box on the Alignment tab of the Format Cells dialog box enables you to mesh together separate cells of a single range to create a mega cell. The purpose for doing this is so you can change the horizontal or vertical alignment of its data entry with regard to the new mega cell's borders. (The data can be either a text or numeric entry as long it was made in the first cell of the erstwhile separate cell range.)

Because your purpose in merging a cell range into a mega cell often is to be able to center a heading within it so that the heading spans several columns, the Formatting toolbar contains a Merge and Center button. By clicking this button, you combine two different controls on the Alignment tab of the Format Cells dialog box:

✔ The Center option in the Horizontal drop-down list box in the Text Alignment section

✔ The Merge Cells check box option in the Text Control section

Figure 21-10 illustrates the most common use for the Merge and Center button. Here, I have centered the spreadsheet title entered into cell A1 over columns A through I by first selecting the cell range A1:I1 and then clicking the Merge and Center button on the Formatting toolbar.

• **Figure 21-10: Sales table after centering the spreadsheet title across columns A:I.**

 The Merge and Center button is a toggle switch. The first time you click it, Excel merges the selected cells and centers the text within it. The second time you click it with the merged cell selected, the program restores the cells that were merged into one and returns the text entry to its original alignment.

Technique 22

Charting Data in a Snap

One of the most effective ways to present your worksheet data is in graphic form using one of Excel's chart formats. By representing the numbers in your spreadsheet in graphic form, users can spot trends and anomalies in the data much more quickly than when perusing the raw figures (no matter how well you've formatted them).

Excel makes it a snap to turn the tables of data in your spreadsheets into vibrant, inspiring charts. When charting data, you can either create the chart on its separate chart sheet or embed the chart as a graphic object on one of the regular worksheets in the workbook. If you choose to embed the chart as a graphic object, you can then modify the chart's size and position as you would a photo or piece of clip art that you add to the worksheet. You can also easily print the chart along with its substantiating data in a report. If you create a chart on a separate chart sheet, you can easily print the chart on a separate page of your report without having to worry about fitting it in with surrounding data.

Instant Charts

If you want your data graphed on a separate chart sheet, you can do this in as little as one keystroke, two tops. If you're dealing with a table of data where you want all the data graphed, you simply position the cell pointer somewhere in the table of data and press F11. If, however, you're dealing with a table of data that includes numbers you don't want graphed (subtotals or grand totals in the table), you need to take the extra step of selecting the range of cells to be graphed (column and row headings including the numbers to be represented) before you press F11.

Figures 22-1 and 22-2 illustrate just how incredibly quick and easy it is to generate a chart on its own sheet. Figure 22-1 shows a production schedule of projected units to be produced in the last nine months of the calendar year (April through December) arranged by part number. When I first open the workbook with the cell pointer automatically saved in cell A1, I just press F11 to graph this table of data.

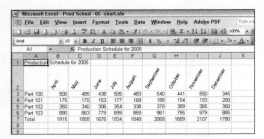

• **Figure 22-1: Data table with production schedule arranged by part number.**

Figure 22-2 shows you the result of pressing F11. As you can see, Excel instantly creates a clustered column chart on its own chart sheet using the rows of data in the production schedule as the data series. This chart sheet is named Chart1 and is placed in front of all the other worksheets in the workbook.

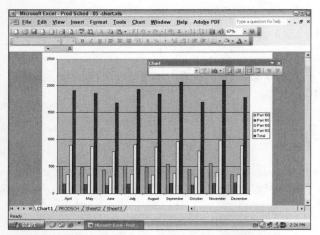

• **Figure 22-2: Clustered column chart created from production schedule on its own chart sheet.**

Because I didn't preselect the range of data to be graphed, Excel automatically selects all the rows of data in the table and represents them as the different data series in the chart. This includes the last row — the one containing the monthly subtotals.

(In the column chart, these totals are represented by the last data series — the tallest bars in each monthly category.)

To prevent Excel from graphing the subtotals row, all I needed to do was to select the cell range A2:J6 before I pressed F11. To eliminate this total data series and have Excel redraw the chart without it, I just click any one of the columns representing individual data points of this total data series and then press the Delete key. Figure 22-3 shows you the column chart after eliminating the totals data series from the chart.

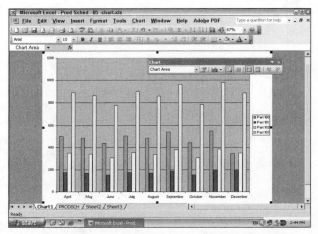

• **Figure 22-3: Clustered column chart after deleting the totals data series.**

After making sure that you have just the data you want represented in the chart, you can get down to the business of enhancing it. Because Excel automatically displays the Chart toolbar (shown in Figure 22-4), you can use its buttons to make many of these chart improvements. For those options that are not readily available from the Chart toolbar, look to the options on the Chart pull-down menu — which is automatically added to the Excel menu bar whenever you make a chart sheet active or select an embedded chart on a regular worksheet.

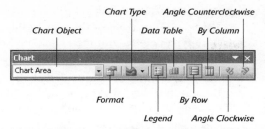

• **Figure 22-4:** Use the buttons on the Chart toolbar to enhance the basic chart.

Typical enhancements that you can make to your new chart include

- ✔ **Change the orientation of the data series in the chart.** By default, Excel generates the data series in the chart from the rows of data. To generate the data series from the columns of data, click the By Column button on the Chart toolbar.

- ✔ **Change the chart type.** By default, Excel represents the data as a Clustered Column chart. To select a new chart type, click the Chart Type drop-down button and then select the new chart type from the pop-up palette. If this palette doesn't have the chart type you want, choose Chart⇨ Chart Type to open the Chart Type dialog box containing all the chart types supported by Excel as well as any custom chart types you create. (See Technique 23 for more on custom chart types.)

- ✔ **Add chart titles.** By default, the new chart has no titles. To add titles, choose Chart⇨Chart Options and then enter the Chart title, the Category (X) axis title, and the Value (Y) axis title as needed.

- ✔ **Format the chart titles and headings.** To do this, select the chart object you want to format (Chart Title, Category Axis Title, Value Axis Title, and so on) in the Chart Objects drop-down list box and then click the Format - button on the Chart toolbar.

- ✔ **Add a data table to the chart that displays the graphed data beneath the chart itself.** Click the Data Table button on the Chart toolbar.

Figure 22-5 shows you the same chart as originally shown in Figure 22-3 after changing the chart type from the default Clustered Column type to a Clustered Bar chart. In addition, I added a data table to the chart to show the underlying values represented in the chart.

 If you decide that you'd like to convert your fully enhanced chart to an embedded chart, choose Chart⇨Location, select the As Object In option button in the Chart Location dialog box — along with the worksheet in which to embed it in the As Object In drop-down list box — and click OK. Excel then converts the chart into a graphic object and adds it to the original worksheet and at the same time deletes the chart sheet.

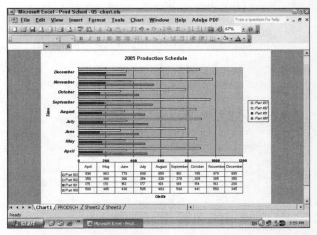

• **Figure 22-5:** Changing the chart type to Clustered Bar and making suggested enhancements.

Chart Wizard Magic

If you're somewhat impatient like me, you probably really appreciate the immediacy of generating a new chart (albeit a somewhat rough one) at literally the press of a button. For those of you who are not quite as impetuous and therefore don't require quite as much immediate gratification, Excel offers a more studied, step-by-step way to generate your charts via its Chart Wizard.

Although creating a new chart with the Chart Wizard is a little slower process, it's also one that gives you the opportunity to make basic enhancements — selecting a new chart type, adding chart titles, and so on — as you create the chart. So, when you're finished, you have a chart that requires much less futzing on your part. When looked at from this perspective, you may find that the Chart Wizard, while not nearly as flashy, may actually prove to be more efficient.

To graph your data with the Chart Wizard, follow these general steps:

1. **Select the data in the spreadsheet that you want represented in the chart and then click the Chart Wizard button (the one sporting the column chart icon) on the Standard toolbar or choose Insert⇨Chart.**

   Excel opens the Step 1 of 4 - Chart Type dialog box, shown in Figure 22-6.

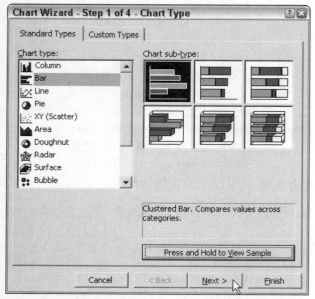

• **Figure 22-6:** Selecting the type of chart in the first Chart Wizard dialog box.

2. **Select the general type of chart in the Chart Type list box, select the specific type in the Chart Sub-type palette, and then click the Next button.**

   To get an idea of how your data will look dressed up in the selected chart type, click and hold down the Press and Hold Down to View Sample button.

   When you click the Next button, Excel opens the Step 2 of 4 - Chart Source Data dialog box, shown in Figure 22-7.

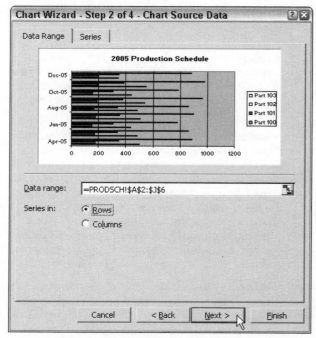

• **Figure 22-7:** Designating the data range and data series to be used in the second Chart Wizard dialog box.

3. **Check that both the range shown in the Data Range text box and the selected worksheet charting are correct. If need be, click the Columns option button to have the data series represented by the columns in the selected range rather than the rows. Then click the Next button.**

   If you need to change the values used for a particular data point in the series or add or delete data points, select the Series tab and then adjust the range assigned to a particular data point or remove or add new ones.

When you click the Next button, Excel opens the Step 3 of 4 - Chart Options dialog box, shown in Figure 22-8.

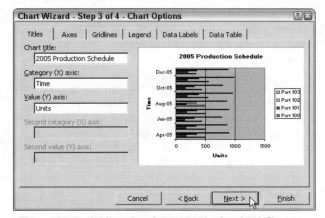

• **Figure 22-8:** Adding the chart titles in the third Chart Wizard dialog box.

4. **Enter the titles for the chart in the appropriate text boxes on the Titles tab and then make any other desired enhancements to the chart using the other tabs in this dialog box. When you're finished, click Next.**

As you enter the titles for the chart, they appear in the preview area on the right side of the dialog box. Use the options on the other tabs — Axes, Gridlines, Legend, Data Labels, and Data Table — to make further enhancements to the basic chart.

When you click Next, Excel opens the Step 4 of 4 - Chart Location dialog box, shown in Figure 22-9.

5. **To place the new chart on a separate chart sheet, select the As New Sheet option button and then click the Finish button. Otherwise, to embed the new chart as a graphic object in a worksheet, leave the default As Object In option button selected and then click Finish. (To embed the chart on another sheet in the workbook, select it on the As Object In drop-down list before you click Finish.)**

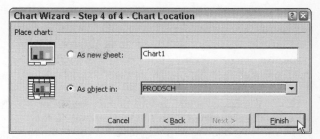

• **Figure 22-9:** Designating the location of the new chart in the fourth Chart Wizard dialog box.

Figure 22-10 shows you how the embedded chart appears in the worksheet after you click Finish to close the Step 4 of 4 - Chart Location dialog box. Note that Excel automatically selects this new graphic object (indicated by the presence of the black square sizing handles at the corners and mid-points of the perimeter of the Chart Area).

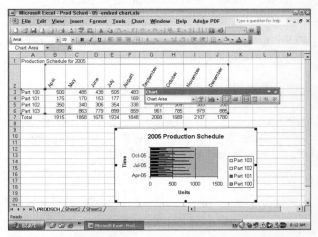

• **Figure 22-10:** Embedded chart created with the Chart Wizard.

Excel also selects the ranges of cells that contain the text and numbers used in the chart. The program encloses the rows or columns of numerical data in a blue rectangle with sizing handles at the four corners.

The program identifies the text entries that, in the case of this type of Clustered Bar chart, contain the data points in each cluster and appear in the legend by enclosing them within a green rectangle with sizing handles at its corners. Excel also identifies the text entries that contain the various clusters along the Category (X) Axis by enclosing them within a cyan-colored rectangle with its own sizing handles.

 You can directly manipulate the contents of the embedded chart simply by dragging the sizing handles for these different chart components. For example, to include an extra row or column of data in the chart, all you have to do is to drag the sizing handles attached to the blue rectangle to include the new row or column within its boundaries.

You should note that whenever an embedded chart is selected in a worksheet, the program displays the floating Chart toolbar and adds the Chart menu to the Excel menu bar. You can use the buttons on the Chart toolbar or menu items on the Chart menu to make any needed modifications to the chart itself.

While the embedded chart is selected in the worksheet, you can resize it and reposition it as needed:

- To resize the chart area, drag the appropriate sizing handle.

- To move the chart, position the mouse pointer within the confines of the chart area (just not directly over a particular component such as

the chart title, legend, and so on) and then drag it to its new position. (The mouse pointer changes from the white cross arrowhead to a four-headed arrow as you drag the dashed outline of the chart.)

Most of the time you'll find that you need to do both some chart resizing and repositioning. Excel has a tendency to draw embedded charts rather small in relation to its identifying elements — the chart title, legend, and Category Axis and Value Axis titles. Often, the chart area is so small that not all of the data elements represented in the chart are even visible. (This is the case in Figure 22-10, where only three of the nine months that have been charted are visible.) The program also tends to place the new embedded chart below the table of supporting data but not directly below so that even if you want the chart beneath the table of data, you often still need to nudge it in slightly to the left.

 The only problem with increasing the size of the embedded chart to make the data elements read better is that Excel makes the text elements proportionately bigger. To deal with this, you need to modify the formatting for these text elements. See Technique 23 for ideas on how to make these modifications most efficiently.

Technique 23

Chart Customization Tricks

Save Time By

- ✔ Efficiently formatting the chart's text elements
- ✔ Scaling and formatting the chart axes
- ✔ Making the chart plot area read better

No one can deny that creating the basic chart in Excel is a fast business. The only problem is that this swiftness comes at the price of truly disproportionate and oftentimes illegible charts. (You only have to take a gander at the charts shown in Figures 22-2 and 22-10 of Technique 22 to bear this out.) This means you spend the bulk of your chart-making time after the fact — doing much needed modifications and enhancements.

This technique looks at three different chart areas — titles and headings, axes, and plot area — that often require some attention in a new chart and shows you how you can efficiently make the needed modifications. In terms of the chart titles and headings and axes, these modifications usually entail basic formatting changes. In terms of the chart plot area, these modifications often entail enhancing the legibility of the data through the additions of elements such as data tables, data labels, and additional gridlines and sometimes adjusting the scale of one or more of the chart axes.

Getting the Chart Titles and Headings in Balance

The first big problem with most Excel charts is that their text elements are way out of balance in relation to the plot area (which is actually the heart of the chart). This is especially true of embedded charts where relatively gigantic titles and legends tend to dwarf the plot area, often making it impossible for the program to display all the data points.

Figure 23-1 is a good example of this kind of problem. Here the plot area of the Clustered Bar chart is so compressed that only three of the nine months plotted can be displayed, and all color differentiation between the individual data points (clearly visible in the huge chart legend) is completely lost.

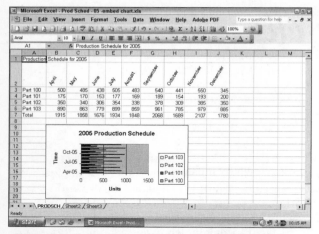

• **Figure 23-1:** This plot area of this embedded chart is dwarfed by the large text elements.

Although increasing the size of the chart area can help this problem, making the chart bigger overall is no real answer. As you can see in Figure 23-2, Excel maintains the same proportions between plot area and the chart titles and headings so that what was originally big text in the chart becomes huge text.

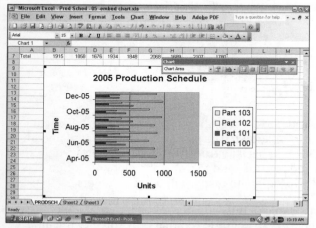

• **Figure 23-2:** Increasing the size of the chart area inflates the size of the text elements as well.

Indeed, the only real answer to this problem is to reduce the size of the chart text. The most efficient way to make this kind of change is to follow these steps:

1. **Select a text element in the chart.**

   You can either do this by clicking the element in the chart itself or by selecting its name on the Chart Objects button's drop-down list on the Chart toolbar.

2. **Click the Format button on the Chart toolbar.**

   Doing this opens a Format dialog box specifically for the particular object.

3. **Use the Size option on the Font tab of this dialog box to select a smaller size font (and, perhaps even select a new font and apply other attributes such as bold and italics to it while you're at it). When you're finished, click OK.**

4. **Repeat these steps for each additional text element.**

Figure 23-3 shows what a difference just reducing the font size of the chart's various text elements has on the plot area and the legibility of the entire chart. This figure is identical to Figure 22-2 shown earlier except that I reduced the font size for the chart title, legend headings, Value Y-axis title and headings, and the Category X-axis title and headings.

Now that the sizes of the text elements are in proportion with the size of the chart area, Excel is able to display all the graphed data in the center plot area. Note that the Value (Y) axis now contains seven tick marks (from 0 to 1200) as opposed to just the four in the original chart (0, 500, 1000, and 1500). Also, the Category (X) axis can display clusters for all nine months (April to December) rather than the five months (April, June, August, October, and December) in the original chart.

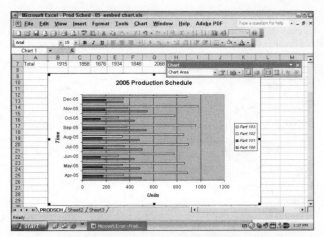

• **Figure 23-3:** Embedded chart after reducing the font size of all the chart titles and axis and legend headings.

Scaling and Formatting the Chart Axes

Another problematic area in new Excel charts — one that often requires your tender touch — is the formatting (or lack thereof) of the chart axes. Most of the two-dimensional column and bar charts that you'll encounter use a numerical scale only for the vertical (Value) Y axis. Other chart types such as XY (Scatter) and Line charts use numerical scales both for the horizontal (Category) X axis and the vertical Y axis.

When Excel generates a new chart, it uses the high and low values in the spreadsheet data to determine the minimum and maximum values used by the Y-axis scale (and sometimes used by the X-axis scale as well). These high and low values also determine the number of tick marks on the scale, the increment between the tick marks, and the headings that each tick mark displays.

Very often, you'll find that reducing the font size of the Y-axis or X-axis headings is not enough; you may also need to select a more truncated number format for your numerical scales, Occasionally, you may even find it beneficial to modify the scale that the chart uses so that your worksheet data are better represented in the plot area.

Figure 23-4 illustrates such a situation. This Clustered Column chart shows the dollar amounts of CG Media's first quarter 2004 sales for CDs and cassette tapes broken down by music category. Excel automatically formatted the Value (Y) axis using the Accounting number format with two decimal places. For this chart (and most of the others you generate), you never need to give up precious chart area real estate to decimal places (no one's concerned about the extra cents), and if you add a Value axis title as I did for indicating the currency, you have no need to select a number format that displays the dollar sign.

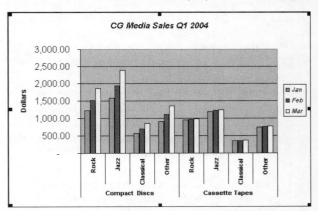

• **Figure 23-4:** Embedded Clustered Column chart with a Value (Y) axis that needs some help.

To modify the scale or format for the Value (Y) axis or Category (X) axis, you simply click the axis in the chart area or select it in the Chart Object button's drop-down list. Then click the Format (Axis) button on the Chart toolbar to open the Format Axis dialog box. Here are some modifications you can make in this dialog box:

- ✔ To assign a new number format to the selected chart axis, select the Number tab (see Figure 23-5) and then choose a new built-in category or develop a custom format of your own. (See Technique 20 for details on developing custom number formats.)

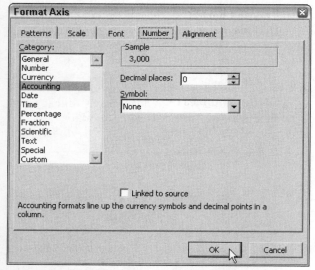

• **Figure 23-5: Modifying the new number format used by the Value (Y) axis.**

- ✔ To make modifications to the Value (Y) axis scale, select the Scale tab (shown in Figure 23-6). This tab contains a number of options that control the scale's display. The most important among these options are the Minimum and Maximum scale values that Excel selects:

  - ▶ The Minimum value determines the bottom tick mark (where the Y axis crosses the X axis).

  - ▶ The Maximum value determines the top tick mark.

Excel then uses this spread to establish the increments for the major and minor tick marks on this scale. (Only the major tick marks are displayed by default.)

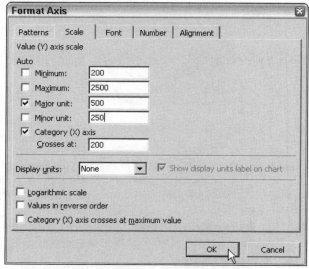

• **Figure 23-6: Modifying the Value (Y) axis scale.**

To help enlarge the plot area for my Area chart, I decided to fine-tune the Minimum and Maximum values for this chart's Y-axis scale. To do this, I created two formulas in the worksheet: one that uses Excel's MIN function to calculate the lowest value in the cell ranges represented in this chart and another that uses the MAX function to calculate the highest value in these ranges. For my example, the lowest sales value turns out to be $350.00 while the highest is $2,382.82.

I then opened the Scale tab of the Format Axis dialog box and took the Y axis scale off autopilot by making the following changes:

- ✔ I entered 200 as the new Minimum and 2500 as the new Maximum (Excel automatically selected 0 as the Minimum and 3000 as the Maximum).

✔ I increased the Minor Unit from Excel's automatic increment of 100 up to 250. (The Minor Unit determines where Excel draws tick marks should you choose to display the minor gridlines for the Y axis.)

Figure 23-7 shows you the results of all this tinkering with both the number formatting of the headings on the Value (Y) Axis and as well as its scale. As you can see, these headings are much cleaner and easier to read without the unnecessary decimal places. Also, modifying where the Y-axis scale begins and ends gives you a much clearer vision of the top and low sellers among the CDs and cassettes.

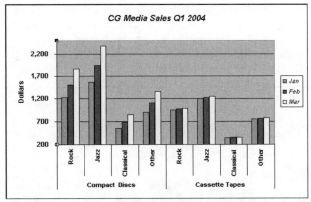

• **Figure 23-7: Clustered Column chart after formatting the Y-axis headings and adjusting its scale.**

Tricks for Making the Plotted Data Easier to Decipher

The last area that often needs improvement is the plot area itself. What you can do to make this area easier to understand is heavily dependent upon the type of chart you're working. Some chart types such as those in the Pie chart category allow for very little improvement to their plot areas, whereas others such as Clustered Column and Clustered Bar charts allow for a great deal.

For charts that use both an X-axis and a Y-axis, sometimes the easiest thing you can do to improve the legibility of the chart is simply to add minor gridlines. Depending upon the type of chart, these extra lines can guide the eye from the tick marks displaying the closest values on the Y-axis to the actual data points in the chart.

To add (or remove) gridlines from a chart that uses them, follow these steps:

1. **Choose Chart⇨Chart Options to open the Chart Options dialog box.**

You need to select the chart to add the Chart menu to the menu bar when working with an embedded chart.

2. **On the Gridlines tab (see Figure 23-8), select (or deselect) the Major Gridlines and/or Minor Gridlines check boxes for the appropriate axis.**

3. **When you're finished, click OK.**

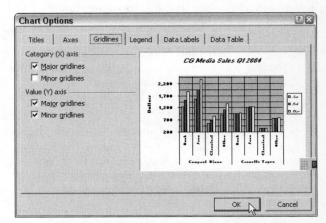

• **Figure 23-8: Displaying major X-axis and major and minor Y-axis gridlines for the chart.**

Figure 23-9 shows the Clustered Column introduced in the previous section after adding both the minor gridlines to the Value (Y) axis and the major gridlines to the Category (X) axis. Note how well the addition of the major vertical gridlines for the X axis clearly delineates the clusters with each data series.

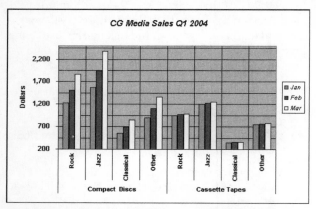

• **Figure 23-9:** Clustered Column chart after adding major X-axis and minor Y-axis gridlines.

When you're dealing with a chart where displaying the underlying numerical data visually represented in the plot area is important to its understanding, you have a couple of choices:

✔ Display a data table that shows all the graphed numbers in a standard row-and-column table format appearing immediately beneath the chart area. To add a data table to a chart, just click the Data Table button on the Chart toolbar.

✔ Add data labels that display the numbers right next to each data point in the graph. To display the values as data labels, select the Data Labels tab of Chart Options dialog box (Chart⇨Chart Options) and then select the Value check box option.

 When Excel adds a data table or displays values as data labels in a chart, it formats these values exactly as they are in the worksheet itself. To apply a more compact number format in these chart elements, you must assign the new truncated number format to the cells in the worksheet that contain the actually graphed numbers.

Figure 23-10 shows the final version of the embedded Clustered Column chart. Here, along with the major X-axis gridlines and the minor Y-axis gridlines, I added a data table and removed the chart's legend. Because the data table automatically includes the legend's color keys as part of its row headings, there is no longer any need to give up any precious chart real estate to the legend. The final version of this embedded chart maintains a balance between the graphic and textual elements while at the same time is easy to read and to interpret.

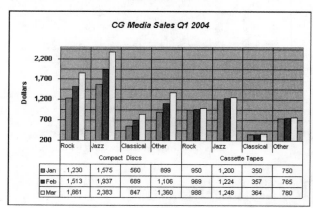

• **Figure 23-10:** Final Clustered Column chart after adding a data table and removing the legend.

Part IV

Worksheet Formula Timesavers

The 5th Wave   By Rich Tennant

"I always back up everything."

Technique 24

Efficient Formula Copying

Save Time By

- Reviewing Excel's different cell references for formulas
- Making efficient one-dimensional copies
- Making two-dimensional copies when possible

Copying formulas is undoubtedly one of the most basic and important functions that you perform when creating a new worksheet. Given that, knowing how to make efficient copies of the formulas you construct goes a long way towards making you an efficient spreadsheet designer.

Whether you use the AutoFill feature or the cut-and-paste method to copy your formulas, you don't save any time if your basic formula doesn't use the correct type of cell references for the kind of copy you're making. Therefore, before revealing some tricks of the trade in making efficient copies of your formulas, I think a quick review of the basic functions of the types of cell references and when they're used may be in order.

Going from Relative to Absolute

One reason why electronic spreadsheet programs such as Excel are so popular is that they're able to handle the cell references in formulas when you make copies. The ability to populate the cells of your worksheet with the appropriate calculations based on a single model formula copied in a few seconds time is a tremendous boon to businesspeople everywhere.

As I'm sure you're well aware, when you reference cells when building a formula, Excel automatically makes those cell references *relative,* meaning that both the row number and column letter of each cell address can be adjusted in formula copies. Although the relative cell reference is the program default, you can override this setting by making the cell reference *absolute* so that neither the row number nor the column letter is adjusted in formula copies. You can also convert to a mixed form of cell address where the row number can't be adjusted but the column letter can or one in which the row number can be adjusted but the column letter can't.

Excel indicates absolute elements in a cell reference by prefacing it with a dollar sign so that $C$79 designates absolute column and row, C$79 relative column and absolute row, and $C79 absolute column and relative row. Use F4 to cycle a cell reference from relative to absolute and through the two mixed modes.

The easiest way to understand what's going on when Excel adjusts a cell reference's row number or column letter is to switch the program out of its row number/column letter default style of cell referencing to the alternate (and much more logical) R1C1 style. With this style, both the rows and columns of the worksheet are numbered so that what you commonly call cell A1 becomes cell R1C1.

 To switch into R1C1 cell addressing, open the General tab of the Options dialog box and select the R1C1 Reference Style check box. To switch back into the normal row number/column letter style, clear this check box.

To see how viewing cell references in the R1C1 style can help you understand how Excel makes formula copies, consider the simple SUM formula shown in Figure 24-1. This formula in cell B8 (R8C2 in R1C1 notation) totals the January 2004 CD sales by summing the range of the four cells immediately above.

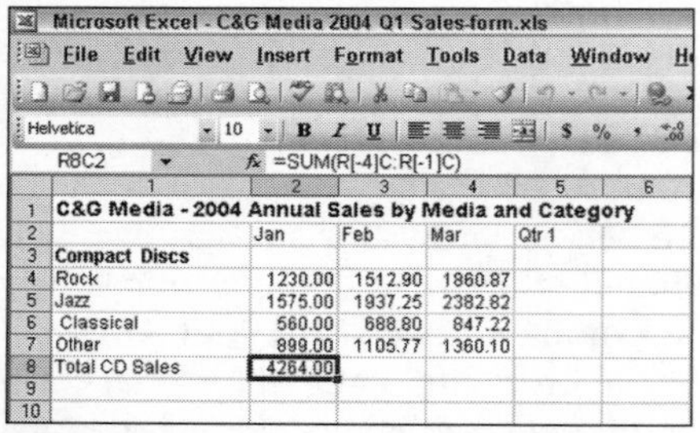

![Figure 24-1 screenshot]

• **Figure 24–1: Viewing a simple SUM formula in the R1C1 cell reference notation.**

In normal row number/column letter notation, this formula reads:

    =SUM(B4:B7)

When you switch into R1C1 notation, this same formula appears as:

    =SUM(R[-4]C:R[-1]C)

All this says in English is "sum the cell that's four rows up from the current row (-4) through and including the cell that is one row up (-1) in the

current column." When I copy the formula across row 8 to the February column (3) and March column (4), you see that in R1C1 notation Excel doesn't really adjust anything. The program simply copies the original R1C1 version of the formula to each cell in the columns on the right. There, the exact copy of the original formula performs the same function: summing the values in its column that are four rows up through and including one row up.

Figure 24-2 confirms this fact. After copying the original formula in cell R8C2 (B8) to the cells R8C3, R8C4, and R8C5 (C8, D8, and E8), I moved the cell pointer one column to the right. As you can verify by looking at the Formula bar in Figure 4-2, Excel really did make an exact copy of the original formula to this cell. When viewed in R1C1 notation, you can understand why the copy calculates the correct sum.

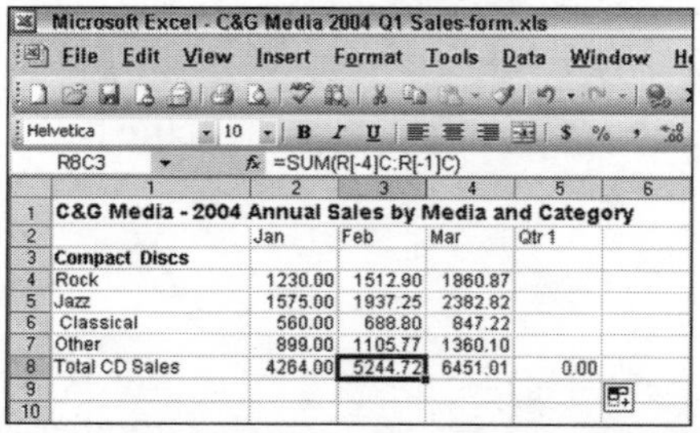

![Figure 24-2 screenshot]

• **Figure 24-2: Verifying that a copy of the SUM formula is exactly the same as the original in the R1C1 notation.**

Next, take a look at a formula that sums the values across different columns in the same R1C1 notation. In Figure 24-3, you see the original formula that sums the three-month CD sales in the Rock category for the first quarter. In R1C1 notation, this SUM formula reads:

    =SUM(RC[-3]:RC[-1])

In English, this formula says "sum from the cell that is three columns to the left (C[-3]) to and including the cell one column to the left (C[-1]) in this row." When I copy this formula down column 5 (E) to rows 5, 6, and 7, the exact copies of this formula sum the monthly sales for the Jazz, Classical, and Other categories, respectively.

Figure 24-3: *Microsoft Excel - C&G Media 2004 Q1 Sales-form.xls*

	1	2	3	4	5	6
1	C&G Media - 2004 Annual Sales by Media and Category					
2		Jan	Feb	Mar	Qtr 1	
3	Compact Discs					
4	Rock	1230.00	1512.90	1860.87	4603.77	
5	Jazz	1575.00	1937.25	2382.82		
6	Classical	560.00	688.80	847.22		
7	Other	899.00	1105.77	1360.10		
8	Total CD Sales	4264.00	5244.72	6451.01	4603.77	
9						
10						

R4C5 ▼ *fx* =SUM(RC[-3]:RC[-1])

• **Figure 24-3:** Copying a SUM formula in R1C1 notation that totals across the columns of a row.

You may be curious about how formulas that contain absolute references work in R1C1 notation. Figure 24-4 shows you the original formula that calculates what percentage of the entire quarter's sales each month's total sales represents. It does this by dividing the January monthly total in row 8 by the quarterly total in cell R8C5 (E8). Because each copy of this formula for the February and March percentages need to divide their specific monthly totals in row 8 by the same quarterly total in cell R8C5 (E8), the reference to this cell needs to be absolute.

R10C2 ▼ *fx* =R[-2]C/R8C5

	1	2	3	4	5	6
1	C&G Media - 2004 Annual Sales by Media and Category					
2		Jan	Feb	Mar	Qtr 1	
3	Compact Discs					
4	Rock	1230.00	1512.90	1860.87	4603.77	
5	Jazz	1575.00	1937.25	2382.82	5895.07	
6	Classical	560.00	688.80	847.22	2096.02	
7	Other	899.00	1105.77	1360.10	3364.87	
8	Total CD Sales	4264.00	5244.72	6451.01	15959.73	
9						
10	% of Total	27%	33%	40%		
11						
12						

• **Figure 24-4:** Copying a formula that uses an absolute cell reference in R1C1 notation.

In R1C1 notation, the original percentage formula with the absolute cell reference appears as:

```
=R[-2]C/R8C5
```

You can see that the first cell reference is relative (it says simply to take the value in the cell two rows above in the current column). You know that the second cell reference following the divisor is absolute because it simply contains the R1C1 cell reference itself. When I copy this formula to the February and March columns in row 10, these copies will perform the proper division, dividing the February monthly total in cell R8C3 (C8) by the quarterly total in R8C5 (E8) and the March monthly total in cell R8C4 (E8) by the quarterly total in R8C5 (E8) as well.

 Even if you don't want to work regularly with Excel in R1C1 notation, you can use this system when you want to verify that all your copies of a formula are correct. With R1C1 turned on, all the copies you make of a given formula should appear identical to the original on the Formula bar as you move the cell pointer through the range.

When It's Copy Time

When it comes to copying your spreadsheet formulas, you have a choice between using AutoFill or cut and paste. Which method I use depends entirely upon where the formula needs to be copied to.

If I'm copying a formula in *one dimension* — that is, down the rows of a single column or across the columns of a single row — I will use AutoFill if I just have to drag the Fill handle down a few blank rows or across a few blank columns. If I have to make a gazillion copies in one or the other dimension, I usually switch to cut and paste.

When copying a formula in *two dimensions* — that is, down the rows of the same column and then across the columns of the selected rows to fill out a schedule or table of data that uses the basic formula to compute all its values — I almost never use AutoFill because this requires two drag operations: the first to copy the formula down the rows and the second to copy it across the columns.

Instead, I cut corners: I copy the formula cell to the Clipboard, select the entire range of the table (including the current cell with formula), and press Enter to paste the formula into the entire range (this takes all of three seconds flat). And, of course, whenever copying a formula from one worksheet to another or one workbook to another, I always use cut and paste because this is the only way you can do it!

Making one-dimensional copies down or across

By far the most common formula copying that you do is one dimensional, either down a single column or across a single row. Formulas that subtotal the columns and rows of values in a simple rectangular table or schedule use this type of one-dimensional copying.

To copy in one dimension, position the cell pointer in the cell with the original formula and then do either of the following:

✔ Drag the Fill handle down the column or across the row.

✔ Copy the formula to the Clipboard and then select the range of blank cells into which you want to paste it. (The pasting itself is the easy part; simply press the Enter key, and your pasting is complete.)

When copying a formula down lots and lots of rows or across bunches and bunches of columns, I want to share a trick with you that can make this entire procedure a whole lot easier. In order for this little trick to work, however, you need to use cut and paste (AutoFill is out), and the row immediately above the one with the formula or the column to the immediate left must be full of data entries all the way down the rows or across the columns into which the copies must be made.

Figure 24-5 illustrates this situation. Here, I want to copy the SUM formula in cell E4 down to the bottom of the sales table to range E5:E8. In order to do so, I use the occupied column to the immediate left (D in this example) to quickly extend the range into which the formula is then pasted.

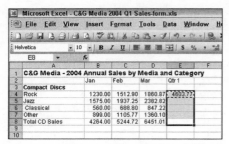

• **Figure 24-5:** Copying a SUM formula down a blank column by using the occupied column to the left.

To see how this works, follow along with my steps:

1. **Position the cell pointer in the cell that contains the original formula to be copied (E4) and then copy it to the Windows Clipboard (Ctrl+C).**

2. **Press the ← key to move the cell pointer one column to the left (D4) and then press Ctrl+↓.**

Excel moves the cell pointer to the last occupied cell in this column (D8 in this example).

3. **Press the → key to move the cell pointer one column to the right to the last cell where the formula is to be copied (E8).**

4. **Hold down the Shift key and press Ctrl+↑ to extend the range up to the cell with the original formula and then press the Enter key.**

When you press Enter, Excel copies the formula to all the cells that you selected with this little sleight of hand. To apply this technique to copying a formula across the columns of a single row, copy the formula to the Clipboard and then press ↑ and Ctrl+→ to reach the end of the occupied row. Then press ↓ and Shift+← to extend the range back to the original formula cell whereupon you press Enter.

 This trick may not seem like much in this example, but when you have to copy a formula down 400 rows instead of 4, it really pays off. And besides, with a little practice, you can make hundreds of copies in seconds. Just remember that you shouldn't press Shift until you're ready to extend the range in the blank column or row back to the cell with the original formula.

Making two-dimensional copies both down and across

Two-dimensional formula copies that go down rows and then across columns (or vice versa) are not nearly as common as one-dimensional copies down the rows of a single column or the columns of a single row. However, when the chance to make a two-dimensional copy comes along, it's the best because you virtually create an entire table of data in a single operation (and you can't beat that for efficiency).

Figure 24-6 shows you a situation that calls for copying a formula in two dimensions: down rows 7 through 16 in column B and across columns C, D, E, F, and G in all these rows. Cell B7 contains the master formula that needs to be copied throughout this range. This formula uses Excel's PMT function to determine a monthly loan payment based on a group of principal amounts in the cell range A7:A16 and annual interest rates in the cell range B6:G6.

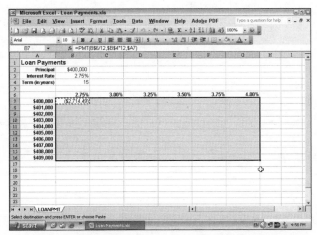

• **Figure 24-6:** Getting ready to copy the formula with the PMT function to the entire data table.

To populate this formula throughout the table, I follow these four simple steps:

1. **Position the cell pointer in the cell containing the formula to be copied (B7).**

2. **Copy the formula to the Clipboard (Ctrl+C).**

3. **Select the cell range into which to paste the copied formula (B7:G16).**

4. **Press the Enter key.**

That's all there is to it. Figure 24-7 shows the same table after pressing the Enter key. Excel copies the master formula in one operation, filling the table with the monthly mortgage payments based on varying principal amounts and annual interest rates.

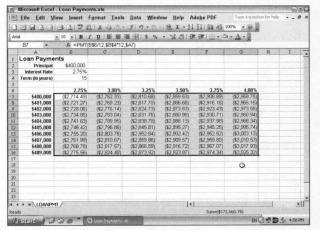

• **Figure 24-7:** Mortgage table after copying the master formula with the PMT function throughout.

Please note that the key to the successful copying of the master formula throughout this table lies in the proper blend of absolute and mixed cell references in it. The PMT function requires three arguments: rate (interest rate per annum), nper (number of periods), and pv (present value, also known as the principal). For the master formula, cell B6 contains the rate argument, B4 the nper argument, and A7 the pv argument. For purposes of copying the formula down the rows and across the columns of the table, the following combination of absolute and mixed cell references has to be used:

```
=PMT(B$6/12,$B$4*12,$A7)
```

The rate argument cell uses a mixed cell reference where the column is relative and the row is absolute so that Excel adjusts the rate as you copy the formula across columns B through G but does not adjust off row 6 when you copy down rows 7 through 16. Likewise, the pv argument cell (the last one in the PMT function) uses the opposite mixed cell reference wherein the column is absolute and the row relative. This allows Excel to adjust the principal when you copy the formula down rows 7 through 16 but not adjust off column A when you copy across columns B through G.

Finally, the nper argument cell (in the second argument in the PMT function) uses an absolute cell reference so that Excel uses the same loan term (in the input cell B4) in every copy of the master formula, regardless of whether this formula is copied down rows 7 through 16 or across columns B through G.

Just in case you're interested, this is how the master formula in cell B7 (er, R7C2) appears in R1C1 notation:

```
=PMT(R6C/12,R4C2*12,RC1)
```

If you were to switch to the R1C1 cell notation and then move the cell pointer through all the columns and rows of the table, you would see that every cell contains an exact copy of this master formula.

25 Technique

Speeding Up Table Creation with Array Formulas

In Technique 24, I make a big deal about making efficient copies of your spreadsheet formulas. In this technique, I make a big deal about using array formulas in tables of data so that you don't have to bother with making a single formula copy. Instead, you input all the formulas you need in a particular cell range in a single operation. Not only does this significantly reduce the amount of formula copying you have to do in a worksheet, but you also get the added benefit of saving computer memory — array formulas take less memory to store than copies of a single formula. (This savings can be significant when you're dealing with huge spreadsheets.)

The key to array formulas is the array, a concept that isn't quite as foreign as it may first sound. In Excel, with its row and column grid, you work with arrays all the time. In fact, you could even go as far as to say that the Excel worksheet itself is nothing more than a humongous 65536 (row) x 256 (column) array!

A Quick Look at Array Ranges

Array formulas that you build in a spreadsheet use one of two types of array ranges:

✔ One-dimensional array range that occupies a single row or column

✔ Two-dimensional array range that occupies more than one row and column

Figure 25-1 illustrates these two types of ranges with four sample array ranges. Each sample range contains a list of simple numerical values known as *array constants*.

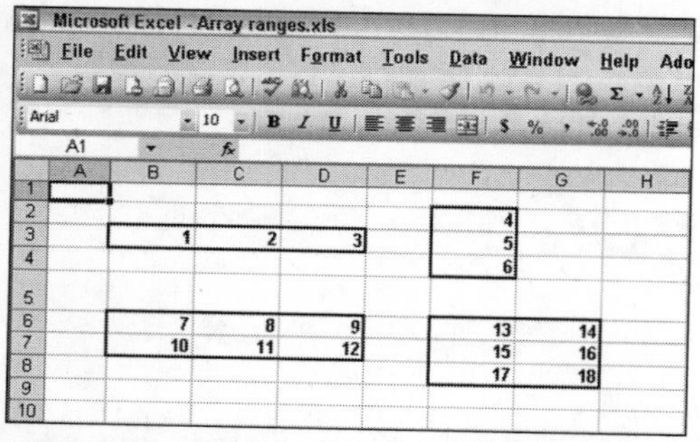

• **Figure 25-1: Sample one- and two-dimensional array ranges.**

The first one-dimensional array in this figure is located in the cell range B3:D3. This array range is a 1 x 3 range (one row across three columns) with three array constants. In an array formula, these constants would appear as:

    {1,2,3}

The second one-dimensional array is in the cell range F2:F4. This array range is a 3 x 1 range (three rows in one column) with three array constants. In an array formula, these constants would appear as:

    {4;5;6}

The first two-dimensional array in Figure 25-1 is in the cell range B6:D7. This array range is a 2 x 3 range (two rows in three columns) with six array constants. In an array formula, these constants would appear as:

    {7,8,9;10,11,12}

The second two-dimensional array is in the cell range F6:G8. This array range is a 3 x 2 range (three rows in two columns) with six array constants. In an array formula, these constants would appear as:

    {13,14;15,16;17,18}

When listing the contents of an array range, the entries are listed across columns and then by rows. Commas are used to separate the columns of a row, and semicolons separate the rows. The entire contents list is enclosed in a closed pair of curly braces.

Hurray for Array Formulas!

Array formulas are easy to build. Just keep in mind that you're creating computations that use complete ranges of cells rather than just individual cells. Because you want to insert the array formula into an entire range of cells rather than just the current one, you can't complete the formula entry either by clicking the Enter button on the Formula bar or by pressing the Enter key. Instead, you must complete the entry by pressing Ctrl+Shift+Enter. This is the only, I repeat, only way to enter the array formula in all the cells of the array range.

Figure 25-2 illustrates a situation where you can use array formulas to good advantage. This figure contains a table that tracks wages for a group of employees in the month of February. These wages are calculated for two periods — the 1st to the 15th and the 16th to the 28th — and then summed to produce monthly totals. To compute the wages for each period, you need to multiply the hours worked by the employee in that period by his or her hourly wage. (Note that, in this figure, columns C through Q and columns S through AH — the columns that record the daily hours worked by each employee within each pay period — are hidden for the purpose of creating the array formulas that calculate their totals.)

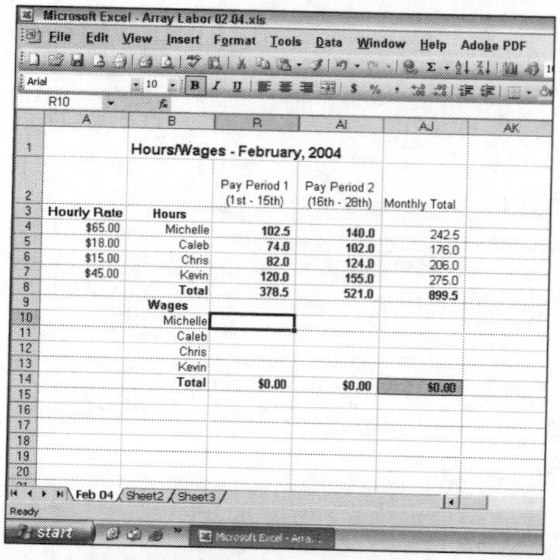

• **Figure 25-2: A worksheet for computing wages that can benefit from array formulas.**

If you were to perform this computation with regular formulas, you would create the following master formula in cell R10:

```
=R4*A4
```

You would then copy this formula down to the range R11:R13. Next, you would perform a similar procedure, creating this type of formula in cell AI10 and then copying it down to the range AI11:AI13. Finally, you would create a master formula in cell AJ10 that summed cells R10 and AI10 and then copy this formula down to the cell range AJ11:AJ13.

Instead, you can accomplish the same thing with three array formulas. In the cell range R10:R13, you create the following array formula that calculates the first-period wages for all the employees:

```
{=R4:R7*A4:A7}
```

Next, in the cell range AI10:AI13, you create this array formula to compute the second-period wages for everyone:

```
{=AI14:AI17*A4:A7}
```

Finally, in the cell range AJ10:AJ13, you create this array formula to compute the monthly wages for all the employees:

```
{=AJ4:AJ7*A4:A7}
```

To see how quick and easy it is to build these array formulas, follow along with these steps:

1. **Select range R10:R13.**

Instead of selecting a single cell, you select the entire range into which the array formula will be entered.

2. **Type = (equal sign) and then select the cell range R4:R7.**

The equal sign followed by the address of the cell range R4:R7 appears in the first cell of the range you selected in step 1.

3. **Type * (asterisk), select the cell range A4:A7, and then press F4 to make the range absolute ($A$4:$A$7).**

When specifying the operations to be performed between array ranges, you use the normal operator (+, -, *, /, ^). You make the second array range absolute so that when you copy the array formula from range R10:R13 to AI10:AI13, Excel does not adjust this range and continues to use the hourly rates established in this range.

4. **Press Ctrl+Shift+Enter.**

To complete the entering of the array formula in the entire selected range (rather than in just the current cell), you must press Ctrl+Shift+Enter. Excel then inserts the array formula enclosed in braces in every cell in the selected range. (See Figure 25-3.)

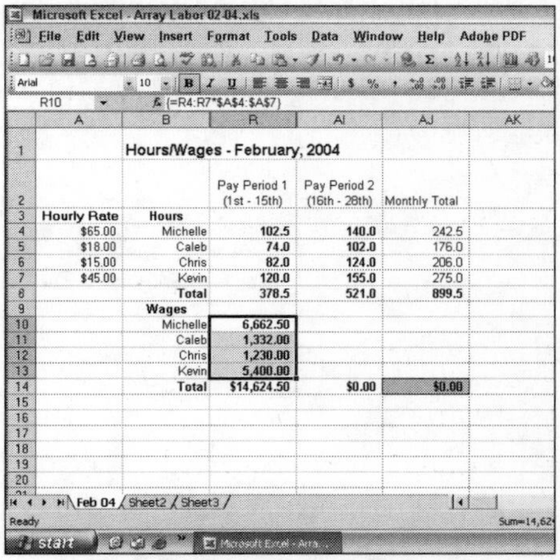

• **Figure 25-3: Worksheet after entering the first array formula in the cell range R10:R13.**

5. **Press Ctrl+C, select cell AI10, and press Enter.**

Excel copies the array formula into the range AI10:AI13, adjusting the first range from R4:R7 to AI4:AI7, without affecting the hourly wage range, $A$4:$A$7 (see Figure 25-4).

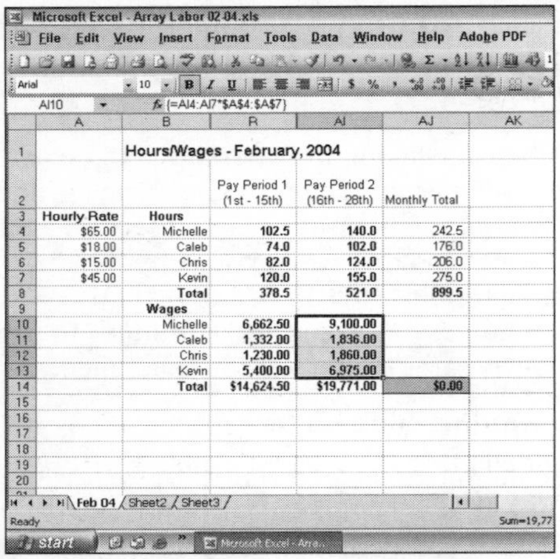

• **Figure 25-4:** Worksheet after copying the first array formula to the cell range AI10:AI13.

6. Press Ctrl+C, select cell AJ10, and press Enter.

Excel copies the array formula in the range AI10:AI13 to the array range AJ10:AJ13 (see Figure 25-5).

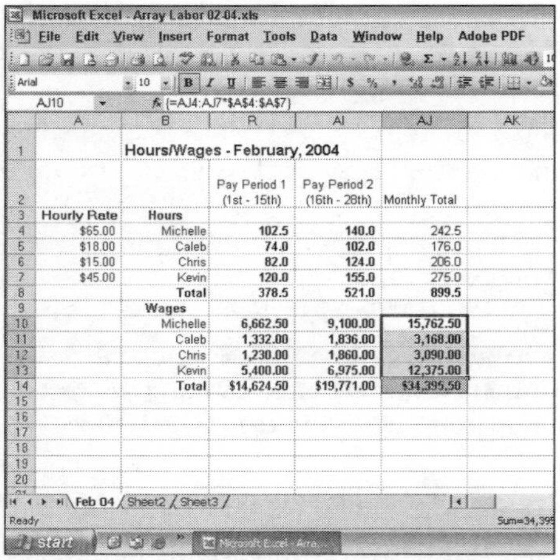

• **Figure 25-5:** Worksheet after creating the array formula that computes the total monthly wages.

Array formulas are great: They save time and computer memory. The only downside is they're not easy to edit (see the following section). Therefore, don't use array formulas in tables that are subject to frequent additions and deletions. Reserve them for tables whose structures are fixed.

Editing Array Formulas

When it comes to editing array formulas, you need to think of the Three Musketeers' motto of "all for one, and one for all." Because the formula was entered as a unit, Excel does not allow you to edit any individual cell in that range. If you try to move, delete, insert, or clear individual cells in a range containing an array formula, Excel displays an alert dialog box that says `You cannot change part of an array.`

If you need to make these kinds of editing changes to an array range, you first need to select all its cells (that is, all the cells containing the array formula). Only then can you complete your editing operation.

> To edit the contents of an array formula, you don't have to select the entire range that contains it. Just double-click one of its cells, or select a cell and press F2. However, in order for you to complete the change you make to the array formula, you must still press Ctrl+Shift+Enter.

If you want to be able to manipulate the cells individually, you need to convert the array formula in the cells to their individual calculated values. To do this, follow these steps:

1. Select the array range and copy the cells into the Clipboard (Edit⇨Copy or Ctrl+C).

2. Open the Paste Special dialog box (Edit⇨Paste Special), click the Values option button, and click OK.

Excel not only replaces the array formula with the calculated values (constants) but also no longer treats the cell range as an array, enabling you to edit its individual cells.

26 Technique

Using Range Names

Save Time By

- Naming ranges that you routinely use
- Naming constants for formulas
- Using range names in your formulas

When working with spreadsheets, naming cell ranges you need to find quickly or print routinely is a really important way to save time. So too, naming cells that are referenced in your master formulas is a really efficient way to document their functioning. Finally, assigning range names to constants that you refer to in formulas (such as a fixed discount rate or rate of growth) is a really resourceful way to have access to a stable value without having to stick it in some cell in the worksheet.

In this technique, you find out how to use all three of these procedures to save time in a worksheet that you access and edit on a somewhat regular basis. As part of this timesaver, I also review the different ways you can name cell ranges and hints on when to use one method over another.

Name That Range!

At the most basic level, naming a range in Excel is no harder than selecting the range of cells (this can be a single cell, cell range, or nonadjacent cell selection), clicking the Name Box (on the same row as the Formula bar that contains the current cell address), typing a unique descriptive name for the range, and then pressing Enter.

 Remember these range name conventions: All range names must begin with a letter of the alphabet, contain no spaces (use underscores, please), and not duplicate any other name in the workbook (keep those names unique).

In fact, I always name single-cell ranges or nonadjacent ranges from the Name Box on the Formula bar. You never see me taking the time to open the Define Name dialog box (Insert⇨Name⇨Define) and enter the descriptive range name there.

To quickly select a cell range or nonadjacent selection after naming it, click the drop-down button on the Name Box and then select the selection's name in the drop-down list. To print the cell selection, choose File➪Print, click the Selection option button in the Print dialog box, and click OK.

Creating names from row and column headings

Instead of taking the time to use individual descriptive names to assign names to ranges in a standard data table, it's almost always more efficient to have Excel do all the naming for you by using a table's existing row and column headings.

To do this, select the table (including the cells with the row and column heading you want assigned) and then choose Insert➪Name➪Create to open the Create Names dialog box (shown in Figure 26-1).

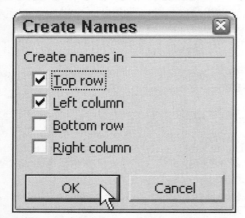

• **Figure 26-1: The Create Names dialog box enables you to assign names from column and row headings.**

When you first open the Create Names dialog box, Excel automatically selects both the Top Row and Left Column check boxes:

✔ When the Top Row check box is selected, Excel assigns the column headings in the first row of your cell selection to the columns of data in the table.

✔ When the Left Column check box is selected, the program assigns the row headings in the first column of the cell selection to the rows of the table. (It also assigns the row heading in the top row of the leftmost column to all the rows of data in the entire table.)

If the top row of your table doesn't contain column headings, clear the Top Row check box. Likewise, if its first column doesn't contain row headings, clear the Left Column check box. Also, if your table uses an unusual layout in which the bottom row contains the column headings, clear the Top Row check box and select the Bottom Row one instead. Finally, if the rightmost column of your table contains the row headings, clear the Left Column check box and select the Right Column one in its place.

The table shown in Figure 26-2 illustrates a situation where you can use the Create Names feature to good advantage. To assign range names to the table (which in turn I can use to assign names to the formulas in the Sales Price column [E]), I select the table including the row headings in column A and the column headings in row 2. Then I open the Create Names dialog box (Insert➪Name➪Create) and accept the default settings (Top Row and Left Column). Note that I don't bother to select the table's title in cell A1.

 The range names you assign with the Create Names feature refer only to cells that contain data of the table and do not include the row and column headings at the top and left or bottom and right of the cell selection.

Figure 26-3 shows a list of the range names (and the cell references to which they refer) created with the Create Names feature. I pasted this list into the cell range B10:C20 by selecting cell B10, choosing Insert➪Name➪Paste, and clicking the Paste List button.

 All the range names you assign with Create Names are added to the Name Box drop-down list (on the Formula bar), meaning that you can select their ranges in the worksheet simply by clicking their names on this drop-down list.

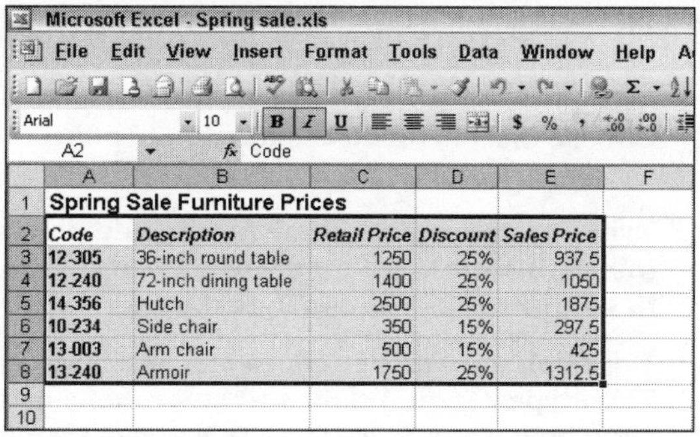

• **Figure 26-2:** Getting ready to create range names for a table by using its row and column headings.

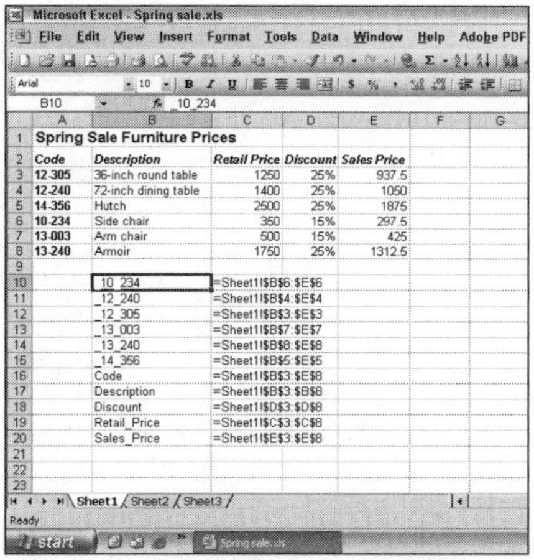

• **Figure 26-3:** Worksheet after pasting a list of the names created with the Create Names feature.

As you can see from the range name list shown in Figure 26-3, when Excel assigns a range name, not only does the program use absolute cell references to specify the cell range that the name references, but it also prefaces the cell range with the sheet name. So, for example, the Sales_Price range name (referring to the cell range E3:E8) is listed at the bottom of the range name table as

```
Sheet1!$E$3:$E$8
```

Note that the sheet name is always separated from the cell range by an exclamation point.

When assigning descriptive names to cell ranges in the Define Name dialog box, you never have to include the sheet name; just make sure that the descriptive names are unique. Likewise, when referring to range names in formulas, don't take time to add the sheet reference because Excel keeps track of this automatically.

Assigning range names that span different sheets

The only time that sheet names are really required as part of the range name is when the cell range it refers to spans different sheets of the workbook. In order to name these so-called *3-D references* (that is, the same cell range that spans multiple adjacent worksheets), you need to specify the different worksheets involved.

The easiest way to do this is by specifying the sheets in the Define Name dialog box as follows:

1. **Make the first worksheet included in the 3-D reference active.**

2. **Choose Insert⇨Name⇨Define to open the Define Name dialog box.**

3. **In the Names in Workbook text box, type the descriptive name for the range that spans more than one sheet.**

4. **Press the Tab key until the Refers To text box is selected and then type = (equal sign).**

5. **Select the tab of the active sheet and then hold down the Shift key as you select the tab of the last worksheet to be included.**

When you select the tab of the active sheet, Excel inserts its sheet reference in the Refers To text box. When you Shift+click the tab of the last sheet in the 3-D reference, Excel inserts its sheet reference after that of the active sheet — separated by a colon.

6. **Select the range of cells in the active sheet to be included in all the sheets in the 3-D reference.**

As you drag through the cells in the active work-sheet, Excel automatically collapses the Define Name dialog box so that you can see what you're doing. As you select the cell range, Excel inserts its range reference (using absolute cell references) after the sheet range, as shown in Figure 26-4.

7. Click OK to close the Define Name dialog box.

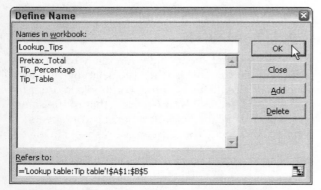

• **Figure 26-4:** Selecting the sheets to be included in the range name.

 After naming a 3-D reference, you can use its range name in formulas instead of having to go to the trouble of manually selecting the individual cell range in each sheet. This is a real timesaver when building formulas that accumulate values from different sheets.

Assigning Range Names to Constants

Not only are range names great for selecting and referring to cell ranges in the worksheet, but you can also use them to good advantage by naming constant values that you need to use in your formulas. For example, in the sample spring sale furniture table (refer to Figure 26-3) instead of listing the 15% and 25% discount rates in column D, you can create a range name that holds these constants and then refer to them in formulas that compute the dollar amount of the discount in the cell range D3:D8.

To assign a constant to a range name, follow these steps:

1. Choose Insert⇨Name⇨Define to open the Define Name dialog box.

2. Type the descriptive name for the new constant (observing the same range-naming conventions) in the Names in Workbook text box.

3. Press Tab until the Refers To text box is selected. Then type = (equal sign) and enter the constant value you want to assign to this name. (See Figure 26-5.)

4. Click OK to close the Define Name dialog box.

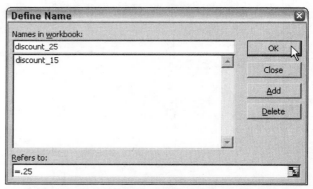

• **Figure 26-5:** Defining the 25% constant in a range name called discount_25.

 If you need to define several constants at once, click Add instead of OK in Step 4 to insert each name in the Names in Workbook list box. When you're finished defining the constants, click OK.

Using Your Range Names in Formulas

The great thing about using range names in your formulas is that they automatically document their function. This is especially helpful to coworkers who have to use your spreadsheets but who had no part in their design. When using names in your formulas, you can assign the names as you construct new formulas in the worksheet, or you can add them after the fact to existing formulas.

Using range names in new formulas

If you named a cell range or constant that you need to refer to in a new formula, you can use its name when building a formula. To enter the name, you can either type it (risky business if you have any trouble remembering the exact name), or you select its name from the Paste Name dialog box, as shown in Figure 26-6.

 Selecting the name from the Paste Name dialog box is much easier — especially when dealing with constants that don't show up anywhere on the worksheet — unless you've pasted a list of range names somewhere within it (Insert⇨Name⇨Paste, Paste List).

Figure 26-6 illustrates how you go about using a range name in a new formula. In this example, I want to multiply the retail price in cell C3 by the discount_25 constant to compute a 25% discount in cell D3. To do this, I follow these steps:

1. **Start the formula by typing = (equal sign), select cell C3, and then type * (asterisk) to indicate multiplication.**

2. **Open the Paste Name dialog box (Insert⇨ Name⇨Paste), select discount_25 in the Paste Name list, and click OK.**

Excel inserts discount_25 into the formula, and then I have to click the Enter button on the Formula bar to complete it.

Figure 26-7 shows the sales table after I finish adding the discount formulas in the cell range D3:D8 that compute the discount amount using either the discount_25 or the discount_15 constant. By adding the range name, I can tell in an instant which percentage I'm using for each item as I move the cell pointer through these cells.

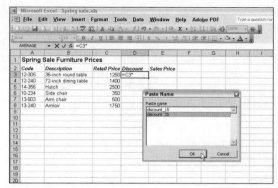

• **Figure 26-6: Inserting a range name into a new formula.**

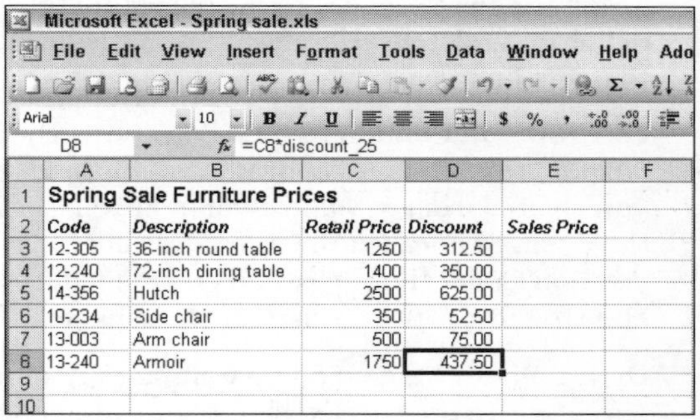

![Microsoft Excel - Spring sale.xls worksheet]

• **Figure 26-7: Worksheet table with formulas using constants saved as range names.**

Assigning range names to existing formulas

Excel doesn't automatically replace cell references with the range names that you assign to them. To replace cell references with their names, you need to use the Insert⇨Name⇨Apply command. Then in the Apply Names dialog box that appears, you select the range names that you want applied in your worksheet formulas by selecting them in the Apply Names list box.

When you first open the Apply Names dialog box, it contains just two check boxes: Ignore Relative/Absolute and Use Row and Column Names (both of which are checked). When you click the Options button, Excel expands the Apply Names dialog box to display additional options that you can use when applying your range names, as shown in Figure 26-8.

The complete Apply Names options include the following:

- ✔ **Ignore Relative/Absolute:** Select this check box to replace cell references with the names that you've selected in the Apply Names list box regardless of the type of reference used in their formulas. Clear this check box if you want to replace only those cell references that use the same type of references as your names (absolute for absolute, mixed for mixed, and relative for relative).

  Most often, you want to leave this check box selected because Excel automatically assigns absolute cell references to the names that you define and relative cell references in the formulas that you build.

- ✔ **Use Row and Column Names:** Select this check box to have the names appear in your formula that you created from row and column headings with the Create Names feature. Clear this check box if you don't want these row and column names to appear in the formulas in your worksheet.

- ✔ **Omit Column Name if Same Column:** Select this check box to prevent Excel from repeating the column name when the formula is in the same column. Clear this check box if you want the program to display the column name even in formulas in the same column as the heading used to create the column name.

- ✔ **Omit Row Name if Same Row:** Select this check box to prevent Excel from repeating the row name when the formula is in the same row. Clear this check box if you want the program to display the row name even in formulas in the same row as the heading used to create the row name.

- ✔ **Name Order:** You have two choices here:

  - ▶ **Row Column:** Click this option button (the default) to have the row name precede the column name when both names are displayed in the formulas.

  - ▶ **Column Row:** Click this option button to have the column name precede the row name.

Figure 26-9 illustrates how the Apply Names feature works. First, I created range names for the sales table by selecting the range A2:E8, opening the Create Name dialog box, and using the Top Row and Left Column defaults (see "Creating names from row and column headings" earlier in this technique). Next, I selected the cell range D3:E8, which contains all the cells with formulas in this table, and then opened the Apply Names dialog box (Insert➪Name➪Apply).

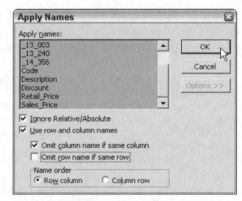

• **Figure 26-8:** Applying range names to the selected formulas in the table.

• **Figure 26-9:** Worksheet table after assigning range names to its formulas.

Because I wanted the row headings included in the formula's range, I clicked the Options button to expand the Apply Names dialog box and then cleared the Omit Row Name if Same Row check box and clicked OK. As a result, Excel inserted the code range name in the formulas. For example, the formula in cell D3 now contains

```
=_12_305 Retail_Price*discount_25
```

If I had left the Omit Row Name if Same Row check box selected in the Apply Names dialog box, the formula in D3 would instead read

```
=Retail_Price*discount_25
```

The problem with omitting the row heading from the formulas is that all the formulas in column D would then read the same as the one in D3. By adding the row heading, anyone using the spreadsheet can easily verify the precise function of each discount formula. For example, when the cell pointer is in cell D6 of the sales table shown in Figure 26-9, the formula on the Formula bar reads

```
=_10_234 Retail_Price*discount_15
```

The only problem with including the row or column headings is that, in formulas that refer to more than one cell in the same row or column, the repeating of these headings can make the formulas long and cumbersome to decipher (thus defeating the goal of using range names to document their function).

For example, the formula in cell E3 that computes the sales price for the 36-inch round table with the code 12-305 now reads

```
=_10_235 Retail_Price-_10_235 Discount
```

In such cases, you may be better off using the Apply Names default settings that omit all repeated headings to create a much cleaner, albeit generic form of the formula. In the case of E3, the sales price formula created by omitting the row heading would be much simpler:

```
=Retail_Price-Discount
```

Just keep in mind that this is how all the rest of the sales price formulas in cells D4, D5, D6, D7, and D8 appear.

27 Technique

Smarter Formula Construction

Save Time By

- ✔ Pointing to cell references when building formulas
- ✔ Using the Insert Function feature
- ✔ Using labels instead of cell references in formulas

Formulas are the lifeblood of spreadsheets. When building new formulas, accuracy always trumps speed because few things can be as time-consuming as trying to clean up a bunch of errors that you've spread everywhere when copying bad formulas. And by far the worst formulas are not those that result in outright error values (the origins of which can be tracked down and eliminated) but those that look fine even though they aren't accurate because they either refer to the wrong cells or are performing the wrong calculations.

To help you to avoid this kind of invisible but nevertheless detrimental error, this technique covers ways you can work smarter in building formulas. These tricks include the basic methods of pointing to formula cell references rather than typing their ranges, relying on the Insert Function feature to find and enter all but the most basic of Excel's built-in functions, and finally, using the row and column table headings in constructing master formulas to ensure that they perform the intended calculations.

Pointing Out Cell References in Formulas

Over my many years as a software trainer, I wish I had a nickel for every student I encountered who wanted to rush into completing a formula by typing in the addresses of the cells and cell ranges used in a new formula. (If I did, I probably would have retired long ago, and I wouldn't be writing this book.) I must say that I've had to work to convince some of the efficacy of always adding cell references to formulas by selecting their cells directly in the worksheet. These are usually those students who, because they're whiz-bang typists, don't want to take the time to point to the addresses that they can type into the formula so much quicker.

The problem with these folks typing in the cell addresses is that they can easily type in the wrong addresses, and if this doesn't result in an outrageous computation or an outright error value, they can speed on their way not realizing that their formula is referring to the wrong cells and that they're results are worthless or, worse, harmful. The chances of this kind of thing happening when you point out the cells or cell range by taking the time to select them is miniscule by comparison.

After nearly 20 years of using electronic spreadsheets, you never see me typing in cell references rather than pointing them out when creating a new formula. The only time I ever type them is on the rare occasion when I'm editing a formula and just need to change a row number or column letter in one of addresses.

Believe me when I say that you can save yourself a lot of heartache (and explaining to the boss) by always pointing out the cell references in the master formulas you build. And just in case your pointing technique has gotten a little rusty, check out Figures 27-1 through 27-4 for a quick refresher.

Figure 27-1 shows the lower part of a balance sheet where I need to enter a master formula that computes the ratio of the gross profit for the Northern region by subtracting the cost of goods sold from the gross sales (B4-B12) and then dividing that result by gross sales. To construct that formula by pointing to the cell references, I follow these steps:

1. **I begin by typing = (equal) followed by the open parenthesis.**

I need to enclose the subtraction in parentheses so that Excel computes this result before doing the division, an operation that has a higher precedence.

Excel evaluates all operations in a formula following a strict left-to-right order of precedence unless you interrupt that order with the use of parentheses. To refresh yourself on this order, press F1 and then search for "calculation operators" and follow the About Calculation Operators link.

2. **Now I'm ready to select the first cell reference. I scroll up and click cell B4 — the cell containing the Northern sales.**

After I click this cell, Excel encloses it in a marquee and enters its cell reference in the formula shown on the Formula bar.

3. **Then I type - (minus) to indicate a subtraction operation.**

Excel responds by removing the marquee from cell B4 (although it remains surrounded by a blue bounding box, indicating that this cell is the first variable in the formula).

	A	B	C	D
22	Central	27554	29482.78	31546.5746
23	Western	16130	17259.1	18467.237
24	International	32361	34626.27	37050.1089
25	Total Operating Expenses	113520	121466.4	129969.048
26				
27	Net Income			
28	Northern	-1534	-938.12	-228.1342
29	Southern	-1920	-1568.16	-1141.758
30	Central	38289	43601.85	49564.2071
31	Western	14376	16937.17	19845.9003
32	International	22064	25964.37	30387.8177
33	Total Net Income	71275	83997.11	98428.0329
34				
35				
36	Regional Ratio Analysis			
37		Jan	Feb	Mar
38	Gross Profit on Sales			
39	Northern	=(		

• **Figure 27-1: Starting the new formula that computes the ratio of gross profit on sales.**

4. **Next, I click cell B12, the cell containing the cost of goods sold for the Northern region.**

Excel encloses cell B12 in a marquee and adds this cell reference to the formula on the Formula bar. (See Figure 27-2.)

5. **Next, I type a closed parenthesis to close off the subtraction operation.**

When I do this, Excel removes the marquee from cell B12 (while at the same time encloses this cell in a green bounding box to indicate that this cell is the second variable in the formula).

6. **All that remains is to type / (slash) to indicate a division operation and click cell B4 again.**

Once again, the program encloses cell B4 in a marquee and adds its cell reference to the Formula bar. (See Figure 27-3.)

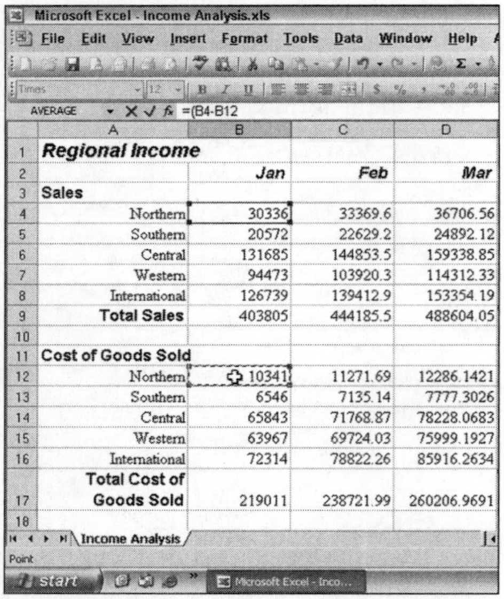

• **Figure 27-2:** Selecting the cells for the subtraction calculation.

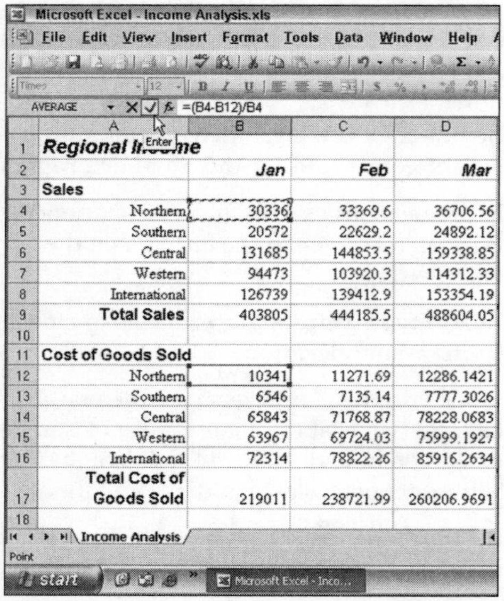

• **Figure 27-3:** Selecting the cell for the division calculation.

7. After checking the final formula on the Formula bar, I'm ready to enter the formula in cell B39.

To do this, I click the Enter button on the Formula bar.

I don't press Enter because I don't want to keep the cell pointer on this cell for copying purposes.

Figure 27-4 shows the computed ratio in cell B39, ready to be formatted with the Percent Style button and then copied across row 39.

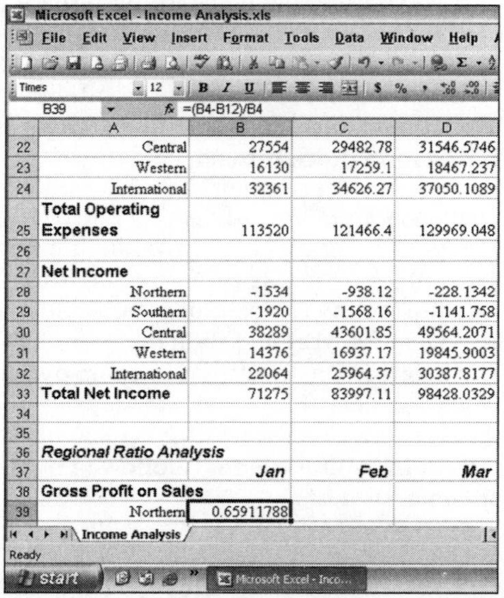

• **Figure 27-4:** Worksheet after completing the formula in cell B39.

Putting the Insert Function Feature at Your Service

As you're undoubtedly aware, Excel offers hundreds of built-in functions that perform all sorts of specialized calculations that you can incorporate into your spreadsheet formulas. To help you with all but the simplest functions (that is, SUM, AVERAGE, COUNT, MAX, and MIN, all of which are available from the AutoSum button on the Standard toolbar), Excel offers the Insert Function button — the one marked *fx* at the beginning of the Formula bar.

When you click this button, Excel opens the Insert Function dialog box, similar to the one shown in Figure 27-5. When the Insert Function dialog box first opens, it displays a list of the functions that you've used most recently (not that that's any indicator of the function you want to use in the present). You can then

- ✔ **Select one of the listed functions.** If you know the function you want to use, enter its name in the Search for a Function text box and then click the Go button to have Excel list this function at the top of the Select a Function list box and select it for use.

- ✔ **Select a new function category.** To list all the functions, select All on the Or Select a Category drop-down list.

- ✔ **Search for a function that performs the type of calculation you need done.** If you don't know the name of the function and need to search for it, enter a brief description of the kind of computation you need to do and then click the Go button.

    For example, in Figure 27-6, I instigated a search for a function that calculates your mortgage payment. As you can see in this figure, Excel recommended a list of financial functions ranging from PV to FV in the Select a Function list box. As soon as I selected the PMT function in this Recommended list, the Insert Function dialog box showed the syntax of the PMT function with all its arguments and also described the purpose of the function below it.

After you select the function you want to insert in the formula you're building and click OK in the Insert Function dialog box, the program opens a Function Arguments dialog box. This dialog box shows all the arguments for the function you selected. (The mandatory arguments are shown in bold, and any optional arguments are shown in regular type.)

Each argument text box enables you to select the cell, cell range, or cell ranges for that argument directly in the worksheet. When you do, the program automatically collapses the Function Arguments dialog box down to the argument text box to make this process as easy as possible.

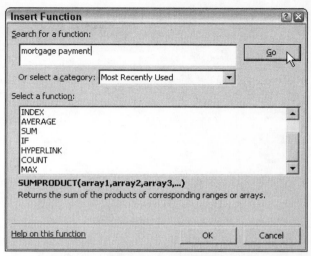

- **Figure 27-5:** Use the Insert Function dialog box to select the proper function and indicate its arguments.

- **Figure 27-6:** Searching for a function in the Insert Function dialog box.

Figure 27-7 shows the Function Arguments dialog box after I selected the three mandatory arguments for the PMT function. I was able to select all three cells — B6 for the rate, B4 for the nper, and A7 for the pv argument (see Technique 24 for information on the reason for the different mixed and absolute cell references) — by selecting these cells directly in the worksheet.

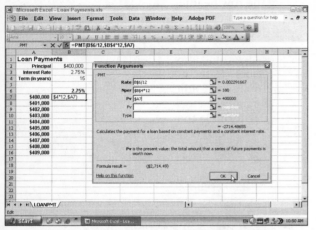

• **Figure 27-7:** Entering the arguments for the PMT function in the Function Arguments dialog box.

 If you've defined a range name (see Technique 26) that you want to insert into an argument of a function, select the appropriate argument text box in the Function Arguments dialog box and then select the range name to use in the Paste Name dialog box (Insert⇨Name⇨Paste).

Figure 27-8 shows the worksheet after entering the PMT master formula into the first cell of that Loan Payments table. Thanks to the Insert Function feature, I was able to quickly and easily locate this function and add the necessary arguments direct from the worksheet.

• **Figure 27-8:** Worksheet after entering the formula with the PMT function.

 When selecting a sizeable range of cells for a formula or the argument of a function, don't forget the tricks for quickly selecting larger cell ranges covered in Technique 10.

Using Labels Instead of Cell References in Formulas

This final method for building formulas with the correct cell references doesn't actually use any cell references at all. This method enables you to build formulas for a data table by using row and column headings that haven't been assigned as actual range names in the sheet (as described in Technique 26).

Before you can use this trick of referring to cells in formulas by their row and column labels, you have to change one of the calculation program options. Open the Calculation tab of the Options dialog box (Tools⇨Options) and then select the Accept Labels in Formulas check box.

If you don't activate the Accept Labels in Formulas check box before you create a formula that uses row and column labels to refer to cells, the formula will return the #NAME? error value as soon as you complete its entry.

Figure 27-9 illustrates how labels work in formulas after you activate the Accept Labels in Formula option. Here, you see the beginnings of a simple table that calculates the total wage due in column D by multiplying the hours worked in column B by the hourly rate in column C. To create the formula that computes Greg's wage in cell D3, I can now use the column headings Hours and Rate in place of B3 and C3, respectively.

In other words, instead of creating in cell D3 the nondescript formula

    =B3*C3

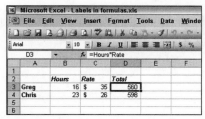

• **Figure 27-9: Using column labels to document a formula's calculation.**

I can create a formula that documents its function, as in

```
=Hours*Rate
```

In fact, I can go even further in documenting the function of the original master formula by using not only the column headings but the row heading as well. In this case, the master formula would read

```
=Greg Hours*Greg Rate
```

By adding the row label that identifies the employee, I can tell at a glance whose wage is being computed. Adding the row heading to each formula reference also enables me to ensure that Excel performs the right calculation.

Another nice thing about adding both the row and column labels to the master formula is that Excel then automatically adjusts the labels as needed when you copy the formula. For example, if I enter the master formula that includes the Greg row label down a row to cell D4 for Chris, the program automatically adjusts the row heading so that the copy reads

```
=Chris Hours*Chris Rate
```

This type of formula not only documents itself but also ensures the spreadsheet user of its accuracy. And the best part is that you can do it all on the fly: You don't have to take the time to first assign range names to the cells before you create these types of self-documenting and self-checking formulas.

Technique 28

Trapping Those Terrible Errors

Save Time By

- ✔ Trapping division by zero errors before they occur
- ✔ Trapping all types of error values

Most of the error values returned by the formulas you put in your worksheets represent bona-fide calculation errors that you need to take care of. (See Technique 29 for some ideas on how to trace and eliminate their source.) Other error values are unavoidable at different stages in spreadsheet development (most notably when you lack certain input values) or in the bare-bones template stage.

One of the most common of the latter type of error values is the #DIV/0! error value. This error crops up whenever you have a division formula that attempts to divide by a cell that either contains the value 0 or is still blank (the equivalent of 0 to Excel) because you haven't had time to input any value into the cell. Another is the #NA (not available) error value. If it gets entered into a cell with the NA function, it spreads to all the other formulas that refer to it either directly or indirectly, giving the faulty impression that not much of anything is currently available in the spreadsheet.

This technique covers ways you can construct formulas that stop these kinds of errors dead in their tracks, preventing them from spreading elsewhere in your worksheet. As part of this technique, I cover the use of the granddaddy of all logical functions: the IF function. If you're already familiar with the working of this function, feel free to skip the next section and dive right into the procedure for stopping those ugly division-by-zero error values.

If I Were a Logical Function

Excel includes a bunch of logical functions that you can use. The hallmark of a logical function is that it returns only one of two answers when calculated:

- ✔ Logical TRUE (also given the value 1)
- ✔ Logical FALSE (also given the value 0)

In other words, taking a page from Ebert and Roeper, with a logical function it's either thumbs up or thumbs down.

The most important logical function, especially in terms of trapping error values, is the basic IF function. The syntax of the IF function is as follows:

```
IF(logical_test,value_if_true,
    value_if_false)
```

The `logical_test` argument sets up some kind of equality (A=B), inequality (A<>B), or comparison (A>B, A<=B, and so on) that either is the case (true) or is not (false):

- ✔ The `value_if_true` argument tells Excel what to calculate or input when the logical test is found to be true.

- ✔ The `value_if_false` argument tells the program how to proceed or what to input when the logical test turns out to be false.

For example, you could use the IF function to create a formula that computes tax for a sale item only when a taxable cell contains the word *Yes:*

```
=IF(A79="Yes",C79+C79*7/5%,C79)
```

In English, this IF construction says if cell A79 (the Taxable? column) contains the word Yes, Excel multiplies the extended price in cell C79 by 7½% and then adds this tax amount to the extended price. Otherwise (that is, if cell A79 contains anything besides the label Yes), Excel just returns the original extended price in cell C79 without adding any tax to it.

Trapping Division by Zero Errors

The #DIV/0! error values are sometimes unavoidable at different stages in your spreadsheet and can benefit from being eliminated from the worksheet. Figure 28-1 shows you such a situation. Here is a blank template that contains a row of formulas (B9 through M9) that calculate what percentage each month's

production total is of the yearly total. And as long as any worksheet generated from this template lacks any kind of production input, all the formulas in the cell range B9:M9 will continue to display these lovely #DIV/0! error values.

• **Figure 28-1: Worksheet template riddled with #DIV/0! errors.**

You can easily eliminate these division-by-zero error values in row 9 with the help of the IF function. All you have to do is have the IF function's `logical_test` argument test the contents of the grand total cell N7:

- ✔ If this cell contains 0, the IF function's `value_if_true` argument inputs 0 (rather than #DIV/0!) in the cell containing the IF formula.

- ✔ If the cell contains anything besides 0, the IF function's `value_if_false` argument calculates the original percentage formula and returns this result to the cell.

This kind of IF formula, entered into cell B9 to calculate the January percent of total, will look like this:

```
=IF($N$7=0,0,=B9/$N$7)
```

Figure 28-2 shows you how the Production Schedule template looks after entering this IF formula into cell B9 and then copying it across row 9 to the cell range C9:M9. As you can see in this figure, the addition of this little IF function to the formulas in row 9 certainly did the trick. Because cell N7 currently contains 0, the `value_if_true` argument for all the IF functions is triggered, and therefore all the percent-of-total cells now contain 0 themselves.

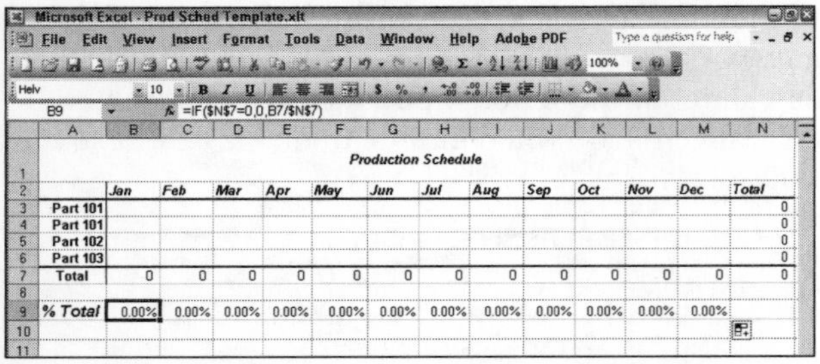

• **Figure 28-2: Worksheet template after eliminating the #DIV/0 errors with the IF formula.**

Trapping All Types of Error Values

The error-trapping formula created with the IF function in cell B9 (see the preceding section) works fine as long as you know that the grand total in cell N7 will contain either 0 or some other numerical value. It does not, however, trap any of the various error values, such as #REF! or #NAME?, or account for the special #NA (Not Available) value. If, for some reason, one of the formulas feeding into the SUM formula in N7 returns one of these beauties, they will suddenly cascade throughout all the cells with the percent-of-total formulas (cell range B9:M9).

Figure 28-3 illustrates this point. As a result of entering the NA function into cell B3, the #NA value has spread to grand-total cell N7 and, from there, to all the cells with the percent-of-total formulas in the cell range B9:M9. Although the original IF formula stops #DIV/0! error values dead in their tracks, it is powerless against any other error value.

To trap all other error values in the grand total cell N7 and prevent them from spreading to the percent-of-total formulas, you need to add the ISERROR function to the basic IF formula. The ISERROR function returns the logical value TRUE if the cell specified as

its argument contains any type of error value, including the special #N/A value. (Note that if you use ISERR instead of ISERROR, the program checks for all types of error values except for #N/A.)

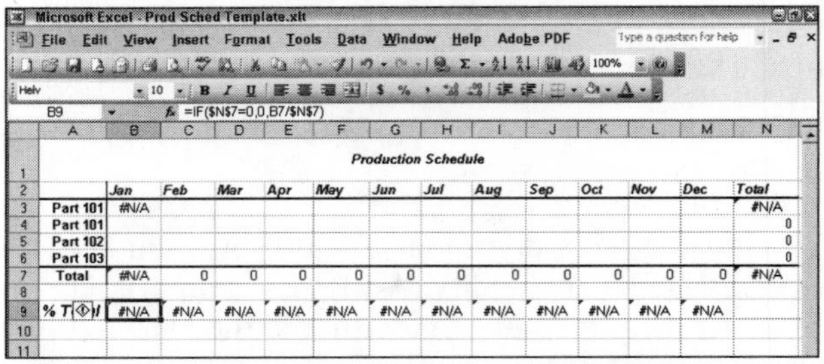

• **Figure 28-3: Worksheet template after #NA values have infected the percent-of-total formulas.**

To add the ISERROR function, you insert it into the IF function as the `logical_test` argument:

- ✔ If N7 contains an error value or the #N/A value at the time the IF function is evaluated, you specify 0 as the `value_if_true` argument so that Excel inputs 0 in cell B9 rather than error value or #N/A.

- ✔ For the `value_if_false` argument, you specify the original IF function that inputs 0 if the cell N7 contains 0; otherwise, it performs the division that computes what percentage the January production figure is of the total production.

This amended formula with the ISERROR as the `value_if_true` argument and with the original IF function nested inside it as the `value_if_false` argument in cell B9 looks like this:

```
=IF(ISERROR($N$7),0,IF($N$7=0,0,B7/$N$7))
```

As soon as you copy this modified version of the original formula into the cell range C9:M9, all the cells with percent-of-total formulas will be protected against those ugly error values, as shown in Figure 28-4.

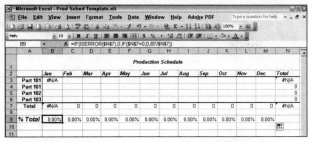

• **Figure 28-4:** Worksheet template after modifying the
original IF formula to trap all error values.

If you want to be alerted when a formula contains an error value even as you suppress its
display with an error-trapping formula, apply
some type of conditional formatting to its cell.
To do this in cell B9 of the example worksheet template, you would set up a Formula
Is ISERROR($N$7) Condition 1 and then
assign some sort of bold font and background
color formatting to signify when the condition
is TRUE. (See Technique 19.)

Technique 29

Eliminating Errors with Error Tracing

Despite your best efforts, it's almost impossible to prevent all formula errors from cropping up. Possibly the worst thing about this is that the errors often tend to spread far and wide, given the web of formula interdependencies in a spreadsheet. The biggest challenge in such situations is to track down the root of the problem — that is, the cell with the original formula error that causes the error values to sprout up all over the place like dandelions over a field after a spring rain.

Fortunately, Excel offers some effective tools for tracking down the cell that's causing your error woes by tracing the relationships among the formulas in the cells of your worksheet. By tracing the relationships, you can test formulas to see which cells, called *direct precedents* in spreadsheet jargon, directly feed the formulas and which cells, called *dependents* (nondeductible, of course), depend upon the formulas' results. Excel even offers a way to visually backtrack the potential sources of an error value in the formula of a particular cell.

Formula Auditing 101

The easiest method for tracing the relationship among cells is offered by the tools on the Formula Auditing toolbar, shown in Figure 29-1. To display the Formula Auditing toolbar, choose Tools⇨Formula Auditing⇨ Show Formula Auditing Toolbar or choose Formula Auditing on the shortcut menu of one of the displayed toolbars. When you first display the Formula Auditing toolbar, Excel automatically makes it a floating toolbar, which you can dock as you see fit.

This versatile toolbar contains the following tools (from left to right) that you can put to good use in your never-ending struggle for truth, justice, and perfection in your Excel workbooks:

- ✔ **Trace Precedents:** When you click this button, Excel draws arrows to the cells (the so-called *direct precedents*) that are referred to in the formula inside the selected cell. When you click this button again, Excel adds tracer arrows that show the cells (the so-called indirect precedents) that are referred to in the formulas in the direct precedents.

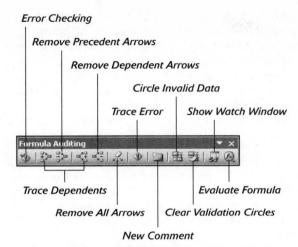

Error Checking

Remove Precedent Arrows

Remove Dependent Arrows

Circle Invalid Data

Trace Error   *Show Watch Window*

Trace Dependents   *Evaluate Formula*

Remove All Arrows   *Clear Validation Circles*

New Comment

• **Figure 29-1: The Formula Auditing toolbar gives you great tools for hunting down and eliminating errors.**

✔ **Remove Precedent Arrows:** Clicking this button gets rid of the arrows that were drawn when you clicked the Trace Precedents button.

✔ **Trace Dependents:** When you click this button, Excel draws arrows from the selected cell to the cells (the so-called *direct dependents*) that use, or depend on, the results of the formula in the selected cell. When you click this button again, Excel adds tracer arrows identifying the cells (the so-called *indirect dependents*) that refer to formulas found in the direct dependents.

✔ **Remove Dependent Arrows:** Clicking this button gets rid of the arrows that were drawn when you clicked the Trace Dependents button.

✔ **Remove All Arrows:** Click this button to remove all the arrows drawn, no matter what button or pull-down command you used to put them there.

✔ **Trace Error:** When you click this button, Excel attempts to locate the cell that contains the original formula that has an error. If Excel can find this cell, it selects it and then draws arrows to the cells feeding it (the direct precedents) and the cells infected with its error value (the direct dependents). Note that you can use this button only on a cell that contains an error value.

✔ **New Comment:** Clicking this button opens a comment box attached to the current cell where you can add a text note.

✔ **Circle Invalid Data:** Clicking this button draws red circles around all the data entries in the worksheet that don't currently contain valid data (as defined with the data validation feature — see Technique 14 for information on using data validation to restrict input in a cell).

✔ **Clear Validation Circles:** Clicking this button removes all circles drawn by clicking the Circle Invalid Data button. (To remove individual circles, select the cell and then enter the data that's required by the data validation assigned to the cell.)

✔ **Show Watch Window:** Clicking this button opens the Watch Window dialog box, which displays the workbook, sheet, cell location, range name, current value, and formula in any cells that you add to the watch list. To add a cell to the watch list, click the cell in the worksheet, click the Add Watch button in the Watch Window dialog box, and then click Add in the Add Watch dialog box that appears.

✔ **Evaluate Formula:** Clicking this button opens the Evaluate Formula dialog box, where you can have Excel evaluate each part of the formula in the current cell. This can be quite useful in formulas that nest many functions within them.

Clicking the Trace Precedents and the Trace Dependents buttons on the Formula Auditing toolbar (or choosing both Trace Precedents and Trace Dependents on the Tools⇨Formula Auditing cascading menus) lets you see the relationship between a formula and the cells that directly and indirectly feed it, as well as those cells that directly and indirectly depend upon its calculation. Excel establishes this relationship by drawing arrows from the precedent cells to the active cell and from the active cell to its dependent cells.

If these cells are on the same worksheet, Excel draws solid red or blue arrows (on a color monitor) extending from the precedent cells to the active cell and from the active cell to the dependent cells. If the cells are not located locally on the same worksheet (they may be on another sheet in the same workbook or even on a sheet in a different workbook), Excel draws a black dotted arrow. This arrow comes from or goes to an icon picturing a miniature worksheet that sits to one side, with the direction of the arrowheads indicating whether the cells on the other sheet feed the active formula or are fed by it.

Tracing Formula Precedents

You use the Trace Precedents button on the Formula Auditing toolbar to trace all the generations of cells that contribute to the formula in the selected cell (something like tracing all the ancestors in your family tree). Many times, finding the original source of the formula leads you right to the source of all the error values in your spreadsheet.

Figures 29-2 and 29-3 illustrate how you can use the Trace Precedents button to quickly locate the cells that contribute, directly and indirectly, to the simple addition formula in cell B9. Figure 29-2 shows the worksheet after I clicked the Trace Precedents button the first time. As you can see, Excel draws trace arrows from cells A5 and C5 to indicate that they are the direct precedents of the addition formula in cell B9.

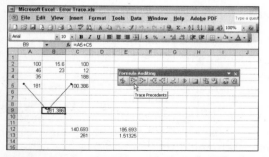

• **Figure 29-2:** Clicking the Trace Precedents button shows the direct precedents of the formula in the current cell.

Figure 29-3 shows you what happens when I click this button a second time to display the indirect precedents of this formula (think of them as being a generation earlier in the family tree). The new tracer arrows show that cells A2, A3, and A4 are the direct precedents of the formula in cell A5 — indicated by a border around the three cells. Remember that cell A5 is the first direct precedent of the formula in cell B9.

Likewise, cells B2, B3, and C4 are the direct precedents of the formula in cell C5. Cell C5 is the second direct precedent of the formula in cell B9. Each time you click the Trace Precedents button, Excel displays another (earlier) set of precedents (until no more generations exist).

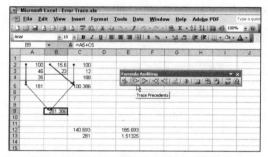

• **Figure 29-3:** Clicking the Trace Precedents button a second time shows the indirect precedents of the formula.

 To speed up the process and display both the direct and indirect precedents in one operation, double-click the Trace Precedents button.

Figure 29-4 shows what happens when I once again click the Trace Precedents button (after clicking it twice before, as shown in Figures 29-2 and 29-3). Clicking the button reveals the indirect precedents for cell C5. The formulas in cells C2 and C3 are the direct precedents of the formula in cell C5. The direct precedent of the formula in cell C2 (and, consequently, the indirect precedent of the one in cell C5) is not located on this worksheet. This fact is indicated by the dotted tracer arrow coming from that cute miniature worksheet icon sitting on top of cell A3.

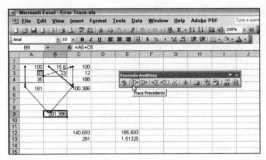

• **Figure 29-4: Clicking the Trace Precedents button a third time shows a precedent on another sheet.**

To find out exactly which workbook, worksheet, and cell(s) hold the direct precedents of cell C2, you double-click somewhere on the dotted arrow. (Clicking the icon with the worksheet miniature doesn't do a thing.). Double-clicking the dotted tracer arrow opens the Go To dialog box, which shows a list of all the precedents (including the workbook, worksheet, and cell references). To go to a precedent on another worksheet, double-click the reference in the Go To list box, or select it and click OK. (If the worksheet is in another workbook, this workbook file must already be open before you can go to it.)

Figure 29-5 shows the Go To dialog box that appears when I double-click the dotted tracer arrow. To jump to the location listed in the Go To list box (cell B4 of Sheet2 in this case), click its name and then click OK.

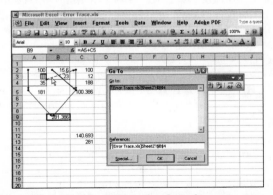

• **Figure 29-5: Double-clicking the dotted tracer arrow opens the Go To dialog box.**

 To display all the direct or indirect precedents or the direct or indirect dependents that are on the same sheet as the formula, click the Special button in the Go To dialog box. Then in the Go To Special dialog box that appears, select either the Precedents or Dependents option button and click either the Direct Only or All Levels option button.

 To clear the tracer arrows a generation at a time, click the Remove Precedent Arrows button on the Formula Auditing toolbar. To remove all tracer arrows at once, double-click this button.

Tracing Formula Dependents

Use the Trace Dependents button on the Formula Auditing toolbar to trace all the generations of cells that either directly or indirectly utilize the formula in the selected cell (kind of like tracing the genealogy of all your progeny). Tracing dependents with the Trace Dependents button is much like tracing precedents with the Trace Precedents button. Each time you click this button, Excel draws another set of arrows that shows a generation of dependents further removed.

 To display both the direct and indirect dependents on the same sheet as the formula, double-click the Trace Dependents button on the Formula Auditing toolbar. Likewise, to remove all the tracer arrows, double-click its Remove Dependent Arrows button.

Figure 29-6 shows what happened after I selected cell B9, double-clicked the Trace Dependents button to display both the direct and indirect dependents, and then clicked the button a third time to display the dependents on another worksheet.

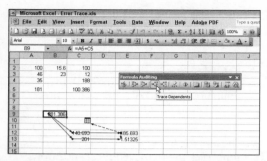

• **Figure 29-6:** Clicking the Trace Dependents button to display all the cells that use the formula's result.

As this figure shows, Excel first draws tracer arrows from cell B9 to cells C12 and C13, indicating that C12 and C13 are the direct dependents of cell B9. Then it draws tracer arrows from cells C12 and C13 to E12 and E13, respectively, the direct dependents of C12 and C13 and the indirect dependents of B9. Finally, it draws a tracer arrow from cell E12 to another sheet in the workbook (indicated by the dotted tracer arrow pointing to the worksheet icon).

Finding the Original Error and Fixing Its Formula

You use the Trace Error button on the Auditing Toolbar when you need to track the source of a formula error so that you can correct it. When you click this button when the cell pointer is in a cell that contains an error value, Excel attempts to track down the source by selecting the cell with the original offending formula and then drawing blue tracer arrows to its direct precedents and red tracer arrows to all its direct dependents.

Figure 29-7 shows the sample worksheet after I made a damaging modification that left three cells — C12, E12, and E13 — with #DIV/0! errors. To find the origin of these error values and identify its cause, I selected cell E13 and then clicked the Trace Error

button on the Formula Auditing toolbar to engage the use of Excel's faithful old Trace Error feature.

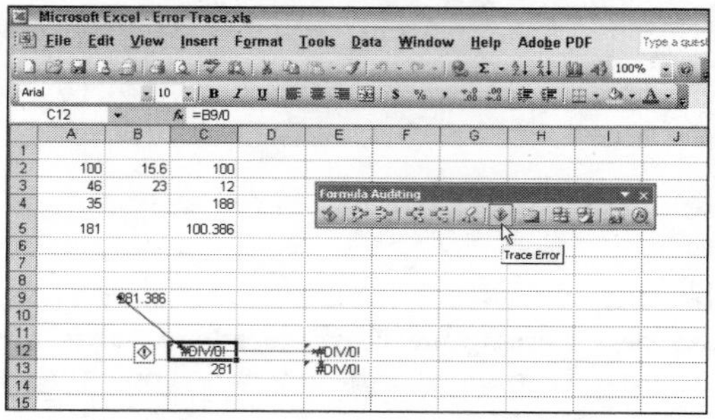

• **Figure 29-7:** Finding the source of a #DIV/0! error with the Trace Error button.

Figure 29-7 shows the result of clicking the Trace Error button (unfortunately without color, so you can't tell which trace arrows were drawn in blue or red). Note that Excel has selected cell C12, although cell E13 was the current one when I clicked the Trace Error button. To cell C12, Excel has drawn a blue tracer arrow (you'll have to take my word for it) that identify cell B9 as its direct precedent. From cell C12, the program has drawn a single red tracer arrow (again, you have to trust me on this) from cell C12 to cell E12 that identifies its direct dependent.

After the Error Trace feature has located the problem formula, you can click the Error Checking button on the Formula Auditing toolbar to fix it. When you click this button, an Error Checking dialog box similar to the one shown in Figure 29-8 appears. This dialog box not only diagnoses the source of the error value but also offers you several choices on how to proceed:

✔ **Help on This Error:** Click this button to display a Microsoft Excel Help window with information on the error.

✔ **Show Calculation Steps:** Click this button to open an Evaluate Formula dialog box that enables you to step through the formula to pinpoint exactly where the computation goes wrong.

✔ **Ignore Error:** Click this button to have the program disregard the error value and pass on to the next error value in the worksheet.

✔ **Edit in Formula Bar:** Click this button to activate the Formula bar so that you can edit the formula and fix the problem.

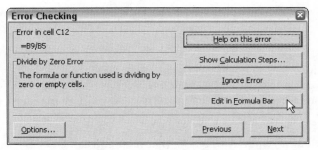

• **Figure 29-8: Correcting the formula error in the Error Checking dialog box.**

If you decide to use the Edit in Formula Bar button, make your changes to the formula on the Formula bar and then click the Enter box on the Formula bar to enter your fix into the cell. You can tell if you corrected the problem because the calculated result will replace the error value in the cell and Excel will remove all the error values in the other dependent cells. Also, the program converts all the red tracer arrows (showing the proliferation trail of the original error) to regular blue tracer arrows, indicating merely that these restored cells are dependents of the formula that once contained the original error.

You can then click the Resume button (which automatically replaces the Help on this Error button) in

the Error Checking dialog box. If the program then finds no other error values in the worksheet, an alert dialog box appears, indicating that the error check of the worksheet is complete. Click OK to close both this alert dialog box and the Error Checking dialog box simultaneously. Finally, you can remove all the tracer arrows from the sheet by clicking the Remove All Arrows button on the Formula Auditing toolbar and close the toolbar by clicking its Close button.

Unfortunately, the Error Trace feature is not infallible. Sometimes this feature can't find the source of a formula error the first time you use it. Trace Error will fail to locate the source of the error if the program encounters one of the following conditions in its search for the current cell's precedents and dependents:

✔ **A branch point with more than one error source:** In this case, Excel doesn't make a determination on its own as to which path to pursue; you have to inspect each path manually.

✔ **Preexisting tracer arrows:** Always click the Remove All Arrows button to remove all preexisting trace arrows before you click the Trace Error button.

✔ **A formula containing a circular reference:** You need to try to resolve the circular reference by recalculating the worksheet by selecting the Iteration check box on the Calculation tab of the Options dialog box and then increasing the number of iterations in the Maximum Iterations text box and perhaps decreasing the amount of change in the Maximum Change text box.

Technique 30

Creating Efficient Date and Time Formulas

Formulas that calculate elapsed times and dates are right up there after financial formulas in terms of spreadsheet popularity. However, unlike financial formulas, which rely on tried-and-true monetary calculations whose functioning is pretty clear to most business folks, the way electronic spreadsheet programs deal with dates and times, especially when used in arithmetic computations, is an almost complete mystery, right up there with where that matching sock disappears to in the wash.

This technique attempts to make clear how Excel sees dates and times so that you can efficiently create formulas that calculate elapsed dates and times. (Where the sock goes is anybody's guess?) Judging from the reader mail I get on dates and times in Excel from my other Excel books, most of you will be happy to just have this one mystery solved!

The Deal with Dates and Times

I must admit that dates and times in an Excel spreadsheet are particularly deceptive. This is because the program is so adept at interpreting almost any entry that even remotely resembles a date or time as a bona fide date and time value. As a result, you don't think twice about dates or times until you try to use them in simple subtraction formulas that compute how much time has elapsed between them. Then, all of a sudden, it seems as though Excel doesn't know jack about dates and times, when, in fact, it is you who lack the necessary understanding.

Figure 30-1 shows a list of date and time entries in column B and C of a sample worksheet. Column B shows you how Excel automatically formats and displays the dates and times that I entered in cells B2:B7. (The date and time in cell B2 is entered via the NOW function, and the rest were typed in more or less as they appear.) Column C shows you the actual values that Excel squirrels away when you make these kinds of date and time entries. (I revealed their true, arithmetical nature by applying the

General number format to exact duplicates copied to the cell range C2:C7.)

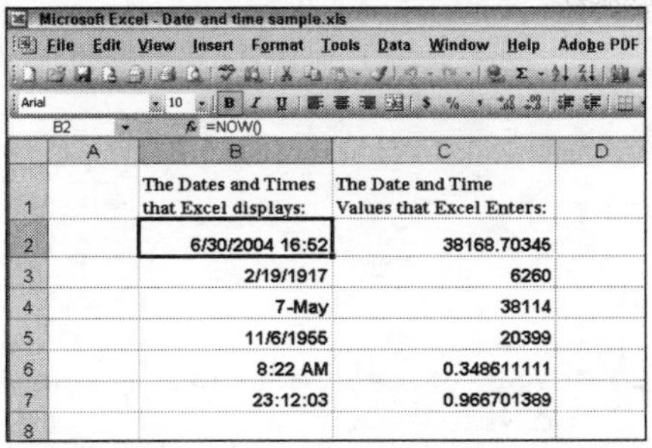

The Dates and Times that Excel displays:	The Date and Time Values that Excel Enters:
6/30/2004 16:52	38168.70346
2/19/1917	6260
7-May	38114
11/6/1955	20399
8:22 AM	0.348611111
23:12:03	0.966701389

• **Figure 30-1: What you see is not always what you get in terms of date and time entries.**

As column C of the sample worksheet shown in Figure 30-1 reveals, Excel doesn't treat the dates and times that you enter as simple text entries. Any entry with a format that resembles one of the date and time number formats utilized by Excel is automatically displayed in that date and time format. At the same time, the entry is converted, quietly behind the scenes, into a serial number.

In the case of dates, this serial number represents the number of days that have elapsed since the beginning of the 20th century so that January 1, 1900, is serial number 1; January 2, 1900, is serial number 2; and so forth. In the case of times, this serial number is a fraction that represents the number of hours, minutes, and seconds that have elapsed since midnight, which is serial number 0.00000000. For example, 12:00:00 p.m. (noon) is serial number 0.50000000; 11:00:00 p.m. is 0.95833333; and so forth.

As long as you make a date or time entry that conforms to a recognized date or time format, Excel enters it as one of these date or time serial numbers. The only time the program doesn't make this adjustment is when you enter a date or time in an unrecognized format or specifically enter or import the date or time as a text entry.

Keep in mind that Excel can still compute elapsed time between date and times entered as text. The program can even do calculations between one date or time entered as text and the other entered as an appropriate date or time value.

You Do the Date Math!

Most of the date formulas that you build are designed to calculate the number of days or years that have elapsed between two dates. To do this, you build a simple formula that subtracts the later date from the earlier date. The only problem is that the result you get from such date arithmetic usually doesn't look like the answer you want. This is because Excel gets on the old automatic-formatting bandwagon and assigns an inappropriate date format to the result that really is the number of elapsed days.

Figure 30-2 illustrates the typical situation. Here, you want to calculate the years of service for a group of employees by subtracting the date of their retirements from their start dates. On the surface, this seems simple enough: All you have to do is subtract the date value in column E from the date value in column F so that the first formula in cell G2 is

```
=E2-F2
```

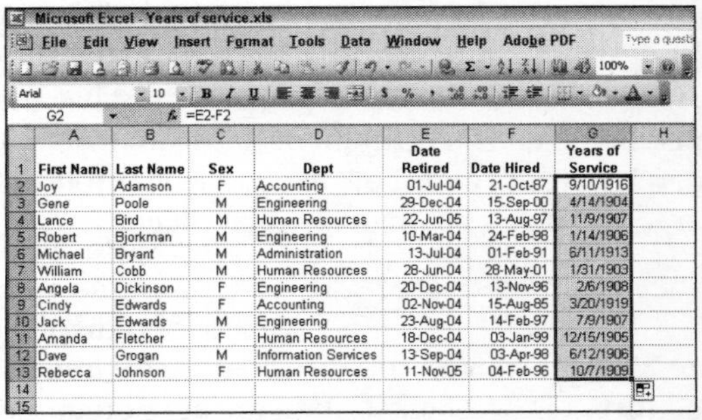

First Name	Last Name	Sex	Dept	Date Retired	Date Hired	Years of Service
Joy	Adamson	F	Accounting	01-Jul-04	21-Oct-87	9/10/1916
Gene	Poole	M	Engineering	29-Dec-04	15-Sep-00	4/14/1904
Lance	Bird	M	Human Resources	22-Jun-05	13-Aug-97	11/9/1907
Robert	Bjorkman	M	Engineering	10-Mar-04	24-Feb-98	1/14/1906
Michael	Bryant	M	Administration	13-Jul-04	01-Feb-91	6/11/1913
William	Cobb	M	Human Resources	28-Jun-04	28-May-01	1/31/1903
Angela	Dickinson	F	Engineering	20-Dec-04	13-Nov-96	2/6/1908
Cindy	Edwards	F	Accounting	02-Nov-04	15-Aug-85	3/20/1919
Jack	Edwards	M	Engineering	23-Aug-04	14-Feb-97	7/9/1907
Amanda	Fletcher	F	Human Resources	18-Dec-04	03-Jan-99	12/15/1905
Dave	Grogan	M	Information Services	13-Sep-04	03-Apr-98	6/12/1906
Rebecca	Johnson	F	Human Resources	11-Nov-05	04-Feb-96	10/7/1909

• **Figure 30-2: Calculating the difference between a stop and start date.**

The only problem, as you can see in Figure 30-2, is that the program applies the most common Date number format to the calculated results so that the difference in cell G2 appears as the date

```
9/10/1916
```

To display the results in column G as whole numbers, as you'd expect, you have to then format the calculated differences with another number format. Figure 30-3 shows the Years of Service column after formatting the range G2:G13 by applying the General number format to these differences. (You can do this quickly by pressing Ctrl+Shift+~.) As you can see, the calculated results in this cell range now appear as the much more sensible number of days.

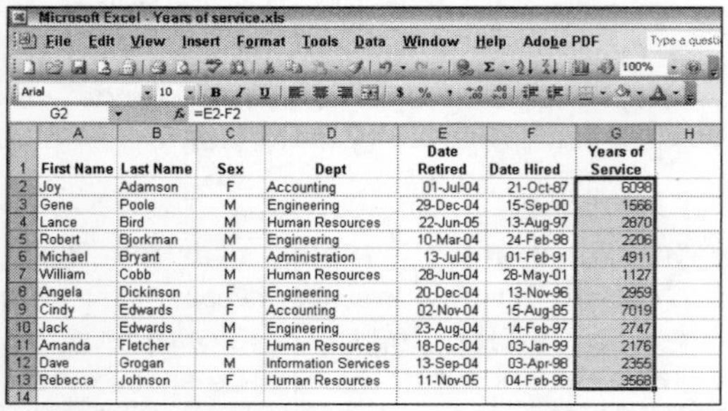

Microsoft Excel - Years of service.xls

G2 =E2-F2

	A	B	C	D	E	F	G	H
1	First Name	Last Name	Sex	Dept	Date Retired	Date Hired	Years of Service	
2	Joy	Adamson	F	Accounting	01-Jul-04	21-Oct-87	6098	
3	Gene	Poole	M	Engineering	29-Dec-04	15-Sep-00	1566	
4	Lance	Bird	M	Human Resources	22-Jun-05	13-Aug-97	2870	
5	Robert	Bjorkman	M	Engineering	10-Mar-04	24-Feb-98	2206	
6	Michael	Bryant	M	Administration	13-Jul-04	01-Feb-91	4911	
7	William	Cobb	M	Human Resources	28-Jun-04	28-May-01	1127	
8	Angela	Dickinson	F	Engineering	20-Dec-04	13-Nov-96	2959	
9	Cindy	Edwards	F	Accounting	02-Nov-04	15-Aug-85	7019	
10	Jack	Edwards	M	Engineering	23-Aug-04	14-Feb-97	2747	
11	Amanda	Fletcher	F	Human Resources	18-Dec-04	03-Jan-99	2176	
12	Dave	Grogan	M	Information Services	13-Sep-04	03-Apr-98	2355	
13	Rebecca	Johnson	F	Human Resources	11-Nov-05	04-Feb-96	3568	
14								

• **Figure 30-3: The differences between two dates after applying the General number format to them.**

However, because you want the results expressed as the number of years of service rather than days, you still have to convert the days to years. To do this, I edited the master formula in G2 so that the difference between the retirement date and hire date is divided by 365.25 and that result is then rounded up to a fraction using a single decimal place:

```
=ROUND((E2-F2)/365.25,1)
```

Figure 30-4 shows you the result after copying this edited form of the elapsed date formula down the column to the cell range G3:G13.

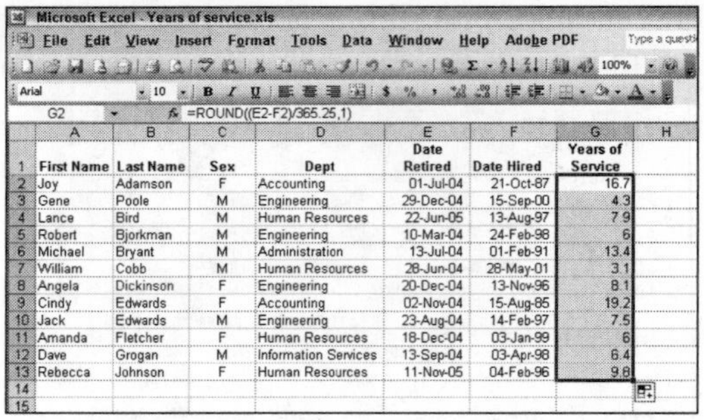

Microsoft Excel - Years of service.xls

G2 =ROUND((E2-F2)/365.25,1)

	A	B	C	D	E	F	G	H
1	First Name	Last Name	Sex	Dept	Date Retired	Date Hired	Years of Service	
2	Joy	Adamson	F	Accounting	01-Jul-04	21-Oct-87	16.7	
3	Gene	Poole	M	Engineering	29-Dec-04	15-Sep-00	4.3	
4	Lance	Bird	M	Human Resources	22-Jun-05	13-Aug-97	7.9	
5	Robert	Bjorkman	M	Engineering	10-Mar-04	24-Feb-98	6	
6	Michael	Bryant	M	Administration	13-Jul-04	01-Feb-91	13.4	
7	William	Cobb	M	Human Resources	28-Jun-04	28-May-01	3.1	
8	Angela	Dickinson	F	Engineering	20-Dec-04	13-Nov-96	8.1	
9	Cindy	Edwards	F	Accounting	02-Nov-04	15-Aug-85	19.2	
10	Jack	Edwards	M	Engineering	23-Aug-04	14-Feb-97	7.5	
11	Amanda	Fletcher	F	Human Resources	18-Dec-04	03-Jan-99	6	
12	Dave	Grogan	M	Information Services	13-Sep-04	03-Apr-98	6.4	
13	Rebecca	Johnson	F	Human Resources	11-Nov-05	04-Feb-96	9.8	
14								
15								

• **Figure 30-4: Years of service column after converting the days to years.**

When Your Time Is Up

Timecard-type spreadsheets routinely require formulas that calculate the amount of elapsed time between a starting and ending time. You might have, for example, a worksheet that records the starting and stopping times for your hourly employees and that also needs to calculate the number of hours and minutes that elapses between these two times to figure their daily and monthly wages.

To build a formula that calculates how much time has elapsed between two different times of the day, you simply subtract the ending time of day from the starting time of day. However, you run into the same problem with time arithmetic as you do with date arithmetic. Although the computation is quite straightforward, you still need to deal with unwanted Time number formatting and with an additional calculation that converts the decimal number result into a comprehensible hour, minute, and second format.

Figure 30-5 illustrates this situation. Here, I've set up a simple formula in cell F2 that calculates the elapsed time between a stop time in cell E2 and a start time in cell D2. I then copied the formula down the column to the cell range F3:F13. As you can see, Excel automatically applies a Time number format to the differences in column F, making them appear as times as well.

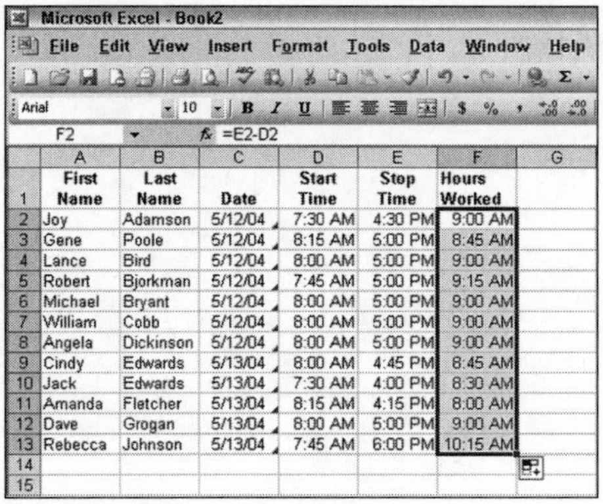

	A	B	C	D	E	F	G
1	First Name	Last Name	Date	Start Time	Stop Time	Hours Worked	
2	Joy	Adamson	5/12/04	7:30 AM	4:30 PM	9:00 AM	
3	Gene	Poole	5/12/04	8:15 AM	5:00 PM	8:45 AM	
4	Lance	Bird	5/12/04	8:00 AM	5:00 PM	9:00 AM	
5	Robert	Bjorkman	5/12/04	7:45 AM	5:00 PM	9:15 AM	
6	Michael	Bryant	5/12/04	8:00 AM	5:00 PM	9:00 AM	
7	William	Cobb	5/12/04	8:00 AM	5:00 PM	9:00 AM	
8	Angela	Dickinson	5/12/04	8:00 AM	5:00 PM	9:00 AM	
9	Cindy	Edwards	5/13/04	8:00 AM	4:45 PM	8:45 AM	
10	Jack	Edwards	5/13/04	7:30 AM	4:00 PM	8:30 AM	
11	Amanda	Fletcher	5/13/04	8:15 AM	4:15 PM	8:00 AM	
12	Dave	Grogan	5/13/04	8:00 AM	5:00 PM	9:00 AM	
13	Rebecca	Johnson	5/13/04	7:45 AM	6:00 PM	10:15 AM	
14							
15							

• Figure 30-5: Calculating the difference between a stop time and a start time.

The way to deal with this is simply to apply another, more appropriate number format to the results. However, if you apply the General format to the result of such time arithmetic, you find that Excel then displays the differences as decimal values representing what fraction of a day (that is, a 24-hour period) that difference represents. If, for example, you apply the General format to cell F2 containing 9:00 AM as the difference between the stop time of 4:30 PM in cell E2 and the start time of 7:30 AM in cell D2, you end up with this decimal number:

```
0.375
```

To convert decimal numbers like this that represent the fraction of an entire day into the number of hours that have elapsed, you simply multiply these results by 24. Figure 30-6 shows you the worksheet after editing the original formula in F2 to do just this:

```
=ROUND((E2-D2)*24,2)
```

Figure 30-6 shows the worksheet after copying this edited formula to the rest of the column in range F3:F13 and formatting all the results in the Hours Worked column with the Accounting number format with two decimal places.

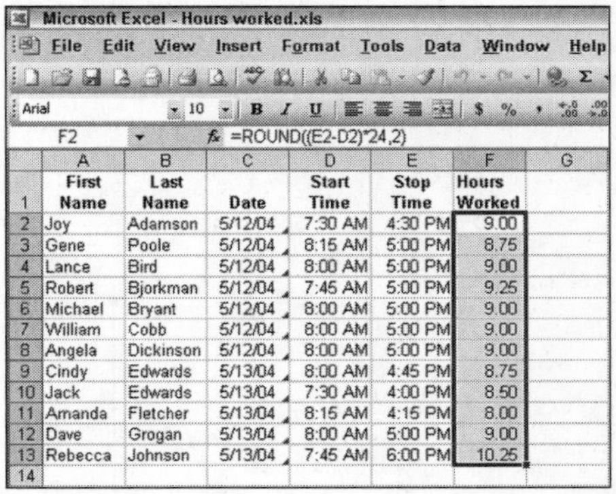

	A	B	C	D	E	F	G
1	First Name	Last Name	Date	Start Time	Stop Time	Hours Worked	
2	Joy	Adamson	5/12/04	7:30 AM	4:30 PM	9.00	
3	Gene	Poole	5/12/04	8:15 AM	5:00 PM	8.75	
4	Lance	Bird	5/12/04	8:00 AM	5:00 PM	9.00	
5	Robert	Bjorkman	5/12/04	7:45 AM	5:00 PM	9.25	
6	Michael	Bryant	5/12/04	8:00 AM	5:00 PM	9.00	
7	William	Cobb	5/12/04	8:00 AM	5:00 PM	9.00	
8	Angela	Dickinson	5/12/04	8:00 AM	5:00 PM	9.00	
9	Cindy	Edwards	5/13/04	8:00 AM	4:45 PM	8.75	
10	Jack	Edwards	5/13/04	7:30 AM	4:00 PM	8.50	
11	Amanda	Fletcher	5/13/04	8:15 AM	4:15 PM	8.00	
12	Dave	Grogan	5/13/04	8:00 AM	5:00 PM	9.00	
13	Rebecca	Johnson	5/13/04	7:45 AM	6:00 PM	10.25	
14							

• Figure 30-6: Hours Worked column after converting the calculated elapsed times to hours.

Part V

Worksheet Editing Timesavers

The 5th Wave — By Rich Tennant

"And tell David to come in out of the hall. I found a way to adjust our project budget estimate."

Technique 31

Quickly Finding the Workbook You Want to Edit

Save Time By

✔ Selecting a workbook from the Recently Used list

✔ Searching for a workbook from the File Search task pane

✔ Searching for a workbook from the Open dialog box

Nothing is quite as vexing as not being able to find the workbook file that you need to print or edit. Wasting time opening spreadsheet after spreadsheet in search of the file you need to work with is not only frustrating but also time-consuming.

This technique covers ways to quickly and easily find the workbook file you want. Heeding this advice is not only a great way to increase your spreadsheet efficiency but a good way to keep that blood pressure in check as well.

Opening Recently Used Files

The first place to look for the workbook you want to open is on the Recently Used file list. This is the list of the last four workbook files that you had open and edited. This list appears at the bottom of the Getting Started task pane (in the Open section), the task pane that opens automatically when you first launch Excel. (See Figure 31-1.) You also have access to this file list on the File menu at anytime when using the program.

If you see the name of the workbook you want to open on this list, just click its filename link to open the workbook in Excel (and automatically close the Getting Started task pane).

 If you routinely edit lots of workbooks in a day, you may want to increase the number of files that appear on the Recently Used list. Open the General tab of the Options dialog box (Tools➪Options) and then increase the value in the Entries text box — the box to the immediate right of the Recently Used File List check box.

Recently Used File List

• **Figure 31-1:** Check the Recently Used file list on the Getting Started task pane for the workbook you want to open.

Making the Most of the File Search Task Pane

If the workbook file you want to work with is not among the four files listed in the Recently Used file list, your next line of defense is the Search feature in the Open dialog box. You can access this feature right from the worksheet window. Just use the Basic File Search task pane (shown in Figure 31-2), which you can open by choosing File➪File Search.

Doing a basic file search

The Basic File Search task pane contains the following three boxes that you can use in conducting your file search:

• **Figure 31-2:** Searching for a workbook file from the Basic File Search task pane.

- ✔ **Search Text** is the text box where you enter one or more words contained in the file that you want to find. If you're unsure of how certain words are spelled, you can use the wildcard characters ? and * when entering the search text:

  - ▶ The ? wildcard stands for a single character so that entering t?m finds files that contain *Tim* and *Tom* but not *team* and *trim*.

  - ▶ The * wildcard character stands for any number of characters so that entering t*m finds files that contain all four words in the preceding example.

✔ **Search In** is the combo box where you can specify the place on your computer system to search. By default, Excel searches everywhere on your computer (including the desktop, My Documents folder, all local disk drives, and all shared document folders).

To restrict the search to just your local hard disk, click the Search In drop-down button, click the My Computer expand button (the one with the +), and then clear the check marks from all the elements except for Local Disk (C:).

To restrict the search on your hard disk to just certain folders, click the Local Disk (C:) Expand button and then clear the check boxes from all the folders that you *don't* want searched.

If you're part of a network and think that the workbook may be saved on a networked drive, select the My Network Places check box. (Note that some networks don't support searching, in which case you'll receive a message telling you that it is an unavailable location when you perform the search.)

✔ **Results Should Be** is the drop-down list box where you can specify what types of files to find. To restrict this list to Excel workbook and template files only, clear the Office Files check box and then select just the Excel Files check box.

When you do a basic search, Excel finds workbook files that contain any form of the words that you enter as the search text. For example, if you enter invest in the Search Text field, Excel finds files that contain *invest, investing, invested, investor,* and *investments*. The program also searches for an occurrence of the words in the cells in all the worksheets in the workbook and in the Keywords and other fields entered on the Summary tab of the file's Properties dialog box. (See Technique 4.)

Conducting the file search and using the results

After you finish specifying the search text, the location to search, and the results to return, you begin the search by clicking the Go button in the Basic File Search task pane. When you click this button, the Basic File Search task pane becomes a Search Results task pane, where Excel shows you all the files that contain your search text, as shown in Figure 31-3. If the workbook that you want to open appears in the Search Results task pane, you can click the Stop button to prevent Excel from doing any further searching.

To open a workbook file displayed in the Search Results task pane, click its file icon or position the mouse pointer on the icon and, when a pop-up button appears, click this button and then click the Edit with Microsoft Excel item on the pop-up menu.

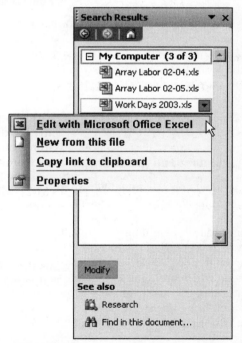

• **Figure 31-3:** Selecting a workbook file to open in the Search Results task pane.

If you're not sure from viewing the filenames alone which of the files displayed is the one that you want to open, position the mouse pointer on the file icon for a few seconds. A ToolTip showing the complete path to the file, along with the date that it was last modified, appears below the file icon. If this information alone isn't enough, click the file's pop-up button and then click Properties at the bottom of the pop-up menu. This action opens a Properties dialog box containing General, Custom, and Summary tabs that give you all sorts of information about the file. (Note that the Summary tab will be empty except for the Author if you didn't fill in this information prior to saving the workbook file.)

If your search returned more files than can be displayed together in the Search Results task pane, a Next *x* Results link (where *x* is the actual number of results) appears when you scroll down to the end of the list. Click this link to display the next group of ten results. If you find that you're not getting the results that you expected, click the Stop button at the bottom of the Search Results task pane and then click the Modify button (this button immediately replaces Stop when you click it) to return to the Basic File Search task pane. There, you can tweak your search criteria or even try narrowing the search by using the Advanced File Search feature.

Doing an advanced file search

Excel supports an Advanced File Search feature, which enables you to add more specific search criteria than just simple words (although it uses exactly the same Search In and Search Results Should Be options). To open the Advanced File Search task pane from the Basic File Search task pane, click the Advanced File Search link in the See Also section at the bottom of the task pane. Note that the Advanced File Search link disappears after you do a basic search. To bring it back, simply click the Modify button at the bottom of the Search Results task pane.

The Advanced File Search task pane (see Figure 31-4) contains a Search For section where you specify the conditions that must be met in order for a file to appear in the Search Results task pane. Here's what you find below this section:

- ✓ **Go button:** Begin the search.

- ✓ **Restore button:** Go back to the Basic File Search task pane.

- ✓ **Search In combo box:** Specify which drives and folders to search.

- ✓ **Results Should Be drop-down list box:** Specify which types of files to search for.

The last two boxes — Search In and Results Should Be — function exactly the same as their counterparts in the Basic File Search task pane.

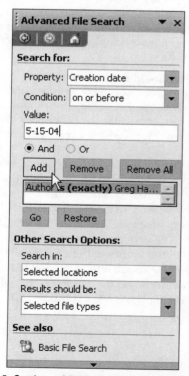

• **Figure 31-4:** Setting additional search criteria in the Advanced File Search task pane.

The Search For section contains the following items for specifying the condition or conditions to be applied in the search:

- **Property** is the combo box where you specify the property to search for. The pop-up menu attached to this box displays a complete list of things that you can specify including the author, keywords, date last saved or printed, file size, and total editing time, as well as the more mundane default of Text or Property.

- **Condition** is the drop-down list box where you select the type of limitation set on the property during the search. The conditions available vary according to the type of property that you select in the Property combo box:

  - For text properties, you can specify Is (Exactly) for exact matches or Includes for partial matches.

  - For date properties, you can specify On, On or After, On or Before, along with a variety of time-specific conditions.

  - For numeric properties, you can specify Equals, Not Equal To, More Than, Less Than, At Least, and At Most.

- **Value** is the text box where you enter the text or value that is used in judging whether the condition that you set up for the property you specified is TRUE or FALSE. You enter the label or number that you want used in the Value text box just as you would enter it in your spreadsheet.

After using these three boxes to specify your search criteria, click the Add button to add them to the list box that appears in the middle of the Advanced File Search task pane.

When specifying search criteria in this task pane, you can apply more than a single set of criteria. After specifying the second set of criteria in the Property, Condition, and Value boxes, choose between the And and the Or option button before you click the Add button:

- When you select And, a file matches only when all the criteria applied to it are TRUE.

- When you select Or, a file matches when any one of the criteria applied to it is TRUE.

After you finish adding criteria in the Search For section, the place to search in the Search In combo box, and the files to search for in the Results Should Be drop-down list box, you begin the advanced searching by clicking the Go button. As when doing a basic search, the Advanced File Search task pane becomes a Search Results task pane where the files that meet your criteria appear. You can then open the files for editing by clicking their file icons.

Searching for Files in the Open Dialog Box

The Basic File Search and Advanced File Search task panes aren't the only places from which you can do searches for the workbooks that you need to open. You can also perform a basic or advanced search from within the Open dialog box itself. To access the Search feature, click the Tools button on the Open dialog box's toolbar and then select the Search item, as shown in Figure 31-5.

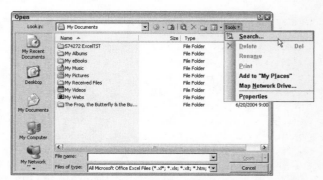

• **Figure 31-5: Doing a basic file search from the Open dialog box.**

Like the File Search task pane, the File Search dialog box enables you to choose between performing a basic or more detailed search with its Basic and Advanced tabs. Each tab contains the same search options as the Basic File Search and Advanced File Search task panes, so searching for files in the File Search dialog box is just like doing a search from those two task panes. (See "Doing a basic file search" and "Doing an advanced file search," earlier in this technique.)

Technique 32

Controlling the Worksheet Window Display

Save Time By

✔ Making effective use of the Zoom feature

✔ Freezing rows and columns of a worksheet on-screen

✔ Saving display settings as a view

The biggest problem with editing is finding and getting to the place in the worksheet that needs modification and then keeping your place in the worksheet as you make the changes. This problem is exacerbated by the fact that you probably often work with really large spreadsheets of which only a small portion can be displayed at any one time on your screen.

This technique looks at a number of features that can help you find your way and keep your place in a spreadsheet. Among these are the Zoom In feature, the Window feature, and the Freeze Panes feature:

✔ The Zoom In feature enables you to increase the magnification of the worksheet window, thus making it possible to switch to a really up-close view for editing.

✔ The Window feature enables you to display different parts of the same — or even a different — worksheet on-screen.

✔ The Freeze Panes feature enables you to keep pertinent information, such as column and row headings, on the worksheet window as you scroll other columns and rows of data into view.

Zooming In for the Edits

In Technique 9, I suggest using the Zoom Out feature to find the place that you need to edit. In this technique, I recommend that you use the Zoom In feature to increase the magnification to a level that makes cell range editing most comfortable. In case you're not that familiar with Excel's Zoom controls, you can access the Zoom feature in one of two ways: the Zoom combo box on the Standard toolbar or the Zoom dialog box, which you can open by choosing View➪Zoom.

When setting a new magnification using the Zoom combo box or the Zoom dialog box, you can select one of the preset magnification percentages — 200%, 100%, 75%, 50%, and 25%, with 100% being the default setting for all worksheets — from its drop-down list. (Of course, the size of the cells at the 100% setting can vary, depending on the current resolution and the overall size of your monitor's screen.)

You can also enter a custom percentage between a minimum of 10% and a maximum of 400%:

✔ To do this in the Zoom combo box, click the combo box, enter the new value, and then press the Enter key.

✔ To set a custom percentage in the Zoom dialog box, open the Zoom dialog box (View➪Zoom), click the Custom text box, type a new percentage, and click OK.

If you have a Microsoft IntelliMouse, you can set it up in Excel so that rolling the wheel back and forth zooms out and in on the current worksheet. On the General tab of the Options dialog box (Tools➪Options), select the Zoom on Roll with IntelliMouse check box. Afterwards, rolling the wheel backward increases the magnification by 15% until you reach the maximum 400%, whereas rolling the wheel forward decreases the magnification by 15% until you reach the minimum 10% value.

When editing a range of cells, I often find the Fit Selection option (abbreviated to Selection on the Zoom pop-up menu) to be the most useful because this feature automatically selects whatever magnification is necessary to display all the cells currently selected. To use this feature, follow these steps:

1. Select the range of cells that must be displayed for the type of editing you're doing.

2. Either select Selection on the Zoom combo box's pop-up menu on the Standard toolbar or click the Fit Selection option button in the Zoom dialog box (View➪Zoom).

Figures 32-1 and 32-2 illustrate this type of situation. In Figure 32-1, I select the cell range J20:L25 — the range that needs editing — and then click the Selection option from the Zoom combo box on the Standard toolbar.

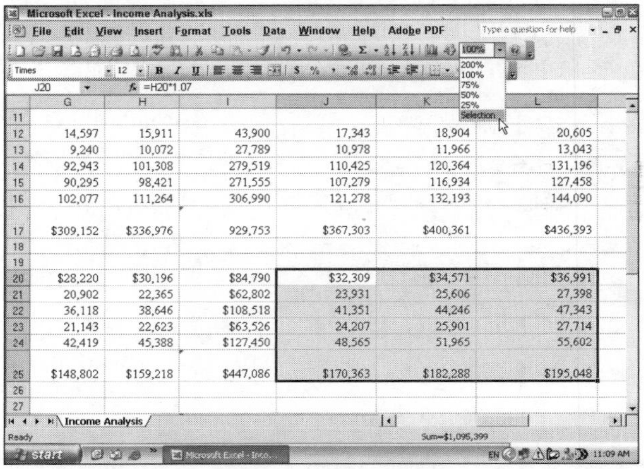

• **Figure 32-1:** Selecting the cell range to zoom in on with the Fit Selection feature.

Figure 32-2 shows the results of this action. To display only this cell range in the worksheet window, Excel automatically selects a new magnification setting of 179%. After editing the cells in this range, I can then return to the normal magnification by selecting 100% from the Zoom combo box.

Zoom out to locate the cell range to be edited on the worksheet. Then select the range and use the Fit Selection feature to display it full-screen as you make the necessary editing changes.

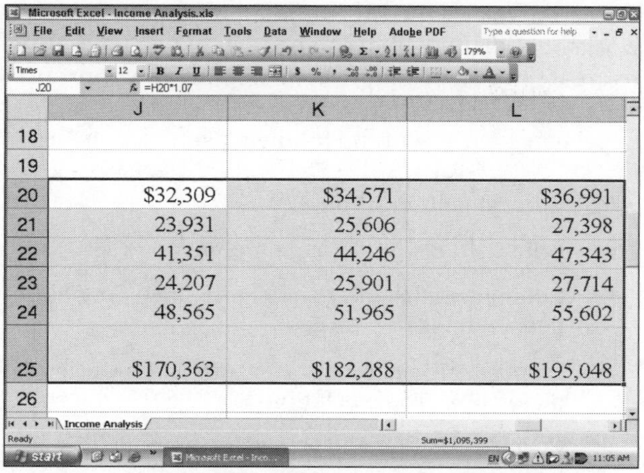

• **Figure 32-2:** Cell range after letting the Fit Selection feature increase the magnification as needed.

Frozen Panes in My Windows

Figure 32-2 could be the poster child for the Freeze Panes feature. Although zooming in on the range of cells that needs editing has made the data entries easy to read, without the column and row headings you haven't a clue as to what kind of data you're looking at. If I had used the Freeze Panes command to freeze column A with the row headings and row 2 with the column headings, you could tell because these headings would still be there on the screen even after I used the Fit Selection feature to increase the magnification.

> Columns and rows that you fix with the Frozen Panes feature stay on the screen regardless of the magnification settings you select or how you scroll through the other cells of the worksheet.

To use the Freeze Panes feature to fix columns and rows with the spreadsheet headings on-screen, you first position the cell pointer in the cell that's located to the immediate left of the column or

columns that you want to freeze and immediately beneath the row or rows that you want to freeze. Then choose Window⇨Freeze Panes.

Figures 32-3 and 32-4 illustrate how this works. Figure 32-3 shows the Income Analysis spreadsheet after freezing column A and rows 1 and 2. To do this, I positioned the cell pointer in cell B3 and then chose Window⇨Freeze Panes. Notice the thin black line that runs down column A and across row 2, marking which column and rows of worksheet are frozen on the display and will now remain in view no matter how far you scroll to the right to new columns or scroll down to new rows.

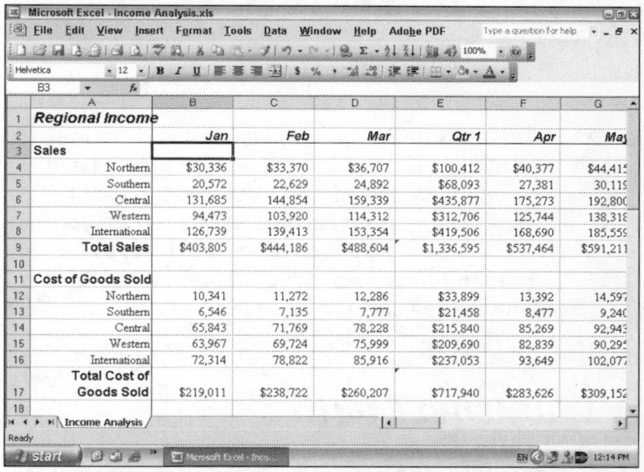

• **Figure 32-3:** Freezing the row headings in column A and the column headings in rows 1 and 2 on the worksheet.

As Figure 32-4 shows, frozen panes stay on the screen even when you zoom in and out on the worksheet. For this figure, I repeated the steps I took in changing the magnification for Figure 32-2 (only this time with the frozen panes in place). First, I selected the range J20:L25 and then clicked Selection on the Zoom combo box's pop-up menu. Now you can tell at a glance what the values in this range refer to as you make the necessary edits.

• **Figure 32-4:** Spreadsheet after zooming in on a cell selection after freezing panes.

Although frozen panes keep row and column headings on the screen at all times, they have no effect on the printed worksheet. To print these headings on each page of a report, you need to set up their columns and rows as the Print Titles before sending the report to the printer. (See Technique 39.)

A Worksheet with a Custom View

In the course of editing a worksheet, you may need to modify the worksheet display many times as you work with the document. For example, you may find at some point that you need to reduce the magnification of the worksheet display to 75% magnification. At another point, you may need to return to 100% magnification and hide different columns in the worksheet. At some later point, you may have to redisplay the hidden columns and then freeze panes in the worksheet.

You can use Excel's Custom View feature to save multiple custom views, each of which contain the display settings you need to use in editing. This way,

instead of taking the time to manually set up the worksheet display that you need, you can have Excel re-create it for you simply by selecting the appropriate custom view. When you create a custom view, Excel can save any of the following settings:

- ✔ Current cell selection

- ✔ Print settings (including different page setups)

- ✔ Column widths and row heights (including hidden columns)

- ✔ Display settings on the View tab of the Options dialog box (Tools⇨Options)

- ✔ Current position and size of the spreadsheet window

- ✔ Window pane arrangement (including frozen panes)

To create a custom view of your worksheet, follow these steps:

1. **Make all the necessary changes to the worksheet display so that the worksheet window appears exactly as you want it to appear each time you select the view. Also select all the print settings in the Page Setup dialog box that you want used in printing the view. (See Technique 39.)**

2. **Choose View⇨Custom Views to open the Custom Views dialog box. (See Figure 32-5.)**

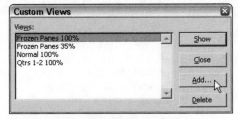

• **Figure 32-5:** Saving display and print settings as a custom view.

3. **Click the Add button to open the Add View dialog box.**

4. Enter a unique descriptive name for your view in the Name text box, as shown in Figure 32-6.

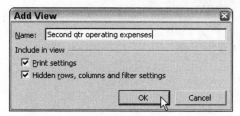

• **Figure 32-6:** Naming the new view and selecting its settings.

5. To include print settings and hidden columns and rows in your view, leave both the Print Settings and Hidden Rows, Columns, and Filter Settings check boxes selected. If you don't want to include these settings, clear either or both check boxes. When you're finished, click OK.

After you define custom views for a spreadsheet, you can invoke their settings by opening the Custom Views dialog box. In the Views list box, either double-click the view to use or select the view and click the Show button.

 Before you define any custom views that hide columns, freeze panes, and mess with the worksheet's magnification, define a Normal 100% custom view that represents the standard view of the worksheet. That way, you can recover from a special view simply by double-clicking Normal 100% in the Views list box of the Custom Views dialog box.

Technique 33

Managing Worksheet Windows

Keeping tabs on your data in a large spreadsheet is a challenge. Comparing the data entered into widely separate parts of the same worksheet can require a lot of scrolling back and forth between regions. The problem is only compounded when you're dealing with a spreadsheet whose data is distributed over different worksheets. There you have to flip between sheets *and* scroll the regions you're comparing into view.

This technique covers ways you can use worksheet windows to compare data, copy and move it between different regions of the same (or different) worksheets, and even move it from one workbook file to another. Two approaches are possible:

✔ **Using a single worksheet:** You split the worksheet window into horizontal or vertical panes and then scroll different sections of the sheet into view.

✔ **Using data on different worksheets:** You open a second window on a second worksheet and then arrange the windows to display data from the desired regions of both worksheets.

Opening Panes in the Worksheet Window

Excel makes it easy to split the worksheet window into two or four panes, each equipped with its own scroll bars. After splitting the window into panes, you can then use each pane's scroll bars to bring different parts of the same worksheet into view. This is great for comparing the data in different sections of a table that wouldn't otherwise be legible if you zoomed out far enough to display both sections in the worksheet window.

To split the worksheet window into panes, you can use a variety of methods. The most direct way when you need to split the window into only two panes is by dragging the window's split bars to the desired row or column. The most direct way when you need to split the window into four panes is to strategically position the cell pointer at the appropriate row and column and then choose Window⇨Split.

To split the window horizontally into two panes (upper and lower), drag the *horizontal split bar* (the thin bar located above the up scroll arrow on the vertical scroll bar) down the worksheet until you reach the row border where you want the window divided (as shown in Figure 33-1).

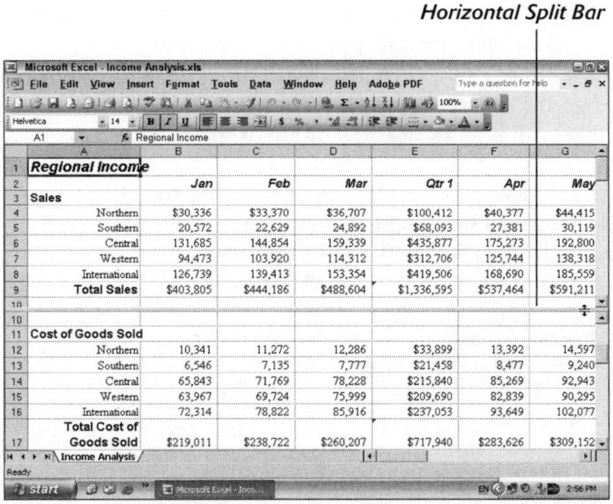

Horizontal Split Bar

• **Figure 33-1:** Drag the horizontal split bar up to divide the window into two panes one on top of the other.

To split the window vertically into two panes (left and right), drag the *vertical split bar* (the thin bar located behind the right scroll arrow on the horizontal scroll bar) to the left on the worksheet until you reach the column border where you want the window divided (as shown in Figure 33-2).

To split the window both horizontally and vertically into four panes (upper-left, upper-right, lower-left, and lower-right), position the cell pointer in the cell whose top border marks the place where you want to divide the worksheet horizontally — and make sure the cell's left border is where you want the vertical division to take place. Then choose Window⇨ Split. (See Figure 33-3 for an example.) You can get the same result by dragging first one split bar and then the other: For example, drag the horizontal split bar down to the desired row and then drag the vertical split bar left until you get to the desired column.

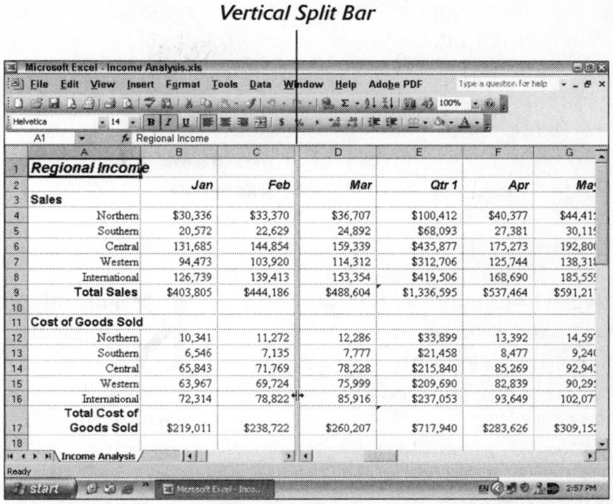

Vertical Split Bar

• **Figure 33-2:** Drag the vertical split bar to the left to divide the window into two side-by-side panes.

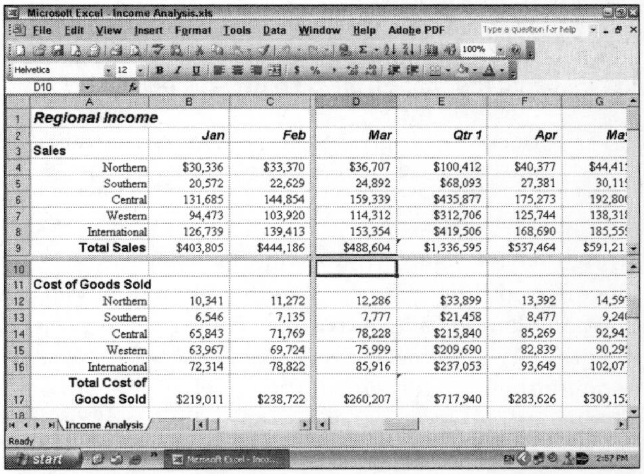

• **Figure 33-3:** Dividing the window into four panes at row 10 and column D.

When you split a window into panes, Excel automatically synchronizes the scrolling, depending on how you split the worksheet. When you split a window into two horizontal panes (as shown in Figure 33-1), the worksheet window contains a single horizontal scroll bar and two separate vertical scroll bars: All horizontal scrolling of the two panes is synchronized;

vertical scrolling of each pane remains independent. When you split a window into two vertical panes (as shown in Figure 33-2), the worksheet window contains a single vertical scroll bar and two separate horizontal scroll bars: All vertical scrolling of the two panes is synchronized; horizontal scrolling of each pane remains independent.

When you split a window into two horizontal *and* two vertical panes (as shown in Figure 33-3), the worksheet window contains two horizontal scroll bars and two separate vertical scroll bars: Vertical scrolling is synchronized in the top two window panes when you use the top vertical scroll bar and synchronized for the bottom two window panes when you use the bottom vertical scroll bar. Likewise, horizontal scrolling is synchronized for the left two panes when you use the horizontal scroll bar on the left and synchronized for the right two panes when you use the horizontal scroll bar on the right.

To move the cell pointer from pane to pane with the keyboard when the window is split into four panes, press F6 (the cell pointer moves to the first cell in each pane, going clockwise) or press Shift+F6 (the cell pointer moves to the first cell in each pane, going counterclockwise).

To remove all panes from a window when you no longer need them, choose Window⇨Remove Split. You can also remove individual panes by dragging the gray dividing bar for the horizontal or vertical pane until you reach one of the edges of the worksheet window — or you can simply double-click the bar that divides that pane.

Comparing Sheets in the Same Workbook

Panes are fine for comparing different sections of the same worksheet, but you need to divide the Excel worksheet into separate windows if you want to compare data from separate sheets or from different workbook files. The easiest way to do this is to use Excel's Compare Side by Side feature to split the worksheet into two horizontal windows (one on top of the other) in which you can display different sheets from the same workbook.

The following steps show how to use this feature to compare data entered in the same regions on separate sheets of a spreadsheet. The example compares revenue figures from two different years, entered on separate sheets of the same workbook:

1. **Open the workbook containing the sheets you want to compare and then activate the worksheet that you want to appear in the topmost window (as shown in Figure 33-4).**

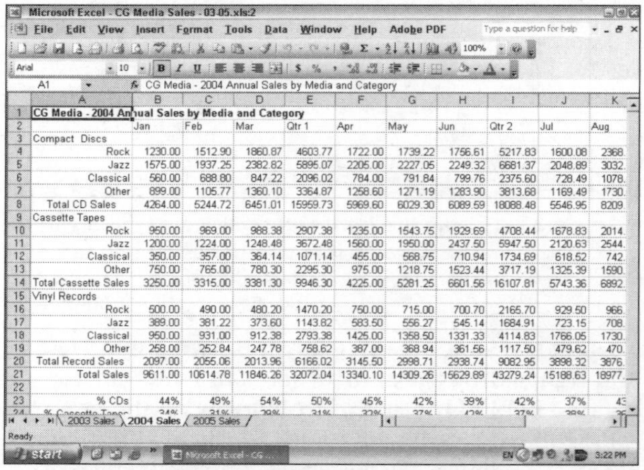

• **Figure 33-4: Spreadsheet with annual revenues on separate worksheets.**

2. **Choose Window⇨Compare Side by Side With.**

Excel creates two horizontal windows numbered 1 and 2, with window 2 on the top and window 1 on the bottom (as shown in Figure 33-5).

3. **Press Ctrl+F6 to activate window 1 (the lower), and then select the sheet tab of the worksheet whose data you're comparing with the data in window 2 (as shown in Figure 33-6).**

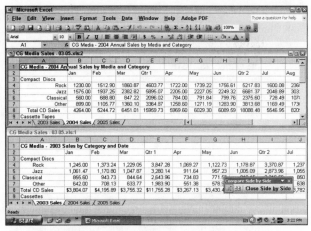

• **Figure 33-5: Spreadsheet after creating horizontal windows.**

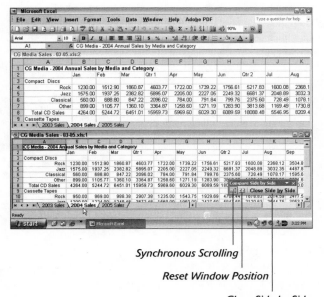

Synchronous Scrolling

Reset Window Position

Close Side by Side

• **Figure 33-6: Spreadsheet after activating a different worksheet in window 1.**

When you choose the Compare Side by Side With command on the Window menu, Excel automatically displays the Compare Side by Side toolbar (shown in the lower part of Figure 33-6) with its three buttons:

✔ **Synchronous Scrolling:** When this button is clicked, any scrolling you do in the worksheet in the active window is mirrored and synchronized in the worksheet in the inactive window beneath it. If you want to scroll the worksheet in the active window independently of the one in the inactive window, deactivate the Synchronous Scrolling button by clicking it.

✔ **Reset Window Position:** Click this button if you manually resize the active window (by dragging its size box) and then want to restore the two windows to their previous side-by-side arrangement.

✔ **Close Side by Side:** When you click this button, Excel returns the windows to the display arrangement as it was before you used the Window⇨Compare Side by Side With command. (If you didn't select a display option in the Arrange Windows dialog box, Excel displays the active window at full size.)

Comparing Sheets in Separate Workbooks

Sometimes you need to compare, move, or copy data between the sheets of two different workbooks. Before you can do so, you have to open windows on each of the separate workbooks. Follow these steps:

1. **Open the two workbooks that contain the data you want to compare and/or move or copy.**

2. **Choose Window⇨Compare Side by Side With. (See Figure 33-7.)**

3. **Press Ctrl+F6 to move the cell pointer between the workbook windows and then select the tab of the sheets that you want to compare.**

When you finish comparing the data on the sheets of the two workbooks, close their windows by clicking the Close Side by Side button in the Compare Side by Side toolbar (or by choosing Window⇨Close Side by Side if the Compare Side by Side toolbar is hidden).

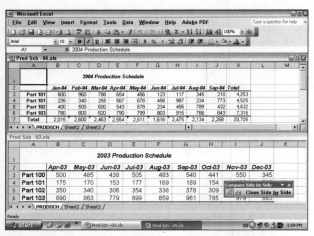

• **Figure 33-7:** Using Compare Side by Side With to create windows on two different workbooks.

To move a cell range from one workbook to another, drag the selection from one window to the other. (Hold down the Ctrl key as you drag to copy the selection.) To move or copy an entire worksheet, drag its sheet tab from one workbook window to the other.

Technique 34

Quick and Easy Insertion and Deletion

Save Time By

✔ Safely inserting cells into (and removing them from) existing ranges

✔ Inserting and deleting entire rows and columns from the worksheet

✔ Inserting and deleting entire worksheets form the workbook

This technique looks at insertion-and-deletion editing that goes beyond the mere cell level — where you're limited to just replacing or deleting a cell's particular contents. Here you get a look at larger insertions and deletions that involve structural changes to the worksheet or workbook.

These larger edits include inserting new cells into — or deleting them from — existing ranges. It also shows how to insert new rows and columns into a worksheet and how to (safely) delete existing ones. Finally, it looks at inserting new sheets into a workbook and deleting the ones you no longer need.

Inserting and Deleting Cells in an Existing Range

Sometimes, after building your spreadsheet, you have to modify its structure slightly by inserting new cells for additional entries in an existing range. To insert new cells without replacing the cells that already have existing entries, just use the Insert⇨Cells command and then indicate whether Excel is to shift the cells down or to the right to make room for the new blank ones.

Figures 34-1 and 34-2 illustrate this situation. Figure 34-1 shows a worksheet that tracks home sales for a parcel known as Paradise Estates. In this case, I need to insert three additional house sales into Column B, in between the $175,000 figure in Row 4 and the $125,000 figure in Row 5. To do this, I select the cell range B5:B7 (which is where I want the new entries to appear), open the Insert dialog box (Insert⇨Cells), select the Shift Cells Down option button (Shift Cells Right is selected by default), and then click OK.

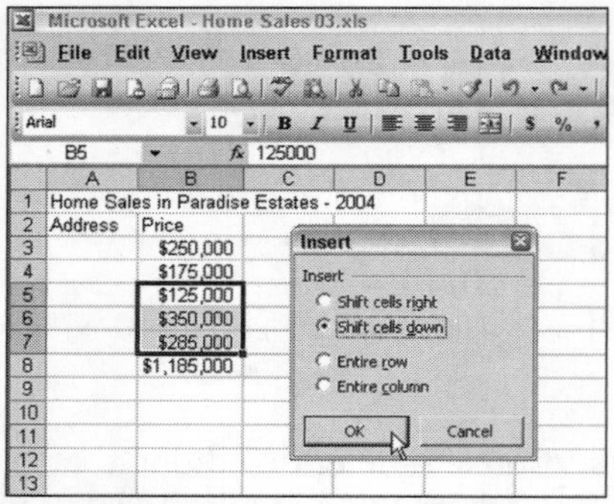

• **Figure 34-1:** Inserting three blank cells in a column of existing entries.

Figure 34-2 shows you the same worksheet after shifting the existing entries down and entering the new home sales figures in cells B5, B6, and B7. Here Excel has automatically updated the SUM function (now in cell B11 but originally entered in cell B8) to include the new cells I squeezed in; now they're part of its range argument.

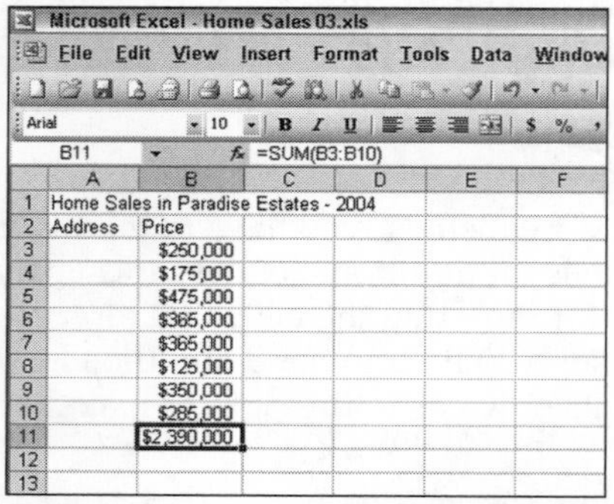

• **Figure 34-2:** Worksheet after making entries in the three inserted cells in column B.

Deleting cells from existing ranges when you don't want to leave empty cells is a similar process: You use the Edit⇨Delete command, as Figures 34-3 and 34-4 demonstrate. In Figure 34-3, I discover that the second $365,000 figure I entered into cell B7 is a duplicate that shouldn't be there — and I don't have to replace it with some other value. I want to delete the duplicate in this cell and pull up the existing entries in the rows below (that is, cell range B8:B11)

so as to leave no gaps in the column. So I select cell B7 before selecting the Shift Cells Up option in the Delete dialog box (Edit⇨Delete).

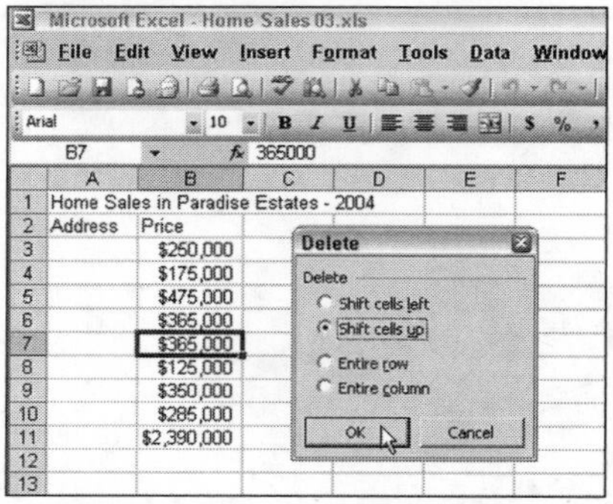

• **Figure 34-3:** Worksheet after making entries in the three blank cells in column B.

Figure 34-4 shows you the result. Here you see the worksheet after removing the mistaken duplicate in cell B7 and shifting the entries in the cells below up one row (from the range B8:B11 up to B7:B10).

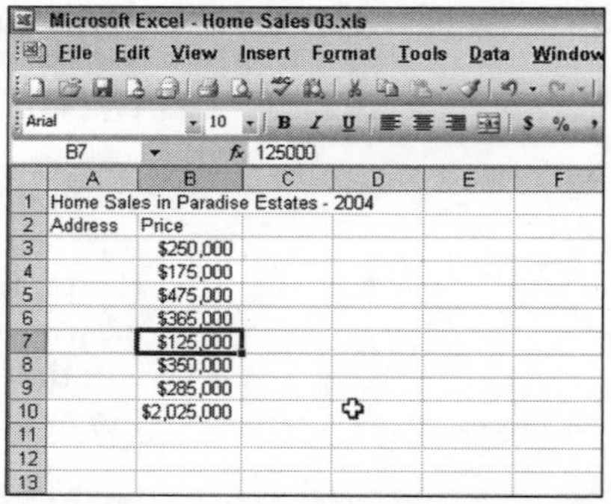

• **Figure 34-4:** Worksheet after making entries in the three blank cells in column B.

Inserting and Deleting Rows and Columns

Inserting and deleting entire rows and columns in a worksheet is very similar to inserting new cells into a range — or deleting cells from the same range. In fact, you can actually insert or delete rows from within the Insert and Delete dialog boxes by selecting their Entire Row or Entire Column option button. There is, however, a big difference in the result:

✔ Inserting or deleting a new row affects all the columns in the worksheet, from column A over to column IV.

✔ Inserting or deleting a new column affects all the rows in the worksheet, from row 1 down to row 65536.

Because these insertions and deletions affect more than the cells in their immediate vicinity, you have to be sure that you're not about to adversely affect data in unseen rows and columns of the sheet before you undertake these operations. Note that, in this regard, inserting columns or rows can be almost as detrimental as deleting them if, by inserting them, you split apart existing data tables or lists whose data should always remain together.

One way to guard against inadvertently deleting existing data or splitting a single range is to use the Zoom feature: You can zoom out and check visually for intersecting groups of data in the hinterlands of the worksheet. The quick way to do this is to enter 10 into the Zoom box (on the Standard toolbar) and then press Enter. Of course, at a zoom setting of 10%, you can't read any of the data entered into the worksheet, but you can tell whether the column or row you intend to fiddle with intersects those data ranges (which you can identify as tiny specks of black).

Another way to check is to use the Ctrl key with the → or ↓ key to move the cell pointer from data range to data range across the column or row affected by the deletion of a column or row. Remember that pressing Ctrl at the same time as an arrow key when the cell pointer is in a blank cell jumps the cell pointer to the next occupied cell in the current row or column. That means if you press Ctrl+→ when the cell pointer is in row 79 and the pointer jumps to cell IV79 (the end of the worksheet in that row), you

know that you won't mess up any data in that row by deleting the row (which would eliminate the data) or inserting a new row (which would shift the data up or down). So, too, if you press Ctrl+↓ when the cell pointer is in column C and the cell pointer jumps down to cell C65536, you're assured that no data is about to be purged — or shifted left or right — if you get rid of that column or insert a new column in its place.

After using one of these methods to ascertain that you won't harm existing data in the hinterland of the sheet, you're ready to insert or delete the row or column. Here are some points to remember:

✔ To insert or delete rows, you first select the row number(s) in the row header where the new rows are to be inserted or existing rows removed.

✔ When you insert rows, the existing data in the rows below shifts downward.

✔ When you delete rows, the existing data in the rows below shifts upward.

✔ To insert blank rows, choose Insert⟿Rows.

✔ To delete the selected rows, choose Edit⟿Delete instead.

The steps for inserting and deleting worksheet columns is almost identical for either procedure:

1. Select the column letters in the column header.

2. Choose Insert⟿Columns (to insert a column) or Edit⟿Delete (to delete a column).

Excel automatically moves any data that's currently in the columns to the right of those you selected:

▶ When you insert new columns, the existing data moves to the right.

▶ When you delete existing columns, the existing data moves to the left.

Inserting and Deleting Worksheets

The most global type of insertion or deletion you make in a spreadsheet is to insert new worksheets or delete existing ones from the workbook file itself. The steps for this type of structural edit look like this:

1. **Select the affected sheet tabs.**

2. **Choose either Insert⇨Worksheet or Edit⇨ Delete Sheet.**

    ▶ If you're inserting worksheets, Excel inserts a number equal to the number of tabs you've selected and places the blank worksheets ahead of them.

    ▶ If you're deleting worksheets that contain data, Excel displays an alert dialog box to warn you of possible data loss. To complete the deletion, click the Delete button in this dialog box.

35 Technique

Outline and Subtotal Magic

Excel's Outline feature enables you to control the level of detail displayed in a table of data or a data list in a worksheet. After outlining a table or list, you can quickly condense or expand the display of the table or list to show specified levels of detail. You can control which outline level is displayed in the worksheet, so it's easy to print summary reports with various levels of data (see Technique 39) or chart just the summary data (see Technique 22).

Excel's Subtotal feature is a quick way to summarize data in a list without having to create and copy the formulas that perform the desired calculations. Using this feature, you determine which groups of records (rows) are summed as well as which fields (columns) are actually computed. When you need to produce an online or printed report from a data list that includes various levels of totals, the Subtotal feature is the way to go.

Adding Outline Levels to a Table or List

When you "outline" a table of data in an Excel worksheet, the program applies a hierarchy of levels to the rows and columns of data — which you can then manipulate to display different degrees of detail in the data. The best way to understand how this works is to see the feature in action.

Figure 35-1 shows the CG Media 2004 sales table after outlining it. To create this outline, all I had to do was to select the cell range A2:R14 — the range containing the data to be outlined — and then choose Data⇨Group and Outline⇨Auto Outline; Excel did the rest. As you can see, when the program outlined this table, it automatically assigned three different summary levels for its rows and columns. (An Excel outline can have up to eight row and column levels, if the table requires it.)

Row Level

Column Level   *Column Level Bar*

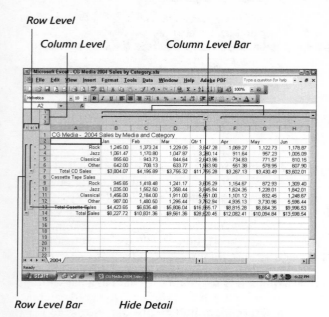

Row Level Bar   *Hide Detail*

• **Figure 35-1: Sales table after applying outline levels with Auto Outline.**

When Excel first outlines the data in your table, the program displays the highest outline level (which is 3 in this example), showing all the detail. To reduce the amount of detail shown, click a lower-numbered Row Level or Column Level button.

Figure 35-2 shows the outlined sales table after I clicked the number-2 Column Level button, which collapsed the outline down to the secondary column level: Excel immediately hides all columns with the monthly sales figures, showing only the quarterly and annual totals. Note that when Excel collapses the outline to the secondary column level, it automatically adds Show Detail buttons above each column that shows a quarterly total. To display the monthly sales detail for any quarter, just click its Show Detail button.

Show Detail Button

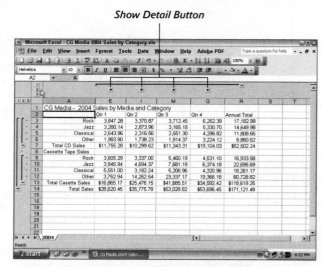

• **Figure 35-2: Collapsed sales table with the number-2 Column Level button selected.**

Figure 35-3 shows the sales table after further collapsing the outline. This time I clicked the number-2 Row Level button, which collapsed the outline down to the secondary row level as well as the secondary column level. Excel now hides all columns containing the categories of CD and cassette sales, while at the same time displaying Show Detail buttons to the immediate left of rows 7 and 13 (which contain the total CD and cassette sales, respectively). To display category sales, either for CDs or cassettes, you have only to click the appropriate Show Detail button.

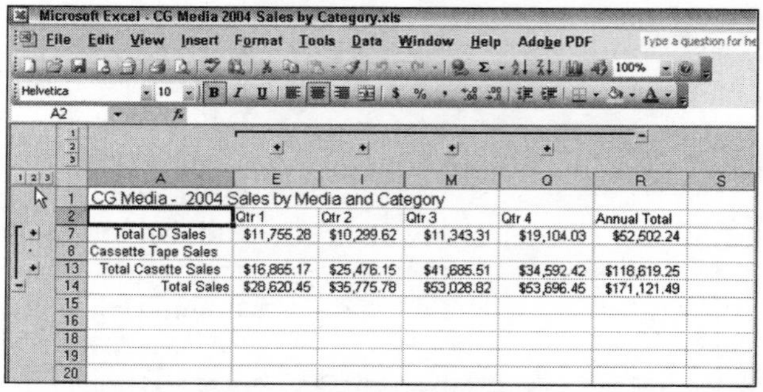

[Figure 35-3 screenshot]

• **Figure 35-3: Collapsed sales table with the number-2 Column Level and Row Level buttons selected.**

Figure 35-4 shows the sales table after collapsing the outline one more time. For this figure, I clicked the number-1 Row Level button to collapse the outline down to the primary row level, while leaving the secondary column level selected. At this point, the table displays only grand totals for each of the four quarters, along with the annual details.

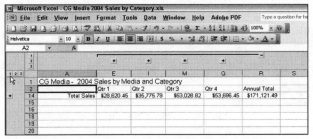

• **Figure 35-4: Collapsed sales table with the number-2 Column Level and number-1 Row Level buttons selected.**

 To chart just the summary details in an outlined table, collapse its row and column levels down until only the necessary subtotals or totals are displayed. Then select these displayed cells in the worksheet and press F11 or click the Chart Wizard button. (See Technique 22.)

 Press Ctrl+8 to immediately hide (and later redisplay) all outline symbols in the worksheet window.

To remove an outline from your worksheet, choose Data➪Group and Outline➪Clear Outline. Note that removing the outline does not affect the data in any way — Excel merely removes the outline structure. Also note that it doesn't matter at what level the outline is displayed at the time you select this command. If the outline is partially or totally collapsed, deleting the outline automatically displays all hidden rows and columns in the data table or list.

 Create custom views (see Technique 32) that display your outlined table in various levels of detail. Then, instead of having to display the

outline symbols and manually click the appropriate Row Level buttons and/or Column Level buttons to view a particular level of detail, you simply select the appropriate custom view. When creating these custom views, be sure that you leave the Hidden Rows, Columns, and Filter Settings check box selected in the Add View dialog box.

Subtotaling a Table or List

You can use Excel's Subtotals feature to subtotal data in a sorted list. (See Technique 44.) To subtotal a data list, first you sort the list on the field (column) for which you want the subtotals; then you designate the field (column) that contains the values you want summed — these don't have to be the same fields in the data list.

When you use the Subtotals feature, you aren't restricted to having the values in the designated field added together with the SUM function. You can instead have Excel return the number of entries with the COUNT function, the average of the entries with the AVERAGE function, the highest entry with the MAXIMUM function, the lowest entry with the MINIMUM function, or even the product of the entries with the PRODUCT function.

Figures 35-5 and 35-6 illustrate how easy it is to use the Subtotals feature to obtain totals in a data list. In Figure 35-5, I sorted the sample Employee data list — first by the Department field (in ascending order) and then by the Salary field (in descending order). Then I chose Data➪Subtotals to open the Subtotal dialog box and made the following choices:

✔ Calculate subtotals for the Department field in the At Each Change In drop-down list box.

✔ Use the SUM function in the Use Function drop-down list box.

✔ Sum the values in the Salary check box in the Add Subtotal To list box.

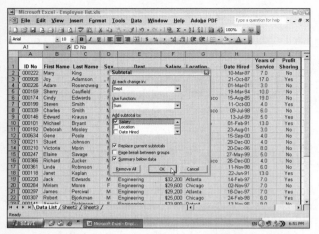

• **Figure 35-5:** Subtotaling the salaries for each department in the Employee data list.

Figure 35-6 shows the results I obtained after clicking the OK button in the Subtotal dialog box. Here, you see the bottom of the data list where it shows the salary subtotals for the Engineering, Human Resources, and Information Services — along with the grand total of the salaries for all the departments. The grand total is displayed at the bottom of the data list because I left the Summary Below Data check box selected in the Subtotal dialog box — if you don't want a grand total, clear this check box.

• **Figure 35-6:** Bottom of the Employee data list showing some of the department salary subtotals and the grand total.

As you can see from this figure, when you use the Subtotal feature, Excel outlines the data at the same time that it adds the rows for the required totals and grand total. In this example, the program created an outline with three row levels. When you click the number-2 Row Level button, the program hides all records (rows) in the data list except for those containing the department salary totals and the salary grand total. When you click the number-1 Row Level button, Excel hides all records (rows) but the one with the salary grand total.

In a really large data list, you may want page breaks every time there is a change in the subtotaled field (the one designated in the At Each Change In drop-down list box). To add those page breaks, select the Page Break between Groups check box in the Subtotal dialog box.

36 Technique

Consolidating Data from Different Worksheets

Excel's Consolidation feature makes short work of combining numerical data in tables stored on several different worksheets or even different workbook files. For example, you can use this feature to total all budget spreadsheets prepared by each department in the company or to create summary totals for income statements for a period of several years.

If you used a template to create each worksheet you're consolidating or an identical layout, Excel can quickly consolidate the values by virtue of their common position in the respective worksheets. However, even if you laid out the data entries differently in each spreadsheet, Excel can still consolidate them provided that you've used the same labels to describe the data entries in their respective worksheets.

Most of the time, you will want to total the data that you're consolidating from the various worksheets. By default, Excel uses the SUM function to total all the cells in the worksheets that share the same cell references (when you consolidate by position) or use the same labels (when you consolidate by category). You can, however, have Excel use any of the following statistical functions when doing a consolidation: COUNT, AVERAGE, MAX, MIN, PRODUCT, COUNTA (referred to as Count Nums), STDEV, STDEVP, VAR, or VARP.

Consolidating Data by Position

You consolidate worksheets by position when they use the same layout (such as those created from a template). When you consolidate data by position, Excel does not copy the labels from the source areas to the destination area, only the values.

To consolidate worksheets by position, follow these steps:

1. **Open all the workbooks with the worksheets you want to consolidate. If the sheets are all in one workbook, open that file in Excel.**

2. **Create a new worksheet to hold the consolidated data.**

If you're consolidating the data in a new workbook, you need to open it (File⇨New). If you're consolidating worksheets generated from a template, use the template to create the new workbook. (See Technique 1.)

3. **Select the cell at the beginning of the destination area in the new worksheet or select the cell range if you want to limit the destination area to a particular region.**

If you want Excel to expand the size of the destination area as needed to accommodate the source areas, just select the first cell of this range.

4. **Choose Data⇨Consolidate to open the Consolidate dialog box, shown in Figure 36-1.**

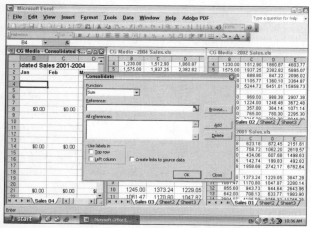

• **Figure 36-1:** Using the Consolidate dialog box to total 2001-2004 sales.

5. **(Optional) Select the function you want to use in the Function drop-down list if you don't want the values in the source areas summed together.**

6. **Select the cell range or type the cell references for the first source area in the Reference text box.**

When you select the cell range by pointing, Excel minimizes the Consolidate dialog box to the Reference text box so that you can see what you're selecting. If the workbook is not visible in a window, choose it on the Window menu and then select the cell selection as you normally would. (Remember that you can move the Consolidate dialog box — the one that's been minimized to the Reference text box — by dragging its title bar.)

If the source worksheets are not open, click the Browse button to select the filename in the Browse dialog box to enter it (plus an exclamation point) into the Reference text box. Then you can type in the range name or cell references you want to use. If you prefer, you can type in the entire cell reference including the filename. Remember that you can use the asterisk (*) and question mark (?) wildcard characters when typing in the references for the source area.

7. **Click the Add button to add this reference to the first source area to the All References list box.**

8. **Repeat Steps 6 and 7 until you add all the references for all the source areas that you want to consolidate, as shown in Figure 36-2.**

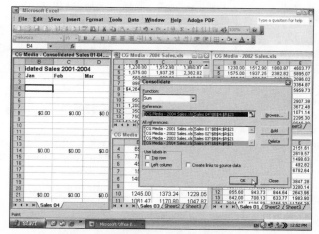

• **Figure 36-2:** The Consolidate dialog box after selecting all the cell ranges to be totaled.

9. **Click the OK button to close the Consolidate dialog box and have Excel consolidate the designated data.**

Figure 36-3 shows you the consolidated worksheet after closing the Consolidate worksheet and then increasing its window to full size. This worksheet now contains the total sales for the last four years, 2001 through 2004.

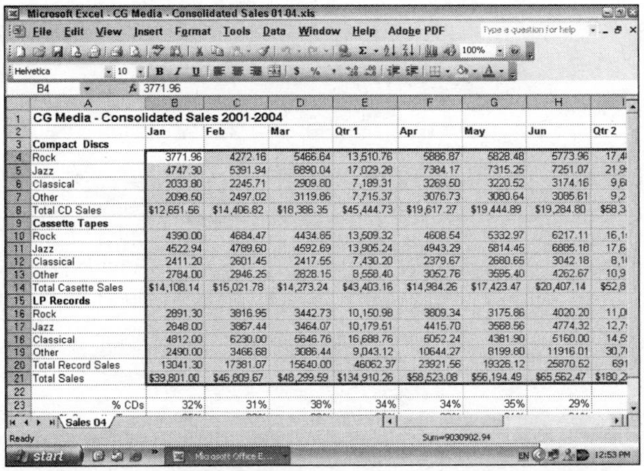

• **Figure 36-3: Full-size worksheet after consolidating the sales data from the last four years.**

Consolidating Data by Category

You consolidate data by category when the source areas do not share the same cell coordinates in their respective worksheets but their data entries do use common row and/or column labels. When you consolidate by category, you include these identifying labels as part of the source areas. Unlike consolidating by position, Excel copies the row labels and/or column labels you specify for use in the consolidation.

When consolidating spreadsheet data by category, you must specify whether to use the top row of column labels and/or the left column of row labels in

determining which data to consolidate. To use the top row of column labels, select the Top Row check box in the Use Labels In section of the Consolidate dialog box. To use the left column of row labels, select the Left Column check box in this area. After you specify all the source areas (including the cells that contain these column and row labels), click the OK button in the Consolidate dialog box to execute the consolidation in the destination area.

Linking Consolidated Data

During a consolidation, Excel enables you to link the data in the source areas specified in the All References list box of the Consolidate dialog box to the destination area in the new worksheet. That way, any changes that you make to the values in the source area will be updated automatically in the destination area of the consolidation worksheet. To create links between the source worksheets and the destination worksheet, you simply select the Create Links to Source Data check box in the Consolidate dialog box prior to performing the consolidation.

When you perform a consolidation with linking, Excel creates the links between the source areas and the destination area by outlining the destination area. (See Technique 35.) Each outline level created in the destination area holds rows or columns that contain the linking formulas to the consolidated data.

Figure 36-4 shows just such an outline created during consolidation. I expanded the level of the outline showing the consolidation of the rock music CD sales.

Here, you can see that during consolidation, Excel created four detail rows for each of the four years of sales (2001, 2002, 2003, and 2004) used in the linked consolidation. These rows contain the external reference formulas that link to the source data. For example, the formula in cell B4 contains the following formula:

```
='[CG Media - 2001 Sales.xls]Sales01'!$B$4
```

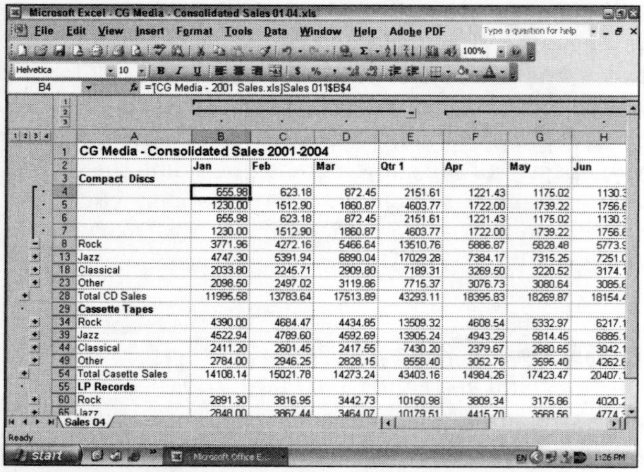

• **Figure 36-4:** Consolidated worksheet with links to sales data from the last four years.

This formula links the value in cell B4 in the Sales 01 sheet of the CG Media - 2001 Sales.xls workbook. If you change this value in that worksheet, the new value is updated automatically in cell B4 in the CG Media - Consolidated Sales 01-04 workbook, which, in turn, changes the subtotal for the January rock music CD sales in its cell B7.

Editing with Search & Replace and Spell Check

No discussion of spreadsheet editing is complete without including something on the Find and Replace and Spell Check features in Excel. You can use the Find and Replace feature to quickly locate every occurrence of a specific *string* (a series of characters) in a work-sheet and then have Excel actually update the cells that it finds with new text or numbers. This feature is a real timesaver when you need to make a global change that affects cells in diverse parts of the spreadsheet.

Excel's Spell Check feature is a real godsend if you're like me and are not the best (that is, most accurate) typist in the world. Spell checking a worksheet can go a long way towards eliminating typos that get by the program's AutoCorrect feature. (See Technique 11.) The only problem with using Spell Check is that many spreadsheets are crammed full of acronyms, technical terms, and formal names that Excel's spelling dic-tionary has never heard of. To prevent the spell checker from really slow-ing you down by stopping at every other word in the spreadsheet to ask if it's misspelled, you need to build custom dictionaries that contain most of these erstwhile unknown terms.

Using Find and Replace

Excel's Find and Replace feature enables you to easily update the con-tents of a single worksheet or all the worksheets in a workbook on either a case-by-case basis or globally. To make quick and easy editing changes with this feature, follow these steps:

1. To perform a search and replace through the entire worksheet, select a single cell. To restrict the search-and-replace operation to a specific cell range or nonadjacent selection, select all the cells to be edited.

2. Choose Edit⇨Replace or press Ctrl+H to open the Find and Replace dialog box. (See Figure 37-1.)

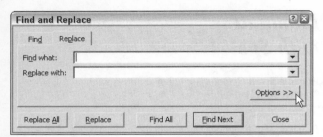

• **Figure 37-1:** Using the Find and Replace feature to make editing changes.

3. Click the Options button to expand the Replace tab.

4. Type the search string that you want to locate in the Find What drop-down list box and specify any formatting to be searched by clicking its Format button.

When entering the search string, you can use the question mark (?) or asterisk (*) wildcards to stand for any characters that you're unsure of. Use the question mark to stand for a single character as in Sm?th, which matches either *Smith* or *Smyth*. Use the asterisk to stand for multiple characters as in 9*1, which locates *91, 94901,* or even *9553 1st Street*. To search for a wildcard character, precede the character with a tilde (~), as in ~*2.5, to locate formulas that are multiplied by the number 2.5. (The asterisk is the multiplication operator in Excel.)

If the cell holding the search string that you're looking for is formatted in a particular way, you can narrow the search by specifying what formatting to search for. When you click the Format button, Excel opens a Find Format dialog box with the same tabs and options as the standard Format Cells dialog box. Select the formatting that you want to search for in this dialog box and then click OK.

5. Type the replacement string in the Replace With drop-down list box and specify any formatting to be added to the replacement string by clicking its Format button.

6. Select any additional options you want:

▶ **Within:** Select the Workbook setting to search all the worksheets within a workbook.

▶ **Search:** Change this setting from By Rows to By Columns to search down the columns and across the rows rather that across the rows and then down the columns.

▶ **Look In:** By default, Excel selects Formulas for this option to look for the search string in the contents of each cell as it's displayed on the Formula bar. To have Excel search for the string in among the values displayed in the cells themselves, select Values on this drop-down list. To have the program look for the search string only in the comments added to the cells, select Comments on this drop-down list.

▶ **Match Case:** Find occurrences of the search string only when it matches the case that you entered.

▶ **Match Entire Cell Contents:** Find occurrences of the search string only when it matches the entire cell entry.

By default, Excel considers any occurrence of the search string to be a match — even when it occurs as part of another part of the cell entry. This means that when you search for 25, Excel considers cells containing 25, 15.25, 25 Main Street, and 250,000 as matches. Select the Match Entire Cell Contents check box to match only complete occurrences of your search string.

7. Click the Find Next button to locate the first occurrence of the search string. When Excel finds an occurrence, click the Replace button to replace the first occurrence with the replacement string or the Find Next button again to skip this occurrence. (See Figure 37-2.)

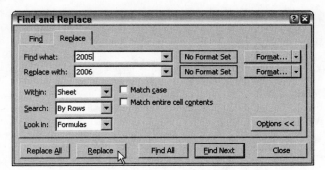

• **Figure 37-2: Finding the first occurrence of the search string for possible replacement.**

Using the Find Next and Replace buttons to search and replace on a case-by-case basis is by far the safest way to use the Find and Replace feature. If you're certain (really certain) that you won't mess anything up by replacing all occurrences throughout the spreadsheet, click the Replace All button to have Excel make the replacements globally without stopping to show you which cells are updated.

8. **When you finish replacing entries on a case-by-case basis, click the Close button to close the Find and Replace dialog box.**

Note that if you globally replace the search string in the worksheet, Excel automatically closes the Find and Replace dialog box when it finishes replacing the last match.

 Be clear about the difference between the Formulas and Values Look In options in the expanded Find and Replace dialog box. When, for example, the default Formulas option is selected and you enter 15 the search string, Excel looks for these two digits only in text entries and within the contents of formulas as they appear on the Formula bar (as in =15+A4). To have the program find the digits 15 when directly entered in a cell or returned as the result of a formula calculation as actually displayed in the cells of the worksheet (as when the formula =A2-A3 returns 15 to a cell), you must select Values as the Look In option before you conduct the search.

Eliminating Typing Errors with Spell Check

Excel's Spell Check feature affords you a quick-and-easy way to check for any typos in your spreadsheets before sending them out for any kind of review. To spell check a worksheet, click the Spelling button on the Standard toolbar, press F7, or choose Tools⇨Spelling.

Excel then looks up each word in the Excel dictionary. If it doesn't find a word (as is often the case with less-common last names, abbreviations, acronyms, and technical terms), Excel selects the cell with the unknown spelling and then displays a Spelling dialog box showing the unknown word in the Not in Dictionary text box, along with suggested correct spellings shown in a Suggestions list box. (See Figure 37-3.)

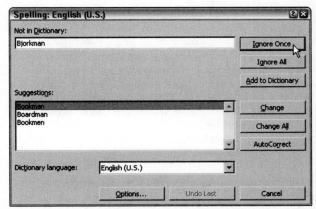

• **Figure 37-3: Flagging a word in the worksheet that's not found in the dictionary.**

You can then take any of the following actions to take care of the unknown word:

✔ Select one of the words in the Suggestions list box and then click the Change button to have Excel replace the unknown word with the selected suggestion and continue spell checking the rest of the worksheet.

✔ Select one of the words in the Suggestions list box and then click the Change All button to have Excel replace all occurrences of the unknown word with the selected suggestion throughout the entire worksheet and then continue spell checking.

✔ Click the Ignore Once button to let the misspelling slide just this once and continue spell checking the rest of the worksheet.

✔ Click the Ignore All button to ignore all occurrences of the unknown word in the worksheet and continue spell checking.

✔ Click the Add to Dictionary button to add the unknown word to a custom dictionary so that Excel knows the word the next time you spell check that or any other worksheet.

✔ Click the AutoCorrect button to have Excel add the unknown word to the AutoCorrect list with the selected suggestion as its automatic replacement.

 Excel checks the spelling of the cells only in the current worksheet (not in all the sheets in the workbook). If you want Excel to spell check another worksheet, you need to select its sheet tab to make it active before you start the spell check. To spell check just a portion of the worksheet, select the range or make a nonadjacent cell selection before you start the spell check.

When Excel finishes checking the current worksheet or cell selection, the program displays an alert dialog box that indicates that the spell checking is complete.

Customizing the Spell Check settings

When you use the Spell Check feature, you can change certain spelling options to better suit the spreadsheet that you're checking. To change the spelling options, click the Options button at the bottom of the Spelling dialog box to open the Options dialog box, shown in Figure 37-4.

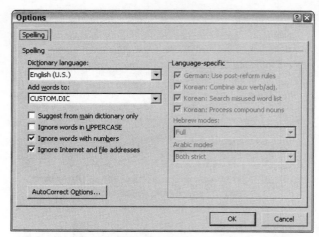

• **Figure 37-4:** Modifying the options for the Spell Check feature.

You can use the controls in the Options dialog box to change the following settings:

✔ **Dictionary Language:** Select a new dictionary language. (This option is especially useful if your spreadsheet contains British English spellings or French or Spanish terms.)

✔ **Add Words To:** Select another custom dictionary to which to add new terms.

✔ **Suggest from Main Dictionary Only:** Select this check box to have Excel use only the main dictionary when doing a spell check (thus, ignoring all words that you add to the custom dictionary).

✔ **Ignore Words in UPPERCASE:** Select this check box to have Excel ignore acronyms in your spreadsheet that use all capital letters.

✔ **Ignore Words with Numbers:** Clear this check box to have Excel flag unknown words that contain numbers.

✔ **Ignore Internet and File Addresses:** Clear this check box to have Excel let unknown words that contain URL and Mailto addresses and file pathnames slide. (You know, stuff such as www. dummies.com and c:\mydocuments\finance.)

✔ **AutoCorrect Options:** Click this button to open the AutoCorrect dialog box where you change the settings that determine when certain words are automatically corrected as well as add new automatic replacements.

Note that Language Specific check boxes and drop-down lists on the right side of the Options dialog box remain grayed out until you select a dictionary in the Dictionary Language drop-down list for German, Korean, Hebrew, or Arabic. Then you can use them (depending on the language you select) to determine how their words are treated during spell checking.

Adding words to a custom dictionary

Click the Add to Dictionary button in the Spelling dialog box to add unknown words to a custom dictionary. By default, Excel (as well as your other Microsoft applications, such as Word) adds words to a custom dictionary file named CUSTOM.DIC. If you want, you can create other specialized custom dictionaries just to use when spell checking particular types of spreadsheets. To create a new custom dictionary, follow these steps:

1. **Begin spell checking your worksheet (press F7 or click the Spelling button on the Standard toolbar).**

You can't start adding words to a new custom dictionary until you spell check a worksheet and Excel starts flagging some unknown words.

2. **As soon as Excel locates an unknown word in the Spelling dialog box that you want to add to a new custom dictionary, click the Options button.**

3. **Click in the Add Word To drop-down list, replace the custom part of the dictionary file-name with a name of your own, and then click OK or press Enter.**

When editing the custom.dic filename to create a name for your new custom dictionary, be sure not to delete the .dic filename extension. As soon as you click OK or press Enter, Excel adds the unknown word to your new custom dictionary.

4. **Continue spell checking your worksheet, clicking the Add to Dictionary button to add all unknown words that you want to be part of your new custom dictionary.**

After creating a custom dictionary, Excel automatically uses the words in this dictionary as well as in the CUSTOM.DIC when spell checking your worksheets.

 You can directly edit the words that you add to your custom dictionary with the Windows Notepad text editor. Open the custom dictionary file (located in the Proof folder on your hard drive) and then make any changes to the entries in this file by saving your changes with Notepad's File⇨Save command.

Part VI

Tips for Printing, Sharing, and Reviewing Workbooks

The 5th Wave · By Rich Tennant

"Get ready, Mona — here come the stats."

Technique 38

Spreadsheet Security

Data security is a big issue on everyone's mind these days. Excel provides you with two levels of security: password-protecting the workbook so that only users who have the password can open the file and spreadsheet protection that limits what kind of editing, if any, users can do to the existing content and structure of its worksheets.

In addition to these two levels of security, Excel also makes it possible for you to hide sensitive data in the worksheet that might not be appropriate for all users (such as employee salaries or performance review codes) but that nevertheless need to be part of the document.

This technique looks at all three aspects of spreadsheet security, giving you pointers on the best ways to preserve the integrity of your spreadsheet as well as guard against its more sensitive information from falling into the wrong hands.

Assigning a Password for Opening a Workbook

When assigning a password to a workbook, you can prevent unauthorized users from opening the workbook and/or editing its file. You set a password for opening the workbook file when you're dealing with a spreadsheet whose data is of a sufficiently sensitive nature that only a select group of employees should have access to it (such as spreadsheets dealing with personnel information). Of course, after you assign a password to the workbook, you must supply this password to the people who need access to make it possible for them to open the workbook file.

You have a couple options for assigning passwords:

✔ **Assign a password for opening the workbook.** You'd assign such a password when you're dealing with a spreadsheet whose data needs to be viewed and printed by different users, none of whom are authorized to make changes to the entries.

✔ **Assign a password for modifying the workbook.** For example, you might assign a password for modifying a workbook before distributing it company wide. This password would be in place while the workbook is being edited and reviewed. (See Technique 42.)

With a spreadsheet that contains data that's for the eyes of only a select few but that is not to be modified even by those authorized to open it for review or printing purposes, you need to assign both a password for opening the file and a password for modifying its contents or structure.

To assign a password to open the workbook and/or a password to modify the file, follow these steps:

1. **Save the workbook by choosing File➪Save As if you've already saved the file at least once or by choosing File➪Save (Ctrl+S) if the file's never been saved.**

The Save As dialog box opens. (See Figure 38-1).

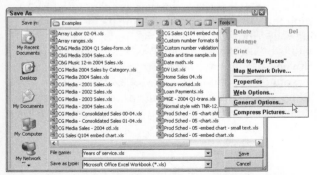

• **Figure 38-1: Opening the Save Options dialog box from the Save As dialog box.**

2. **Select General Options on the Tools pop-up menu to open the Save Options dialog box, shown in Figure 38-2.**

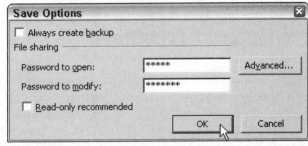

• **Figure 38-2: Assigning the passwords to open and modify in the Save Options dialog box.**

3. **To assign a password to open the file, type the password in the Password to Open text box.**

When entering the password, it can be up to 255 characters long and consist of a combination of letters and numbers with spaces. Keep in mind when using letters, however, that passwords are case-sensitive, so *opensesame* and *OpenSesame* are not the same password because of the different use of upper- and lowercase letters. As you type the password, Excel masks the actual characters you type by rendering them as asterisks (*) in the text box.

Note that Excel automatically assigns an Office 97/2000 Compatible–type encryption when you assign a password to open the file. You can use the Advanced button to assign another type of encryption, but I wouldn't fool with these options unless you really know what you're doing or have been instructed to use another type by someone in your IT department.

 When entering passwords, make sure that you don't enter something that you can't easily reproduce or something that you can't remember. You must be able to immediately reproduce the password in order to assign it, and you must be able to reproduce it later if you ever want to be able to open or change the darned workbook ever again.

4. To assign a password to modify the file, select the Password to Modify text box and then type in this password.

When entering the password for modifying the workbook, be sure that you assign a different password from the one you just assigned for opening the file (if you did assign a password for opening the file in the previous step).

5. (Optional) If you want Excel to automatically create a backup of the workbook each time it's saved, select the Always Create Backup check box. If you want the password-protected workbook to open in read-only mode (so that changes can only be saved a in new file), select the Read Only – Recommended check box.

6. Click OK to open the Confirm Password dialog box, shown in Figure 38-3.

• **Figure 38-3:** Confirming the password to open in the Confirm Password dialog box.

7. Type the password exactly as you entered it in the Password to Open text box (or the Password to Modify text box, if you didn't use the Password to Open text box) and then click OK.

If you just entered a password in the Password to Open text box, you need to reenter this password in the Confirm Password dialog box.

If you just entered a password in the Password to Modify text box, you need only to reproduce this password in the Confirm Password dialog box.

However, if you entered a password in both the Password to Open text box and the Password to Modify text box, you must reproduce the password entered in the Password to Open text box in the first Confirm Password dialog box and then reproduce the password you entered in the Password to Modify text box in the second Confirm Password dialog box, which appears after you click OK in the first Confirm Password dialog box.

8. To save the password-protected version of the file under a new filename or in a different folder, edit the name in the File Name text box and then select the new folder on the Save In drop-down list.

9. Click the Save button to save the workbook with the password to open and/or password to modify.

Excel then saves the file if this is the first time you've saved it. If not, the program displays an alert dialog box indicating that the file you're saving already exists and asking you if you want to replace the existing file.

10. If the alert dialog box asking you if you want to replace the existing file appears, click Yes.

Opening a password-protected workbook

After saving a workbook file to which you've assigned a password for opening it, you must thereafter be able to faithfully reproduce that password to open the file (at least until such time as you change or delete the password). When you next try to open the workbook, Excel opens a Password dialog box like the one shown in Figure 38-4, where you must enter the password exactly as it was assigned to the file.

• **Figure 38-4:** Entering the password to open a file in the Password dialog box.

If you mess up and type the wrong password, Excel displays an alert dialog box letting you know that the password you entered is incorrect, as shown in Figure 38-5. After you click OK to close the alert dialog box, you must repeat the entire file-opening procedure (hoping that this time you're able to enter the correct password).

• **Figure 38-5: Oops! Entering anything other than the exact password gives you this alert dialog box.**

When you do enter the correct password, Excel immediately opens the workbook for viewing and printing (and editing as well, unless you've also assigned a password for modifying the file).

 If you're unable to successfully reproduce the password, you are unable to open the file and put it to any use! Excel doesn't provide any sort of command for overriding the password and opening a protected workbook, nor does Microsoft offer any such utility. If there's any danger of forgetting a workbook's password, be sure to write it down somewhere and keep it in a secure place, preferably under lock and key.

If your workbook is protected from modifications and you attempt to open its file, Excel immediately displays a Password dialog box where you have to choose between opening the file with write privileges and opening it in read-only mode. (See Figure 38-6.) To be able to make changes to the original workbook file with write privileges, you must be able to accurately enter the password in the Password text box and then click OK. To open the workbook as a read-only file, click the Read Only button in this dialog box.

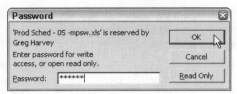

• **Figure 38-6: Opening a workbook file that has been protected against modifications.**

If you don't have access to the modification password and choose to open the file in read-only mode (indicated by [Read-Only] appended to the filename on the title bar), you can review the file and print its worksheets, but you can't save any editing changes that you make to it. If you try to save changes with the File⇨Save command, Excel displays an alert dialog box indicating that the file you're working with is read-only (see Figure 38-7).

• **Figure 38-7: The alert dialog box that appears when you try to save a file opened as read-only.**

After you click OK to close this alert dialog box, Excel opens the Save As dialog box where you can save your changes. Rename the workbook file in the File Name text box or select a new folder in which to save the file in the Save In list box; then click Save.

Changing or deleting passwords

Sometimes you may find that having to cough up a password each time that you need to open or modify an often-used spreadsheet is just not worth all the effort. You may then decide to remove the passwords that you've assigned to a workbook. In some cases, you may just want to change the passwords assigned to open or modify the workbook (either to passwords that are easier to remember or to ones that you want to distribute to a new list of users).

To delete or change a password for opening or modifying a workbook, open the Save As dialog box (File⇨Save As) and then open the Save Options dialog box (Tools⇨General Options on the Save As dialog box's toolbar).

To delete the password to open the file, simply press the Delete key to remove all the asterisks from the Password to Open text box (automatically selected when you open the Save Options dialog box). To reassign the password, replace the current password with the new one you want to assign by typing it over the original one. Then when you click OK, you need to reenter the new password in the Confirm Password dialog box and click OK.

To delete or change the password for modifying the workbook, you follow the same procedure, except that you have to be able to successfully reproduce the password for modifying the workbook after opening it and then change or delete the password that's entered into the Password to Modify text box in the Save Options dialog box.

Finally, after closing the Save Options dialog box, you simply click the Save button in the Save As dialog box and then click the Yes button in the alert dialog box that asks you if you want to replace the existing file.

Protecting the Worksheet Against Unwanted Changes

Even spreadsheets that need to be updated on a regular basis (and therefore are not candidates for passwords to open or modify the workbooks) often need protection. This is especially true with spreadsheets where routine data entry is entrusted to users with little or no understanding of Excel's workings who, if they inadvertently replaced a formula with an entry, would have no idea how to restore it. To keep the formulas and standard text in a spreadsheet safe from such unwarranted changes, you need to protect its worksheet.

Before you rush off to take me at my word and turn protection on in all the worksheets you entrust to this type of data-entry person, you need to have a rudimentary understanding of how worksheet protection operates in Excel.

First off, be aware that any cell in any Excel workbook can have one of two different protection formats assigned to them: either locked or unlocked, and hidden or unhidden. Whenever you begin a new spreadsheet, all the cells in the workbook have the locked and unhidden protection formats assigned to them. However, this particular formatting doesn't come into play until you turn on protection in the worksheet by choosing Tools⇨Protection⇨Protect Sheet. At that time, you are then prevented from making any editing changes to all locked cells and from viewing the contents of all hidden cells on the Formula bar when they contain the cell pointer.

Practically speaking, this means that you need to go through the sheet removing the Locked protection format from all the cell ranges where you or your users still need to be able to do data entry and editing even when protection is turned on in the worksheet.

 When setting up spreadsheet templates, unlock all the cells where users need to input new data and keep locked all the cells that contain headings and formulas that never change. Then turn on worksheet protection prior to saving the file in the template file format. (See Technique 1.) Formulas and stock text in all spreadsheets generated from the template will automatically be protected but still give users access to the areas that require data entry.

Unlocking cells for data entry

To remove the Locked protection status from a cell range or nonadjacent selection, follow these steps:

1. **Select the range or ranges to be unlocked.**

To select multiple ranges to create a nonadjacent cell selection, hold down the Ctrl key as you drag through each range.

2. Choose Format⇨Cells or press Ctrl+1 to open the Format Cells dialog box.

3. Select the Protection tab and then clear the Locked check box, as shown in Figure 38-8.

4. Click OK to close the Format Cells dialog box.

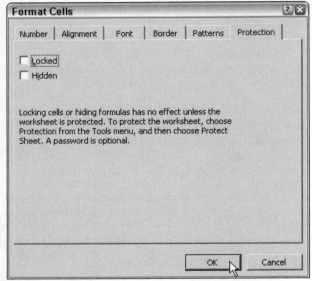

• **Figure 38-8: Unlocking cells for data entry on the Protection tab of the Format Cells dialog box.**

 Keep in mind that unlocking cells does nothing in and of itself. It's not until you turn on the protection for your worksheet that your unlocked cells work any differently from the locked ones. At that time, only unlocked cells accept the edits that you specify. (See the next section for details.)

Turning on worksheet protection

When all cell ranges where you want to allow editing are unlocked, you're ready to turn on protection. To do this, you choose Tools⇨Protection⇨Protect Sheet to open the Protect Sheet dialog box, shown in Figure 38-9.

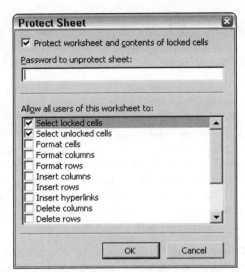

• **Figure 38-9: Enabling protection in the Protect Sheet dialog box.**

When you first open this dialog box, the following check boxes are selected:

✔ The Protect Worksheet and Contents of Locked Cells check box at the very top

✔ The Select Locked Cells and Select Unlocked Cells check boxes in the Allow All Users of This Worksheet To list box

All the other check box options (including several that are not visible without scrolling up the Allow All Users of This Worksheet To list box) are unselected.

This means that if you click OK at this point, the *only* things that you'll be permitted to do in the worksheet are to edit *unlocked* cells and to select cell ranges of any type (both locked and unlocked alike).

 If you really want to keep other users out of all the locked cells in a worksheet, clear the Select Locked Cells check box in the Allow All Users of This Worksheet To list box. That way, your users are restricted to just those unlocked ranges where you permit data input and contents editing.

Don't ever clear the Select Unlocked Cells check box and the Select Locked Cells check box at the same time. Doing so renders the worksheet completely useless by removing the cell pointer from the worksheet and making it impossible for the user to edit even the unlocked cells of the spreadsheet.

In addition to enabling users to select locked and unlocked cells in the worksheet, you can enable the following actions in the protected worksheet by selecting their check boxes in the Allow All Users of This Worksheet To list box:

- ✔ **Format Cells:** Enables the formatting of cells (with the exception of changing the locked and hidden status on the Protection tab of the Format Cells dialog box).

- ✔ **Format Columns:** Enables formatting so that users can modify the column widths and hide and unhide columns.

- ✔ **Format Rows:** Enables formatting so that users can modify the row heights and hide and unhide rows.

- ✔ **Insert Columns:** Enables the insertion of new columns in the worksheet.

- ✔ **Insert Rows:** Enables the insertion of new rows in the worksheet.

- ✔ **Insert Hyperlinks:** Enables the insertion of new hyperlinks to other documents, both local and on the Web. (See Technique 52.)

- ✔ **Delete Columns:** Enables the deletion of columns in the worksheet.

- ✔ **Delete Rows:** Enables the deletion of rows in the worksheet.

- ✔ **Sort:** Enables the sorting of data in unlocked cells in the worksheet. (See Technique 44.)

- ✔ **Use AutoFilter:** Enables the filtering of data in the worksheet. (See Technique 45.)

- ✔ **Use Pivot Table Reports:** Enables the manipulation of pivot tables in the worksheet. (See Technique 48.)

- ✔ **Edit Objects:** Enables the editing of graphic objects, such as text boxes, embedded images, and the like, in the worksheet. (See Technique 56 for details.)

- ✔ **Edit Scenarios:** Enables the editing of what-if scenarios, including modifying and deleting them. (For details of what-if scenarios, see Technique 48.)

In addition to enabling particular actions in the protected worksheet, you can also assign a password that's required in order to remove the protections from the protected worksheet. When entering a password in the Password to Unprotect Sheet text box of the Protect Sheet dialog box, you observe the same guidelines as when assigning a password to open or to modify the workbook (a maximum of 255 characters that can consist of a combination of letters, numbers, and spaces, with the letters being case sensitive).

When you enter a password in the Password to Unprotect Sheet text box and then click OK, Excel displays the Confirm Password dialog box. Here, you must accurately reproduce the password you just entered (including upper- and lowercase letters) before Excel turns on the sheet protection and assigns the password to its removal.

 If you don't assign a password to unprotect the sheet, any user with a modicum of Excel knowledge can turn off the worksheet protection and start making all manner of changes to its contents, including wreaking havoc on its formulas. It makes little sense to turn on the protection in a worksheet if you're going to permit anybody to turn it off by simply choosing the Tools➪Protection➪Unprotect Sheet command.

Removing protection from a worksheet

When you turn on protection in a worksheet, your data input and editing are restricted solely to unlocked cells in the sheet, and you can perform only those additional actions that you enabled in the Allow Users of this Worksheet To list box. If you try to replace, delete, or otherwise modify a locked cell in the protected worksheet (assuming that the Select Locked Cells check box is selected), Excel displays an alert dialog box with the following message:

```
The cell or chart you are trying to change
is protected and therefore read-only
```

The message then goes on to tell you that to modify a protected worksheet, you must first remove the protection by choosing the Tools➪Protection➪ Unprotect Sheet command. If you've assigned a password to unprotect the sheet, the program displays the Unprotect Sheet dialog box where you must enter the password exactly as you assigned it. After you enter the correct password and click OK, Excel turns off the protection in the sheet, and you can once again make any modifications to its structure and contents in both the locked and unlocked cells.

 When you protect a worksheet, only the data and graphics on that particular sheet are protected. This means that you can mess with the contents of other sheets of the same workbook without removing protection. To protect the contents on another sheet, you need to activate it and then repeat the entire procedure for protecting it as well (including unlocking cells that need to be edited and selecting which other formatting options to enable in the worksheet and whether or not to assign a password to unprotect the sheet) before distributing the workbook.

Enabling cell range editing by certain users

If you're running Excel 2000 or 2003 on a network or a machine that's being shared with other users, you can enable the editing of individual ranges in the protected worksheet for just certain users. When you use this feature, you give particular users permission to edit particular cell ranges, provided that they can correctly provide the password you assign to that range.

To give access to particular ranges in a protected worksheet, follow these steps:

1. **Choose Tools➪Protection➪Allow Users to Edit Ranges to open the All Users to Edit Ranges dialog box, shown in Figure 38-10.**

Note that if the worksheet is currently protected, the Allow Users to Edit Ranges menu item is grayed out and unavailable. In that case, you must remove protection with the Tools➪Protection➪ Unprotect Sheet command before you follow Step 1.

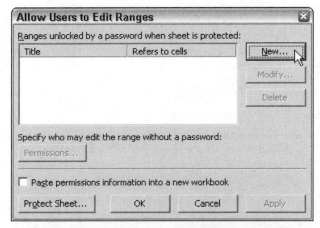

• **Figure 38-10:** Designating the unlocked ranges and the users who can edit them when the sheet is protected.

2. **Click the New button to open the New Range dialog box, shown in Figure 38-11.**

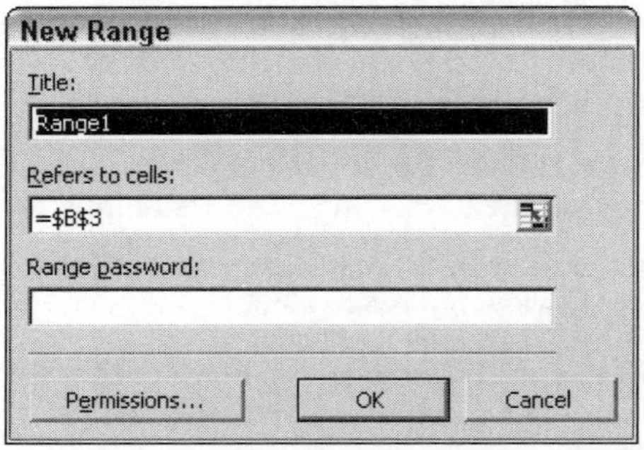

• **Figure 38-11:** Designating the first unlocked range in the New Range dialog box.

3. Type a descriptive name for the range in the Title text box (or accept the name Excel assigns to the range such as Range1, Range2, and so on).

4. Select the Refers to Cells text box and then type in the address of the cell range (without removing the = sign) or select the range or ranges in the worksheet.

If you select the range by dragging through its cells, Excel automatically reduces the New Range dialog box to the Refers to Cells list box.

5. Type in the password for accessing the range in the Range Password text box.

6. Click the Permissions button to open the Permissions for Range1 (or whatever you've named the range).

7. Click the Add button to open the Select Users or Groups dialog box, shown in Figure 38-12.

• **Figure 38-12:** Designating the users who can edit the range in the Select Users or Groups dialog box.

8. Select the name of the user in the Enter the Object Names to Select list box. To select multiple users from this list, hold down the Ctrl key as you click each user name.

If this list box is empty, click the Advanced button to expand the dialog box and then click the Find Now button to locate all the users for your location. You can then click the name or Ctrl+ click the names you want to add from this list, and then when you click OK, Excel returns you to the original form of the Select Users or Groups

dialog box and adds these names to its Enter the Object Names to Select list box.

9. Click OK in the Select Users or Groups dialog box to close it and return to the original Permissions dialog box.

10. Click the name of the first user who must know the password and then select the Deny check box in the Permissions For list box. (See Figure 38-13.)

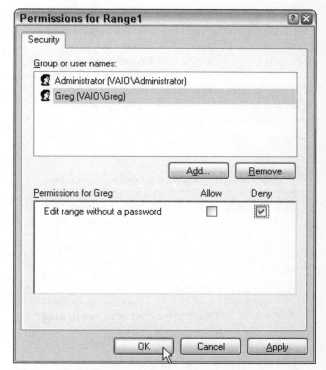

• **Figure 38-13:** Designating which users must have the password in order to edit the range.

11. Repeat Step 10 for each user who must know the password and then click OK.

Excel then displays a warning alert dialog box, letting you know that you're setting a deny permission that takes precedence over any allows entries. That mean that if the person is a member of two groups, one with an allow entry and the other with a deny entry, the deny entry permission rules (meaning that the user must know the range password).

12. Click the Yes button in the Security alert dialog box to close it and return to the New Range dialog box.

13. Click OK in the New Range dialog box to close it and open the Confirm Password dialog box.

14. Type the range password in the Reenter Password to Proceed text box and then click OK to close it and return to the Allow Users to Edit Ranges dialog box.

The Allow Users to Edit Ranges dialog box now contains the name and reference of the new range you just specified as one that can be unlocked when the worksheet is protected, as shown in Figure 38-14.

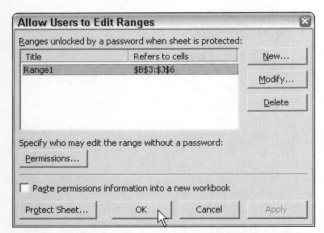

• **Figure 38-14: Allow Users to Edit Ranges dialog box with the first range unlocked by password.**

If you need to define other ranges available to other users in the worksheet, you can do so by repeating Steps 2 through 14.

When you finish adding ranges to the Allow Users to Edit Ranges dialog box, you're ready to protect the worksheet. If you want to retain a record of the ranges you've defined, follow Step 15. Otherwise, skip to Step 16.

15. Select the Paste Permissions Information Into a New Workbook check box if you want to create a new workbook that contains all the permissions information.

When you select this check box, Excel creates a new workbook whose first worksheet lists all the ranges you've assigned, along with the users who may gain access by providing the range password. You can then save this workbook for your records. Note that the range password is not listed on this worksheet; if you want to add it, be sure that you password-protect the workbook so that only you can open it.

Now, you're ready to protect the worksheet. If you want to do this from within the Allow Users to Edit Ranges dialog box, click the Protect Sheet button to open the Protect Sheet dialog box. If you want to protect the worksheet later on, click OK to close the Allow Users to Edit Ranges dialog box and then choose the Tools⇨Protection⇨ Protect Sheet whenever you're ready to turn on the worksheet protection.

16. Click the Protect Sheet button to protect the worksheet; otherwise, click OK to close the Allow Users to Edit Ranges dialog box.

If you click the Protect Sheet button, Excel opens the Protect Sheet dialog box where you can set a password to unprotect the sheet as well as to select the actions that you permit all users to perform in the protected worksheet (as outlined earlier in this chapter). After you turn on protection in the worksheet, only the users you've designated are able to edit the cell range or ranges you've specified. Don't forget to supply the range password to all the users who are allowed to do editing in the range or ranges at the time you distribute the workbook to them.

Protecting the structure of the workbook file

You can apply one last level of protection to your spreadsheet files: protecting the entire workbook. When you protect the workbook, you ensure that its users can't modify the file's structure by adding, deleting, or even moving and renaming any of its worksheets. To protect your workbook, choose Tools➪Protection➪Protect Workbook to open the Protect Workbook dialog box, shown in Figure 38-15.

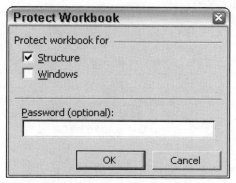

• **Figure 38-15: Protecting the workbook file from structural changes.**

The Protect Workbook dialog box contains two check boxes: Structure (which is automatically checked) and Windows (which is not selected). This dialog box also contains a Password (Optional) text box where you can enter a password that must be supplied before you can unprotect the workbook. Like every other password in Excel, the password to unprotect the workbook can be up to 255 characters — consisting of a combination of letters, numbers, and spaces, with all the letters being case sensitive — and must be replicated exactly before it is put into effect.

When you protect a workbook with the Structure check box selected, Excel prevents you from doing any of the following tasks to the file:

- ✔ Inserting new worksheets.
- ✔ Deleting existing worksheets.
- ✔ Renaming worksheets.
- ✔ Hiding or viewing hidden worksheets.
- ✔ Moving or copying worksheets to another workbook.

- ✔ Displaying the source data for a cell in a pivot table or displaying a table's page fields on separate worksheets. (See Technique 48.)

- ✔ Creating a summary report with the Scenario Manager. (See Technique 49.)

When you turn on protection for a workbook after selecting the Windows check box, Excel prevents you from changing the size or position of the workbook's windows (which is not usually something you need to control).

After you enable protection in a workbook, you can then turn it off by choosing Tools➪Protection➪ Unprotect Workbook. If you assigned a password to unprotect the workbook, you must accurately reproduce it in the Password text box in the Unprotect Workbook dialog box that appears.

Hiding Sensitive Worksheet Data

In addition to protecting locked cells from editing changes when the worksheet is protected, you can also ensure that their contents do not show up on the Formula bar when their cells contain the cell pointer. You might add this, for example, to cell ranges that contain long, complex formulas so that they don't clutter the Formula bar by adding to the busyness of the screen when you move the cell pointer through their cells. (Let's face it. Because they're protected from changes, there's really no reason to look at them anyway.)

To suppress the display of a cell range from the Formula bar, select the range, open the Protection tab of the Format Cells dialog box (Ctrl+1), select the Hidden check box, and click OK. Then turn on the worksheet protection (Tools➪Protection➪ Protect Sheet).

Don't ever select the Hidden check box on the Protection tab to hide a range of formulas when the Locked check box is not also selected. If you do, you're enabling users to replace or delete a cell's contents right at the time that its contents no longer appear on the Formula bar — a recipe for disaster!

Sometimes your spreadsheet may contain sensitive data that isn't proper for certain data-entry operators to see, either on the Formula bar when the cell pointer is in their cells or in the worksheet itself. For those cases, you not only need to assign the Hidden protection format to these cell ranges (as described above) but also need to apply a custom number format that hides the cells in the worksheet itself. (See Technique 20.)

 Be sure to lock any cell ranges that you render completely invisible in the worksheet by applying the Hidden protection format that hides their contents on the Formula bar and a custom number format that hides their display in the worksheet. This prevents users from making changes to these cells that now appear for all intents and purposes to be blank.

Technique 39

Printing Tricks for Flawless Reports

Save Time By

- Previewing the report before printing it
- Using Page Break Preview to manage page breaks
- Adding headers and footers to your report
- Adding print titles to your report
- Printing formulas in your report
- Printing charts in your report

Printing your spreadsheets is probably the most important task that you perform in Excel. This technique looks at all the little things you can do to ensure that your printed reports not only contain all the necessary information but also present it in the clearest possible manner.

Among the tricks of the spreadsheet printing trade of which you should be aware are how to use Excel's Page Preview feature — to check how the report will print and to take care of any last-minute problems with the page elements — and how to use the Page Break Preview to take care of any nasty page-break problems. This technique also covers how to use the Header and Footer feature to create custom running heads for the report as well as how to use the Print Titles feature to ensure that row and column headings from the worksheet are printed on each page of spreadsheet data. Finally, this technique looks at how to obtain a quick printout of your worksheet data showing the formulas used rather than their results so that you can check the integrity of the computations and have a printed record of them.

Making Last-Minute Adjustments with Print Preview

Using the Print Preview feature to preview your report and catch any last-minute problems saves you lots of trips to the printer and tons of wasted paper as well as affords you a way to make most of the necessary last-minute adjustments to the printout. These adjustments can include such things as resetting the margins and column widths, modifying headers and footers, and changing the page order, size, orientation, and scaling.

In Print Preview, text and graphics elements assigned to the cells in the *Print Area* (that is, the section of the current worksheet included in the printout) appear more-or-less as they will print. Unlike the standard on-screen view of the worksheet, Print Preview shows you the headers and footers defined for the report and allows you to page through the report one page at a time so that you can check the page breaks.

If you find any data errors when previewing a report, you can then edit them before you send the job to the printer by clicking the Close button to exit Print Preview and return to the normal worksheet view. If you don't find any problems, you can then send the job to the printer directly from the Print Preview window.

You can open the Print Preview window from the normal worksheet window, the Page Setup dialog box, or the Print dialog box:

✔ **From the worksheet:** Click the Print Preview button on the Standard toolbar or choose File⇨Print Preview.

✔ **From the Page Setup dialog box (File⇨Page Setup):** Click the Print Preview button on the right side of the dialog box beneath the Print button.

✔ **From the Print dialog box (File⇨Print):** Click the Preview button located in the lower-left corner of the dialog box.

When you first open the Print Preview window, the window displays a full-page view of the report's first page, as shown in Figure 39-1. To increase the page size to 100 percent, click the Zoom mouse pointer on the section of the page that you want to see in detail.

When the page is enlarged to 100 percent (see Figure 39-2), you can use the scroll bars to bring new parts of the page into view in the Print Preview window. Or, if you prefer, you can use the keyboard:

✔ To scroll up or down, press the ↑ and ↓ keys or Page Up and Page Down.

✔ To scroll left to right, press ← and → or Ctrl+Page Up and Ctrl+Page Down.

✔ To position the left edge of the page on the screen, press the Home key.

✔ To position the right edge of the page on the screen, press End.

✔ To position the upper-left corner of the page on the screen, press Ctrl+Home.

✔ To position the lower-right corner on the screen, Press Ctrl+End.

✔ To position the left, right, top, or bottom corner of the page on the screen from whatever part of the page is displayed, press Ctrl+ an arrow key (←, →, ↑, or ↓).

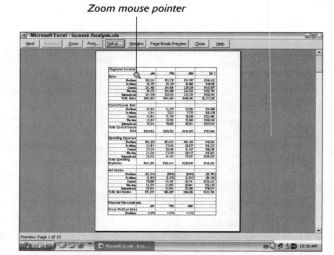

Zoom mouse pointer

• **Figure 39-1:** First page of a ten-page report in the Print Preview window.

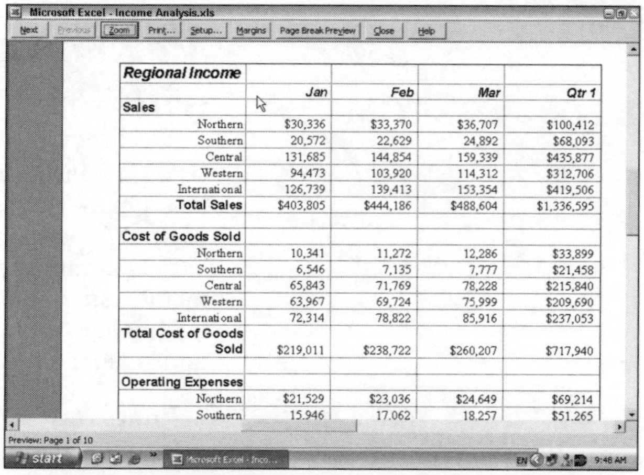

• **Figure 39-2:** First page of the report enlarged to 100 percent in the Print Preview window.

To return to full-page view in the Print Preview window, click the arrowhead pointer somewhere on the page or click the Zoom button located at the top of the Print Preview window. If your report consists of more than one page, you can view succeeding pages by clicking the Next button, located at the top of the window, or by pressing the Page Down key. To review pages that you've already seen, click the Previous button or press Page Up.

Manipulating the margins and column widths

If you detect problems with the margins as you preview the pages in your report, you can change them. Click the Margins button to display top, bottom, left, and right margin markers along with column indicators in the Print Preview window (see Figure 39-3).

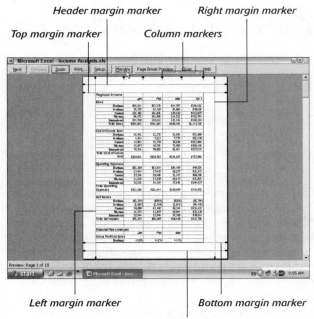

• **Figure 39-3:** Displaying the margins and column-width markers in Print Preview.

To change the margins and/or adjust the column widths, position the mouse pointer on the margin or column marker and then, when the pointer changes to a double-headed arrow, drag the marker in the appropriate direction. When you release the mouse button, Excel redraws the data on the page that you're previewing to suit the new margin settings. Note that changing the margins has no effect on the positioning of the header or footer text, only the data in the body of the report.

To change a column width, you position the mouse pointer on the marker of the column border that you want to increase or decrease and then drag it with the double-headed mouse pointer in the appropriate direction. (See Figure 39-4.) After you finish modifying the margins or column widths, remove the on-screen markers by clicking the Margins button again.

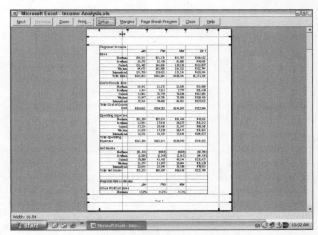

• **Figure 39-4:** Decreasing the width of the first column in Print Preview.

Manipulating the page settings

If you identify a problem with the page settings while previewing the pages of a report, you can open the Page Setup dialog box by clicking the Setup button on the Print Preview toolbar. You can then use the controls on the Page, Margins, Header/Footer, or Sheet tab to fix the problem without having to close the Print Preview window.

For example, in the first page of my previewed sample report shown in Figure 39-1, I notice that the report is going to include cell gridlines without the worksheet's row and column headings. Luckily, I can remove the cell gridlines and add back the row and column headings while still being able to see how this all looks in Print Preview. I just need to open the Sheet tab of the Page Setup dialog box and then clear the Gridlines check box and select the Row and Column Headings check box, as shown in Figure 39-5.

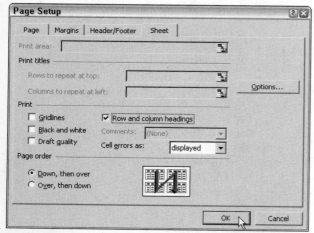

• **Figure 39-5:** Changing Print settings on the Sheet tab of the Page Setup dialog box.

Figure 39-6 shows the first page of the report in Print Preview after making these changes to the print settings on the Sheet tab and then closing the Page Setup dialog box to return to the Print Preview window.

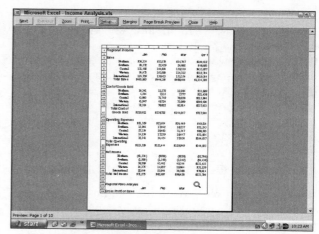

• **Figure 39-6:** First page of the report in the Print Preview window after changing some print settings.

Controlling Bad Page Breaks

Page breaks that split up important information that should appear together on the same page are probably the most prevalent type of problem you're likely to notice in the Print Preview window. Fortunately, Excel offers a variety of methods for taking care of the different sorts of paging problems that tend to crop up.

If you have page break problems for a printout that features lots of tables of data that are much wider than they are tall, often the best way to try to solve this problem is simply to change the orientation of the printed report from the default Portrait mode (where the printing runs with the short edge of the paper) to Landscape mode (where the printing runs with the long edge). To try out this solution, open the Page tab of the Page Setup dialog box (File⇨ Page Setup or the Setup button in Print Preview) and then select the Landscape option button.

Figure 39-7 shows the effect that changing from Portrait to Landscape mode has on the sample ten-page report shown in the earlier figures. In this orientation, you get several more columns of data printed on each page with fewer rows.

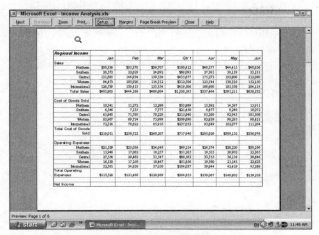

• **Figure 39-7:** Switching from Portrait to Landscape mode in the Print Preview window.

Using the Page Break Preview feature

You can use the Page Break Preview feature to try and manually adjust the bad page breaks that you identify in the report. You can access Page Break Preview from either the normal worksheet window or the Print Preview window:

- ✔ **From the normal worksheet:** Choose View⇨ Page Break Preview.

- ✔ **From the Print Preview window:** Click the Page Break Preview button on the toolbar located at the top of the window.

When you choose Page Break Preview, Excel displays the worksheet at a somewhat reduced magnification with the page breaks clearly identified in the worksheet window. Page borders appear as heavy blue dashed lines, and the page numbers appear in the middle of the page in light gray. The first time you choose Page Break Preview, Excel displays a Page Break Preview Welcome information dialog

box, shown in Figure 39-8, which informs you that you can adjust the page breaks displayed on the screen by dragging them.

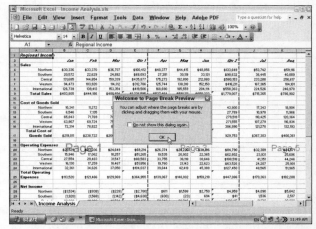

• **Figure 39-8:** Using Page Break Preview to identify and fix bad page breaks.

After closing this dialog box, you can examine the page breaks (indicated by the dotted lines) by scrolling through the worksheet. Note that you can use the Zoom button on the Standard toolbar to reduce the magnification on the worksheet even further so that you can see all the pages and the order in which they will be printed (indicated by the page numbers displayed in the center of the page).

Figure 39-9 shows the Page Break Preview display shown in Figure 39-8 after reducing the magnification setting in the Zoom control from the default 60% of normal setting to 35%. At this reduced magnification setting, the breaks for all ten pages of the report are now visible. In the Page Break Preview display at this zoom setting, you can also see clearly how Excel pages the data in your worksheet proceeding down the rows of data before going across the columns (so that all the even-numbered pages are below rather than to the right of odd-numbered pages).

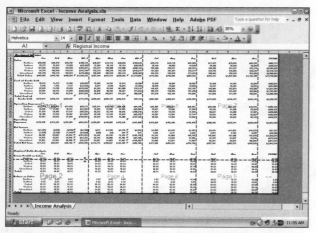

• **Figure 39-9: Page Break Preview display showing all ten pages of the report.**

After examining the page breaks in the Page Break Preview display, you can then decide which page breaks, if any, to adjust. When deciding how to adjust page breaks, keep in mind that Excel won't allow you to drag the page breaks to include more columns to the right or more rows lower in the worksheet because these represent the limit of columns and rows that fit on the page, given the current page and printing settings. (To be able to include more of these columns or rows on a page, you'd have to adjust the margin settings, column widths, or the scaling of the printing.)

To manually adjust a page break in the Page Break Preview display, drag its page border to the column or row where you want the page to break. Note that Excel distinguishes the page breaks that you adjust in the Page Break Preview display from the ones that the program put in by displaying yours as blue solid lines (rather than blue dashed lines).

After you finish adjusting the bad page breaks in the Page Break Preview display, return to the normal worksheet display by choosing View⇨Normal.

Changing the scale of the printing

Oftentimes, especially with one- or two-page printouts, you can solve paging problems by making a slight adjustment to the printing scale. Excel offers two controls for scaling the size of the printing in your report, both of which are located on the Page tab of the Page Setup dialog box, as shown in Figure 39-10.

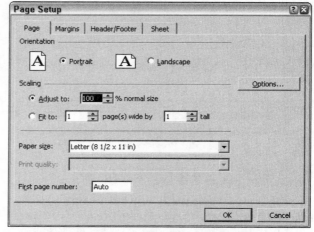

• **Figure 39-10: Adjusting the scale of the printing on the Page tab of the Page Setup dialog box.**

You can use the Adjust To option button and associated text box to set the printing at a particular magnification (between 10% and 400% of normal). When modifying the scale of the printing, you can either enter this new percentage into this text box or select it with its spin buttons.

Perhaps more practical, at least in the case of printouts with few pages, is the Fit To control, which gives Excel the responsibility for selecting the scale of the printing in order to fit a set number of pages. When you select the Fit To option button, you can then select the final number of pages in the report by designating the number of pages in the Page(s) Wide and Tall text boxes.

When deciding what values to enter or select for the Wide and Tall text boxes, refer to the original page layout that Excel came up with in the Page Break Preview display and then adjust its number of pages across (wide) and down (tall) accordingly. If, for example, you find that the original page layout had five pages across with two down and that there were just a couple of columns of data appearing alone on the last two pages (9 and 10), you could then dispense with those last two pages by selecting the Fit To option button and then entering 4 in the Page(s) Wide text box and 2 in the Tall text box. Excel would then reduce the size of the printing as necessary to achieve this new layout, and you could then verify the page breaks in this new eight-page report layout before sending it to the printer.

Adding Headings to Your Report

Running heads — headings that appear in the same position on each page of the printed report — can go a long way towards making the data and charts in your report more comprehensible to the reader. Excel supports two types of running heads in the reports you print:

- **Headers and footers:** Headings that appear in the top and bottom margins respectively on each page of the report.

- **Print titles:** Headings that repeat rows and columns from the worksheet containing the actual column and row headings that identify the worksheet data in the table or list that's being printed. Print titles appear at the left and top of each page in the body of the report.

Headers and footers made to order

The Header/Footer tab of the Page Setup dialog box (see Figure 39-11) contains the controls for defining or removing a header and footer from the printed report. The *header* contains the information that

you want printed at the top of every page of the report, and the *footer* contains the information that you want printed at the bottom of each page. Note that Excel doesn't automatically assign either a header or footer when you first print a report from a workbook.

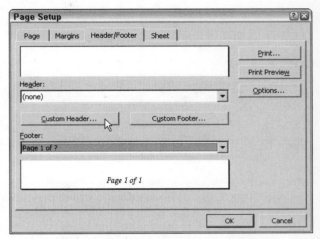

• **Figure 39-11: Defining a header and footer on the Header/Footer tab of the Page Setup dialog box.**

When assigning a header or footer for your report, you can either select one of the stock headings (such as those that print the current page number or date, or those that print the name of the workbook or worksheet, and so forth) or create a custom heading of your own. To select a stock heading on the Header/Footer tab, click the heading in the Header and/or Footer drop-down list box to replace the default setting of (none).

To create a custom heading for the header and/or footer, click the Custom Header or Custom Footer button on this tab to open the respective Header or Footer dialog box. Figure 39-12 shows the Header dialog box. (The Footer dialog box is almost a carbon copy of the Header dialog box.) As you can see, a custom header and footer can consist of up to three parts:

✔ A Left Section in which all the items are left-justified

✔ A Center Section in which the elements are centered between the left and right margins

✔ A Right Section in which they are right-justified

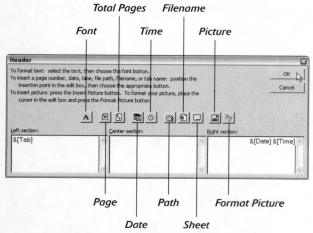

• **Figure 39-12:** Defining a custom header for a report in the Header dialog box.

When you create a custom header or footer, you can mix your text with stock information, such as the current page number, total number of pages, date, path to the folder containing the file, workbook filename, and worksheet name. To do this, click the insertion point in the section where you want to add text and then type your text interspersed with the stock information whose code you insert. To insert the code for a piece of stock information, click the appropriate button in the Header or Footer dialog box. (Refer to Figure 39-12.)

Table 39-1 shows you the codes that Excel inserts into the text of your custom header or footer when you click the various buttons in the Header or Footer dialog box. Note that when you click the Font button, Excel opens the Font dialog box where you can select a new font, font size, or font style for the

selected text without inserting any codes into the current section of the custom header or footer.

TABLE 39-1: HEADER AND FOOTER CODES

Button	Code	What It Does
Page Number	&[Page]	Inserts current page number
Total Pages	&[Pages]	Inserts the total number of pages
Date	&[Date]	Inserts current date in the form 9/15/04
Time	&[Time]	Inserts current time in the form 10:02 AM
Path	&[Path]	Inserts the complete pathname for the file in the form C:\mydocuments\finances\budget04
Filename	&[File]	Inserts the workbook filename
Sheet	&[Tab]	Inserts the worksheet name
Picture	&[Picture]	Inserts the graphic image you select

Also note that when you click the Picture button, Excel opens the Insert Picture dialog box, where you choose the graphics file whose image you want to appear in the header or footer (normally a logo or other mark that fits well within the top or bottom margin). This file is represented in the header or footer by the &[Picture] code. When you click the Format Picture button (available only after you've inserted the &[Picture] code in the header or footer), Excel opens the Format Picture dialog box, which enables you to modify the image's size and appearance.

Print titles on every page

You can use the text boxes in the Print Titles section on the Sheet tab of the Page Setup dialog box to add row and column headings from tables in a worksheet as headings that appear on each page of the report. Select the Rows to Repeat at Top text box and then select the row(s) in the worksheet that contain the column headings you want to appear in the upper portion of each page. Select the Columns to Repeat at Left text and then select the column(s) in the worksheet that contain the row headings you want to appear on the left side of each page.

Figures 39-13 and 39-14 illustrate the use of both a row and column print title in a report. In Figure 39-13, I designate rows 1 and 2, which contain the worksheet title and the column headings respectively — as the row print titles. I also designate column A, which contains the row headings for the Income Analysis table, as the column print titles.

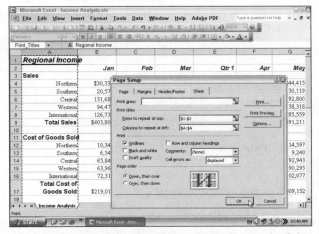

• **Figure 39-13:** Defining print titles on the Sheet tab of the Page Setup dialog box.

Figure 39-14 shows the result. Here, you see the third page of the six-page report in the Print Preview window after designating rows 1 and 2 as the row print titles and column A as the column print titles. As you can see, column print titles repeated from the first page of the report immediately identify the type of the income and expenditure just as the row print titles identify the time frame.

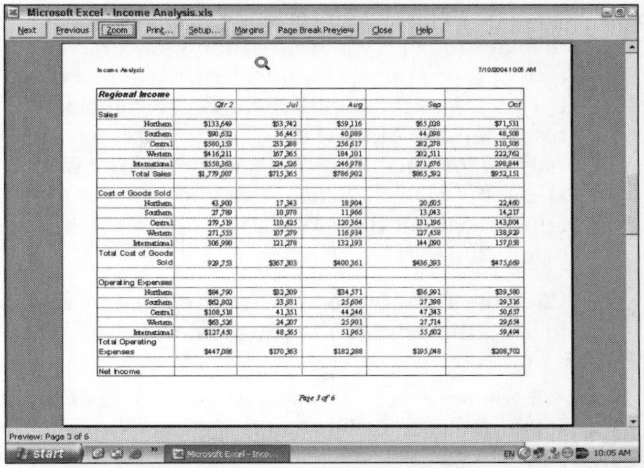

• **Figure 39-14:** Preview of Page 3 of the report showing the row and column print titles.

Printing the Formulas in the Report

Normally, whenever you print a worksheet, Excel prints the entries exactly as they appear in their cells of the worksheet. As a result, when you print a section of worksheet that contains formulas, the printout shows only the results of the calculations performed by the formulas and not the contents of the formulas themselves. In addition to a printout showing the results, you may also want to print a hard copy of the worksheet showing all the formulas by which these results were derived. You can then use this printout of the formulas when double-checking the formulas in the worksheet to make sure that they're designed correctly.

To print a copy of the worksheet with the formulas displayed in the cells, follow these steps:

1. Choose Tools⇨Options to open the Options dialog box.

2. Select the View tab, select the Formulas check box, and click OK.

When the Formulas check box is selected, Excel displays the entry in each cell in the worksheet as it appears on the formula (as well as the Formula Auditing toolbar which you can close by clicking its Close button). In this state, not only do formulas appear as entered in the worksheet, but also all values (text and numeric) appear without their formatting, as shown in Figure 39-15.

3. Click the Print button on the Standard toolbar to send the print job to the printer.

If you need to print only a particular area of the worksheet, select that range and then designate that section as the Print Area (File⇨Print Area⇨Print Area) before you click the Print button on the Standard toolbar.

Figure 39-15 shows the Production Schedule sample worksheet after displaying its formulas. Note that Excel automatically adjusts the column widths to display the contents of their formulas and displays the Formula Auditing toolbar (which I docked above the Formula bar). Note too, that the program automatically replaces all formatted numbers with their raw values, including the dates in row 2 that now display their serial numbers. (Excel restores all number formatting as soon as you clear the Formulas check box.)

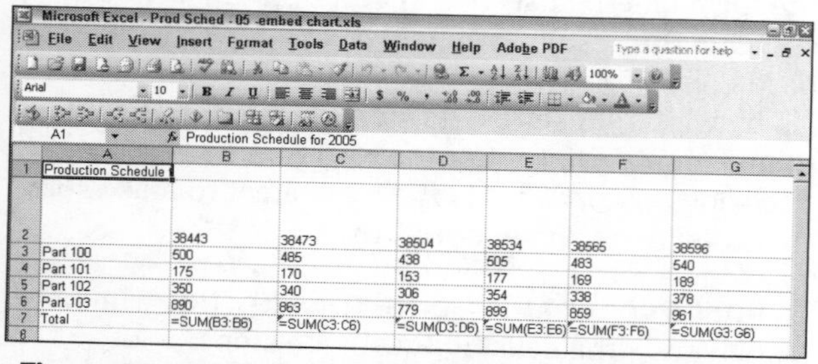

• Figure 39-15: Worksheet table after displaying the formulas in the worksheet.

After printing the formulas in the worksheet, you can return the worksheet to its Normal view without the formulas displayed in the cells by clearing the Formulas check box on the View tab of the Options

dialog box. Excel returns the worksheet display to normal so that only the results of formulas are displayed in the cells and all entries are displayed with their formatting.

You can instantly switch between displaying and hiding formulas in a worksheet by pressing the Ctrl+` keyboard shortcut — Ctrl plus the accent key with the tilde (~) symbol above it. This shortcut acts as a toggle; the first time you press it, all formulas are displayed in the cells of your worksheet, and the second time you press it, they are once again hidden.

To help you identify the cell reference of each formula in your printout, print the version of the worksheet that displays the formulas in the cells with the column letters and row numbers on the top row and leftmost column of each page. To do this, you need to open Sheet tab of the Page Setup dialog box (File⇨Page Setup) and select the Row and Column Headings check box. Then you can print the worksheet by clicking the Print button in the Page Setup dialog box or, if you need to return to the worksheet to display the formulas in the worksheet before sending the job to printer, click the dialog box's Close button instead.

Printing the Charts in the Report

To print an embedded chart as part of the surrounding data on the same worksheet, you simply print the worksheet (File⇨Print or Ctrl+P). To print an embedded chart by itself without the supporting worksheet data, click the chart to select it and then choose File⇨Print. Note that you can also print the embedded chart by putting it in its own window (right-click on the embedded chart and then select Chart Window on its shortcut menu) before you select the Print command. (See Figure 39-16.) To print a chart that's on a separate chart sheet, activate its chart sheet tab and then choose File⇨Print or press Ctrl+P.

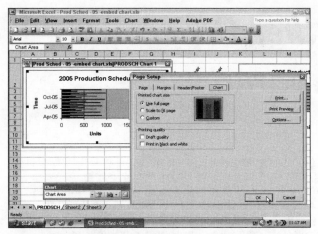

• **Figure 39-16: Getting ready to print an embedded chart in its own chart window.**

When printing a chart alone — that is, without its supporting data or in its own chart sheet or chart window — the Page Setup dialog box includes a Chart tab that contains its own special chart printing options:

✔ **Use Full Page:** Click this option button to print to scale the chart so that it takes up the entire page.

✔ **Scale to Fit Page:** Click this option button to have Excel scale the chart so that it prints on the page size you've selected.

✔ **Custom:** Click this option button to print the chart in the size it assumes on the screen.

✔ **Draft Quality:** Select this check box to print the chart by using your printer's draft-quality setting.

✔ **Print in Black and White:** Select this check box to have your color printer print the chart in black and white.

Note that when you place an embedded chart in its own chart window (refer to Figure 39-16), you can open the Page Setup dialog box to change these print settings on the Chart tab by right-clicking on the title bar and then clicking Page Setup on the window's shortcut menu.

Technique 40

Sharing Data with Other Office Programs

This technique covers data sharing between Excel and other Windows programs that you or your coworkers use. In many cases, data sharing involves getting Excel data tables, data lists, and charts into other Office programs that you use, especially Microsoft Word documents and PowerPoint presentations. In other cases, data sharing involves getting data generated in other programs, such as in tables and lists created in Microsoft Word and contacts maintained in Microsoft Outlook, into an Excel worksheet.

Sometimes, data sharing involves importing text files into Excel worksheets. As part of this process, you *parse* the text entries — that is, you tell Excel how to split up the individual pieces of information in each line of the text file so that these items are entered into separate cells (making it possible to sort and filter the list by various data items).

Swapping Data via the Clipboard

The key to swapping blocks of data or discrete objects in or out of Excel is the Windows Clipboard. Excel gives you access to contents of the Clipboard in the form of the Clipboard task pane, which you can quickly open by pressing Ctrl+CC (that is two Cs in a row all the while holding down the Ctrl key).

With the Clipboard task pane open, you can copy its objects or blocks of text into cells of the open worksheet simply by clicking the item in this task pane. Figures 40-1 and 40-2 illustrate this situation. Figure 40-1 shows the Clipboard task pane open in a new worksheet window. At this time, the Clipboard contains four items: a URL copied from Internet Explorer, a list of names from a Word document, an endless knot, and a Mind Over Media logo graphic copied from a PowerPoint presentation.

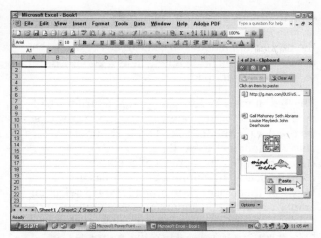

• **Figure 40-1:** Open the Clipboard task pane to see the contents of the Windows Clipboard.

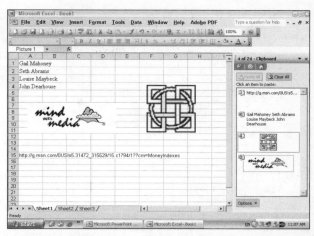

• **Figure 40-2:** Worksheet after importing various Clipboard objects into a new worksheet.

Figure 40-2 shows the new worksheet after pasting all four Clipboard objects into the new worksheet. (To do this, you simply click each object in the Clipboard task pane.) As you can see, Windows pasted the four names entered on separate lines of the Word document into the worksheet as separate cell entries in the range A1:A4 (A1 was the current cell when I clicked this item in the Clipboard task pane). The URL is entered in cell A15 as a long text entry when that cell was current, and the two graphic files were pasted in as sizable and movable graphic objects as Excel saw fit.

In addition to using the Windows Clipboard to paste information into an Excel spreadsheet from other Windows programs, you can also use the Clipboard to take worksheet data and charts from a spreadsheet for use in another Windows program. Figures 40-3 and 40-4 illustrate this situation.

Figure 40-3 shows the CG Media 2004 Sales worksheet after copying the table of data in the range A1:F11 (with the first quarter sales figures) and the embedded chart directly beneath it into the Windows Clipboard (shown as the first two items in the Clipboard task pane on the right).

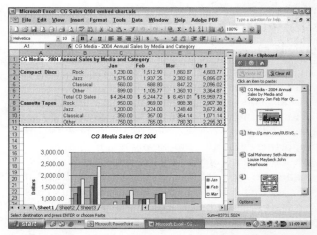

• **Figure 40-3:** Copying Excel data and an embedded chart to the Windows Clipboard.

Figure 40-4 shows the 2003 Word window after pasting the worksheet data and accompanying chart from Word's Clipboard task pane into a new document. As you can see, Word automatically formats the Excel worksheet data as a Word table, while taking the Excel Clustered Column chart in as a separate graphic object that you can resize and move within the document.

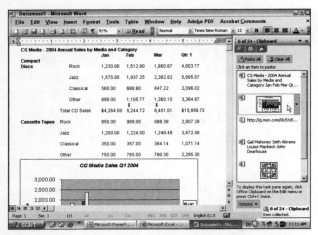

• **Figure 40-4:** New Word document after pasting in the Excel worksheet data and chart.

Importing Text Files into Excel

Text files used to be the preferred format for data sharing on personal computers — way back in the Dark Ages before the universal adoption of Microsoft Windows on the PC platform and the widespread use of the Internet. Therefore, it should come as no surprise to find out that Excel is totally at home with importing data from almost any text file. To do this job, Excel relies on its Text Import Wizard, which enables you to tell Excel exactly how to split up the data on each line of the text file into separate cells in the worksheet (a process technically known as *parsing* the text file).

Most text files containing lists of related data use some sort of standard character to separate each data item (such as a comma or tab) in every line, just as the file uses the character representing the pressing of the Enter key to mark the separation of each line of data within the file. Those text files that use the comma to separate data items are known as *CSV (comma-separated values) files.* Those that use

tabs to separate the individual data items are known as *tab-delimited files.* Note that some programs use the term *delimited files* to refer to any text file that uses a standard character, such as a comma or tab, to separate its individual data items.

The Text Import Wizard analyzes the structure of incoming text files to help you determine how to split up the data in the text file. The Text Import Wizard always imports the text data into the current worksheet starting at the active cell and then uses as many subsequent columns and rows as are necessary. For this reason, you should always select an empty cell at the beginning of a blank region in the worksheet (or better yet, in a blank worksheet) before you try to open a text file, a process that automatically launches the Text Import Wizard. That way, you never run the risk of the incoming text file data wiping out existing data in the worksheet.

To use the Text Import Wizard, follow these steps:

1. **Open the text file in the Open dialog box (File⇨Open) as you would any bona fide Excel file.**

   Remember that to display the text files in one of the folders on your computer, you must select Text Files (*.prn; *.txt; *.csv) in the Files of Type drop-down menu. (By default, the Excel Open dialog box shows only the Excel files in a folder.)

   Note that Excel displays an alert dialog box indicating that the program cannot load the file directly and telling you to click OK to open the file in a different format.

2. **Click OK in the alert dialog box.**

   The Text Import Wizard - Step 1 of 3 dialog box appears, as shown in Figure 40-5.

   In the Step 1 of 3 dialog box, the Text Import Wizard analyzes the data in the text to try and determine whether or not it separates the data item with some sort of delimiting character.

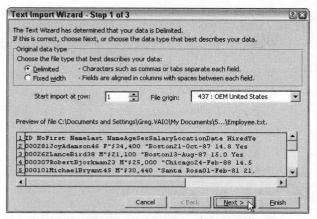

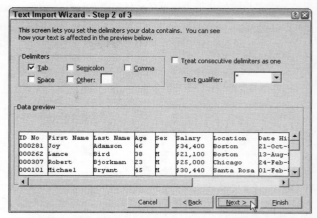

• **Figure 40-5:** Selecting between a delimited and fixed width text file in the Text Import Wizard.

• **Figure 40-6:** Previewing the way the text information is parsed into columns.

3. If the wizard decides the file uses some sort of delimiting character, Excel selects the Delimited options button. If, instead, you're dealing with a text file in which the data items all use the same number of characters (such as 11 spaces for SSN and 10 spaces for ID number), click the Fixed Width options button.

4. The Text Import Wizard always assumes that you want to start importing the data from the first to the very last line in the text file. If you don't need the first line or lines imported, use the preview list box to determine the number of the first line to import and then enter that number in the Start Import at Row text box.

You may not want to import the first line few lines if they contain stuff like document titles that you'd only have to eliminate from the worksheet if you did bring them in.

5. Click Next when you're finished in the Step 1 of 3 dialog box.

The Text Import Wizard - Step 2 of 3 dialog box appears, as shown in Figure 40-6. This dialog box contains a Data Preview section that shows your text data aligned (simulating the column arrangement in your Excel worksheet).

6. Select the delimiting character in the event that the wizard selects the wrong character in the Delimiters section:

▶ If your text file uses a custom delimiting character, select the Other check box and then enter that character in its text box.

▶ If your file uses two consecutive characters (such as a comma and a space), select both of their check boxes as well as the Treat Consecutive Delimiters as One check box.

7. The Text Import Wizard treats any characters enclosed in a pair of double quotes as text entries (as opposed to numbers). If your text file uses a single quote, click the single quote (') character in the Text Qualifier drop-down list box. Then click Next.

The Text Import Wizard - Step 3 of 3 dialog box appears, as shown in Figure 40-7. In this dialog box, you can assign a data format to the various columns of text data or indicate that a particular column of data should be skipped and therefore not imported into your Excel worksheet.

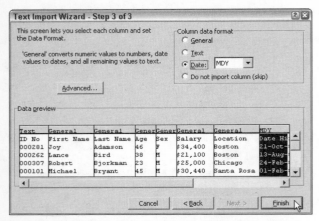

• **Figure 40-7:** Assigning a data format to the columns of parsed data.

8. **To assign a data type to a column, click its column in the Data Preview section and then click the appropriate option button (General, Text, or Date) in the Column Data Format section in the upper-right corner.**

You can choose among the following three data types:

▶ **General** (the default) to convert all numeric values to numbers, entries recognized as date values to dates, and everything else in the column to text

▶ **Text** to convert all the entries in the column to text

▶ **Date** to convert all the entries to dates by using the date format shown in the associated drop-down list box

In determining values when using the General data format, Excel uses the period (.) as the decimal separator and the comma (,) as the thousands separator. If your text data uses these two symbols in the opposite order (the comma to indicate the decimal point and the period as the thousands separator), as is the case in many European countries, follow these steps:

i. Click the Advanced button to open the Advanced Text Import Settings dialog box.

ii. Select the comma (,) in the Decimal Separator drop-down list box and the period (.) in the Thousands Separator drop-down list box and then click OK.

If your text file uses trailing minus signs (as in 100-) to represent negative numbers (instead of -100), make sure that the Trailing Minus for Negative Numbers check box is selected before you close this dialog box.

9. **If you want to change the date format in a column to which you've assigned the Date data format, select its MDY code in the Date drop-down list box (where *M* stands for the month, *D* for the day, and *Y* for the year).**

10. **To omit a particular column when importing the text file, click its column in the Data Preview and then click the Do Not Import Column (Skip) option button at the bottom of the Column Data Format section.**

11. **After you've formatted all the columns as you want them, click Finish to import and parse the text file data starting at the current cell.**

Figure 40-8 shows the rows of the imported and parsed text data that appear in the new worksheet starting at cell A.

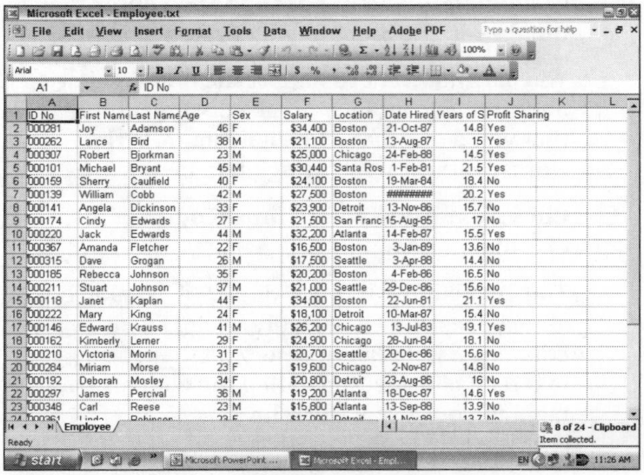

• **Figure 40-8:** New worksheet with parsed data.

Don't forget to change the type of file from text to Microsoft Excel Workbook when you first save your imported text file. Choose File⇨Save As from the Excel menu bar, select Microsoft Excel Workbook (*.xls) in the Save as Type drop-down list box, and click Save.

Embedding Excel Data in Other Office Documents

Because almost everybody purchases Excel as part of the Microsoft Office suite nowadays, it should come as no surprise to discover that most of the file sharing that takes place between Excel and other programs ends up being between Excel and one of the other major Microsoft Office applications such as Word, PowerPoint, and Access.

When sharing Excel data with another type of Office document, Microsoft offers you a choice in the way that you exchange the application data. You can either *embed* the worksheet or chart in the other program's document or set up a *link* between the Excel-generated object in the other program and Excel itself:

- ✔ **Embedding** means that the Excel object (whether it's a worksheet or a chart) actually becomes part of the Word document or PowerPoint presentation. Any changes that you then need to make to the worksheet or chart must be made within the Word document or PowerPoint presentation. This presupposes that you have Excel on the same computer as Word or PowerPoint and that your computer has enough memory to run them both.

- ✔ **Linking** means that the Excel object (worksheet or chart) is only referred to in the Word document or PowerPoint presentation. Any changes that you make to the worksheet or chart must be made in Excel. They are then automatically updated in the Word document or PowerPoint presentation to which it is linked when you open the document and/or presentation.

I recommend the embedding method when the Excel object (worksheet or chart) is not apt to change very often, if at all. Reserve the linking method for an Excel object that changes fairly often, when you always need the latest and greatest version of the object to appear in the other program's document, or when you don't want to make that document any larger by actually embedding and saving the Excel data in it.

 Use the embedding or linking techniques only when you're pretty sure that the Excel data is far from final and that you need to be able to update the data either manually (with embedding) or automatically (with linking). If your Excel data is bound to remain unchanged, just use the old standby method of copying the Excel data to the Clipboard and then pasting it in place in the other program's document. (See "Swapping Data via the Clipboard," earlier in this technique.)

Embedded worksheet data

The easiest way to embed a table of worksheet data or a chart in another Office document is to use the good old drag-and-drop method. Just drag the selected cells or chart from Excel to their place in the other open Office program window. The only trick to dragging and dropping the data is getting the windows set up. (You can set up the windows after opening the Excel workbook and the other Office document by choosing the Tiles Windows Horizontally or the Tile Windows Vertically items on the task bar's shortcut menu.)

Figures 40-9 and 40-10 illustrate the procedure for embedding a table of worksheet data (with January sales for the Mission Street store) from its worksheet (named Mission Street) in a memo started in a new Word document. After selecting the table in range A1:B6 in the Excel window, I dragged this selection to the beginning of a new paragraph in the Word memo. (Hold down the Ctrl key to copy the data rather than move it from Excel to Word.)

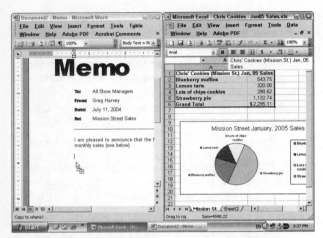

• **Figure 40-9:** Dragging a table of worksheet data to embed it in a new Word memo.

Figure 40-10 shows the memo after dropping the copied worksheet table into place at the beginning of a new paragraph in the Word window. Note that the table with the worksheet data contains cell gridlines just like the worksheet from which it was copied.

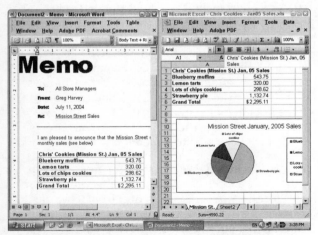

• **Figure 40-10:** Word memo after embedding the worksheet table.

 If you don't want gridlines to appear in the worksheet data that you copy to the Word document, you need to remove their display in the Excel window before you do the drag-and-drop. To remove gridlines from a worksheet, clear the Gridlines check box on the View tab of the Options dialog box (Tools⇨Options).

The really cool thing about embedding Excel stuff is that you can edit the data from within Word. Figure 40-11 shows the copied table after I indented it with the Increase Indent button on Word's Formatting toolbar. This figure shows what happens when I double-click the embedded table: A frame with columns and rows, scroll bars, and sheet tabs appears around the table. Notice, also, that the pull-down menus and toolbars in the Word window have miraculously changed to Excel's menus complete with the Excel Standard and Formatting toolbars. (It's like being at home when you're still on the road.) At this point, you can edit the table's contents in Word by using the Excel commands with which you're thoroughly familiar.

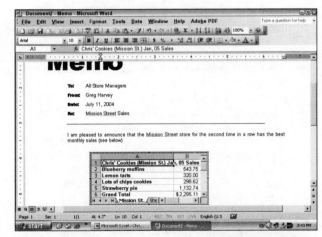

• **Figure 40-11:** Editing the embedded worksheet table in Word.

Linking worksheet data

As cool as embedding is, you do find occasions when linking the Excel data to the Word document is the preferred method and is, in fact, even easier to do. Remember that when you link the worksheet data or charts that you paste into other Office documents, changes made to the data or charts in the original worksheet are automatically updated if the document is open at the time you make the modifications in Excel; otherwise, you're prompted to update the links when you next open the document.

Figures 40-12 and 40-13 illustrate how the linking process works. For this example, I want to copy the pie chart showing the January 2005 sales at the Mission Street store into the Word memo, while at the same time create a link between this copy of the chart and the worksheet from which it came. To create this link, I follow these steps:

1. **Select the pie chart and then copy it to the Clipboard (Ctrl+C).**

2. **Switch to the Word memo, position the Insertion point cursor at the beginning of a new paragraph, and choose Edit⇨Paste Special on the Word menu bar.**

    Doing this opens the Paste Special dialog box, shown in Figure 40-12.

3. **To create the link, select the Paste Link option button and then click OK to paste the copy of the pie chart into place in the memo.**

Figure 40-13 shows what happens after I update the embedded chart in the original Chris' Cookies worksheet, changing its chart type from the normal two-dimensional pie chart to a three-dimensional pie chart. As you can see, this chart-type change is immediately reflected in the chart in the Word memo when I switch from Excel to Word.

Suppose that the Office document into which you've linked the Excel data or graphic object is not open at the time you update the workbook to which it is linked. When you next open the document with its Office program, an alert dialog box appears, indicating that the document contains links and asking you if you want to update the document with data from the linked files. All you have to do is to click the Yes button to have the worksheet data or chart in the open document updated so that it reflects its current state in the original Excel workbook.

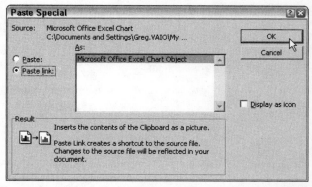

• **Figure 40-12:** Linking a chart being pasted into the Word memo with its original worksheet.

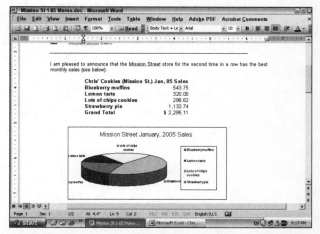

• **Figure 40-13:** Changes made to the original pie chart are automatically updated in the Word memo.

Technique 41

Sharing Workbooks on a Network

Save Time By

✔ Turning on file sharing for a workbook

✔ Setting up the workbook share options

✔ Merging changes from different users

If you use Excel on a computer connected to a network, you can share the spreadsheets that you create with other users who have network access. Workbook sharing is perfect for spreadsheets that require frequent or regular data updates, especially those whose data comes from several departments. For example, spreadsheets that track budgets or schedule projects that rely on input from many departments can benefit from workbook sharing.

This technique covers the different ways you can share a workbook so that different people can edit its contents at the same time. It also covers how to set the sharing options that control how Excel handles conflicting updates that users make to the same cells of a worksheet.

Let's All Learn to Share

To facilitate workbook sharing, start by saving the spreadsheet file in a folder on a network drive to which everyone that needs to edit the spreadsheet has access. After doing that, you can turn on workbook sharing in one of the following ways:

✔ Set up file sharing for the workbook by choosing Tools⇨ Share Workbook.

✔ Turn on change tracking for the workbook by choosing the Tools⇨Track Changes⇨Highlight Changes.

Whenever you use one of these methods to share a workbook, Excel indicates that the workbook is now shared by appending [Shared] to the workbook's filename as it appears on the title bar of the Excel program window. When a second person on another computer on the network opens the shared workbook file, Excel opens a copy of the workbook file, and the [Shared] indicator also appears on the title bar of his or her Excel program window appended to its filename.

This is different from the way Excel treats a regular, unshared workbook on your computer. When you try to open an unshared file that's already open, Excel displays a File in Use alert dialog box informing you that the workbook you want to open is already open. You can then choose between just opening the file in read-only mode (in which you can't save your changes under the original filename) and having the program first open the file in read-only mode and then notify you when the other person closes the workbook so you can save your changes.

 All users don't have to be running the latest or the same version of Excel on their computers in order to edit a shared workbook. Workbook sharing is supported by Excel versions 97 through 2003. (You can't save changes to a shared workbook when using any earlier version of Excel.) Also, when you make changes to a shared workbook, Excel uses your user name to identify the modifications that you made. To modify your user name, edit the name in the User Name text box on the General tab of the Options dialog box (Tools⇨Options).

Editing changes not available to a shared workbook

When you share a workbook, Excel disables some of the program's editing features so they're not available when making changes to the shared spreadsheet. The following tasks are disabled in a shared workbook:

- Deleting worksheets from the workbook

- Merging cells in the worksheets of a workbook

- Applying conditional formats to the cells of the worksheets (although any conditional formats assigned before you share the workbook remain in effect)

- Setting up or applying data validation to cells of the worksheets (although all data validations restrictions and messages assigned before you share the workbook remain in effect)

- Inserting or deleting blocks of cells in a worksheet (although you can insert or delete entire columns and rows from the sheet)

- Drawing shapes and adding text boxes with the tools on the Drawing toolbar

- Assigning passwords for protecting individual worksheets or the entire workbook (although all protection and passwords assigned prior to sharing the workbook remain in effect)

- Grouping or outlining data in a worksheet

- Inserting automatic subtotals in a worksheet

- Creating data tables or pivot tables in a worksheet

- Creating, revising, or assigning macros (although you can run macros that were created in the worksheet before it was shared, provided that these macros don't perform any operations that aren't supported in a shared workbook)

Sharing a workbook

The first way to share a workbook is by turning on file sharing as follows:

1. **Open the workbook you want to share.**

Remember to save the workbook you want to share in a folder on your network so it's available to all the potential users.

2. **Choose Tools⇨Share Workbook to open the Share Workbook dialog box, shown in Figure 41-1.**

The Share Workbook dialog box contains two tabs:

- ▶ The Editing tab, which enables you to turn on file sharing and shows you all the users who have the file open

- ▶ The Advanced tab, where you control how long changes are tracked and how updates are handled

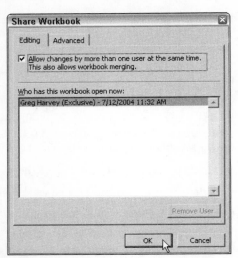

• **Figure 41-1:** Turning on file sharing by allowing changes by more than one user.

3. On the Editing tab, select the Allow Changes by More Than One User at the Same Time check box.

4. To change the settings that affect how long a change log is maintained and how editing conflicts are handled, select the Advanced tab and use those options.

By default, Excel maintains a Change History log for 30 days. If you wish, you can modify whether or not Excel maintains this Change History log at all (necessary if you want to reconcile and merge changes), or you can just change how long the program saves this log.

You can also change when changes are updated, how conflicts are handled, and whether or not your print settings and data-filtering settings are shared. See the following section, "Setting your sharing options," for more on modifying these options.

5. Click OK to close the Share Workbook dialog box.

An alert dialog box appears, indicating that Excel is about to save the workbook and asking you if you want to continue.

6. Click OK in the alert dialog box to save the workbook with the file-sharing settings.

Upon closing the alert dialog box and saving the workbook, the [Shared] indicator is appended to the filename that appears in the title bar of the Excel program window.

Setting your sharing options

After you turn on file sharing for a workbook, Excel creates a Change History log that records all the changes made by different individuals to the same workbook file. You can then use the Change History log to review the various changes made to a shared workbook and to determine which changes to retain in the event that conflicting changes are made to the same cells. You can also use this log when merging changes from different copies of the same workbook into a single file.

By default, Excel maintains the Change History log for a period of 30 days from the date that you first share the workbook. If you wish, you can change the length of time that Excel maintains the Change History log or even, in rare circumstances, elect to not keep the log. To make changes to the length of time that Excel maintains the Change History log and make other changes to the sharing settings, select the Advanced tab of the Share Workbook dialog box, shown in Figure 41-2.

The Advanced tab is divided into the following sections, each with its own options for not only changing how long the Change History log is maintained but also when and how updates are handled:

- ✔ **Track Changes:** Enables you to modify how long Excel keeps the Change History log. Just enter a new value in the Keep Change History For text box or select a new value with the spin buttons. Select the Don't Keep Change History option button if you don't need the Change History log.

- ✔ **Update Changes:** Determines when changes made by different users are saved. By default, Excel saves changes when the file is saved. To have the program save changes at a set interval, select the Automatically Every option button and then enter the number of minutes for the save interval in the Minutes text box or select it with the spin buttons.

When automatically saving changes at a set time interval, by default Excel saves only your changes while showing you changes made to the workbook by others. To have the program display the changes made to the file by others when the save interval is reached and not save your changes, select the Just See Other Users' Changes option button.

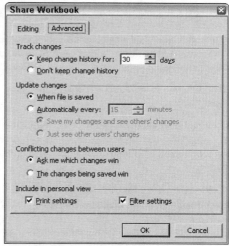

• **Figure 41-2:** Modifying the file-sharing settings on the Advanced tab of Share Workbook dialog box.

✔ **Conflicting Changes between Users:** Determines how changes made to the same cells of a shared workbook by different users are treated. By default, Excel asks you which user's changes to accept and which to deny. If you want Excel to accept the changes made by any user at the time she or he saves the workbook, select The Changes Being Saved Win option button.

✔ **Include in Personal View:** Determines which of your personal settings are saved when you save the workbook. By default, Excel saves both your

personal print settings (including such things as page breaks, changes to the print area, and changes to the printing settings in the Page Setup dialog box) and the filtering settings you select with the Data⇨Filter command. Clear the Print Settings and/or Filter Settings check boxes if you don't want these settings saved as part of the shared workbook.

Turning on change tracking

The other way to share a workbook on your network is simply by turning on change tracking. When you do this, Excel tracks all the changes you make to the shared workbook's cells by highlighting the cells and adding comments that summarize the type of change you make. Whenever you enable change tracking, Excel automatically turns on file sharing and creates a Change History log for the workbook in which the changes are recorded.

To share a workbook by turning on change tracking, follow these steps:

1. **Open the workbook for which you want to track changes.**

This assumes that you've already saved the workbook in a folder on your network that's available to all the potential users.

2. **Choose Tools⇨Track Changes⇨Highlight Changes to open the Highlight Changes dialog box, shown in Figure 41-3.**

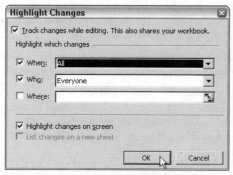

• **Figure 41-3:** Sharing a workbook by turning on change tracking.

3. **Select the Track Changes While Editing check box.**

By default, Excel selects the When combo box and chooses the All option from its pop-up menu to have all changes made to the workbook tracked. Excel also selects the Who combo box and chooses Everyone from the pop-up menu, meaning it automatically tracks the changes made by anybody who opens and edits the workbook (including you).

4. **If you don't want to track all the changes in the workbook, select one of the following options from the When pop-up menu:**

▶ **Since I Last Saved:** Select this option to track the changes only from the time you last saved the workbook.

▶ **Not Yet Reviewed:** Select this option to track all the changes that you've not yet reviewed (and decided whether or not to accept).

Most often, you want to select this option so that you can use the Tools⇨Track Changes⇨ Accept or Reject Changes command to review each user's changes and decide whether or not to keep them.

▶ **Since Date:** Select this option to track changes from a particular date. Excel then inserts the current date into the When combo box, which you can then edit as necessary.

5. **If you want to exempt yourself from change tracking, select Everyone but Me from the Who pop-up menu. Or, if you want to restrict change tracking to a particular user, select the user's name on the Who pop-up menu.**

Change tracking automatically traces changes made to any cells in any sheet in the workbook.

6. **If you want to restrict change tracking to a particular cell range or cell selection in the workbook, select the Where check box and then select the cell range or nonadjacent cell selection in the workbook.**

7. **If you don't want changes displayed in the cells on-screen, clear the Highlight Changes on Screen check box.**

Note that after you finish saving the workbook as a shared file, you can return to the Highlight Changes dialog box and then select its List Changes on a New Sheet check box to have all your changes listed on a new worksheet added to the workbook.

Note too, that if you select this check box when the Highlight Changes on Screen check box is selected, Excel marks the changes in their cells and lists them on a new sheet. If you clear the Highlight Changes on Screen check box while the List Changes on a New Sheet check box is selected, Excel just lists the changes on a new worksheet without marking them in the cells of the worksheet.

8. **Click OK to close the Highlight Changes dialog box.**

After Excel closes the dialog box, an alert dialog box appears, telling you that Excel will now save the workbook and asking you if you want to continue.

9. **Click OK in the alert dialog box to save the workbook with the change tracking and file-sharing settings.**

After you turn on change tracking in a shared workbook (indicated by [Shared] appended to the filename on the Excel program title bar), the program highlights all the following changes in the workbook:

✔ Changes made to the cell contents, including moving and copying the contents to new cells in the worksheet

✔ The deletion of the cell contents

✔ The insertion of new rows, columns, or cells in a worksheet

When change tracking is turned on in a workbook, the program does *not* highlight any of the following changes:

✔ Formatting changes made to the cells

✔ Hidden or unhidden rows and columns in the worksheet

✔ Renamed sheet tabs in the workbook

✔ The insertion or deletion of worksheets in the workbook

✔ Comments added to the cells

✔ Changes to cell values resulting from recalculating their formulas or in cells whose values depend directly or indirectly upon the results of these formulas

To highlight changes you make to the shared workbook, Excel draws a thin line (in another color — usually blue) around the borders of the cell, places a triangle of the same color in the cell's upper-left corner, and changes the color of the cell's column letter and row number to red. When you position the thick white cross pointer on a highlighted cell, Excel displays a comment indicating the change made to the cell, along with the date and time it was made and who it was made by, as shown in Figure 41-4.

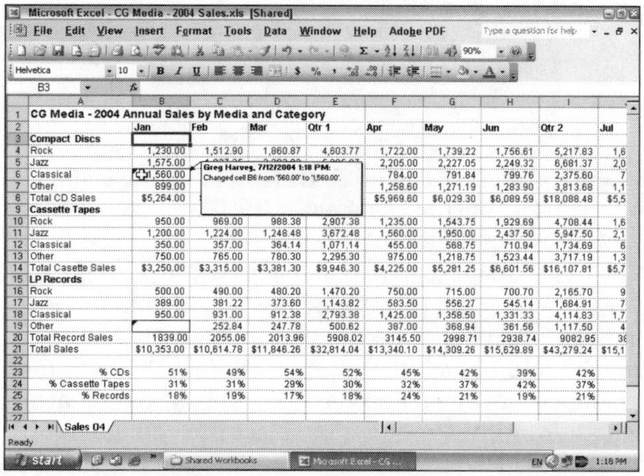

• **Figure 41-4: Displaying the comment describing the change made to a cell highlighted by change tracking.**

When you turn on change tracking, you turn on file sharing, and while file sharing is in effect, you can't make certain kinds of editing changes. For a complete list of these unavailable changes, see the section "Editing changes not available to a shared workbook," earlier in this technique.

Merging Changes from Different Users

At some point in the sharing of a workbook, you'll want to update the workbook to incorporate the changes made by different users. When merging changes, you may also have to deal with conflicting changes made to the same cells and decide which changes to accept and which to reject. After you've merged all the input and decided how to deal with all the conflicting changes, you may want to turn off file sharing to prevent users from doing any further editing.

Conflict resolution worksheet style

While file sharing is turned on in a workbook, Excel automatically updates the changes made to the shared workbook whenever anybody who's editing the same file saves his or her changes. If the program identifies cells in the workbook that contain conflicting changes (that is, different values placed in the same cell by different users) when you go to save a copy of the shared workbook, Excel flags the cell in the workbook with a marquee and then displays the conflict in the Resolve Conflicts dialog box, as shown in Figure 41-5. To accept your change to the cell in question, click the Accept Mine button. To accept the change made by another user, click the Accept Other button instead.

After you accept your change or the other user's change in the case of the first conflict, Excel moves on to flag the next case and displays a description of the conflicting values in the Resolve Conflicts dialog box. When you finish accepting or rejecting your change or the one made by another user for the last conflicting value, Excel automatically closes the Resolve Conflicts dialog box and saves your changes to the workbook.

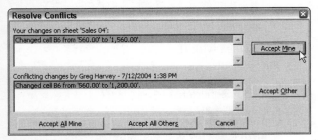

• **Figure 41-5: Deciding which change to accept in the Resolve Conflicts dialog box.**

 If you want Excel to accept only your changes in all cases of conflicting values, click the Accept All Mine button. To have Excel reject all your changes and accept all those made by others, click the Accept All Others button instead.

Accepting or rejecting highlighted changes

When you share a workbook file by turning on change tracking for a workbook, you can decide which changes to accept or reject by choosing Tools⇨Track Changes⇨Accept or Reject Changes. When you first choose this command, Excel displays an alert dialog box informing you that the program will save the workbook. When you click OK to close this alert dialog box, the program looks for conflicts and, if it finds any, opens the Resolve Conflicts dialog box (refer to Figure 41-5) where you decide whose changes to use.

After resolving all the conflicts in the workbook, Excel then opens the Select Changes to Accept or Reject dialog box, shown in Figure 41-6. This dialog box contains the same three check boxes and associated drop-down items (When, Who, and Where) as the Highlight Changes dialog box (refer to Figure 41-3).

By default, the When check box is selected along with the Not Yet Reviewed setting. When this setting is selected, Excel displays all the changes in the

workbook that you haven't yet reviewed for everyone who has modified the shared file. Here are the settings that you can change:

✔ To review only those changes you made on the current date, select Since Date on the When drop-down list.

✔ To review changes made since a particular date, edit the current date in the Since Date drop-down list.

✔ To review changes that everyone has made except you, only those changes you've made, or only those changes a particular coworker has made, click the appropriate item (Everyone But Me, your name, or another user's name) on the Who drop-down list.

✔ If you want to restrict the review to a particular range or region of a worksheet, select the Where check box and then select the range or nonadjacent cell ranges with the cells to review.

• **Figure 41-6: Deciding which changes to review in the shared workbook.**

After you select which changes to review, click OK. Excel then closes this dialog box, highlights the cell in the worksheet that contains the first change to review, and opens the Accept or Reject Changes dialog box (shown in Figure 41-7), where you indicate whether or not to accept or reject the change.

Here's how to accept or reject changes in this dialog box:

✔ To accept a change when there are multiple modifications, select the one you want to use and then click the Accept button.

✔ To reject all the changes and keep the original value, select the original value and then click the Accept button.

✔ If only one change has been made to a cell, you can keep its original value by clicking the Reject button.

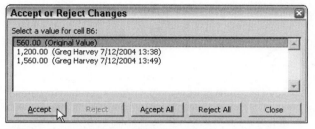

• **Figure 41-7:** Deciding which changes to accept in the shared workbook.

After you accept or reject the modification made to the first highlighted cell, Excel flags the next cell in worksheet that needs reviewing and, at the same time, displays a description of the change in the Accept or Reject Changes dialog box.

 If you know ahead of time that you want to accept or reject all the changes that have been made since you last reviewed the workbook, click the Accept All button or the Reject All button, respectively.

After you accept or reject the last change that Excel identifies in the shared workbook, the Accept or Reject Changes dialog box automatically closes, and you can then save the workbook (Ctrl+S) with the editing changes that you made as a result of this review.

Turning off file sharing

When you no longer need to share a particular workbook, you can turn off file sharing. To do this, open the Share Workbook dialog box (Tools⇨Share Workbook), clear the Allow Changes by More Than One User at the Same Time check box on the Editing tab, and click OK.

After you stop sharing a workbook, all other users who have it open are automatically prevented from saving the workbook in the same folder under the same name. To save their changes to the erstwhile shared workbook, they must now save the workbook with a new filename. You can then merge the changes in their new files with the original workbook (see the following section).

 It's a good idea to inform the users of a shared workbook of your intention to remove the file from shared use. E-mail all the users and let them know the date and time after which the workbook will no longer be shared and open to their edits. That way, all the team members know the exact time after which their modifications will no longer be accepted (often a good inducement for the procrastinators to get their editing changes done).

Merging Different Copies of a Shared Workbook

Instead of sharing a single workbook with other users on the network and then doing a review in which you accept or reject their changes when you save the file or at some predefined time interval, you can distribute copies of a shared workbook and then merge the changes made by different people into one version.

Distributing the copies

The key elements for successfully merging different copies of a shared workbook are that each copy must have the Change History log turned on and each copy must be saved under a different filename. This means that in order to create the copies of the workbook you want to distribute, you need to follow these steps:

1. **Turn on the Change History log in the original by opening the Share Workbook dialog box (Tools⇨Share Workbook) and then selecting** the Allow Changes by More Than One User at the Same Time check box.

2. **Create copies of the original shared workbook by saving them under slightly different filenames (File⇨Save As).**

You may want to append numbers or the initials of the people doing the review to the filenames.

3. **Distribute these different copies to the intended users — usually by attaching the workbook files to e-mail messages.**

These users can then make their edits and save their changes to the shared copy of the original workbook that they receive from you (which they can then return to you as e-mail attachments).

 All editing in the copies you distribute must be made before the time period for keeping the Change History log expires (30 days by default). If you have any doubt that 30 days is enough time, increase the number of days in the Keep Change History For text box on the Advanced tab of the Share Workbook dialog box before you save copies of the original workbook and distribute them to your users.

Merging the changes

When you've received the edited copies you distributed and are ready to merge the changes they contain into one version, follow these steps:

1. **Open the original shared workbook into which you want to merge changes from the other copies.**

Note that the copies of the original workbook whose changes will be merged into the original workbook must *not* also be open in Excel and they must have different filenames.

2. **Choose Tools⇨Compare and Merge Workbooks.**

Doing this opens the Select Files to Merge Into Current Workbook dialog box, shown in Figure 41-8, where you indicate the workbook files to merge.

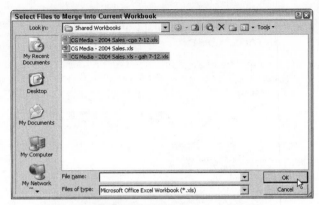

• **Figure 41-8:** Selecting the files to merge into the workbook open in Excel.

3. **Select the folder that contains the workbook(s) to be merged and then select the files.**

Ctrl+click to select more than one file.

4. **Click OK to close the Select Files to Merge into Current Workbook dialog box.**

After you click OK, Excel merges the disk version(s) of the selected workbook(s) into the version you have open in Excel (without prompting you to review or accept or reject any of the updates). All changes in the disk version(s) are merged to the workbook open on your screen. You can then save this single, updated version of the workbook under the same name (Ctrl+S) or under a new filename (File⇨Save As).

 Merging changes from copies of the same shared workbook involves no conflict resolution. If users change the same cell in the copies, the program simply replaces the value in the original shared workbook in turn with the value in each merged copy. Don't use this feature if you want to be able to decide which value to accept and which to reject in such conflicts.

Technique 42

Sending Workbooks Out for Review

Save Time By

- Adding comments to get a workbook ready to send out
- Sending out a workbook for review

Excel makes it easy to send out spreadsheets for review by clients, coworkers, and managers who need to give you their input or approval after reviewing their contents. When getting spreadsheets ready to send out for this type of review, you can annotate them by attaching your comments to key cells that require particular attention.

When sending out a workbook for review, you can either send the workbook embedded within the body of an e-mail message or send it as an attachment to an e-mail message. If you're part of a Microsoft Exchange Server system, you can place a copy of the workbook in a public folder so that all users who have permission to access that folder can open the workbook for review.

Getting a Workbook Ready for Review

In getting a workbook file ready to send out for review, you'll want to add your comments to the workbook's cells. These comments can ask for clarification or suggest changes to the cells' contents. One of the best ways to add comments to a workbook is with the buttons on the Reviewing toolbar (View➪Toolbars➪Reviewing). The Reviewing toolbar, shown in Figure 42-1, also contains buttons that make it easy to review these notes, e-mail the workbook as an attachment to others who have to review the comments, and even reply to suggested changes.

If you have a Tablet PC, you can use the tablet pen to annotate your spreadsheet with handwritten notes. Click the Hide Ink Annotations button on the Reviewing toolbar to temporarily remove their display and the Delete All Ink Annotations button to get rid of them permanently.

New Comment
Next Comment
Show/Hide All Comments
Hide Ink Annotations
Create Microsoft Office Outlook Task
Send to Mail Recipient (as Attachment)
Reviewing
Reply with Changes... End Review...
Update File
Reply with Changes
Hide All Ink Annotations
End Review
Delete Comment
Show/Hide Comments
Previous Comment

• **Figure 42-1: Use the Reviewing toolbar to create and edit comments you add to cells.**

Getting your two cents in

Comments are like electronic sticky notes that you can attach to the cells of your worksheet. You can add comments to the current cell either by clicking the New Comment button on the Reviewing toolbar or by choosing Insert⇨Comment.

Excel responds by adding a comment box (see Figure 42-2) with your name listed at the top (or the name of the person who shows up in the User Name text box on the General tab of the Options dialog box). You can then type the text of your comment in this box. When you finish typing, click any cell in the worksheet to close the Comment box.

Excel indicates the presence of a comment in a cell by displaying a red triangle in its upper-right corner. To display the comment box with the text of its note, position the thick, white cross mouse pointer on this red triangle, or position the cell pointer in its cell and click the Show Comment button on the Reviewing toolbar.

Microsoft Excel - CG Media Sales - 2003 (annotated).xls [Shared]
2003 Sales by Category and Date
Greg Harvey:
Please check this number as it seems too high.

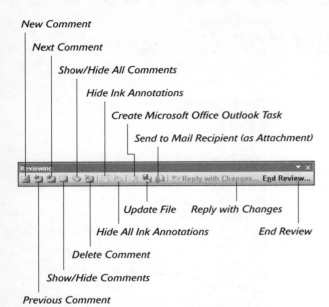

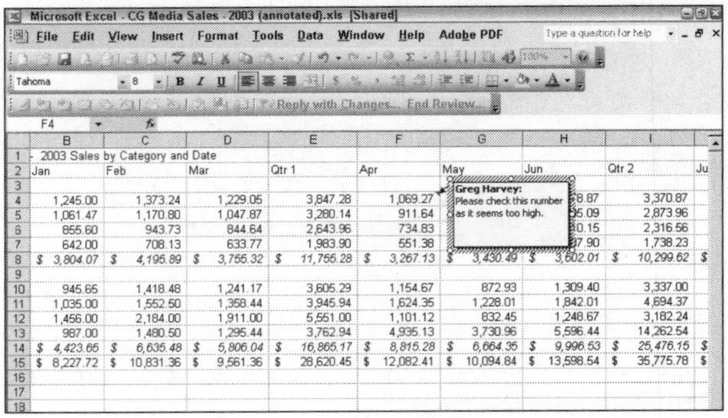

• **Figure 42-2: Adding comments to a spreadsheet being readied for review.**

Comments: Now you see them, now you don't

Most of the time, you see the text of a comment you've added to a cell only when you position the mouse pointer somewhere in its cell (as soon as you move the pointer out of the cell, the comment text magically disappears). If you want to display all the comments you've added to cells in the worksheet at one time, click the Show All Comments button on the Reviewing toolbar or choose View⇨Comments. The comment boxes for all your cell notes appear in the worksheet until you click the Show All Comments button or choose View⇨Comment again.

If you want to keep the text of a single comment displayed in the sheet, select the cell containing the comment and then click the Show Comment button on the Reviewing toolbar. Excel will continue to display the comment even after you vacate the cell. To get rid of the display of the comment box, you must select the cell and then click the Show Comment button a second time.

Editing and formatting comments

Comments normally appear to the right of the cell to which they've been assigned in a box with an arrow pointing to the comment indicator (the red triangle in the cell's upper-right corner). If you want, you can reposition a cell's comment box and/or resize it so that it doesn't obscure certain cells in the immediate region. You can also edit the text in the comment box and change the formatting of its text.

To make any of these editing changes, first position the cell pointer in the cell and then click the Edit Comment button on the Reviewing toolbar. (This button replaces the Add Comment button as the first button on the toolbar.) If the Reviewing toolbar isn't currently displayed on-screen, you can also do this by right-clicking on the cell and selecting Edit Comment on the shortcut menu.

Excel then displays the cell's comment box and positions the insertion point at the end of the comment text, as shown in Figure 42-3.

To reposition the comment box, follow these steps:

1. **Position the mouse pointer on the edge of the comment box (indicated with cross-hatching and open circles around the perimeter).**

2. **When the mouse pointer assumes the shape of white arrowhead pointing to a black double cross, drag the outline of the comment box to a new position in the worksheet.**

   After you release the mouse button, Excel draws a new line ending in an arrowhead from the repositioned comment box to the red triangle in the cell's upper-right corner.

To resize the comment box, follow these steps:

1. **Position the mouse pointer on one of the open circles at the corners and in the middle of each edge on the box's perimeter.**

2. **When the mouse pointer changes into a double-headed arrow, drag the dotted outline of the comment box until it's the size and shape you want.**

   Excel automatically reflows the comment text to suit the new size and shape of the box.

To edit the text of the comment while the insertion point is positioned somewhere in it, drag the I-beam mouse pointer through the text that needs to be replaced or press the Backspace key (to remove characters to the left of the insertion point) or Delete key (to remove characters to the right). You can insert new characters by simply typing them.

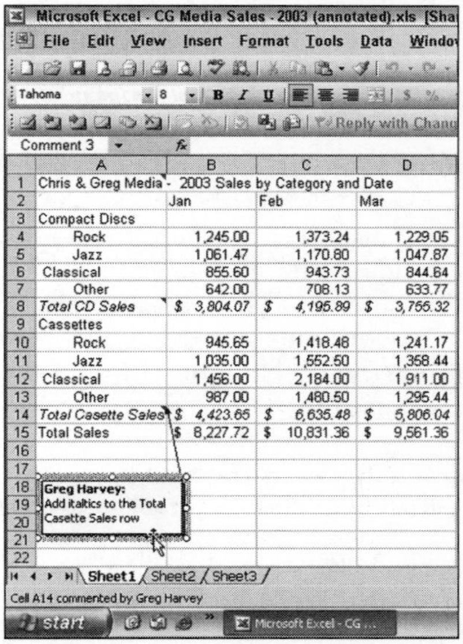

• **Figure 42-3:** Editing a comment by resizing its box and pulling it away from the existing data.

To change the formatting of the comment text, select the text by dragging through it and then right-click on the text and select Format Comment. Excel opens the Format Comment dialog box (containing the same options as the Font tab of the Format Cells dialog box). Here, you can change the font, font style, font size, font color, or add special effects including underlining, strikethrough, and super- and subscripting to the text.

When you finish making your changes to the comment box and text, close the comment box by clicking any cell in the worksheet.

Deleting comments in a worksheet

If you no longer need a particular comment, you can delete it by selecting its cell and then doing any of the following:

✔ Choose Edit➪Clear➪Comments.

✔ Click the Delete Comment button on the Reviewing toolbar.

✔ Right-click on the cell and then select Delete Comment on its shortcut menu.

Sending Out a Workbook for Review

Excel makes it a snap to send out the workbooks that you've annotated for review to all the people who should comment and make changes. Prior to sending out a workbook for review, you need to turn on file sharing. (See Technique 41 for all the details.) Then follow these steps:

1. **Choose File➪Send To➪Mail Recipient (For Review).**

   Excel then opens your e-mail program (such as Outlook or Outlook Express), starts a new e-mail message, and attaches the current workbook as an e-mail attachment. The program also automatically fills in the Subject line of the message, asking the recipient to review the attached file, and inserts the following text into the body of the message:

   `Please review the attached document.`

2. **Fill in the recipient's e-mail address in the To text box, along with the addresses of any other people you want to copy in the Cc text box. (See Figure 42-4.)**

3. **Click the Send button to send it off to your recipient(s).**

Replying with changes

When your recipients receive the e-mail message and open the attached workbook file in Excel, the program automatically opens the Reviewing toolbar (if it's not already displayed in the Excel window) as it opens the file.

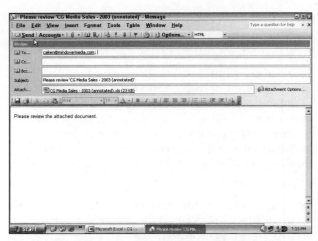

• **Figure 42-4: Sending out a shared workbook for review.**

The reviewers can then use the Next Comment and Previous Comment buttons on this toolbar to jump from comment to comment in the workbook. They can then respond to your comments by making changes to cells that have been flagged or by adding comments of their own.

When they're ready to send their changes and responses back to you, they click the Reply with Changes button on the Reviewing toolbar. Excel then opens their e-mail programs with a new message to which your modified version of the workbook is automatically attached. This new message also has the Subject field filled in and sports a short message in the body stating that they have reviewed the attached workbook. All they have to do is fill in your e-mail address (as the original sender) in the To field and then click the Send button to send the modified workbook back to you.

Merging changes into the original workbook

When you open the modified workbook attached to the response e-mail in Excel, the program immediately displays a Microsoft Excel alert dialog box informing you that the workbook was sent for review and asking you if you want to merge the changes in this workbook back into the original workbook file. To do this, click the Yes button in the alert dialog box.

As soon as you do so, Excel merges all the changes made by the reviewer into the original workbook. Before you save the changes, you can use the Next Comment and Previous Comment button on the Reviewing toolbar to jump to and review the annotated cells (those with comments you originally attached and any that the reviewer attached in response).

If you and all your recipients use Outlook as your e-mail program on a network running the Microsoft Exchange Server, you can use the File⇨Send To⇨Routing Recipient command in Excel to create a routing slip that indicates all the people you want to review the workbook as well as the order in which they're to receive it and comment on its contents. This command enables you to have a group of people give their feedback to a workbook, all of which is automatically merged into the document by the time it returns to you.

Part VII

Streamlining Data Listing and Data Analysis

Technique 43

Adding and Editing Data Lists with the Data Form

Maintaining a large quantity of related information in a special format known as a *data list* (also occasionally referred to somewhat erroneously as a database) is one of the more important things you can do with Excel. This technique covers how to use the data form that Excel automatically creates for any data list you generate to add, edit, and find the information you need to maintain. (See Technique 44 for information on sorting the information in your data lists and Technique 45 for information on filtering out all but the information you're interested in at the time).

Creating a New Data List and Data Form

Excel automatically creates a data form for any data list that you create in Excel. All you have to do is enter the headings for the columns in the data list (known as *fields*) in the first row and a row of data entries (that make up the first record of the data list) in the row immediately below (see Figure 43-1) and then assign to their cells whatever alignment and number formatting you want the rest of the entries in that column (field) to have.

 If your data list contains calculated fields, be sure to enter the formulas necessary for doing these computations in the appropriate cells of the first record. (See the Formula bar entry for cell I2 in Figure 43-1.) Also be sure to assign the desired number format to these results in the calculated fields. Both the formula and the formatting assigned to the calculated fields are picked up in the data form.

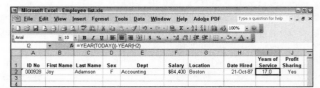

• **Figure 43-1:** Creating a new data list and data form by entering the fields and first record.

Figure 43-2 shows the data form that Excel created for the new Employee data list shown in Figure 43-1, using the field names in the cell range A1:J1 and the first data record in the cell range A2:J2. To display the data form for any data list, position the cell pointer in any cell of the list (either in the top row of field names or in any of field entries in records below) and then choose Data➪Form.

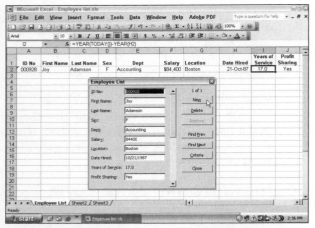

• **Figure 43-2:** Data form created for the Employee list using the field names and showing the first data record.

In the data form, the program automatically assigns hot keys to the various field names (indicated by the underscores) that you can then select by combining with the Alt key. (For example, pressing Alt+E selects the Sex field in this data form.)

Also note that all the field names in the Employee list — with the exception of the Years of Service field that appears near the bottom of the data form — are followed by text boxes in which you can add or edit their particular entries. Because the Years of Service field is computed by a formula, the data form displays the computed result after the field name without providing a text box in which you can edit it. (To modify this field entry, you'd have to edit the original formula in cell I2 of the worksheet.)

When the data form is displayed, you can use the scroll bar to the right of the fields to move through the records in the data list, or you can use various direction keys. Table 43-1 lists the navigating functions of the scroll bar and these keystrokes. For example, to move to the next record in the data list, press the ↓ or Enter key or click the scroll arrow at the bottom of the scroll bar. To move to the previous record in the data list (assuming that there's more than one), press the ↑ key or Shift+Enter key or click the scroll arrow at the top of the scroll bar. To select a field in the current record for editing, click that field's text box or press Tab (next field) or Shift+Tab (previous field) until you select the field (and its current entry).

TABLE 43-1: TECHNIQUES FOR NAVIGATING THE FIELDS IN THE DATA FORM

To Move Here	Do This
Next record, same field in the data list	Press the ↓ or Enter key, click the downward-pointing scroll arrow, or click the Find Next button.
Previous record, same field in the data list	Press the ↑ key or Shift+Enter, click the upward-pointing scroll arrow, or click the Find Prev button.
Next field in the data form	Press Tab.
Previous field in the data form	Press Shift+Tab.
Ten records forward in the data list	Press Page Down.
Ten records backward in the data list	Press Page Up.
First record in the data list	Press Ctrl+↑ or Ctrl + Page Up, or drag the scroll box to the top of the scroll bar.
Last record in the data list	Press Ctrl+↓ or Ctrl+Page Down, or drag the scroll box to the bottom of the scroll bar.

To Move Here	Do This
Within a field	Press ← or → to move one character at a time, press Home to move to the first character, and press End to move to the last character.

Adding new records with the data form

To add a new record to the data list with the data form, follow these steps:

1. **Either move to the end of the data list (by dragging the scroll box to the very bottom of the scroll bar or by pressing Ctrl+↓ or Ctrl+Page Down) or simply click the New button on the data form.**

Excel then displays a blank data form (marked New Record at the right side the dialog box), which you can then fill in.

2. **Fill in the information in the data form (see Figure 43-3).**

After entering the information for a field, press the Tab key to advance to the next field in the record. (Be careful not to press the Enter key yet because this inserts the new record into the data list.)

 You can copy the entry from the same field in the previous record into the current field by pressing Ctrl+" (double quotation mark). You would use this keystroke shortcut, for example, to carry forward entries for the State field when you're entering a bunch of records that all have the same state.

3. **After you've entered all the information you have for the new record, press the ↓ or Enter key or click the New button again.**

Excel then inserts the new record as the last record in the data list and displays a blank data form where you can enter the next record.

4. **Insert additional records to the data list, as desired.**

5. **When you finish adding records, press the Esc key or click the Close button to close the data form dialog box.**

Figure 43-4 shows the new Employee data list after filling in the information for the second record and then pressing the Enter key to enter the record into the third row of the data list. Not only does Excel automatically add the new record to the last row of your data list, but it also presents you with a clean data form that you can then use to fill in the information for the next record.

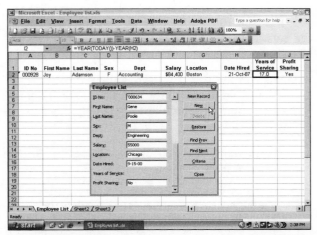

• **Figure 43-3:** Adding the second record for the Employee data list with the data form.

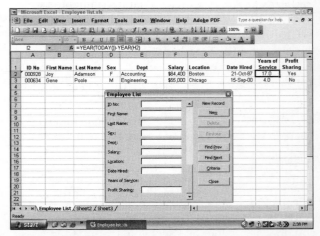

• **Figure 43-4:** Employee data list with the second record entered from the data form.

Some fields require you to enter their numbers as text rather than as values. For example, if you're entering part numbers or other identification numbers that use leading zeros, you need to preface the field entries with an apostrophe (') as in '00210. Note that Excel does not copy this very important punctuation from the previous entry when you press Ctrl+" to copy into the current field, so you must do it manually. For zip code fields, assign the Special Zip Code number format to retain leading zeros.

Finding records with the data form

You can use the Criteria button in the data form to find the records in your data list that you need to edit or delete (as described in the next sections). When you click the Criteria button, Excel clears all the field text boxes so that you can enter the criteria to search for. For example, say that you need to edit Sherry Caulfield's profit-sharing status. You don't have her paperwork in front of you, so you can't look up her employee number. You do know, however, that she works in the Boston office, and although you don't remember exactly how she spells her last name, you do know that it begins with a *C* instead of a *K*.

To locate her record, you can at least narrow the search to all the records where the Location field contains Boston and the employee's Last Name begins with the letter C, as shown in Figure 43-5. To do this, open the data form for the Employee data list, click the Criteria button, and then enter the following text in the Last Name field:

    C*

Then, in the Location field you enter

    Boston

When entering the criteria for locating matching records in the data form, you can use the question mark (?) and asterisk (*) wildcard characters just as you do when using the Excel Find feature to locate cells with particular entries.

• **Figure 43-5: Entering the search criteria to find records where the last name starts with C and the location is Boston.**

Then click the Find Next button or press the Enter key, and Excel locates the first record in the data list where the last name begins with the letter C and the location is Boston. This is William Cobb's record, shown in Figure 43-6.

To locate the next record that matches your criteria, click the Find Next button or press Enter, which brings you to Sherry Caulfield's record, shown in Figure 43-7. Having located Sherry's record, you can then change her profit-sharing status by selecting the Profit Sharing text box and replacing No with Yes. To insert the editing change that you make in the data form into the data list itself, close the data form's dialog box by clicking the Close button.

When using the Criteria button in the data form to find records, you can use the following logical operators when entering search criteria in fields that use numbers or dates:

- ✔ **Equal to (=):** Finds records the same as the text, value, or date you enter.

- ✔ **Greater than (>):** Finds records after the text characters (in the alphabet) or the date, or larger than the value you enter.

- ✔ **Greater than or equal to (>=):** Finds records the same as the text characters, date, or value you enter or after the characters (in the alphabet), after the date, or larger than the value.

- ✔ **Less than (<):** Finds records before the text characters (in the alphabet) or date or smaller than the value you enter.

- ✔ **Less than or equal to (<=):** Finds records the same as the text characters, date, or value you enter or before the characters (in the alphabet) or the date, or smaller than the value.

- ✔ **Not equal to (<>):** Finds records not the same as the text, value, or date you enter.

• **Figure 43-6: Locating the first matching record for William Cobb.**

• **Figure 43-7: Locating the next matching record for Sherry Caulfield.**

For example, to find all the records where an employee's annual salary is $50,000, you can enter =50000 or simply 50000 in the Salary field text box. However, to find all the records for employees whose annual salaries are less than or equal to $35,000, you enter <=35000 in the Salary field text box. To find all the records for employees with salaries greater than $45,000, you would enter >45000 in the Salary field text box instead. If you wanted to find all the records where the employees are male *and* make more than $50,000, you would enter M in the Sex field text box and >50000 in the Salary field text box in the same Criteria data form.

When specifying search criteria that fit a number of records, you may have to click the Find Next or Find Prev buttons several times to locate the record you want to work with. If no record fits the search criteria you enter in the Criteria data form, the computer beeps at you when you click the Find Next or Find Prev button.

To change your search criteria, select the appropriate text box or boxes, delete the old search criteria, and then enter the new criteria. To switch back to the current record without using the search criteria you enter, click the Form button. (This button replaces the Criteria button as soon as you click the Criteria button.)

Editing records in the data form

The Criteria data form makes it easy to locate the records that need editing in your data list. After you've displayed the data form for a record that needs editing, you can then make the editing changes by selecting the text boxes of the effected fields and making your changes, just as you would edit the entry in its cell in the worksheet. (Refer to Table 43-1.)

To complete the editing changes you make to a record, you can click the New, Find Next, Criteria, or Close button (when you don't need to do any more editing to the records in the data list).

Removing records from the data list with the data form

In addition to adding and editing records with the data form, you can also delete them. To remove a record from the data list, you simply display the record in the data form and then click the Delete button.

Be careful when deleting records, however, because you can't restore the records you delete with Excel's Undo feature. For this reason, Excel always displays an alert dialog box whenever you click the Delete button indicating that the record displayed in the data form is about to be permanently deleted. To continue and remove the record, you need to click OK or press Enter. If you change your mind and decide to keep the current record, press the Esc key or click the Cancel button instead.

 Although you can use the Criteria data form to locate a group of records that you want to delete, you can remove only one record at a time with the Delete button. To delete a whole set of records, you might be better off selecting them in the worksheet and then removing them with the Edit➪Delete command (using the Shift Cells Up option).

Technique 44

Sorting Worksheet Data

Save Time By

✔ Sorting the records of a data list

✔ Sorting on three or more fields

✔ Sorting the field names in a list

Being able to properly sort your worksheet data, whether in a standard table or data list, is one of the more important operations that you can perform on the data. When you sort worksheet data in Excel, you rearrange the rows or columns of the original data table or list so that they appear in a particular preferred order. To achieve this preferred order, you designate the column or rows in the table or list whose entries are to be used in determining the new data arrangement.

This technique introduces you to the process of sorting worksheet data. It begins by covering the basic sorting of the records in a data list (see Technique 43) using one, two, or even three fields in the list. The technique then shows you how to add a number field to the data list so that you can use that field to restore the sorted records to the order in which they were originally entered. Finally, you get the lowdown on doing more complex sorts of data lists that involve more than three fields and how to use the Sort feature to rearrange the columns (fields) in an existing table of data or data list.

Don't Be Out of Sorts

Excel's Sort feature makes it easy to rearrange the records or even the fields in your table of data or data list. To sort your data, Excel uses sorting keys to determine how the records or fields should be reordered in the data list:

✔ When sorting records, you indicate by cell address which field (that is, column) contains the first or primary sorting key.

✔ When sorting fields, you indicate which record (row) contains the primary sorting key.

Excel then applies the selected sort (ascending or descending) to the data in the key field or row to determine how the records or fields will be reordered during sorting.

When a key field contains duplicate entries, Excel lists these records in the order in which they were entered in the table or data list. To indicate how Excel should order records with duplicates in the primary key, you define a secondary key. For example, if, when organizing the data list in alphabetical order by the Last Name field, you have several records where the last name is Smith, you can have Excel sort the Smiths' records in alphabetical order by first name. To do so, you define the First Name field as the secondary key. If the secondary key contains duplicates (say you have two John Smiths in your company), you can define a third key field (the Middle Name field, if your data list has one) that determines how the duplicate John Smith records are to be arranged when the data list is sorted.

When defining the key fields or rows for a sort, you can specify either an ascending or descending sort order for its data:

✔ When you specify ascending order (which is the default), Excel arranges text in A-to-Z order and values from smallest to largest.

✔ When you specify descending order, Excel reverses this order and arranges text in Z-to-A order and values range from largest to smallest.

When sorting on a date field, keep in mind that ascending order puts the records in least-recent-to-most-recent date order, whereas descending order gives you the records in most-recent-to-least-recent date order.

When you choose the ascending sort order for a field containing many different kinds of entries, Excel places numbers (from smallest to largest) before text (in alphabetical order) followed by logical values (TRUE and FALSE), error values, and, finally, blank cells. When you're using the descending sort order, the program uses the same general arrangement for the different types of entries, but numbers go from largest to smallest, text runs from Z to A, and the FALSE logical value precedes the TRUE logical value.

Sorting records in a data list

To sort the records in your data list with the Sort feature, follow these steps:

1. **Position the cell pointer somewhere in one of the cells in the data list.**

As long as the cell pointer is in any cell in the data list, Excel automatically selects all the records in the list when you perform the next step. Note that you can manually adjust this range if you want to sort less than all the records in the list.

2. **Choose Data⇨Sort to open the Sort dialog box, shown in Figure 44-1.**

• **Figure 44-1: Using the Sort dialog box to sort the records of the Employee data list.**

Excel selects all the rows (records) in the list (excluding the row of field names at the top) and opens the Sort dialog box. If the list of data you're sorting doesn't have a row of headings in the top row and you want to include the top row's data in the sort, you need to select the No Header Row option button near the bottom of the Sort dialog box.

3. In the Sort By drop-down list, select the name of the field you want used as the primary key in sorting the records.

4. If you want to sort the records in descending order (rather than the default ascending order) using the primary key, click the Descending option button.

5. If the primary key field contains duplicates and you want to specify how these records are to be sorted, select the name of the field to sort by in the first Then By drop-down list.

6. If you want to sort the records in descending order using the secondary key, click the Descending option button to the right of the first Then By drop-down list box.

7. If the secondary key field contains duplicates and you want to specify how these records are to be sorted, select the name of the field to sort by in the second Then By drop-down list.

8. If you want to sort the records in descending order using the tertiary key, click the Descending option button to the right of the second Then By drop-down list.

9. When you finish defining all the keys you need to use in sorting the records in your data list, click OK or press Enter to perform the sort.

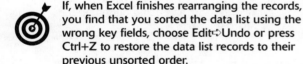 If, when Excel finishes rearranging the records, you find that you sorted the data list using the wrong key fields, choose Edit➪Undo or press Ctrl+Z to restore the data list records to their previous unsorted order.

Note that the Sort dialog box contains an Options button that, when clicked, opens the Sort Options dialog box, shown in Figure 44-2. This dialog box contains options for doing a case-sensitive sort on fields that contain text and options for changing the orientation of the sort from the normal top-to-bottom order to left-to-right order when you want to sort columns in a list.

Figure 44-3 illustrates sorting the Employee data list first in ascending order by location and then in descending order by salary. For this sort, I selected the Location field as the primary key and the Salary field as the secondary key in the sort. Also, to have the records within each location sorted from highest to lowest salary, I chose the Descending option button next to the first Then By drop-down list box. Note in Figure 44-3 how the records are now organized first in ascending order by city listed in the Location field (Atlanta, Boston, Chicago, and so on) and within each city in descending order by Salary (38,900, 32,200, 29,200, and so on).

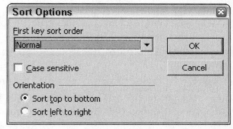

• **Figure 44-2:** Using the Sort Options dialog box to refine the sort order.

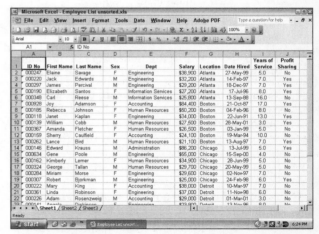

• **Figure 44-3:** Employee data list sorted by location and salary.

To quickly sort records in the data list by using any single field in the list as the sorting key, use the Sort Ascending button (the one with A above Z) or the Sort Descending button (the one with Z above A) on the Standard toolbar. To sort the data list using these buttons, position the cell pointer somewhere in the field on which the records are to be sorted and then click the Sort Ascending button or Sort Descending button (depending upon which order you want to use).

Sorting on a record number field to restore a list to its original order

In some data lists, you may want to be able to restore the records to the order in which they were originally entered (which may not necessarily be an order that you achieve through sorting). To return a list to its original order after doing any amount of sorting, you assign sequential numbers to the records before you ever sort them. To do so, follow these steps:

1. **Position the cell pointer in the first cell of the list and then choose Insert⇨Column.**

Excel inserts a blank column where you can assign the sequential numbers for the records.

2. **Type** `Record No.` **as the field name in the blank cell in the new column and then press Enter.**

3. **Type** 1 **in the blank cell beneath the Record Number field name and then click the Enter button on the Formula bar.**

Clicking the Enter button ensures that the cell pointer stays in the cell that now contains record number 1.

4. **Position the mouse pointer on the Fill handle of the current cell, press and hold down the Ctrl key, and then drag the Fill handle down the column until you reach the row with the last record of the data list.**

When you release the mouse button, Excel fills the Record Number field with sequential numbers starting with 1, as shown in Figure 44-4.

5. **Save the workbook containing the data list (Ctrl+S).**

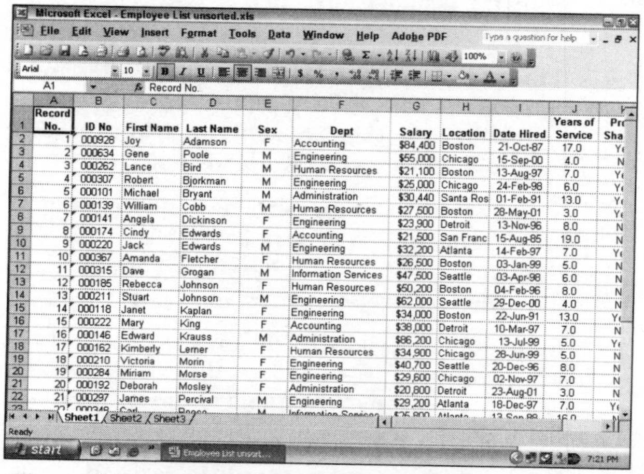

• **Figure 44-4: Employee data list after adding and filling in the new Record No. field.**

After adding the Record No. field with the record numbers to the data list, you can return the list to its original data-entry order (which you would do before adding any new records) by positioning the cell pointer in the cell containing the Record No. field name and then clicking the Sort Ascending button on the Standard toolbar.

Sorting a list on more than three key fields

On rare occasions, you may need to sort a data list on more than three fields (the maximum you can define in one sorting operation). For example, suppose you're working with a personnel data list like the one shown in Figure 44-5 and you want to organize the records in alphabetical order, first by department, then by supervisor, and finally by last name, first name, and middle name. To sort the records in this data list by these five fields, you have to perform two sorting operations:

- In the first sorting operation, define the Last Name field as the primary key, the First Name field as the secondary key, and the Middle Name field as the tertiary key.
- In the second sort, define the Department field as the primary key and the Supervisor field as the secondary key.

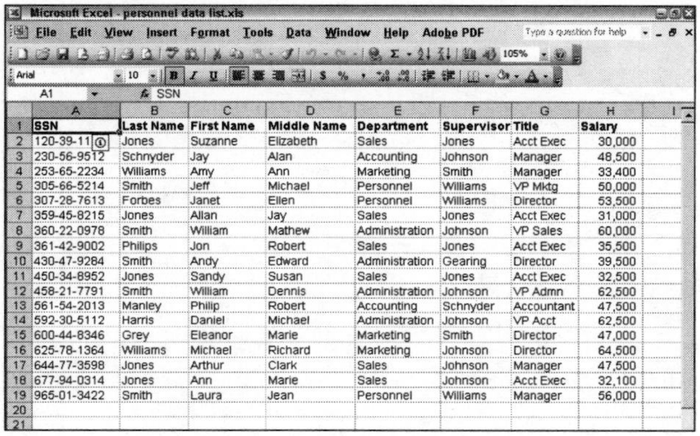

	SSN	Last Name	First Name	Middle Name	Department	Supervisor	Title	Salary
2	120-39-11	Jones	Suzanne	Elizabeth	Sales	Jones	Acct Exec	30,000
3	230-56-9512	Schnyder	Jay	Alan	Accounting	Johnson	Manager	48,500
4	253-65-2234	Williams	Amy	Ann	Marketing	Smith	Manager	33,400
5	305-66-5214	Smith	Jeff	Michael	Personnel	Williams	VP Mktg	50,000
6	307-28-7613	Forbes	Janet	Ellen	Personnel	Williams	Director	53,500
7	359-45-8215	Jones	Allan	Jay	Sales	Jones	Acct Exec	31,000
8	360-22-0978	Smith	William	Mathew	Administration	Johnson	VP Sales	60,000
9	361-42-9002	Philips	Jon	Robert	Sales	Jones	Acct Exec	35,500
10	430-47-9284	Smith	Andy	Edward	Administration	Gearing	Director	39,500
11	450-34-8952	Jones	Sandy	Susan	Sales	Jones	Acct Exec	32,500
12	458-21-7791	Smith	William	Dennis	Administration	Johnson	VP Admn	62,500
13	561-54-2013	Manley	Philip	Robert	Accounting	Schnyder	Accountant	47,500
14	592-30-5112	Harris	Daniel	Michael	Administration	Johnson	VP Acct	62,500
15	600-44-8346	Grey	Eleanor	Marie	Marketing	Smith	Director	47,000
16	625-78-1364	Williams	Michael	Richard	Marketing	Johnson	Director	64,500
17	644-77-3598	Jones	Arthur	Clark	Sales	Johnson	Manager	47,500
18	677-94-0314	Jones	Ann	Marie	Sales	Johnson	Acct Exec	32,100
19	965-01-3422	Smith	Laura	Jean	Personnel	Williams	Manager	56,000

• **Figure 44-5: Personnel data list before sorting.**

Figure 44-6 shows you the personnel data list after performing the second sorting operation. As you can see, the records are now arranged in ascending order by department, then by supervisor within department, and finally by the last name, first name, and middle name of the individuals under each supervisor.

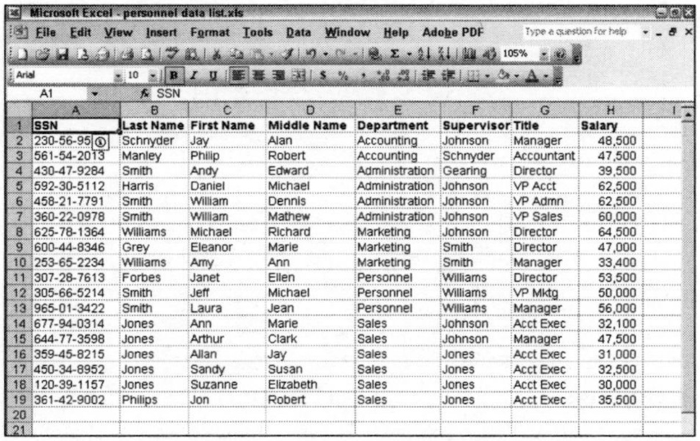

	SSN	Last Name	First Name	Middle Name	Department	Supervisor	Title	Salary
2	230-56-95	Schnyder	Jay	Alan	Accounting	Johnson	Manager	48,500
3	561-54-2013	Manley	Philip	Robert	Accounting	Schnyder	Accountant	47,500
4	430-47-9284	Smith	Andy	Edward	Administration	Gearing	Director	39,500
5	592-30-5112	Harris	Daniel	Michael	Administration	Johnson	VP Acct	62,500
6	458-21-7791	Smith	William	Dennis	Administration	Johnson	VP Admn	62,500
7	360-22-0978	Smith	William	Mathew	Administration	Johnson	VP Sales	60,000
8	625-78-1364	Williams	Michael	Richard	Marketing	Johnson	Director	64,500
9	600-44-8346	Grey	Eleanor	Marie	Marketing	Smith	Director	47,000
10	253-65-2234	Williams	Amy	Ann	Marketing	Smith	Manager	33,400
11	307-28-7613	Forbes	Janet	Ellen	Personnel	Williams	Director	53,500
12	305-66-5214	Smith	Jeff	Michael	Personnel	Williams	VP Mktg	50,000
13	965-01-3422	Smith	Laura	Jean	Personnel	Williams	Manager	56,000
14	677-94-0314	Jones	Ann	Marie	Sales	Johnson	Acct Exec	32,100
15	644-77-3598	Jones	Arthur	Clark	Sales	Johnson	Manager	47,500
16	359-45-8215	Jones	Allan	Jay	Sales	Jones	Acct Exec	31,000
17	450-34-8952	Jones	Sandy	Susan	Sales	Jones	Acct Exec	32,500
18	120-39-1157	Jones	Suzanne	Elizabeth	Sales	Jones	Acct Exec	30,000
19	361-42-9002	Philips	Jon	Robert	Sales	Jones	Acct Exec	35,500

• **Figure 44-6: Personnel data list sorted by department; supervisor, last name, first name, and middle name.**

When sorting data list records on more than three key fields, you need to determine the order of the key fields from most general to most specific. In the preceding example, this arrangement would be as follows:

```
Department, Supervisor, Last Name, First
   Name, Middle Name
```

After arranging the fields in this manner, you then perform your first sort operation with the more specific key fields at the end of the list. In this example, these fields include the following fields as the primary, secondary, and tertiary keys:

```
Last Name, First Name, Middle Name
```

Next, you perform your second sorting operation with the more general key fields at the beginning of the list. In this example, the primary and secondary fields are

```
Department, Supervisor
```

Sorting the Field Names in a Data List

You can use Excel's column-sorting capability to change the order of the fields in a data list without having to resort to cutting and pasting various columns of data. To sort the columns (fields) in a data list, you need to add a row at the top of the list that you then define as the primary sorting key. The cells in this row contain numbers (from 1 to the number of the last field in the data list) that indicate the new order of the fields.

Figures 44-7 and 44-8 illustrate how you can use column sorting to modify the field order of a data list in the sample personnel data list. In Figure 44-7, I inserted a new row (row 1) above the row with the field names for this data list. As you can see, the cells in this row contain numbers that indicate the new field order. After the fields are sorted using the values in this row (see Figure 44-8), the ID No field remains first (indicated by 1), the First Department field becomes the second (2), the Supervisor field is third (3), followed by the First Name (4), Middle Name (5), Last Name (6), Title (7), and Salary (8) fields.

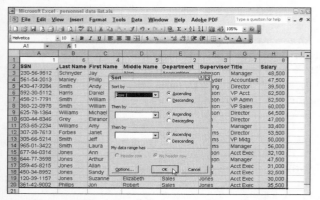

• **Figure 44-7:** Personnel data list before sorting the columns according to the numbers in the top row.

When I opened the Sort dialog box (Data⇨Sort), Excel automatically selected Column A as the primary sort key in the Sort By drop-down list box. I then selected the No Header Row option button and clicked the Options button to open the Sort Options dialog box. Here, I selected the Sort Left to Right option button and then clicked OK. Excel changed Column A to Row 1 in the Sort By drop-down list box.

Figure 44-8 shows the personnel data list after clicking the OK button in the Sort dialog box and sorting its fields according to the values in the first row. After sorting the data list, you then delete this row and modify the column widths to suit the new arrangement before saving the data list with its new field arrangement.

• **Figure 44-8:** Personnel data list after sorting its column in ascending order of the top row numbers.

When sorting the columns in a data list, you must remember to click the Options button in the Sort dialog box and then select the Sort Left to Right option button in the Sort Options dialog box. Otherwise, Excel sorts your records instead of your columns, and in the process, the row of field names becomes sorted in with the other data records in your list!

Technique 45

Quick and Easy Basic Data List Filtering

Save Time By

- ✔ Using AutoFilter to display just certain records in a data list

- ✔ Using AutoFilter to find records with the top or bottom ten items in a list

- ✔ Using custom views to re-create subsets of a data list

- ✔ Using the Custom AutoFilter feature to create a subset for a range of values in a field

Filtering refers to the process of sifting through all the records in a data list to display only those records that meet the particular criteria that you specify. In database lingo, this process is also known as *querying the database*. The records that meet the filtering criteria you set up for the query (and which are subsequently the only ones that are displayed in the list in the worksheet) are referred to as a *subset* of the database.

Excel's AutoFilter feature makes the filtering of most lists you create a real snap, enabling you to quickly alternate between a subset of the data list containing only the filtered records and the full list with all the records. This technique covers how to use AutoFilter to do basic and custom filtering of the data list. It also covers using the Advanced Filter feature to perform more sophisticated queries that use any number of criteria producing the subset of the data list.

AutoFilter Basics

Excel's AutoFilter feature is so simple to use that you can set up the filtering criteria and display the subset of the data list that meet those criteria in literally a few button clicks after turning the feature on. To turn AutoFilter on, position the cell pointer somewhere in one of the cells of the list and choose Data⇨Filter⇨AutoFilter. When you select this command, Excel indicates that AutoFilter is on by displaying drop-down buttons to the right of each field name (column heading) in the data list, as shown in Figure 45-1.

To filter the list, you simply click the drop-down button for each field (column) that you want to use as filtering criteria and then select the entry you want to use on its drop-down list. For example, to filter the Employee list so that you only see records where the Dept field is Accounting, click the Dept field's drop-down button and then select Accounting in its drop-down list. Excel then hides the rows for all records where the department is not Accounting, leaving only those where the Dept field contains Accounting displayed. (See Figure 45-2). The program also colors the downward-pointing triangle in the Dept field's drop-down button blue to indicate that the field is being used in filtering the data list.

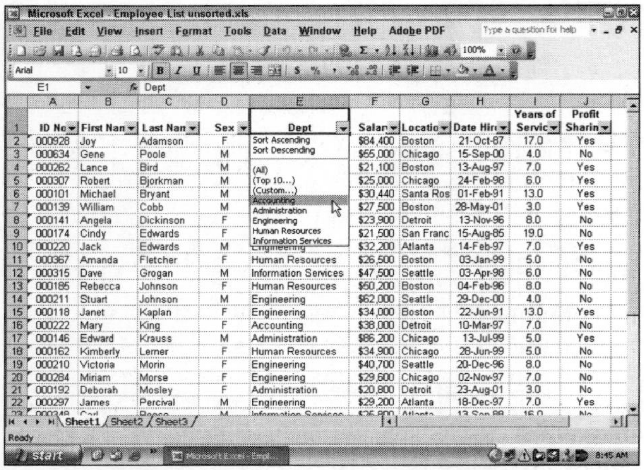

• **Figure 45-1: Turning on AutoFilter in the Employee data list.**

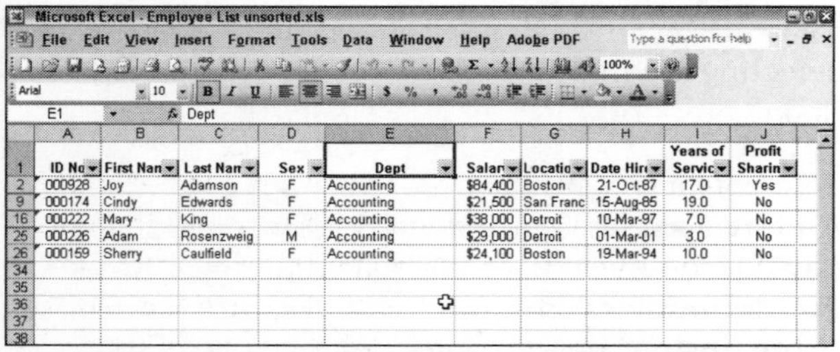

• **Figure 45-2: The Employee data list after filtering out all records except those where the Dept field is Accounting.**

To further filter the list and display only those records where the Dept is Accounting and the Profit Sharing is No, click the drop-down button on the Profit Sharing field name and then select No in its drop-down list. If you then want to filter the list even further to display only the records where the Dept is Accounting, Profit Sharing is No, and the Location is Detroit, click the Location field's drop-down button and select Detroit in its drop-down list.

When you filter a data list to create a subset in this manner, Excel only hides the records that don't meet your filtering criteria — no rows are actually deleted from the workbook. To redisplay all the hidden rows with the missing records, choose Data➪Filter➪Show All. If you're filtering the list using the criteria from only one field (column), you can also do this by clicking (All) near the top of that field's drop-down list.

You can also redisplay all the records in the data list by turning AutoFilter off (Data➪Filter➪AutoFilter).

If you filter your data list with multiple criteria and only want to redisplay the records hidden by a particular criterion, click the (All) item in that field's drop-down list.

Excel's AutoFilter buttons enable you to sort a subset of the data list on different sorting keys. To sort a subset in ascending order on a particular field, select the Sort Ascending item at the top of its drop-down list. To sort in descending order, select Sort Descending instead. To sort the subset on more than one key, select either the Sort Ascending or Sort Descending item on the various fields' drop-down lists in the order appropriate for sorting duplicates. (See Technique 44.)

Making it into the top-ten list

You can select the (Top 10 . . .) item at the top of a particular field's AutoFilter drop-down list to filter out all records except for those whose entries in that field are at the top or bottom of the list by a certain number (10 by default) or in a certain top or bottom percent (10 by default).

You can only use the (Top 10 . . .) item on numerical and date fields. When you select this kind of filtering in a text field, Excel's only response is to beep at you as if to say, "Don't you know that top-ten filtering doesn't make any sense here?"

When you select the (Top 10 . . .) item on a numeric or date field's drop-down list, Excel opens the Top 10 AutoFilter dialog box, shown in Figure 45-3. Here, you can specify your filtering criteria. By default, the Top 10 AutoFilter dialog box is set to filter out all records except those whose entries are among the top ten items in that field. If you want to use this default filtering criteria, simply click OK.

• **Figure 45-3: Using the Top 10 AutoFilter settings to display the records with the top ten years of service.**

You can also change the filtering criteria before you filter the data. You can choose between Top and Bottom in the leftmost drop-down list and between Items and Percent in the rightmost one. You can also change the number in the middle drop-down list by selecting the box and entering a new value or choosing one from its list.

When assigning a new value in this combo box, you can enter a value from 1 on up. Of course, you want to enter a number less than the total number of records in the list when Items is selected in the rightmost combo box and less than 100 when Percent is selected there or else what's the point of using the Top 10 AutoFilter at all?

Figure 45-4 shows the Employee data list after using the default settings for the Top 10 AutoFilter in the Years of Service field to display the records for the employees with the top ten years of service and then sorting the ten records in this subset in descending order by these years (by clicking Sort Descending in the Years of Service field's drop-down list).

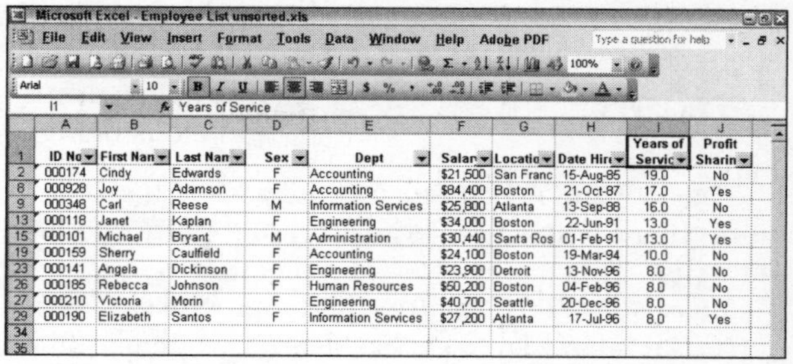

• **Figure 45-4: The Employee data list showing the records for the employees with the top ten years of service.**

Saving subsets of a data list as custom views

In Technique 32, I introduce custom views and how they enable you to save different worksheet screen display settings so that you can instantly put all those settings into effect just by selecting the name of its view. Custom views are perfect for saving subsets of a data list using different filtering criteria. That way, instead of having to go through all the tedium of turning on AutoFilter and then selecting the filtering criteria in all the relevant fields, you can re-create and display the subset in a flash simply by selecting the name of its view in the Custom Views dialog box (View⇨Custom Views).

To create a custom view that re-creates and displays a filtered subset of your data list, you need to manually turn on AutoFilter, select the filtering criteria for the appropriate fields, and then click the Add button in the Custom Views dialog box. (See Technique 32 for the details.)

 When creating a new custom view that shows a subset of a filtered data list, you must be careful not to clear the Hidden Rows, Columns, and Filter Settings check box in the Add View dialog box (refer to Figure 32-6). Otherwise, you are unable to turn on AutoFilter and hide the rows with records that don't meet your filtering criteria for the view you create.

Customizing the AutoFilter Settings

The basic AutoFilter feature doesn't let you select more than a single filtering criterion for any one field in the list. This means, for example, that you can use the basic AutoFilter to filter the Employee list for a particular salary such as $55,000 but you can't filter the list for salaries in the range between $55,000 and $75,000. To filter a data list for a range of values in a particular field, you need to use the Custom AutoFilter feature.

To invoke Custom AutoFilter, you need to select the (Custom) item at the top of the field's drop-down list. For the salary example, for example, you do this by clicking (Custom) in the Salary field's drop-down list. When you select this item, a Custom AutoFilter dialog box similar to the one shown in Figure 45-5 appears.

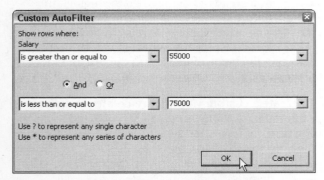

• **Figure 45-5: Using Custom AutoFilter to filter out records except for those within a range of salaries.**

Here, you select the type of operator to use in evaluating the first and the second condition in the top and bottom drop-down lists and the values to be evaluated in the first and second condition in the combo boxes. You also specify the type of relationship between the two conditions with the And or Or options. (The And option is selected by default.)

When selecting the operator for the first and second condition in the leftmost drop-down lists, you have the following choices:

- ✔ Equals
- ✔ Does Not Equal
- ✔ Is Greater Than
- ✔ Is Greater Than or Equal To
- ✔ Is Less Than
- ✔ Is Less Than or Equal To
- ✔ Begins With
- ✔ Does Not Begin With
- ✔ Ends With
- ✔ Does Not End With
- ✔ Contains
- ✔ Does Not Contain

Note that you can use the Begins With, Ends With, and Contains operators and their negative counterparts when filtering a text field. You can also use the question mark (?) and asterisk (*) wildcard characters when entering the characters for use with these operators. (The question mark wildcard stands for individual characters, and the asterisk stands for one or more characters.) You use the other logical operators when dealing with numeric and date fields.

When specifying the values to evaluate in the associated combo boxes, you can type in the text, number, or date, or you can select an existing field entry by selecting one from the drop-down list.

Figure 45-6 shows the subset of the Employee data list after using the Custom AutoFilter (refer to Figure 45-5) that sets up the AND condition that filters out all records except those where the salaries are between $55,000 and $75,000, inclusive and after sorting these remaining records on the Salary field in descending order.

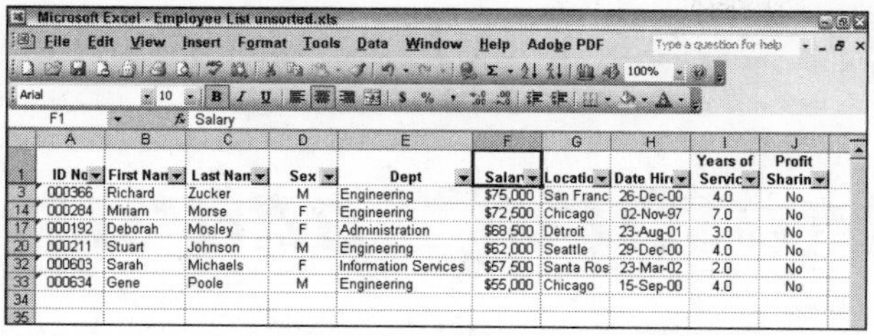

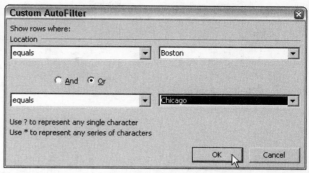

• **Figure 45-6:** A subset of data list where salaries are between $55,000 and $75,000, inclusive.

You can also use the Custom AutoFilter feature to create an OR condition where records appear if they contain either a value or entry that you specify in any one of the two conditions. For example, suppose that you want to create a subset with the records in the data list where the location is Boston or Chicago. To do this, you open the Custom AutoFilter dialog box from the Location field's drop-down list. Then select the Equals operator in both condition top and bottom drop-down lists, select Boston and then Chicago in the respective combo boxes, and then select the OR condition, as shown in Figure 45-7.

Figure 45-8 shows the subset of the Employee data list after using the Custom AutoFilter (refer to Figure 45-7) that sets up the OR condition that filters out all records except those where the location is Boston or Chicago and after sorting these remaining records on the Location field in ascending order.

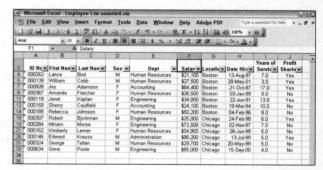

• **Figure 45-7:** Using Custom AutoFilter to filter out records except for those where the city is Boston or Chicago.

• **Figure 45-8:** A subset of the data list where the location is Boston or Chicago.

Technique 46

More Data List Filtering plus Statistical Analysis

Save Time By

- Using the Advanced Filter to create a subset of a data list
- Setting up AND and OR filtering criteria
- Setting up calculated filtering criteria
- Using database functions to compute statistics about a data list

Technique 45 introduces you to basic data list filtering, which enables you to create a subset of all the records in the list using filtering criteria you select with either the AutoFilter drop-down lists for individual fields or the Top 10 or Custom AutoFilters. This technique takes you to the next step: using the Advanced Filter to create a subset using various filtering criteria entered into a separate range in the worksheet.

The great thing about using the Advanced Filter feature is that it enables you to set up calculated criteria for filtering the data list and creating the subset. Also, instead of just having Excel hide rows in the original list to create the subset, you can have the program actually copy the matching records that make up the filtered subset into a new part of the worksheet. That way, you can sort, print, and perform any other needed manipulations on the subset without affecting the records in the original data list.

In addition to the Advanced Filtering feature, this technique introduces you to Excel's database functions that enable you to compute various statistics about its data based on criteria that you set up in a range just as you do with the Advanced Filter feature.

Putting the Advanced Filter in Service

In order to use the Advanced Filter feature to filter the data list, you need to specify two ranges: a List range containing all the records in the data list — including the top row with the field names — and a Criteria range containing a copy of the row of field names with the various filtering criteria entered into the appropriate cells. Optionally, you can specify a third Copy To range that indicates where Excel begins copying the records in the subset of the filtered data when you use the Copy to Another Location option.

If you're using the Advanced Filter feature to copy records to a new location, you can locate the Criteria range in the top rows of columns to the right of the actual data list and then specify the Copy To range as the first cell underneath the Criteria range, similar to the arrangement shown in Figure 46-1.

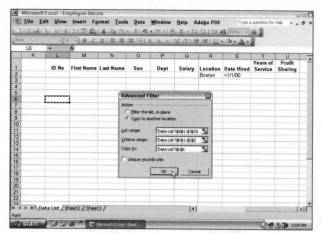

• **Figure 46-1:** Copying records that aren't filtered out by the criteria entered in the Criteria range.

For this figure, I copied the field names in the original data list in the range A1:J1 to the range L1:U1. I then entered Boston in the copy of the Location column (cell R2) and <1/1/00 in the copy of Date Hired column (cell S2). After setting up the Criteria range in cells R2:S2, I then positioned the cell pointer in cell L6 (where I want the Copy To range to begin) and opened the Advanced Filter dialog box (Data⇨Filter⇨Advanced Filter).

Here, I specified the range A1:J33 containing the original records of the Employee data list as the List range. (Note that Excel automatically adds the sheet name to this range and expresses its address as absolute references when you select the range with the mouse.) I then selected the Criteria Range text box and selected range R1:S2. (Again, Excel adds the sheet name and expresses its address as absolute references.)

Finally, I selected the Copy to Another Location option, which makes the Copy To text box available. I then selected the Copy To text box and selected the single cell L6 (which Excel enters as 'Data List'!$L$5).

Figure 46-2 shows you the result of this *query* (the technical name for copying a subset of a data list using filtering criteria) after you click OK in the Advanced Filter dialog box. Excel copies the records that match the criteria where the location is Boston and the Date Hired is prior to January 1, 2000, from the original data list in the range A1:J33 into the Copy To range starting with cell L6 and extending to cell U12.

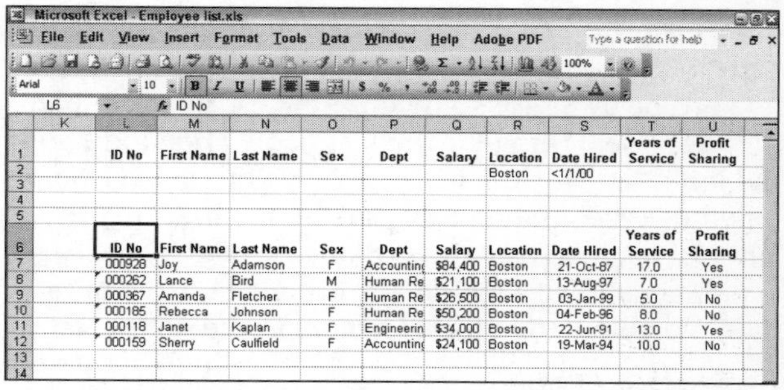

	ID No	First Name	Last Name	Sex	Dept	Salary	Location	Date Hired	Years of Service	Profit Sharing
2							Boston	<1/1/00		
7	000928	Joy	Adamson	F	Accounting	$84,400	Boston	21-Oct-87	17.0	Yes
8	000262	Lance	Bird	M	Human Re	$21,100	Boston	13-Aug-97	7.0	Yes
9	000367	Amanda	Fletcher	F	Human Re	$26,500	Boston	03-Jan-99	5.0	No
10	000185	Rebecca	Johnson	F	Human Re	$50,200	Boston	04-Feb-96	8.0	No
11	000118	Janet	Kaplan	F	Engineerin	$34,000	Boston	22-Jun-91	13.0	Yes
12	000159	Sherry	Caulfield	F	Accounting	$24,100	Boston	19-Mar-94	10.0	No

• **Figure 46-2:** A subset with the records where the Location is Boston and the Date Hired is before Jan. 1, 2000.

If you want, you can then sort the records in the subset by turning on AutoFilter (Data⇨Filter⇨ AutoFilter) and then selecting the Sort Ascending or Sort Descending item at the top of the Date Hired field's drop-down list. You can also print this subset by selecting its range, L6:U12, and then choosing the Selection option in the Print dialog box (File⇨Print) before clicking OK.

If you don't want to copy the records that meet your filtering criteria to a new place in the workbook, you can just filter the original data list. To do this, leave the Filter the List, In-Place option selected when you specify the List range and Criteria range in the Advanced Filter dialog box. When you filter the list, Excel simply hides the rows of the records that don't meet the filtering criteria specified in your Criteria range, leaving just those that do meet the criteria displayed in the worksheet. To redisplay all the records in the data list, choose Data⇨Filter⇨Show All.

To weed out any duplicate records that match your filtering criteria from the Copy To range, be sure to select the Unique Records Only check box in the Advanced Filter dialog box before you click OK.

Specifying filtering criteria

Entering filtering criteria in the Criteria Range of the worksheet for advanced filtering is very similar to entering criteria in the data form after clicking the Criteria button. (See Technique 43.) However, you need to be aware of some differences. For example, if you are searching for the last name *Paul* and enter the label `Paul` for the Criteria range in the Last Name column, Excel matches any last name that begins with *P-a-u-l* such as Pauley, Paulson, and so on. To avoid having Excel match any other last name beside Paul, you have to enter a formula in the cell, as in

```
="Paul"
```

When entering filtering criteria for advanced filtering, you can also use the question mark (?) or the asterisk (*) wildcard character in your selection criteria, just like you do when using the data form to find records. If, for example, you enter `J*n` in the First Name column, Excel considers any characters between *J* and *n* in the First Name field to be a match, including Joan, Jon, or John as well as Jane or Joanna. To restrict the matches to just those names with characters between *J* and *n* and to prevent matches with names that have trailing characters, you need to enter the following formula in the cell:

```
="J*n"
```

When you use a selection formula like this one, Excel matches names like Joan, Jon, and John but not names such as Jane or Joanna that have a character following the *n*.

When setting up your filtering criteria in the Criteria range, you can also use the other logical operators, including >, >=, <, <=, and <>. See Table 46-1 for descriptions and examples for each of these logical operators.

TABLE 46-1: THE LOGICAL OPERATORS IN THE SELECTION CRITERIA

Operator	Meaning	Example	Locates
=	Equal to	="CA"	Records where the state is CA (California)
>	Greater than	>m	Records where the name starts with a letter after M (that is, N through Z)
>=	Greater than or equal to	>=11/6/02	Records where the date is on or after November 6, 2002
<	Less than	<d	Records where the name begins with a letter before D (that is, A, B, or C)
<=	Less than or equal to	<=12/12/04	Records where the date is on or before December 12, 2004
<>	Not equal to	<>"OR"	Records where the state is not equal to OR (Oregon)

To find all the records where a particular field is blank in the data list, enter = and press the spacebar to enter a space in the cell. To find all the records where a particular field is *not* blank in the list, enter <> and press the spacebar to enter a space in the cell.

Setting up AND and OR filtering criteria

When you enter two or more filtering criteria in the same row in the Criteria range, Excel treats the criteria as a logical AND condition and selects only those records that match all the criteria. Figure 46-3 shows an example of a query that uses a logical AND condition. Here, Excel copies only those records where the department is Human Resources *and* the years of service are greater than 4 because both the criteria Human Resources and >4 are placed in the same row (row 2) for their respective field names, Dept and Date Hired.

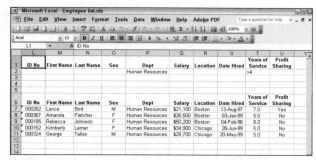

• **Figure 46-3:** A subset with the records where the Department is Human Resources and Date Hired is before Jan. 1, 2000.

Note that in order to perform this query right after performing the one shown in Figure 46-2, I had to modify the Criteria range from 'Data List'!$R$1:$S$2 to 'Data List'!$P$1:$T$2 (so that the range now contains both Human Resources in cell P2 and >4 in cell T2) and had to modify the Copy To range from 'Data List'!$L$6 to 'Data List'!$L$6:$U$6 (so that it includes all the field names).

If you don't specify all the field names in a range where they already exist, Excel only copies the entries from the matching records in the field or fields specified as part of the Copy To range. In other words, if I leave the Copy To range set at the single cell ('Data List'!$L$6), Excel copies only the ID numbers for the five records that match the filtering criteria where the department is Human Resources and the years of service are greater than 4. All the rest of the fields in the matching records are left blank!

You can reuse a Copy To range for your queries without having to first delete the matching records from a previous query. Excel automatically removes all the records from the previous query before copying in the records that match the query you're currently conducting.

When you enter two or more criteria in different rows of the Criteria range, Excel treats the criteria as a logical OR and selects records that meet any one of the criteria they contain. Figure 46-4 shows you an example of a query using a logical OR condition. In this example, Excel copies records where the location is either San Francisco or Chicago. To make this happen, I entered San Francisco in the Location column in the second row (row 2) of the Criteria range and Chicago in the third row (row 3).

Microsoft Excel - Employee list.xls

	ID No	First Name	Last Name	Sex	Dept	Salary	Location	Date Hired	Years of Service	Profit Sharing
1	ID No	First Name	Last Name	Sex	Dept	Salary	Location	Date Hired	Years of Service	Profit Sharing
2							San Francisco			
3							Chicago			
4										
5										
6	ID No	First Name	Last Name	Sex	Dept	Salary	Location	Date Hired	Years of Service	Profit Sharing
7	000634	Gene	Poole	M	Engineering	$55,000	Chicago	15-Sep-00	4.0	No
8	000307	Robert	Bjorkman	M	Engineering	$25,000	Chicago	24-Feb-98	6.0	Yes
9	000174	Cindy	Edwards	F	Accounting	$21,500	San Francisco	13-Aug-85	19.0	No
10	000146	Edward	Krauss	M	Administration	$86,200	Chicago	13-Jul-99	5.0	Yes
11	000162	Kimberly	Lerner	F	Human Resources	$34,900	Chicago	28-Jun-99	5.0	No
12	000284	Miriam	Morse	F	Engineering	$29,600	Chicago	02-Nov-97	7.0	No
13	000339	Charles	Smith	M	Administration	$87,800	San Francisco	09-Jul-98	6.0	No
14	000324	George	Tallan	M	Human Resources	$29,700	Chicago	20-May-99	5.0	No
15	000366	Richard	Zucker	M	Engineering	$37,500	San Francisco	26-Dec-00	4.0	No

• **Figure 46-4:** A subset with the records where the Location is either Chicago or San Francisco.

To perform this query, I only had to modify the Criteria range in the Advanced Filter dialog box to 'Data List'!$R$1:$R$3 to include the field name in cell R1 and the two OR criteria in cells R2 and R3, respectively, before clicking OK.

When setting up your filtering criteria, you can combine logical AND and logical OR conditions (again, assuming that you expand the Criteria range sufficiently to include all the rows containing criteria). For example, if you edit the Criteria range used in the previous query by entering >1/1/99 in cell S2 (in the Date Hired column) in row 2 and then expand the Criteria range to 'Data List'!$R$1:$S$3 when redoing the query, Excel copies the records where the location is San Francisco *and* the date hired is after January 1, 1999, as well as the records where the location is Chicago (regardless of the date hired).

Setting up calculated filtering criteria

You can use calculated criteria to filter or query your data list. To do this, you need to enter a logical formula that Excel can evaluate as either TRUE or FALSE in the Criteria range. You must also enter this formula under a text entry that is *not* used as a field name in the data list. (I repeat, is *not* a field name in the data list.)

Figure 46-5 shows an example of using a calculated criterion that compares values in the Salary field to a calculated value that isn't actually entered in the data list. Here, I performed a query that copies all the records from the Employee data list where the employee's salary is above the average salary (which happens to be $41,098). In this example, cell V2 contains the formula that uses the AVERAGE function to compute the average employee salary and then compares the first salary entry in cell F2 of the data list to that average. In the case of the value in cell F2, this particular condition happens to be true. (The salary $84,400 is indeed greater than the average salary of $41,098.)

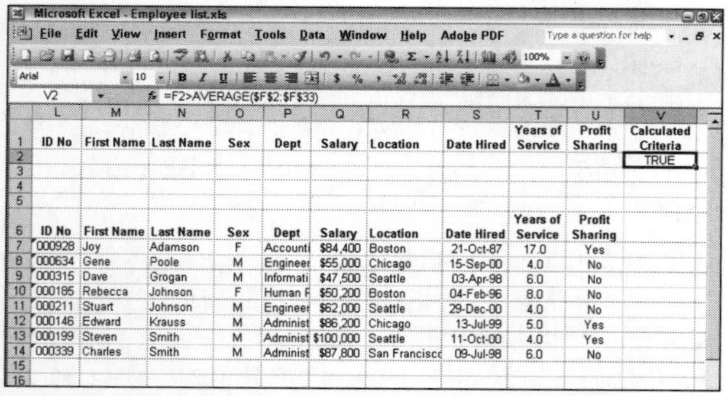

• **Figure 46-5:** A subset with the records where the salary is greater than the average salary in the data list.

Note that this logical formula is placed in cell V2 of the Calculated Criteria column — a cell added to the end of the row of copied field names. In the logical formula, cell F2 is referred to because it is the first

cell in the data list containing a salary entry. The cell range ($F$2:$F$33) used as the argument of the AVERAGE function is the range in the Salary field containing all the salary entries.

To use a calculated criterion like this one, you must remember to place the logical formula under a label that isn't used as a field name in the data list itself (in this example, the label Calculated Criteria does not appear anywhere in the row of field names). You must include this label and formula in the Criteria range (for this query example, the Criteria range is defined as the cell range 'Data List'!$V$1:$V$2).

When you then perform the query by using the Advanced Filter feature, Excel applies this calculated criterion to every record in the database. Excel does this by adjusting the first Salary field cell reference F2 (entered as a relative reference) as the program examines the rest of the records. Note, however, that the range reference specified as the argument of the AVERAGE function is entered as an absolute reference ($F$2:$F$33) in the criterion formula so that Excel doesn't adjust this reference but rather compares the Salary entry for each record to the AVERAGE computed salary for this entire range.

You can also set up calculated criteria that compare entries in one or more fields to other entries in the data list. For example, to copy the records where the Years of Service entry is at least two years greater than the record before it (assuming that you have sorted the data list in ascending order by years of service), you enter the following logical formula in the cell beneath the Calculated Criteria cell:

```
=I3>I2+2
```

Most often, when referencing to cells within the data list itself, you want to leave the cell references relative so that they can be adjusted. However, you keep references to the cells outside the database absolute so that they aren't changed when making the comparison with the rest of the records.

When you enter the logical formula for a calculated criterion, Excel returns the logical value TRUE or FALSE. This logical value applies only to the field entry for the first record in the data list that you refer to in the logical formula. By inspecting this field entry in the data list and seeing if it does indeed meet your intended selection criteria, you can usually tell whether your logical formula is correct.

You can also use Excel's AND, OR, and NOT functions with the logical operators in calculated criteria to find records that fall within a range. For example, to find all the records in the Employee data list where the salaries range between $55,000 and $75,000, you enter the following logical formula with the AND function in the cell beneath the Calculated Criteria cell:

```
=AND(F2>=55000,F2<=75000)
```

To find all the records in the Employee data list where the date hired is either before January 1, 1998, or the salary greater than $85,000, you enter the following logical formula with the OR function in the cell beneath the Calculated Criteria cell:

```
=OR(H2<1/1/98,F2>85000)
```

Note that H2 is the first cell that contains the first date hired entry in the Employee data list just as F2 is the first cell that contains a salary entry.

Getting Data List Statistics

Excel includes a number of database functions that you can use to calculate statistics, such as the total, average, maximum, minimum, and count in a particular field of the data list when the criteria that you specify in a Criteria range are met. For example, you could use the DSUM function in the sample Employee data list to compute the sum of all the salaries for employees hired after January 1, 2000, or you could use the DCOUNT function to compute the number of records for the Human Resources department.

The database functions, regardless of the difference in names (and they all begin with the letter D) and the computations that they perform, all take the same three arguments, as illustrated by the DAVERAGE function:

```
DAVERAGE(database,field,criteria)
```

The arguments for the database functions require the following information:

- ✔ **Database** is the argument that specifies the range containing the data list. The range must include the row of field names.

- ✔ **Field** is the argument that specifies the field whose values are calculated by the database function (averaged in the case of the DAVERAGE function). You can specify this argument by enclosing the name of the field in double quotes (as in `"Salary"` or `"Date Hired"`), or you can enter the number of the column in the data list (counting from left to right with the first field counted as 1).

- ✔ **Criteria** is the argument that specifies the address of the range containing the criteria you're using to determine which values are calculated. This range must include at least one field name indicating the field whose values are to be evaluated and one cell with the values or expression to be used in the evaluation.

Note that in specifying the *field* argument, you must refer to a column in the data list that contains numeric or date data for all the database functions. With the one exception of the DGET function, Excel can't perform computations on text fields. If you mistakenly specify a column with text entries as the field argument, Excel returns an error value or 0 as the result. Table 46-2 lists the various database functions available in Excel along with an explanation of what each one calculates. (You already know what arguments each one takes.)

TABLE 46-2: EXCEL'S DATABASE FUNCTIONS

Database Function Name	What It Calculates
DAVERAGE	Averages all the values in a field of the data list that match the criteria you specify.
DCOUNT	Counts the number of cells with numeric entries in a field of the data list that match the criteria you specify.
DCOUNTA	Counts the number of nonblank cells in a field of the data list that match the criteria you specify.
DGET	Extracts a single value from a record in the data list that matches the criteria you specify. If no record matches the criteria, the function returns the #VALUE! error. If multiple records match, the function returns the #NUM! error.
DMAX	Returns the highest value in a field of the data list that matches the criteria you specify.
DMIN	Returns the lowest value in a field of the data list that matches the criteria you specify.
DPRODUCT	Multiplies all the values in a field of the data list that match the criteria you specify.
DSTDEV	Estimates the standard deviation based on the sample of values in a field of the data list that match the criteria you specify.
DSTDEVP	Calculates the standard deviation based on the population of values in a field of the data list that match the criteria you specify.
DSUM	Sums all the values in a field of the data list that match the criteria you specify.
DVAR	Estimates the variance based on the sample of values in a field of the data list that match the criteria you specify.

Database Function Name	What It Calculates
DVARP	Calculates the variance based on the population of values in a field of the data list that match the criteria you specify.

Figure 46-6 illustrates the use of the database function DSUM. Cell B2 contains the following formula:

```
=DSUM(A3:J35,6,C1:C2)
```

This DSUM function computes the total of all the salaries in the data list that are above $55,000. This total is shown in cell B2 as $468,500.

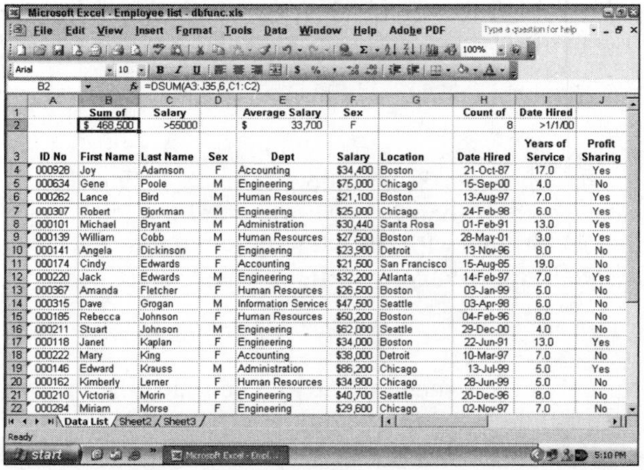

• **Figure 46-6:** A subset with the records where the salary is greater than the average salary in the data list.

To perform this calculation, I specified the range A3:J35 containing the entire Employee data list — including the top row of field names — as the *database* argument. I then specified 6 as the *field* argument of the DSUM function because the sixth field in the data list (as counted from the left) contains the salary values that I want totaled. Finally, I specified the range C1:C2 as the *criteria* argument of the DSUM function. These two cells contain the Criteria range that designate that only the values in the Salary field exceeding 55000 are to be summed.

Figure 46-6 also contains an example of using the DAVERAGE database function in the cell range E1:F2. This DAVERAGE function calculates the average salary for the female employees (employees where the Sex field contains F). To get Excel to perform this calculation, I entered the following database function formula into cell E2:

```
=DAVERAGE(A3:J35,6,F1:F2)
```

This DCOUNT function uses the same *database* argument A3:J35 and the *field* argument 6. The *criteria* argument for this DAVERAGE function is F1:F2, the range that contains the Sex field name.

Finally, Figure 46-6 also contains an example of the DCOUNT function in the cell range H1:I2. This DCOUNT function calculates the number of employees hired since January 1, 2000. To do this calculation, I entered the following database function formula into cell H2:

```
=DCOUNT(A3:J35,8,I1:I2)
```

Again, this DCOUNT database function uses the same *database* argument, A3:J35, but instead of 6 as the *field* argument designating the column whose entries are to be computed as in the other two examples, I specified 8 because the Date Hired field is in the eighth column in the data list as counted from the left. The *criteria* argument for this DCOUNT function is I1:I2, the range that contains the Date Hired field name above the logical formula >1/1/00 in I2.

Technique 47

Doing What-if Analysis in a Snap with Data Tables

What-if analysis, a kind of financial fortune-telling that attempts to project future returns based on various assumptions, has always been the strong suit of electronic spreadsheet programs such as Excel. This technique covers the basic what-if analysis that you can perform with Excel's Data Table feature. (See Technique 48 for information on doing slightly a more sophisticated what-if analysis using the Goal Seeking and Scenario features.)

As part of creating a data table, you enter a series of input values in the worksheet, and Excel uses each of them in the formula that you specify. When Excel finishes computing the data table, you see the results produced by each change in the input values in a single range of the worksheet. You can then save the data table as part of the worksheet if you need to keep a record of the results.

When using Excel's Data Table feature, you have a choice between creating a one-variable and a two-variable data table. In a one-variable data table, Excel substitutes a series of different values for a single input value in a formula. In a two-variable data table, Excel substitutes a series of different values for two input values in a formula.

Creating a One-Variable Data Table

To create a one-variable data table, you need to set up the master formula in your worksheet and then, in a different range of the worksheet, enter the series of different values that you want substituted for a single input value in that formula. Figures 47-1 and 47-2 demonstrate how you go about doing this.

In Figure 47-1, cell B5 contains a simple formula for computing the projected sales for 2005, assuming an annual growth rate of 1.75% over the annual sales in 2004. The 2005 projected sales in this cell are calculated with the following formula:

```
=Sales_04+(Sales_04*Growth_05)
```

This formula adds the original sales amount entered in cell B2 (given the range name Sales_04) to the amount of projected growth (calculated by multiplying the sales amount in B2 by the growth rate of 1.75% entered in cell B3 and given the range name Growth_05). Cell B5 shows you that, assuming an annual growth rate of 1.75% in the year 2005, you can project total sales of $890,312.50.

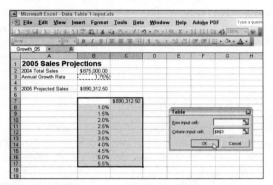

• **Figure 47-1:** Setting up a one-variable data table.

But what if the growth rate in 2005 is not as low as 1.75%, or what if the growth rate is even (heaven forbid) lower than anticipated? To create the one-variable table to answer these questions, you first bring forward the master formula in cell B5 to cell C7 with the formula =B5. Then you enter the series of different growth rates as the input values in column B, starting in cell B8. (Cell B7, at the intersection of the row with the master formula and the column with the input values, must be left blank in a one-variable data table.)

You can create this series of input values for the data table quickly with the AutoFill feature. (See Technique 13.) For this example, I created a data series that increments each succeeding value by 0.5% in the cell range B8:B17, starting at 1% and ending at 5.5%.

After generating the growth rate series in the cell range B8:B17, select the cell range B7:C17 and choose Data⇨Table. The blank cell range C8:C17 is where Excel puts the projected sales figures based on the growth rate entered into the comparable cell in column B.

Excel opens the Table dialog box, shown in Figure 47-1, where you must specify the row input cell in the Row Input Cell text box and/or the column input cell in the Column Input Cell. The cell that you designate must correspond to the cell in the worksheet that contains the original input value that is fed into the master formula.

In the data table in this example, you only need to designate B3 as the column input cell. (In the case of Figure 47-1, when you click in this cell or use an arrow key to select this cell, Excel enters the absolute cell reference, as in $B$3.) You choose cell B3 because it contains the growth rate value used in the master formula.

After indicating the row or column input cells, Excel computes the data table when you click OK. In this example, the program creates the data table by substituting each input value in the data series (the range B8:B17) into the column input (cell B3). The input value is used in the master formula to calculate a new result, which is entered in the corresponding cell (in the cell range C8:C17). After the program finishes calculating the data table, Excel returns the original value to the row or column input cell (in this case, 1.75% in cell B3).

Figure 47-2 shows the completed data table. Here, you can see at a glance the effect on the projected sales for 2005 of changing a half percentage point for the growth rate. After creating the data table, you can then format the results and save the table as part of the worksheet.

If you want to see the effect on the results in the table of using a different range of variables, you only need to enter the new input values in the existing range. By default, Excel automatically recalculates the results in the output range of a data table whenever you change any of its input values. If you want to control when each data table in the spreadsheet is recalculated, while still allowing the formulas in the worksheet to be automatically recalculated, select the Automatic Except Tables option on the

Calculation tab of the Options dialog box (Tools⇨ Options). You then manually recalculate the values in the data table by pressing F9.

• **Figure 47-2:** A worksheet with a completed one-variable data table.

Excel computes the results in a data table by creating an array formula that uses the TABLE function. (See Technique 25 on array formulas.) In this example, the array formula entered into the cell range C8:C17 is as follows:

```
{=TABLE(,B3)}
```

The TABLE function can take two arguments, *row_ref* and/or *column_ref*, which represent the row input cell and column input cell for the data table, respectively. In this example, the data table uses only a column input cell, so B3 is listed as the second and only argument of the TABLE function. Because Excel enters the results in a data table by using an array formula, Excel doesn't allow you to clear individual result cells in its output range. If you try to delete a single result in the data table, Excel displays an alert dialog box, stating that you can't change part of a table.

> To delete just the results in the output range of a data table, select all the cells in the output range (cell range C8:C17, in the current example) before pressing the Delete key or choosing Edit⇨Clear⇨All.

Creating a Two-Variable Data Table

When you have a master formula in a spreadsheet in which you want to see the effect of changing two of its input values, you can create a two-variable data table. When you create a two-variable data table, you enter two ranges of input values to substitute in the master formula: a single-row range in the first row of the table and a single-column range in the first column of the data table. When you create a two-variable data table, you place a copy of the master formula in the cell at the intersection of this row and column of input values.

Figure 47-3 shows the typical setup for a two-variable data table. This figure uses the projected sales worksheet from the previous section on a one-variable data table. Here, I added a second variable to project the total sales in 2005. This worksheet contains a value in cell B4 (given the range name Expenses_05) that shows the projected percentage of expenses to sales. This value is used, in turn, in the master formula in cell B5 as follows:

```
=Sales_04+(Sales_04*Growth_05)-(Sales_04*
    Expenses_05)
```

Note that when you factor in the expenses, the projected sales amount at an annual growth rate of 1.75% falls in cell B5 from $890,312.50 to $864,062.50.

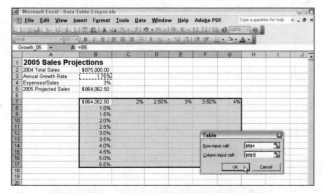

• **Figure 47-3:** Setting up a two-variable data table.

To determine how changing both the growth rate and the percentage of expenses to sales affect the projected sales for 2005, you create a two-variable data table. In setting up this table, you still enter the variable growth rates down column B in the cell range B8:B17. Then you enter the variable expense rates across row 7 in the range C7:G7. This time, you bring forward the master formula by entering the formula =B5 in cell B7, the cell at the intersection of the row and column containing the two input variables.

After setting up the two series of variables in this manner, you're ready to create the table by selecting the cell range B7:G17 and opening the Table dialog box (Data⇨Table). For a two-variable data table, you must designate both a row and column input cell in the worksheet. In this example, the row input cell is B4, which contains the original expense-to-sales percentage. The column input cell remains B3, which contains the original growth rate. After entering these two input cells, you're ready to generate the two-variable data table by clicking OK.

Figure 47-4 shows the completed two-variable data table with the results of changing both the projected growth rate and the projected expenses. As with a one-variable data table, you can format the projected results and save this two-variable data table as part of your worksheet. You can also update the table by changing any of the (two types of) input variables.

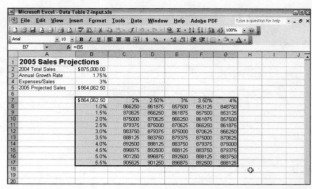

• **Figure 47-4: The worksheet with completed two-variable data table.**

The array formula entered in the output range (C8:G17) to create this two-variable data table is very similar to the one-variable data table array formula, only this time the TABLE function uses both a *row_ref* and *column_ref* argument as follows:

    {=TABLE(B4,B3)}

Because this data table uses an array formula, you must select all the cells in the output range to delete them.

Technique

48

Easy What-if Analysis through Scenarios and Goal Seeking

In Technique 47, I introduce the rudiments of what-if analysis using Excel's Data Table feature, which enables you to project results based on the substitution of either one or two input variables in a master formula. In this technique, I acquaint you with Excel's Scenario Manager, a feature that also enables you to generate different projected results based on sets of input variables. The variables used to generate the projected results are saved as part of named scenarios that you can then reuse in the spreadsheet whenever you need them. After you finish applying the various scenarios to your spreadsheet, the Scenario Manager enables you to generate a summary report that shows both the input variables used by your scenarios as well as the projected results they produce.

In addition to the Scenario Manager, this technique covers Excel's Goal Seek feature that enables you to find the key input value necessary to achieve a projected goal. If you've created a two-dimensional chart representing the projected data, I show you how you can even perform this type of rudimentary goal seeking by directly manipulating particular data markers in the chart.

Exploring Different Scenarios

To create various scenarios for your spreadsheet with Excel's Scenario Manager, you build a worksheet that uses certain cells that change in each scenario (appropriately enough referred to as the *changing cells*). To make it easier to identify the changing cells in each scenario that you create (especially in any scenario summary reports that you generate), assign range names to the variables in the spreadsheet before you create your scenarios. (See Technique 26.)

To create your different scenarios with the Scenario Manager, follow these steps:

1. **Select the changing cells in the spreadsheet — that is, the cells whose values vary in each of your scenarios.**

Remember that you can select nonadjacent cells in the worksheet by holding down the Ctrl key as you click them.

2. **Choose Tools⇨Scenarios to open the Scenario Manager dialog box, shown in Figure 48-1.**

• **Figure 48-1: Adding a new scenario to a worksheet.**

3. **Click the Add button to open the Add Scenario dialog box, shown in Figure 48-2.**

• **Figure 48-2: Naming a new scenario and designating its changing cells.**

This dialog box also contains a Changing Cells text box that contains the addresses of the variable cells that you selected in the worksheet and a Comment box that contains a note with your name and the current date so you always know when you created the particular scenario.

4. **Type a descriptive name for the new scenario in the Scenario Name text box.**

Verify the cell references in the Changing Cells text box to make sure that they're correct — you can modify them if necessary by first clicking in the text box and then clicking the cells in the worksheet while holding down the Ctrl key. You can also edit the note in the Comment box if you want to add more information about your assumptions as part of the new scenario.

5. **Choose what kind of scenario protection, if any, you need with the Prevent Changes and Hide check boxes.**

By default, Excel protects a scenario from changes when you turn on protection for the worksheet (see Technique 38) so that you can't edit or delete the scenario in any way. If you want Excel to hide the scenario as well when worksheet protection is turned on, select the Hide check box. If you don't want to protect or hide the scenario when worksheet protection is turned on, clear the Prevent Changes check box and leave the Hide check box as it is.

6. **Click OK.**

Excel then opens the Scenario Values dialog box, shown in Figure 48-3.

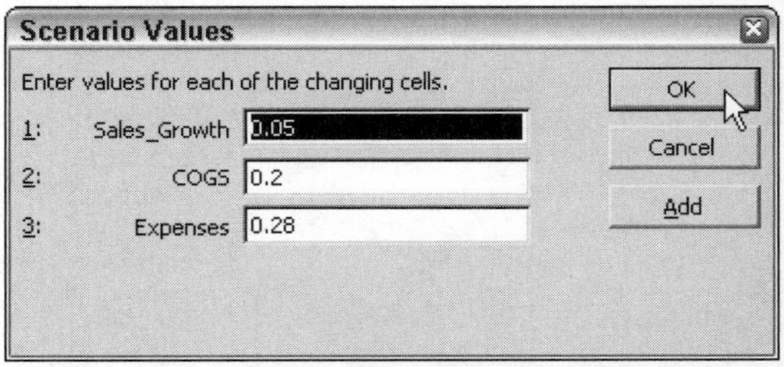

• **Figure 48-3: Entering the values for the changing cells appropriate to the new scenario.**

The Scenario Values dialog box lists the range names (assuming that you named each of the cells), followed by the current value for each of the changing values that you selected in the worksheet before starting to define different scenarios for your spreadsheet.

7. **Modify the values in each of the changing cells' text boxes as needed.**

You can accept the values shown in the text box for each changing cell if it suits the current scenario that you're defining, or you can increase or decrease any or all of them as needed to reflect the scenario's assumptions.

8. **Click the Add button.**

Excel again opens the Add Scenario dialog box, which now displays the name of the scenario you just defined.

9. **Repeat Steps 3 through 7 to add all the other scenarios that you want to create.**

After you finish defining all the scenarios you want to apply to the changing values in the spreadsheet, the Scenario Manager dialog box displays the names of all the scenarios that you added. For example, in Figure 48-4, you see that three scenarios — Most Likely, Best Case, and Worst Case — are now listed in the Scenarios list box.

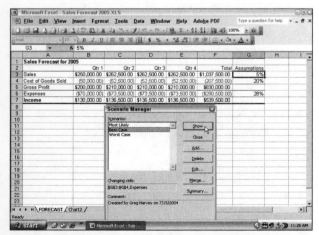

• **Figure 48-4: Selecting the Best Case scenario to apply to the Sales Forecast table.**

To show a particular scenario in the worksheet that uses the values you entered for the changing cells, simply double-click the scenario name in this list box or select the scenario and then click the Show button. Figure 48-5 shows the recalculated forecast table after applying the input values used in the Best Case scenario.

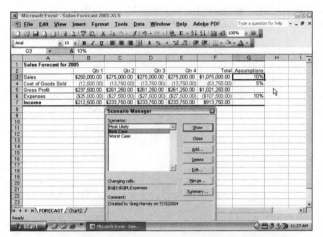

• **Figure 48-5: The Sales Forecast table after applying the Best Case scenario.**

If, after creating the scenarios for your worksheet, you find that you need to use different input values or you want to add or remove scenarios, you can edit the scenarios in the Scenario Manager dialog box (Tools⇨Scenarios). To modify the scenario's name and/or the input values assigned to the changing cells of that scenario, select the scenario name in the Scenarios list box and then click the Edit button so that you can make the appropriate changes in the Edit Scenario dialog box.

To remove a scenario from a worksheet, select the scenario name in the Scenarios list box and then click the Delete button. Note, however, that if you delete a scenario in error, you can't restore it by choosing Edit⇨Undo Clear. Instead, you must re-create the scenario from scratch.

You can also merge scenarios from other Excel workbook files that are open. (Of course, their worksheets should share the same spreadsheet layout and changing cells.) To merge a scenario into the current worksheet from another workbook, click the Merge button in the Scenario Manager dialog box. In the Merge Scenarios dialog box that appears, select the workbook in the Book drop-down list, the worksheet in the Sheet list, and then click OK. Excel then copies all the scenarios defined for that worksheet and merges them with any scenarios that you've defined for the current worksheet.

After creating the different scenarios for your worksheet, you can use the Summary button in the Scenario Manager dialog box to create a summary report that shows the changing values used in each scenario and, if you want, key resulting values that each produces. When you click the Summary button, Excel opens a Scenario Summary dialog box, as shown in Figure 48-6. Here, you select cells that contain the formulas that are recalculated using the changing cells when you apply your various scenarios.

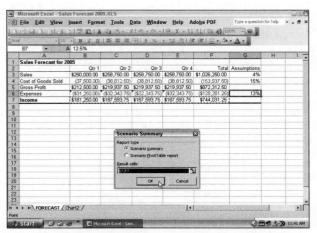

• **Figure 48-6:** Designating the result cells for the scenario summary.

After selecting the result cells for the summary report, click OK to have Excel generate the summary report and display it in a new worksheet window, as shown in Figure 48-7.

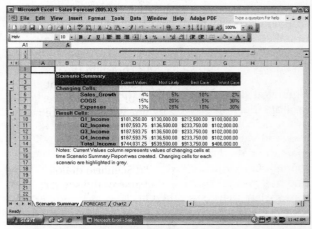

• **Figure 48-7:** A scenario summary report for the three scenarios defined for the Sales Forecast table.

Note in this summary report that, because all the changing and result cells in this table are named, the summary report uses their range names in place of their cell references. Also, when the Scenario Manager generates a summary report, it automatically outlines the summary data, thus creating two vertical levels: one for the changing cells and another for the result cells. To hide the changing cells in this table, simply click its Hide Detail button (the one with the minus sign above the row level bar that encompasses the rows with the changing cell values).

 The Scenario Summary dialog box contains a Scenario Pivot/Table Report option that you can select to produce the summary report on a new worksheet in the form of a pivot table that you can manipulate directly. (See Technique 49.)

Reaching a Target with Goal Seeking

In some what-if scenarios, you know the projected outcome that you want to realize in a worksheet and need Excel's help in finding the input values necessary to achieve those results. This kind of data analysis is known as *goal seeking*.

When you simply need to find the value for a single variable that will give the desired result in a particular formula, you can perform a simple type of goal seeking by using Excel's Goal Seek feature. If you chart the data using some sort of two-dimensional column, bar, or line chart, you can also perform this kind of goal seeking by directly manipulating the appropriate marker on the chart.

Performing goal seeking

To use the Goal Seek feature, you simply select the cell containing the formula that will return the result you're seeking (referred to as the *set cell*), designate the target value you want this formula to return, and then indicate the changing cell containing an input value that Excel can modify to return the targeted result.

Figures 48-8 and 48-9 illustrate how you can use the Goal Seek feature to find how much sales must increase to realize first quarter income of $300,000 (given certain growth, cost of goods sold, and expense assumptions).

To find out how much sales must increase to return a net income of $300,000 in the first quarter, you first select cell B7 — which contains the formula that calculates the first quarter income — and then open the Goal Seek dialog box (Tools⇨Goal Seek). Because cell B7 is the active cell when you open this dialog box, the Set Cell text box already contains the cell reference B7. You then select the To Value text box and enter 300000 as the goal. Then select the By Changing Cell text box and select cell B3 in the

worksheet, the cell that contains the first quarter sales. (See Figure 48-8.)

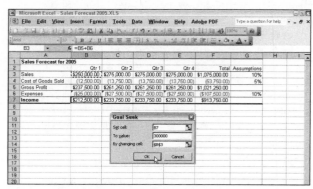

• **Figure 48-8:** Using the Goal Seek feature to find out how much sales must increase to reach a target income.

When you click OK in the Goal Seek dialog box to have Excel go ahead and adjust the sales figure to reach your desired income figure, you see the Goal Seek Status dialog box, shown in Figure 48-9. As this figure shows, Excel increases the sales in cell B3 from $250,000 to $352,941.18, which, in turn, returns $300,000 as the income in cell B7. The Goal Seek Status dialog box informs you that goal seeking has found a solution and that the current value and target value are now the same. (If this were not the case, the Step and Pause buttons in the dialog box would become active, and you could have Excel perform further iterations to try to narrow and ultimately eliminate the gap between the target and current value.)

If you want to keep the values entered in the worksheet as a result of goal seeking, click OK to close the Goal Seek Status dialog box. If you want to return to the original values, click the Cancel button instead.

 To flip back and forth between the "after" and "before" values after you click OK to enter the goal seeking solution, press Ctrl+Z to redisplay the original values before goal seeking and then Ctrl+Y to display the values entered by the goal seeking solution.

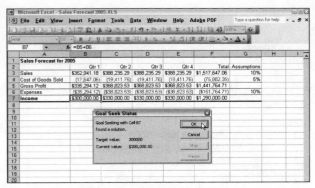

• **Figure 48-9:** A worksheet with goal seeking solution and Goal Seek Status dialog box.

Goal seeking graph style

If you create an embedded two-dimensional line, column, or bar chart for your data, you can perform goal seeking from the chart window by directly manipulating the line or bar. Figures 48-10 through 48-12 illustrate how this process works.

In Figure 48-10, you see a two-dimensional bar chart embedded below the Sales Forecast table that graphs the projected sales and income for all four quarters. The top bar in each cluster represents the quarterly income, and the lower bar represents the quarterly sales. To find out how much sales must increase to realize an income of $300,000 in the first quarter, follow these steps:

1. Click the border of the bar chart to select its Chart Area and display the Chart toolbar.

2. Select the Series "Income" option on the Chart Objects pop-up menu on the Chart toolbar.

Excel selects all the bars in the chart representing the Income data series. Now, you need to select just the one for the first quarter.

3. Hold down the Ctrl key as you click the bar representing the first quarter income — the top bar in the first cluster near the bottom of the bar chart — as shown in Figure 48-10.

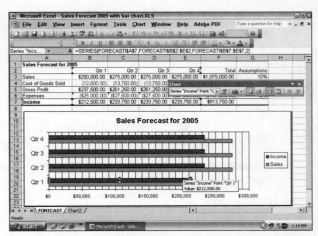

• **Figure 48-10:** Selecting the bar representing the first quarter income in the Clustered Bar chart.

When you select this bar while pressing the Ctrl key, Excel selects only this bar (as opposed to all the bars representing income in the chart) and draws handles around the bar.

4. Release the Ctrl key and then position the mouse pointer at the right end of the bar so that the mouse pointer becomes a double-headed arrow.

Now you're ready to extend the first quarter Income bar by dragging the pointer to the right.

5. Drag the double arrow to the right until the accompanying ToolTip reads 300000.

When you release the mouse button, Excel automatically opens the Goal Seek dialog box with the Set Cell and To Value text boxes already filled in.

6. Click cell B3 to insert its cell address ($B$3) in the By Changing Cell text box, as shown in Figure 48-11.

7. Click OK.

The dialog box closes.

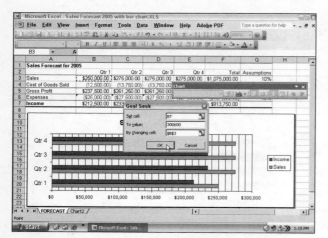

• **Figure 48-11:** Selecting the bar representing the first quarter income in the Clustered Bar chart.

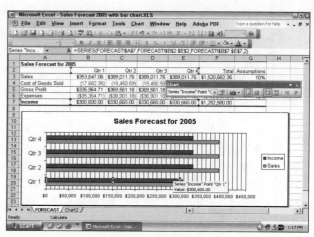

• **Figure 48-12:** Selecting the bar representing the first quarter income in the Clustered Bar chart.

As soon as Excel closes this dialog box, the program updates the embedded chart as well as changes the value in the Sales Forecast table, as shown in Figure 48-12.

Technique 49

Summarizing Data with Pivot Tables and Pivot Charts

The subject of this technique is pivot tables and pivot charts. A *pivot table* represents a very special kind of data table that summarizes different types of data (such as the records of an Excel data list) and enables you to dynamically analyze the relationships between them. Pivot tables are great because they calculate all their summary data without making you create the formulas that perform the computations.

Pivot tables are quite versatile because they enable you to summarize data using any of the standard summary functions, including COUNT, AVERAGE, MAX, MIN, and the like (although totals created with the SUM function will probably remain your old standby). Best of all, you can also use pivot tables to cross-tabulate one set of data in your data list with another. For example, you can use this feature to create a pivot table from an employee list that totals the salaries for each job category cross-tabulated (arranged) by department or job site.

In addition to generating a pivot table to summarize and analyze your data, you can also create a *pivot chart* that represents the data summaries graphically. Like pivot tables, pivot charts are also dynamic, enabling you to explore and display different relationships between the various types of data, all on the fly.

Creating Pivot Tables

To create a pivot table for a data list, open the worksheet with the list and then choose Data⇨Pivot Table and PivotChart Report. The PivotTable and PivotChart Wizard launches, which contains the following three dialog boxes:

✔ **Step 1 of 3** (see Figure 49-1) is where you indicate the source of the data that you want to summarize as well as choose between creating a simple pivot table or a pivot chart, which represents the summary data graphically with a supporting pivot table. The data source options here are Microsoft Excel List or Database, an External Data Source (see Technique 58), Multiple Consolidation Ranges, or Another PivotTable or PivotChart Report.

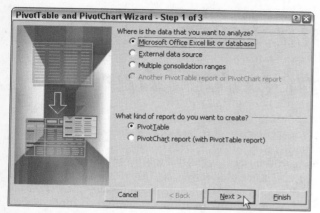

• **Figure 49-1:** Indicating the source of the data and the type of report to create.

✔ **Step 2 of 3** (see Figure 49-2) is where you indicate the data — including field names — that you want to use in the Excel worksheet (when specifying a Microsoft Excel List or Database, Multiple Consolidation Ranges, or Another PivotTable or PivotChart Report as the data source), or execute an external data query that gets the data (when specifying an External Data Source).

• **Figure 49-2:** Indicating the range of the data to use for the new pivot table.

✔ **Step 3 of 3** (see Figure 49-3) is where you indicate whether to place the pivot table in a new worksheet or in a cell range somewhere in the current worksheet. When generating a pivot chart, Excel places the chart on its own chart sheet and places the support pivot table on the sheet that you specify.

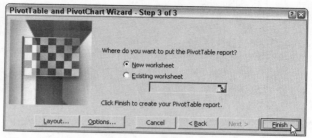

• **Figure 49-3:** Selecting the location of the new pivot table.

After you finish going through the options offered in the three dialog boxes of the PivotTable and PivotChart Wizard, you end up with a blank pivot table, as shown in Figure 49-4.

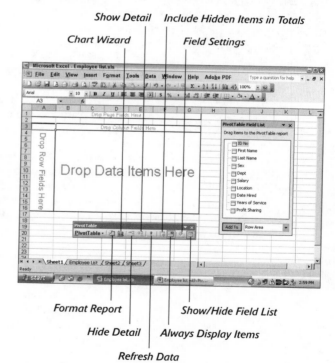

• **Figure 49-4:** New worksheet with blank pivot table complete with PivotTable Field List task pane and toolbar.

This new pivot table contains a blank framework with the various areas of the pivot table identified in light gray type. Excel opens a floating PivotTable Field List task pane that contains a complete list of the field names in your data source. You use these field names to bring the blank pivot table to life. In addition to the PivotTable Field List task pane, Excel also displays a floating PivotTable toolbar in the Excel window.

The key to completing the new pivot table is to assign the fields in the Field List task pane to the various parts of the table. You can do this job one of two ways: by dragging a field name from the task pane and then dropping it on a particular part of the pivot table; or by selecting the field name in the Field List task pane, selecting the part of the table to which to attach the field from the task pane's drop-down list, and then clicking the Add To button.

Before you begin this procedure, however, you need to understand the use and significance of the various areas of a pivot table:

✔ **Drop Page Fields Here:** This area contains the fields that enable you to page through the data summaries shown in the actual pivot table by filtering out sets of data. For example, if you designate the Date Hired field from the sample Employee data list as a Page Field, you can display data summaries in the pivot table for individual years entered into this field or for all years it contains.

✔ **Drop Column Fields Here:** This area contains the fields that determine the arrangement of data shown in the columns of the pivot table.

✔ **Drop Row Fields Here:** This area contains the fields that determine the arrangement of data shown in the rows of the pivot table.

✔ **Drop Data Items Here:** This area contains the fields that determine which data are presented in the cells of the pivot table and then summarized in its last column (totaled by default).

To better understand how you can use these various areas in a pivot table, consider the pivot table shown in Figure 49-5. For this pivot table, I assigned the Profit Sharing field from the data list (a logical field that contains Yes or No to indicate whether an employee is currently enrolled in the company's profit-sharing plan) as the Page Field, the Dept field (containing the names of the various departments in the company) as the Column Field, the Location field (containing the names of the various cities with corporate offices) as the Row Field, and the Salary field as the table's sole Data Item. As a result, the pivot table now displays the sum of the salaries for the employees in each department (across the columns) and then presents these sums by their corporate location (in each row).

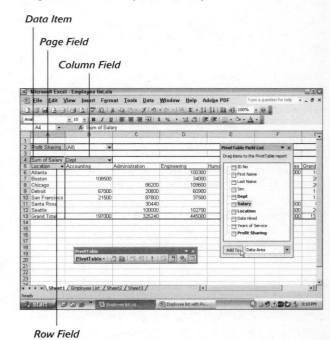

Data Item

Page Field

Column Field

Row Field

• **Figure 49-5: A pivot table after selecting its field and data items from the PivotTable Field List.**

Figure 49-6 shows you the pivot table after I change the Page Field from its default setting of All, which displays the sums for all employees regardless of whether they're currently part of profit sharing, to Yes, which displays only the totals of the salaries for employees who are now part of the plan. For this figure, I also closed the Field List task pane (by clicking the Hide Field List button on the PivotTable toolbar) and narrowed the columns in the table so that they now all appear in the Excel window.

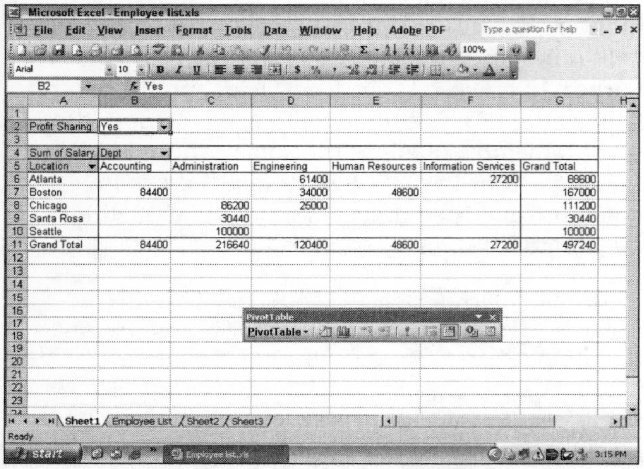

• **Figure 49-6:** The pivot table after changing the Page Field from All to Yes.

To change the Profit Sharing Page Field from All to Yes, you simply click the drop-down button attached to the cell, select Yes, and then click the OK button at the bottom of the drop-down list. (To display the salary totals in the pivot table for those that aren't yet enrolled in the profit-sharing plan, select No in this list instead.)

In addition to changing the way the data in the pivot table is filtered by selecting a new item in the Page Field's drop-down list, you can also collapse and expand the summary data in the body of the pivot table itself by selecting or unselecting particular items from the Column fields' and Row fields' drop-down list.

When you click one of these drop-down buttons, Excel displays a drop-down list box showing each unique item in that field following a Show All item

at the very top. Each item in this list is preceded by a check box. To remove items that are currently shown in the pivot table, you clear check boxes. To clear all the check boxes in one of these drop-down lists, clear the Show All check box. You can then individually select the check boxes of the items whose values you still want displayed in the pivot table before clicking OK.

Pivoting the fields in the table

As the name *pivot* implies, the real fun of pivot tables comes from changing how and what data appears in the table at any time. Because the pivot table remains dynamic, you can quickly and easily change what data the table contains as well as how the table presents the data by manipulating its fields.

For example, suppose that, after making the Dept field the pivot table's Column Field and the Location field the Row Field, you decide that you now want the Location field to be the Column Field and the Dept field to be the Row Field? No problem: All you do is drag the Dept Field label from the top row of the table and drop it in the first column and then drag the Location Field label from the first column and drop it on the first row. Presto! — Excel rearranges the totaled salaries so that the rows of the pivot table show the departmental grand totals and the columns now show the location grand totals, as shown in Figure 49-7.

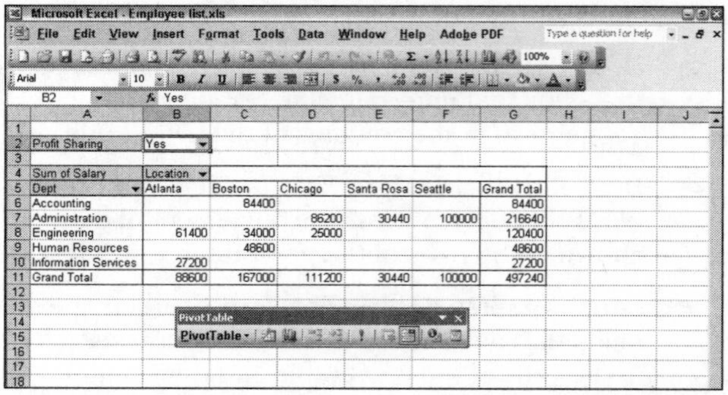

• **Figure 49-7:** Pivoting the table so that Location is now the Column Field and Dept the Row Field.

Pivoting existing fields within a table is not the only change you can make: You can also add new data items to the body of the pivot table or assign more fields to its Column Field and Row Field areas. Figure 49-8 illustrates this situation.

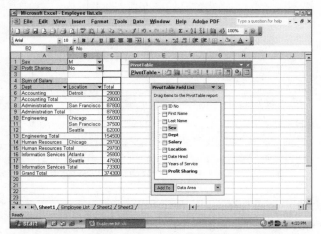

• **Figure 49-8:** A pivot table after adding Sex as a Page Field and adding Location as another Row Field.

This figure shows the same pivot table after making a couple of key changes to the table structure. First, I added the Sex field from the PivotTable Field List as a second Page Field by dragging it from the PivotTable Field List task pane (which I redisplayed by clicking the Show Field List button) and dropping this field on top of the Profit Sharing Page Field. Then I added the Location field as a second Row Field by dragging it from the top row of the pivot table (as shown in Figure 49-7) and dropping it on top of the Dept Row Field. Finally, for this figure, I changed the setting in the Sex Page Field from the default of All to M and the Profit Sharing Page Field from Yes to No.

As a result, the modified pivot table shown in Figure 49-8 now shows the salary totals for all the men in the corporation arranged first by their department and then by location. Because I added Sex

as a second Page Field, you can now see the totals for just the men or just the women who are or aren't currently enrolled in the profit-sharing plan simply by selecting the appropriate Page Field settings.

Formatting the values in the pivot table

One thing that stands out like a sore thumb in pivot tables is the lack of number formatting for the values it summarizes. When Excel creates a new pivot table, it doesn't pick any formatting from the original data source. You have to manually apply whatever number formats and other kinds of table formatting that you want. Fortunately, Excel makes it easy to format both the individual fields of the pivot table as well as the overall table itself.

To format a particular pivot table field, double-click one of the field labels in the table or select the label and then click the Field Settings button on the PivotTable toolbar to open the PivotTable Field dialog box for that field. To format the values summarized in the body of the pivot table, double-click the label that says "Sum of" followed by the name of the field whose values are being summarized in the body of the table to open the PivotTable Field dialog box (see Figure 49-9).

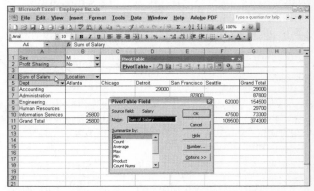

• **Figure 49-9:** Using the PivotTable Field dialog box to format the sums in the pivot table.

If you're formatting a numeric field whose data is presented in the body of the table (as a Data Item) and you want to assign a number format to this data, click the Number button. A simplified version of the Format Cells opens that contains only a Number tab from which you can select the type of number format that you want to use.

If you're formatting a text field used as a Column or Row Field in the pivot table and want to sort the field labels in ascending or descending order across the top row or down the first column, click the Advanced button in its PivotTable Field dialog box. Click the Ascending or Descending option button in the AutoSort section of the PivotTable Field Advanced Options dialog box.

To select an AutoFormat for the pivot table, position the cell pointer in any of the table's cells and then click the Format Report button. (If the PivotTable toolbar is not displayed, choose Format⇨AutoFormat.) The program selects all the cells in the pivot table and opens up an AutoFormat dialog box. This AutoFormat dialog box contains a list with ten different sample Report formats followed by ten different sample Table formats, along with a sample PivotTable Classic format and a None format. (Use the final option to remove any other Report or Table formatting.)

To assign a particular Report or Table format to your pivot table, select its sample and click OK. Excel assigns all the formatting in the selected Report or Table format to your pivot table. If you find that you're not happy with the format you selected, press Ctrl+Z to remove all the new formatting from the table and select another one from the AutoFormat dialog box.

Figure 49-10 shows the sample pivot table I originally generated from the Employee data list after formatting the Salary field (assigned as the table's Data Item) with the Accounting number format with zero decimal places and assigning the Table 8 AutoFormat to the entire table.

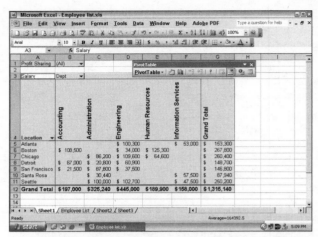

• **Figure 49-10:** The pivot table after formatting the Salary Data Item and assigning an AutoFormat.

Selecting new summary functions

By default, Excel uses the SUM function to total the values in the numeric field(s) that you assign as the Data Items in the pivot table. Some data summaries require the use of another summary function, such as the AVERAGE or COUNT function. To change the summary function that Excel uses, open the Field dialog box for one of the Data Items fields (double-click the field's label at the intersection of the first Column Field label and the Row Field label).

After you open the Field dialog box, you can change its summary function from the default SUM to any of the following functions by selecting it in the Summarize By list box:

- ✔ **COUNT:** Displays the count of the records for a particular category. (Note that COUNT is the default setting for any text fields that you use as Data Items in a pivot table.)

- ✔ **AVERAGE:** Calculates the average (that is, the arithmetic mean) for the values in the field for the current category and page filter.

- ✔ **MAX:** Displays the largest numeric value in that field for the current category and page filter.

✔ **MIN:** Displays the smallest numeric value in that field for the current category and page filter.

✔ **PRODUCT:** Displays the product of the numeric values in that field for the current category and page filter. (All non-numeric entries are ignored.)

✔ **COUNT NUMS:** Displays the number of numeric values in that field for the current category and page filter. (All non-numeric entries are ignored.)

✔ **STDDEV:** Displays the standard deviation for the sample in that field for the current category and page filter.

✔ **STDDEVP:** Displays the standard deviation for the population in that field for the current category and page filter.

✔ **VAR:** Displays the variance for the sample in that field for the current category and page filter.

✔ **VARP:** Displays the variance for the population in that field for the current category and page filter.

After you select the new summary function, click OK to have Excel apply the new function to the data presented in the body of the pivot table.

Creating a calculated field for the pivot table

In addition to selecting among the various summary functions to use on the data, you can create your own calculated fields for the pivot table. Calculated fields are computed by a formula that you create by using existing numeric fields in the data source. To create a calculated field for your pivot table, follow these steps:

1. Select any of the cells in the pivot table.

2. Click the PivotTable button on the PivotTable toolbar, and then from the pop-up menu, choose Formulas⇨Calculated Field to open the Insert Calculated Field dialog box, shown in Figure 49-11.

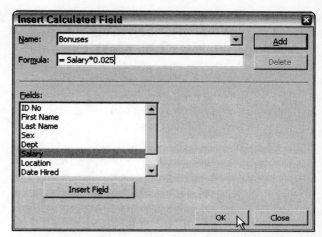

• **Figure 49-11: Creating a calculated field for the pivot table.**

3. Enter the name for the new field in the Name text box.

4. Select the Formula text box and then delete the zero (0) after the equal sign (=) and position the insertion point immediately following the equal sign.

Now you're ready to type in the formula that performs the calculation.

5. Enter the formula to perform the new field's calculation in the Formula text box, inserting whatever fields you need by selecting the name in the Fields list box and then clicking the Insert Field button and indicating the operation to be performed on the fields with the appropriate arithmetic operators (+, -, *, or /).

For example, in Figure 49-11, I created a formula for the new calculated field called Bonuses that multiplies the values in the Salary field by 2.5 percent (0.025) to compute the total amount of annual bonuses to be paid. To do create this formula, I selected the Salary field in the Fields list box to show =Salary. Then I typed *0.025 to complete the formula (=Salary*0.025).

6. **When you finish entering the formula for your calculated field, click the Add button to add the calculated field to the Pivot Table Field List.**

After you click the Add button, it changes to a grayed-out Modify button. If you start editing the formula in the Formula text box, the Modify button becomes active so that you can click it to update the definition.

7. **Click OK to close the dialog box.**

As soon as you close the Insert Calculated Field dialog box, Excel automatically adds its name to the PivotTable Field List task pane and assigns it as a Data Item in the data area. The program also adds a new Data Field and makes it the first Column Field in the pivot table, as shown in Figure 49-12.

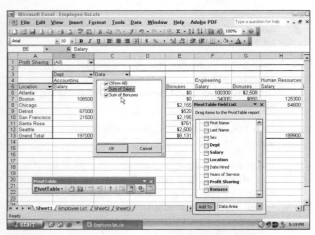

• **Figure 49-12:** A sample pivot table after adding the Bonuses calculated field as a **Data Item.**

If you want to hide a calculated field from the body of the pivot table, click the Data Field's drop-down button to open the drop-down list showing all the Data Fields (both calculated and not) and then clear the calculated field's check box before you click OK. To then add the calculated field back into the pivot table, select its field name in the PivotTable Field

List task pane and then select Data Area in the drop-down list at the bottom of the task pane before you click the Add To button.

Creating a Pivot Chart

Data tables aren't the only things that Excel knows how to pivot. In addition to creating a pivot table that summarizes information in a data list, you can also have the program create a pivot chart as well. When you elect to create a pivot chart along with a pivot table by selecting the PivotChart Report (with PivotTable Report) option button in the Step 1 of 3 PivotTable and PivotChart Wizard dialog box (refer to Figure 49-1), Excel always places the pivot chart on a new chart sheet. This happens regardless of whether you choose to place the associated pivot table on a new worksheet or somewhere on the worksheet that's current when you open the PivotTable and PivotChart Wizard.

Figure 49-13 shows how a typical pivot chart appears in its own chart sheet right after you click the Finish button in the PivotTable and PivotChart Wizard.

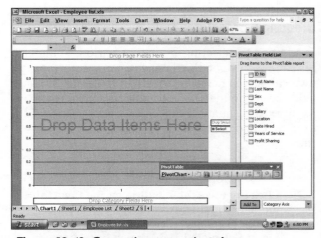

• **Figure 49-13:** Generating a new pivot chart.

Note that when you choose to generate a pivot chart with a pivot table, you actually generate the pivot table by building the chart on its chart sheet. Building a pivot chart is very similar to building a new pivot table: You assign fields from the data source (an Excel data list in this example) shown in the PivotTable Field List task pane (which I docked to the right of the chart area for this figure).

As with the pivot table, you can assign fields to the pivot chart either by dragging them to the designated areas in the chart (Drop Page Fields Here, Drop Data Items Here, Drop Series Fields Here, or Drop Category Fields Here) or by selecting the field name in the Task Pane Field List, and then selecting the name of the chart area to which to assign the field in the drop-down list and, finally, clicking the Add To button.

Figure 49-14 shows the same chart sheet shown in Figure 49-13 after assigning the data fields to the various areas of the chart. In this example, I assigned the Sex field as the chart's Page Field, the Salary field as the Data Item, the Profit Sharing field as the Series Field, and the Location field as the Category Field. As a result, Excel generated a Stacked Column chart that shows the total salaries for each corporate location, differentiated in each column by those who are and those who are not enrolled in the profit-sharing plan. Because I designated the Sex field as the Page Field, I can restrict the chart to show only the sum of the men's or women's salaries at each location (differentiated by profit-sharing status) simply by selecting the M or F option on the pop-up menu that appears when I click the Sex field's drop-down button.

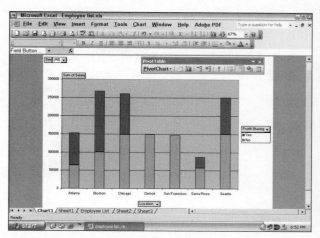

• **Figure 49-14: A completed pivot chart.**

Although Excel always chooses the Stacked Column chart as the basic chart type for each new pivot chart that you generate, you can select another chart type for the pivot chart. To do so, simply click the Chart Wizard button on the PivotTable toolbar or on the Standard toolbar to open the Chart Wizard - Step 1 of 4 dialog box.

Here, you can select a new chart type from among the types displayed on the Standard Types or the Custom Types tab. When selecting a new chart type on the Standard Types tab, be sure that you select the Press and Hold to View Sample button so that you can see exactly how your pivot chart appears in the selected type. (You may be surprised to see how Excel has to "pivot" the chart's fields to accommodate the chart type you selected.) You can also use the Chart Wizard and Chart pull-down menu to enhance and further format your pivot chart. (See Technique 23.)

Part VIII

Internet-Related Timesavers

The 5th Wave   By Rich Tennant

"No, it's not a pie chart, it's just a corn chip that got scanned into the document."

Technique 50

Saving Worksheets as Web Pages

Save Time By

✔ Saving worksheets as static Web pages

✔ Saving worksheets as dynamic Web pages

The subject of this technique is turning your worksheets into Web pages that you can publish to your Web site, either publicly on the World Wide Web or on your company's more private intranet.

When you convert worksheets into Web pages, you have a choice between saving their data in *static* HTML (Hypertext Markup Language) tables or lists or in *interactive* ones that users can manipulate online — as long as they're running Microsoft's Internet Explorer 4.0 or later (6.0 is the current version as of this writing). Interactive Web pages use special programs called *Office Web Components* that provide the person browsing the Web pages with a set of limited controls for making basic changes to the worksheet data and charts online.

Saving Worksheets as Web Pages

Converting your favorite spreadsheet into a Web page ready for publishing on a Web site is no more complicated than opening the worksheet in Excel and then choosing File➪Save as Web Page.

To help you visualize how the spreadsheet-as-Web-page will appear when viewed in your default Web browser, you can use the Web Page Preview feature. To do this, choose File➪Web Page Preview. This action launches your computer's default Web browser (usually this is Internet Explorer unless you've specifically installed and selected a different browser) and displays the spreadsheet more or less as it will appear in that browser when saved as an HTML file. Figure 50-1 shows a preview of the sample CG Media — 2003 Sales worksheet previewed in Internet Explorer 6.0.

 You can't save your spreadsheet as a Web page if the file is password-protected. If you've assigned a password to open the workbook or to modify the worksheet, you need to remove the password before you try saving the worksheet as a Web page. (See Technique 38).

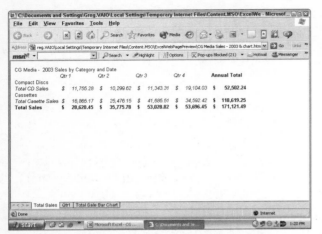

• **Figure 50-1:** Previewing the worksheet to save as a Web page.

If you decide that you want to save the spreadsheet as a Web page after previewing it in your Web browser, follow these steps to save the current worksheet or entire workbook as a Web page:

1. **Choose File⇨Save as Web Page to open a special version of the Save As dialog box, shown in Figure 50-2.**

2. **In the Save In drop-down list box, select the folder in which you want to save the HTML file.**

3. **Enter the filename for the new HTML file in the File Name text box.**

   Note that Excel automatically appends the filename extension .htm (Hypertext Markup) to whatever filename you enter here if you're saving only the current worksheet. If you're saving an entire workbook that has data on more than one worksheet, Excel appends the filename extension .mht (Multiple Hypertext). When selecting a filename, keep in mind that some file servers (especially those running some flavor of UNIX) are sensitive to upper- and lowercase letters in the name.

4. **If you want to save only the current worksheet in the new HTML file, click the Selection: Sheet option button.**

Note that the Selection option button changes name depending upon if anything is selected in the worksheet and whether or not the sheet has previously been saved as a Web page (in which case, the button becomes Republish: Sheet).

By default, Excel selects the Entire Workbook option button, meaning that all the worksheets in the workbook that contain data will be included in the new HTML file.

5. **If you want to add a page title to your HTML file, click the Change button, type the heading in the Page Title text box of the Set Page Title dialog box, and click OK.**

   A page title appears centered at the top of the page right above your worksheet data. Don't confuse the page title with the Web page header that appears on the Web browser's title bar. (The only way to set the Web page header is to edit its HTML tag after the HTML file is created.)

6. **Click the Save button to save the file and close the Save As dialog box.**

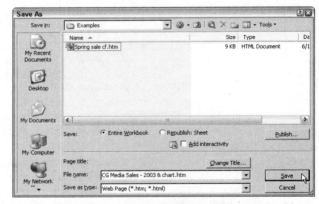

• **Figure 50-2:** Saving a worksheet as a Web page in this version of the Save As dialog box.

Excel saves the file and returns you to the Excel window (which now contains the HTML version of your workbook or worksheet in place of the original .xls file). You can then open the new HTML file in your Web browser by launching the browser, choosing File⇨Open on its menu bar, and navigating to the file you just saved.

Opening your new Web page at the time you save it

If you want, you can open your new Web page in your computer's Web browser immediately after saving it. To do this, click the Publish button in the Save As dialog box after specifying what part of the workbook to save. When you click this button, Excel opens the Publish as Web Page dialog box, shown in Figure 50-3.

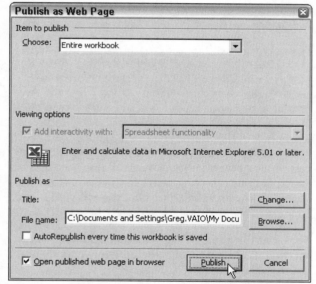

• **Figure 50-3:** Saving the entire workbook as a Web page to be immediately opened in the Web browser.

You then need to follow these steps:

1. **In the Item to Publish drop-down list box, select what part of the workbook you want to save in the HTML file.**

By default, Excel selects Items on Sheet1 (or whatever your first worksheet is named). To save all the worksheets in the workbook, select Entire Workbook on this drop-down list. To save only the range of cells you've selected, select Range of Cells.

2. **To make the Web page interactive, select the Add Interactivity With check box and then select the type of interactivity (Spreadsheet, Chart, or PivotTable) in the drop-down list box to its right.**

See the section "Creating Interactive Web Pages," later in this technique, for details on the various types of Web interactivity that Excel supports.

3. **To add a page title or to edit the one you added in the Save As dialog box, click the Change button, make the changes in the Set Title dialog box, and then click OK.**

4. **To select a new folder and assign a new filename (other than Page.htm, which Excel assigns by default), edit the pathname in the File Name text box; or, click the Browse button select the appropriate folder, enter the desired filename, and click OK.**

5. **Select the AutoRepublish Every Time This Worksheet Is Saved check box if you want Excel to automatically save all changes you make in the Excel worksheet or workbook in the HTML file that you create with its data.**

6. **Clear the Open Published Web Page in Browser check box only if you don't want to open the HTML file that you're creating in your Web browser as soon as you click the Publish button.**

7. **Click the Publish button to close the Publish as Web Page dialog box.**

If you kept the Open Published Web Page in Browser check box selected, Windows then launches your computer's Web browser and opens the newly saved HTML version of the worksheet or workbook in this program. When you finish reviewing the Web page, close your browser to return to Excel with your original worksheet.

Saving all the worksheets in a workbook

When you save an entire workbook containing several sheets of data, Excel saves all the data on each sheet. If you then open the new HTML file in Internet Explorer, the Web page retains its original sheet structure and layout.

Figure 50-4 illustrates this situation. This figure shows a Web page created from an Excel workbook that contains two worksheets (Total Sales and Qtr1) plus a single chart sheet (Total Sale Bar Chart). As this figure shows, when Excel converted this workbook to HTML, it retained the original three-sheet layout, which is then reproduced when the Web page is opened in Internet Explorer. For this figure, I clicked the Total Sale Bar Chart sheet tab to display the first part of the chart saved on its own chart sheet in the original Excel workbook.

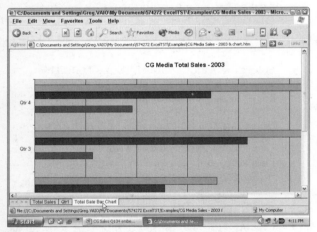

• **Figure 50-4: Entire workbook saved as a Web page showing the chart sheet.**

To display the table of data on the Qtr1 sheet or Total Sales sheet, you simply click its tab in Internet Explorer. You can also page through the sheets in the HTML file by using the buttons shown to the immediate left of the first sheet tab:

- ✔ The Next Sheet (>) button displays the next sheet.

- ✔ The Previous Sheet (<) button displays the previous sheet.

- ✔ The First Sheet (<<) button to displays the very first sheet.

- ✔ The Last Sheet (>) button displays the very last sheet of the file in the browser window.

Saving just part of a worksheet

You don't have to save all the data and charts in a particular worksheet in a new HTML file. You can select just the particular data table, cell selection, or embedded chart that you want and save it in the Web page.

The only thing you do differently when you want to save just part of a worksheet is to select the cell range or embedded chart to include before you choose File➪Save as Web Page. Then when the Save As dialog box opens, you need to remember to click the Selection option button instead of the Entire Workbook option button before you click the Save or Publish button. If you open the Publish as Web Page dialog box from the Save As dialog box, the Range of Cells option appears in the Choose drop-down list box and the address of the selected range appears in the text box immediately below.

Note that the name of the Selection option changes according to the type of selection you've made in the worksheet:

- ✔ When you select a named range to save in the new Web page, Excel displays the name of the range after Selection, as in `Selection: employee_list`.

- ✔ When you select a cell range to save in the new Web page, Excel displays the range address after Selection, as in `Selection: $A$1:$C$79`.

- ✔ When you select an embedded chart to save as a Web page, Excel changes the option button name to `Selection: Chart`.

Adding data to an existing Web page

Sometimes you'll want to save a worksheet as part of an existing HTML file rather than as a new HTML file.

Just keep in mind that anytime you add a worksheet to an existing Web page, Excel appends the worksheet data to the very bottom of the existing Web page.

The steps for saving a worksheet as part of an existing HTML file are virtually the same as for saving a worksheet in a new file. The only difference is that in the File Name text box in Save As dialog box, you enter or select the name of the existing file to which the new HTML version of the worksheet will be appended. Also, when you click the Save button, an Alert dialog box appears in which you click the Add to File button rather than the Replace File or Cancel button.

You can't save an entire workbook as part of an existing Web page. When you select the name of an existing HTML file when the Entire Workbook option button is selected, your only choices are to replace the file or cancel the action of saving it. If you click the Replace File button in the Alert dialog box that appears, you end up getting rid of the original file rather than adding new data to it!

Creating Interactive Web Pages

If you know that the users of your Web pages containing Excel data will be using Internet Explorer (Version 4.0 or later) to view them, you can make it possible for them to manipulate the data and make modest modifications to the worksheet data when viewing the pages in their Web browser. All you need to do to make this happen is to select the Add Interactivity check box in the Save As dialog box at the time you save the worksheet as a Web page.

The types of manipulations and changes that users can make to the spreadsheet data of an interactive Web page in Internet Explorer depend upon the type of data that the page contains:

- ✔ **Worksheet data tables:** Users can edit the cell entries and have the table's formulas updated either automatically or manually as well as modify the formatting of the cells in the table.

- ✔ **Data lists:** Users can sort and filter the data in the list as well as modify field entries and make formatting changes to the list.

- ✔ **Pivot tables:** Users can pivot the fields in a table as well as add new fields. They can also refresh the table data from the external data source (assuming that this source is accessible from the Web page), show details for any of the summarized data in the table, add calculated fields to the table, and page through the summaries by using different items in the Page Fields. (See Technique 49.)

- ✔ **Charts:** Users can edit supporting data (shown beneath the chart as an attached data table) and have the chart automatically updated on the page.

Figure 50-5 shows you how a typical interactive data table appears on a new Web page after opening it in Internet Explorer 6. Notice that the interactive table is self-contained with a toolbar at the top, a facsimile of the worksheet row and column header at the top, and vertical and horizontal scroll bars on the right and the bottom. Notice also that this table uses gridlines to demarcate the cells and sports a sheet tab at the bottom, just like a regular Excel workbook window.

The Office Web Components add horizontal and vertical scroll bars to the interactive table because you have no way to resize the table. You must use the scroll buttons to bring new parts of the data table into view on the Web page. Likewise, the row and column headers are automatically displayed to give you a way to widen or narrow the columns and heighten or shorten the rows by dragging the appropriate border of a column letter or row number.

Despite the obvious similarities to the Excel worksheet window, you can see some noticeable differences as well. The most significant difference is that the interactive spreadsheet table has no Formula bar or menu bar.

Without a Formula bar, you can't tell which values in the table are calculated by formulas and which are input as constants. Also, the only way to edit a table cell is by double-clicking the cell and then editing the entry there (at which time, you can immediately tell whether it's a value or a formula that you're editing).

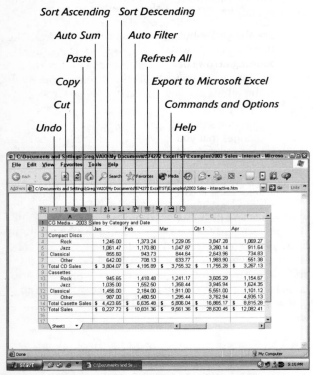

• **Figure 50-5: Interactive HTML worksheet opened in Internet Explorer.**

Without a menu bar, you must pretty much rely upon the buttons on the toolbar to make changes that affect the entire table. The only other way to access commands that affect the table is by right-clicking on one of the table cells to display its short-cut menu. The items on this shortcut menu duplicate the functions of the buttons at the top of the table, with the exception of the Insert and Delete items. These menu items both lead to the Rows and Columns submenu options that enable you to either insert or delete the columns or rows that are currently selected.

To make up for the lack of a menu bar, the toolbar above the interactive worksheet contains a Commands and Options button. When you click this button, a Commands and Options dialog box with four tabs — Format, Formula, Sheet, and Workbook — appears, as shown in Figure 50-6.

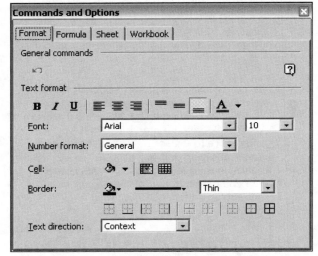

• **Figure 50-6: Use the controls in this dialog box to make changes to an interactive worksheet table.**

These four tabs enable you to make the following types of changes:

- ✔ **The Format tab** contains buttons and boxes for changing the font, size, alignment, border, and cell and text color of any cells that you've selected.

- ✔ **The Formula tab** contains boxes that enable you to see the contents (very helpful when dealing with long formulas) and value of the active cell, along with all the range names defined in the table. You can even use its Define button to define a new range name for the current cell selection.

✔ **The Sheet tab** is divided into Find What and Show/Hide sections. To find some text or values in the table, enter the search text in the Find What text box and then click the Find Next button (using the Match Case and Entire Cell Only check boxes if you need to refine the search). Select or deselect the Show/Hide check box options (Row Headers, Column Headers, Gridlines, and Display Right to Left) to control which interior table elements to display or hide.

✔ **The Workbook tab** is divided into Calculation, Show/Hide, and Worksheets sections. Use the Manual and Automatic option buttons to switch from automatic recalculation (the default) to manual recalculation (in which case, you click the Calculate button to update table formulas).

Use the Show/Hide check box options (Horizontal Scrollbar, Vertical Scrollbar, Sheet Selector, or Toolbar) to control which overall table elements to display or hide. (Note that you can't remove the scroll bars when the table is too large to show all the data in the table.)

Use the Sheet Name text box to rename the table sheet that's selected in the list box below, the Insert button to insert a new sheet into the table, the Delete button to remove the current sheet, and the Hide button to hide the current sheet in the table.

Use the Order buttons to move the current sheet ahead of (with the button with the upward-pointing arrow) or behind (with the button with the downward-pointing arrow) the other sheets in the table.

Unfortunately, you can't save any of the changes that you make to an interactive Web page in Internet Explorer. The only way to save any formatting or editing changes you make to an interactive data table, data list, or pivot table is to export the page back to Excel as an XML (Extensible Markup Language) file and then save the changes there. See Technique 51 for more on using XML data in Excel.

Technique

51

Importing Web Data into the Worksheet

Save Time By

- Importing Web page text or tables via a Web query
- Importing XML data into Excel

The subject of this technique is getting Web data from the Internet or some other source into your Excel worksheets. The first technique I cover is called a Web query. Web queries enable you to import text and tables from a Web page directly into the worksheet. The great thing about Web queries is that once you set them up, you can save them and then use again and again to import the data (which, like stock quotes used in the example, are subject to rapid change).

For those of you using Excel 2003 (the latest and greatest version of the program), I offer you another way to get Web data into your worksheet by using the program to open an XML (Extensible Markup Language) data file. Excel 2003 supports the use of this relatively new Web file format that is on the way to becoming the new *lingua franca* (universal language) for all types of computers (all the way from PCs to mainframes and everywhere in between). In practice, using XML files enables you (with the help of your friendly IT department) to effectively use the Excel worksheet as a front end for your company's database and/or intranet.

Capturing Information for the Spreadsheet with Web Queries

You can use Excel's Web Query feature to extract text or tables (or a combination of the two) from Web pages on the World Wide Web and bring their data into an Excel worksheet. Doing a Web query is a lot like performing an external database query (see Technique 59) except that instead of extracting data from an external database, you're taking it out of a Web page on the Internet.

The key to being able to do a Web query is having the URL of the Web site whose data you want to query. (You know, the `http://`-type address that appears on the Address bar of your Web browser when you visit a site.) You must have this address handy at the time you start the new Web query because the New Web Query dialog box doesn't provide a way to search the Internet, nor does it give you access to your Web favorites as you have in your Web browser.

 To capture a URL for the page that you want to query, visit the Web site in your Web browser by using your Web favorites or its search capability. Then highlight the URL that appears in the Web browser's Address bar and copy it into the Clipboard before you switch back to Excel. There, select the text currently displayed in the Address bar of the New Web Query dialog box (refer to the steps that follow) and paste the page's URL address into this text box by pressing Ctrl+V.

To perform a new Web query in Excel, follow these steps:

1. **Open the worksheet where you want the Web data to reside and position the cell pointer in the first cell where you want the imported data to appear.**

2. **Choose Data⇨Import External Data⇨New Web Query to open the New Web Query dialog box, shown in Figure 51-1.**

When the New Web Query dialog box opens, Excel connects you to the Internet and displays your Web browser's home page.

3. **Enter the URL address of the Web site whose data you want to extract.**

4. **Click the Go button to visit the page.**

The first part of the page that you visit appears within the body of the New Web Query dialog box.

5. **Click somewhere on the Web page to make it active.**

After the Web page is active, Excel shows which elements on the page you can import by displaying yellow buttons with black arrows pointing to the right in front of each table or text, and you can then move new parts of the Web page into view by pressing the arrow keys (→, ↓, ←, or ↑).

• **Figure 51-1: Starting a new Web query.**

6. **Select all the tables and text on the Web page that you want to import into your Excel worksheet, as shown in Figure 51-2.**

To select a table or text on the page for importing, click its yellow button, whereupon it changes to a green button containing a black check mark indicating that it's selected.

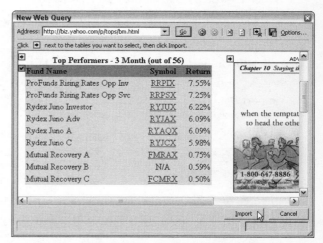

• **Figure 51-2: Selecting the Web data to import into the Excel worksheet.**

After you select all the elements on the Web page, you can either click the Import button to go ahead and bring in the selected text and data or first save the Web query in a separate query file (with an .iqy filename extension for an Internet query).

To save your query for reuse, follow Step 7. Otherwise, skip to Step 8.

7. **Click the Save Query button to open the Save Query dialog box, enter the name for your Web query in the File Name text box, and click the Save button.**

When importing data and text from Web pages into a worksheet, Excel doesn't bother to retain the Web page formatting. If you want the data in your worksheet to look exactly as it does on the Web page with all its fonts and colors, you need take Step 8. If you're only concerned with the raw data, skip to Step 9.

8. **Click the Options button, select either the Full HTML Formatting or the Rich Text Formatting Only option in the Web Query Options dialog box, and then click OK.**

When choosing between the HTML Formatting and Rich Text Formatting Only options, keep in mind that Excel renders RTF formatting more faithfully than the HTML formatting.

9. **Click the Import button.**

The New Web Query dialog box closes, and the Import Data dialog box opens, where you indicate where to import the data, as shown in Figure 51-3.

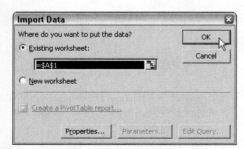

• **Figure 51-3: Selecting where in the Excel worksheet to import the Web data.**

10. **Select the appropriate option in the Where Do You Want to Put the Data section and then click OK.**

By default, Excel selects the Existing Worksheet option and selects the current cell as the place at which to starting importing the Web data. If you want to import the Web data at the beginning of a new worksheet, select the New Worksheet option instead. If you want to import the data in the current worksheet but starting at a different cell, enter its cell address in the text box or click it directly in the worksheet.

As soon as Excel closes the Import Data dialog box, the program begins importing the selected Web data. Because this procedure can take some time, depending upon how much data you're importing and how fast your Internet connection is, Excel inserts a temporary message Getting data in the current cell. The actual Web data replaces the message as it's imported.

After the data is imported into the worksheet, Excel displays the External Data toolbar in the window, as shown in Figure 51-4. You can then click its Edit Query button to revisit the Web page in the Edit Web Query dialog box. You can modify which tables and text to import or click its Refresh button to update the data — a very important feature when you import data such as stock quotes that you definitely want to keep up-to-date.

 If you save the Web query, you can redo the query at any time simply by choosing Data⇨Important External Data⇨Import Data and then selecting its .iqy file. When opening a saved Web query, all you have to do is specify where to place the imported data in the Import Data dialog box to once more get the data from the Web page.

Data Range Properties   Refresh Data

Edit Query   Refresh All

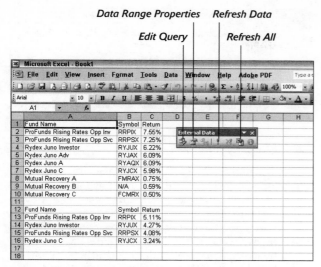

• **Figure 51-4:** The worksheet after importing the Web data selected in a new Web query.

Importing XML Data into a Worksheet

XML (*E*xtensible *M*ark*U*p *L*anguage) is a markup language that is used just like its cousin, HTML (*HyperT*ext *M*arkup *L*anguage) to render Web pages on the Internet. This means that it uses codes called *tags* to define a document's structure and appearance. Unlike HTML, whose tags are all predefined and set in stone (at least until a new version comes out), XML is extensible in the sense that you (well, actually not you, but a trained programmer) can define and create new tags as needed for any particular project.

Another difference between HTML and XML is that XML actually describes the structure and meaning of its data whereas HTML defines only how its data looks (and beauty, as they say, is only skin-deep). It is this quality that makes XML so valuable in terms of sharing data among different incompatible systems

because it makes it easy to reuse the data wherever it's needed.

XML has three distinct types of files to accomplish its magic:

- ✔ **XML Data** files (using the .xml filename extension) containing your data plus XML tags that describe its meaning and structure

- ✔ **XML Schema** files (using the .xsd filename extension) defining the rules for what you can and can't put in your XML data files

- ✔ **XML Transform** files (using the .xsl filename extension) that enable the use of the XML data in a variety of programs or files and can automate data exchange between different applications and control its visual display

 The XML features I describe in this section — except for the option of saving files in the XML spreadsheet format — are available only if you're using Excel 2003 either as part of the Microsoft Office Professional Edition or purchased as a stand-alone unit. If you aren't using this version, you can't import XML data files.

In Excel 2003, you need to create an XML map that links certain cells in your worksheet to the schema used by your XML file. If an outside source such as your IT department hasn't provided you with an XML schema file, Excel infers one from the structure of the XML file itself. You can then use the schema that Excel creates to make your map and into which you then load the XML data as an Excel 2003 list. (See Technique 53.)

 You can't save a workbook as an XML file until you create an XML map.

When you first open an XML data file in Excel, the Open XML dialog box appears. This dialog box gives you the following choices to open the file:

✔ **As an XML List:** Select this option to view the XML data as an Excel 2003 list. (See Technique 53.)

✔ **As a Read-Only Workbook:** Select this option to open the XML data file in *read-only* mode — a mode that doesn't enable you to save any changes you make to the original file.

✔ **Use the XML Source Task Pane:** Select this option to map the data to a schema into which you can then load its data.

To see how easy you can generate an XML schema and then use it to create an XML map into which to load its data, follow along with these steps:

1. **Open a new workbook in Excel and then choose File⇨Open.**

2. **Select XML Files (*.xml) in the Files of Type drop-down list, select the XML file you want to open in the Look In list box, and then click the Open button.**

This action opens the Open XML dialog box, where you indicate how to open the XML file. (See Figure 51-5.)

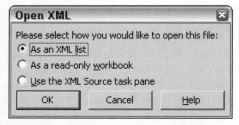

• **Figure 51-5: Deciding how to open the XML file.**

3. **Select the Use the XML Source Task Pane option and then click OK.**

An alert dialog box appears if the XML data file does not refer to an XML schema file or the file does not exist (see Figure 51-6). This dialog box indicates that Excel will create the necessary schema from the XML source data.

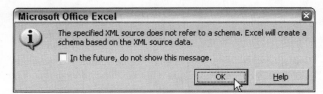

• **Figure 51-6: The alert dialog box indicating that Excel will create the necessary XML schema file.**

4. **Click OK.**

The XML Source task pane appears on the right side of the Excel window, as shown in Figure 51-7. Note that the XML Source task pane shows the schema created from the XML data file and that a floating List toolbar appears in the body of the worksheet. You then create the XML map by dragging the pertinent fields from the XML Source task pane to the desired cells in the worksheet.

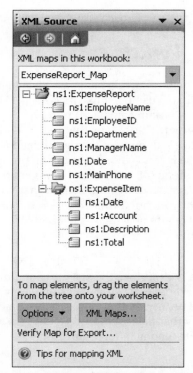

• **Figure 51-7: The XML Source task pane shows the schema file.**

5. Enter labels in the worksheet to identify the fields in the schema that you want to map. Enter these labels in the cells above or to the left of those cells where you intend to map their fields.

6. Drag the name of the field from the schema to the cell in the worksheet (next to its identifying label) where you want the data to appear, as shown in Figure 51-8.

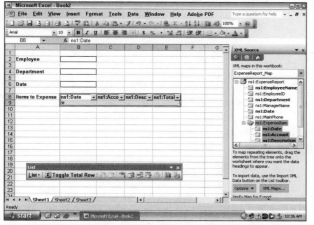

• **Figure 51-8:** The worksheet after mapping the data fields in the schema to the worksheet.

7. Make sure that one of the mapped cells is selected and then choose Data⇨XML⇨Import to open the Import XML dialog box.

8. Select the XML file whose data you want to import into the worksheet with the XML map in the Look In drop-down list and then click the Import button.

Excel imports the data from the XML file into the appropriate mapped cells in the worksheet. (See Figure 51-9.)

9. Choose File⇨Save As to open the Save As dialog box, select the appropriate folder, edit the filename, and click the Save button.

After saving the XML data as an Excel workbook, you can reopen it and refresh the data from the XML source at anytime. Note, however, that by default,

when updating data from an XML source, the program overwrites the original data in the worksheet. If you want Excel to add to the existing information, you must change this setting.

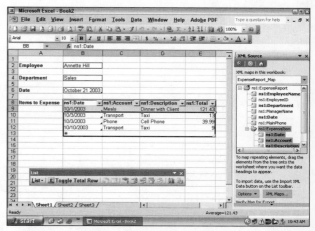

• **Figure 51-9:** The worksheet after populating the map by importing the XML data.

To do this, choose Data⇨XML⇨XML Map Properties to open the XML Map Properties dialog box. Select the Append New Data to Existing XML Lists option (see Figure 51-10) and click OK.

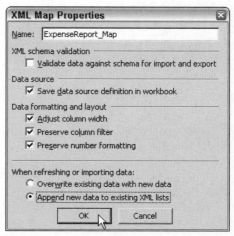

• **Figure 51-10:** Changing the refresh data setting for XML lists.

To refresh the data from an updated XML source file (assuming that it has the same name as the original file), open the worksheet containing the mapped XML data and then choose Data➪XML➪ Refresh XML Data.

Technique 52

Using Hyperlinks to Make Jumps in Workbooks

Nowadays, everybody knows that hyperlinks are the underlined text or graphics on Web pages that you click to take you directly to some other part of the Web site or even, in some cases, to a new Web site on the Internet. What you may not know is that you can add these kinds of links in your worksheet that connect to a favorite Web page on the Internet or just your company's intranet. In addition, you can create hyperlinks that take you to a different part of the same worksheet, to another worksheet in the same workbook, or to another workbook or other type of document on your hard disk or on a network drive to which you have access.

This technique covers the creating and editing of all these types of hyperlinks. It also shows you how you can assign these links not just to the text entries you make in the worksheet or one of its graphic objects but also to custom menus and toolbars that you build.

Adding Hyperlinks to a Worksheet

To add hyperlinks to your Excel worksheet, you must define two things:

✔ The object to which the link is anchored and which you must click to activate

✔ The destination where the link takes you when you activate it

You can attach hyperlinks to any text entry you make in a worksheet cell or to any graphic object that you draw or import into the worksheet. (See Technique 56.) The destinations that you can specify for your hyperlinks can be inside the workbook or outside of it (including another Excel workbook or other type of document, Web page, or even an e-mail address).

The destinations inside the workbook with the links can include

- ✔ **Cell reference** of a cell in any of the worksheets in the workbook.

- ✔ **Range name** of the group of cells that you want to select when you click the hyperlink. (The range name must already exist at the time you create the link — see Technique 26.)

The destinations outside the workbook with the links can include

- ✔ **Filename** of an existing file that you want to open when you click the hyperlink. This file can be another workbook file or any other type of document that your computer can open.

- ✔ **URL** of a Web page that you want to visit when you click the link. This page can be on your company's intranet or on the World Wide Web and is opened in your Web browser.

- ✔ **New document** that you want to create in Excel or some other program on your computer when you click the hyperlink. You must specify the file-name and file extension, which indicates what type of document to create and what program to launch.

- ✔ **E-mail address** for a new message that you want to create in your e-mail program when you click the hyperlink. You must specify the recipient's e-mail address and the subject of the new message when creating the link.

The steps for creating a new hyperlink in the worksheet are very straightforward. The only thing you need to do beforehand is either to add the text entry to the cell to which you want to anchor the link or to draw or import the graphic object to attach the link to. Then to add a hyperlink to the text in this cell or the graphic, follow these steps:

1. **Position the cell pointer in the cell containing the text or click the graphic object to which you want to anchor the hyperlink.**

2. **Choose Insert➪Hyperlink and click the Insert Hyperlink button. Or press Ctrl+K to open the Insert Hyperlink dialog box. (See Figure 52-1.)**

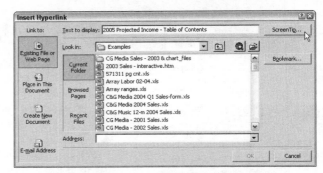

• **Figure 52-1:** Adding a new hyperlink in the Insert Hyperlink dialog box.

If you selected a graphic object or a cell that contains some entry besides text before opening this dialog box, you notice that the Text to Display text box contains <<Selection in Document>> and that this box is grayed out (because there isn't any text to edit when anchoring a link to a graphic). If you selected a cell with a text entry, that entry appears in the Text to Display text box. You can edit the text in this box; however, be aware that any change you make to the text here is also made to the entry in the current cell as soon as you close the Insert Hyperlink dialog box.

3. **Click the ScreenTip button located to the immediate right of the Text to Display text box and then type the text that you want to appear next to the mouse pointer in the Set Hyperlink ScreenTip dialog box (see Figure 52-2). Then click its OK button to return to the Insert Hyperlink dialog box.**

A ScreenTip is text describing the function of the link when you position the mouse pointer over the cell or graphic object to which the link is attached. Note that if you don't add your own ScreenTip, Excel automatically creates its own ScreenTip that lists the destination of the new link when you position the mouse pointer on its anchor.

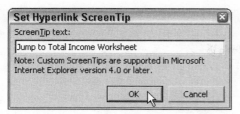

• **Figure 52-2: Adding a custom ScreenTip for the new hyperlink.**

4. **Select the type of destination for the new link by clicking its button in the Link To panel. Your choices are**

▶ **Existing File or Web Page:** Assign the link destination to a file on your hard drive or to a Web page. This option is the default.

▶ **Place in This Document:** Link to a cell or cell range in the current workbook.

▶ **Create New Document:** Link to a new document.

▶ **E-Mail Address:** Link to a new e-mail message.

5. **Specify the destination for the new hyperlink by using the text boxes and drop-down lists that appear for the type of link destination that you selected.**

How you specify this destination depends upon which type of link you're adding; see the following instructions for details.

▶ **Existing File or Web:** To link to an existing file, open its folder in the Look In drop-down list and then select its file icon in the list box. If you're linking to a Web page, enter the URL (as in `http://` and so on) in the Address text box. If the file or Web page that you select contains bookmarks (or range names in the case of another Excel workbook) that name specific locations in the file to which you link, click the Bookmark button, select the name of the location (bookmark) in the Select Place in Document dialog box, and click OK.

▶ **Place in This Document:** To link to a cell address or name range in the current workbook, enter the address of the cell to link to in the Type the Cell Reference text box. Select the name of the sheet that contains this cell. The sheet name may be listed under the Cell Reference range or the Defined Names heading that appears in the Or Select a Place in This Document list box.

▶ **Create New Document:** To create a new document to link to, enter a filename for the new document in the Name of New Document text box. Include the three-letter filename extension if this new document is not an Excel workbook — `.doc` to create a new Word document, for example, or `.txt` to create a new text file. To specify a different folder in which to create the new document, click the Change button to the right of the current path and then select the appropriate drive and folder in the Create New Document dialog box. If you want to edit the contents of the new document right away, leave the Edit the New Document Now option selected. If you prefer to edit the new document at a later time, select the Edit the New Document Later option instead.

▶ **E-Mail Address:** To create a new e-mail message in your e-mail program when the hyperlink is clicked, enter the e-mail address (as in `gharvey@mindovermedia.com`) in the E-Mail Address text box and then enter the subject of the new e-mail message in the Subject text box.

6. **Click OK.**

Excel closes the Insert Hyperlink dialog box and returns you to the worksheet with the new link (unless you specified that the new link is to create a new document *and* you left the Edit New Document Now option selected, in which case, you're in a new document, possibly in another application program such as Microsoft Word). If you anchored your new hyperlink to a graphic object, that object is still selected in the worksheet. (To deselect the object, click a cell outside of its boundaries.) If you anchored your hyperlink to text in the current cell, the text now appears in blue and is underlined. (You may not be able to see the underlining until you move the cell pointer out of the cell.)

 Whenever you position the mouse pointer over the cell or the graphic object with the hyperlink, the mouse pointer changes from the thick, white cross pointer to a hand with the index finger pointing up, and the ScreenTip that you assigned appears below and to the right of the hand.

If you didn't assign a custom ScreenTip to the hyperlink, Excel displays a text box containing the URL or pathname of the link's destination. If the link is a hypertext link (that is, if it's anchored to a cell containing a text entry), the program appends the following message to the end to the URL or pathname that's listed:

```
Click once to follow. Click and hold to
    select this cell.
```

Figure 52-3 shows a table of contents worksheet that contains a bunch of hyperlinks to the various sheets and charts in the workbook. As you can see, when I position the hand mouse pointer on the hypertext of the first of the many links, Excel displays the long pathname to the cell A1 on the Total Income worksheet, followed by the message about clicking once to follow the link and clicking and holding to select its cell instead.

 You can also assign a hyperlink to a spreadsheet cell or graphic object (see Technique 56) by right-clicking on it and then selecting Hyperlink on the shortcut menu. Excel opens the Insert Hyperlink dialog box where you define the destination and ScreenTip for the new link as described earlier in this section.

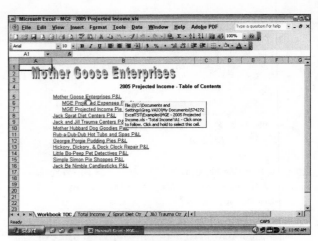

• **Figure 52-3: A table of contents worksheet with hyperlinks to the other sheets in the workbook.**

Following Links in a Worksheet

After you follow a hypertext link to its destination, the color of its text changes from the traditional blue to a dark shade of purple (without affecting its underlining). This color change indicates that the hyperlink has been followed. (Note, however, that graphic hyperlinks don't show any change in color after you follow them.) Followed hypertext links regain their original blue color when you reopen their workbooks in Excel.

To help navigate the links in your workbook, you can display the Web toolbar and use its buttons. To open the Web toolbar, choose View⇨Toolbars⇨Web. Figure 52-4 shows the Web toolbar and identifies each of its unnamed buttons.

The Address combo box on the Web toolbar not only shows you the address of the current workbook but also stores all the addresses of the various documents that you've opened and Web pages that you've visited. You can then reopen a document or revisit a Web page simply by clicking its path or URL on the Address drop-down list.

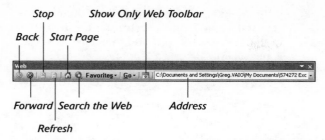

• **Figure 52-4: You can use the buttons on the Web toolbar to navigate the links in a workbook.**

When you follow a link that opens a Web page or another Office document, you can use the Back and Forward buttons to go back and forth between the Excel workbook with your hyperlinks and the destination document or Web page. For example, suppose that you create a hypertext link in a cell of your spreadsheet that opens your favorite financial page on the World Wide Web. When you click the hyperlink text, Excel launches Internet Explorer, connects you to the Internet, and takes you directly to that page.

After browsing the information on the financial Web page, you may need to return to your Excel spreadsheet to check some data. Without closing the Internet Explorer window, click the Back button on the Internet Explorer's toolbar to return to the worksheet. From there, you can go right back to your financial Web page by clicking the Forward button on the Web toolbar.

 You can continue going back and forth between the Web page and the Excel spreadsheet as long as you like just by using the Back and Forward buttons on their respective toolbars. This way is perfect to go to and fro when you're copying and pasting information from the Web page into your worksheet.

Editing Links in a Worksheet

The only trick to editing a link is that you have to be really careful not to activate the link during the editing process. You must always remember to Ctrl+click

or right-click on the link's hypertext or graphic to select the link that you want to edit because simply clicking activates the link.

When you right-click a link, Excel displays its shortcut menu. If you want to modify the link's destination or ScreenTip, select the Edit Hyperlink option. The Edit Hyperlink dialog box opens with the same options as the Insert Hyperlink dialog box. (Refer to Figure 52-1.) You can then use the Link To buttons on the left side of the dialog box to modify the link's destination or the ScreenTip button to add or change the ScreenTip text.

If you want to remove the hyperlink from a cell entry or graphic object without getting rid of the text entry or the graphic, right-click on the cell or graphic and then select the Remove Hyperlink item. If you want to clear the cell of both its link and text entry, select the Delete item. To get rid of a graphic object along with its hyperlink, Ctrl+click the object and press the Delete key.

Creating Hyperlinks for Custom Menus and Toolbars

Technique 2 covers how to customize the Excel pull-down menus and toolbars. As part of this process, I describe in general terms how to assign new hyperlinks to a custom menu item or toolbar button.

To give you an idea of how easy it is to create a hyperlink and attach it to a custom menu or toolbar, follow along with the instructions for assigning a new hyperlink (which opens the home page of my Web site) to a custom button on the toolbar I created in Technique 2 called Choice Tools:

1. **Display the custom toolbar with the custom button to which you want to assign the hyperlink.**

   You can do this by choosing View⇨Toolbars followed by the name of the custom toolbar on the cascading menu.

2. Right-click on the custom toolbar and then select Customize to open the Customize dialog box.

3. Right-click on the custom button (the one with the Happy Face icon) and then choose Assign Hyperlink⇨Open on the shortcut menu (see Figure 52-5).

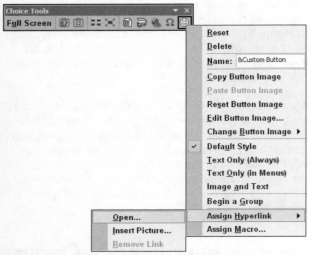

• **Figure 52-5:** Assigning an existing hyperlink to a custom button.

Excel opens the Assign Hyperlink: Open dialog box that uses the same general layout and contains most of the same options (except for those used to add a custom ScreenTip) as the Insert Hyperlink dialog box you use to create hyperlinks you don't assign to custom menus and toolbars.

4. With the Existing File or Web Page button selected in the Link To section, enter the URL in the Address text box and then click OK (see Figure 52-6).

• **Figure 52-6:** Creating the hyperlink to assign to the custom button.

For this example, I enter the URL of my Web site, `http://www.mindovermedia.com` in the Address text box.

5. Click the Close button in the Customize dialog box.

The procedure for assigning a new hyperlink to a custom menu item is almost the same. The only difference is that you open the Assign Hyperlink: Open dialog box in this case by right-clicking on the Custom Menu item (when the Customize dialog box is displayed) and choosing Assign Hyperlink⇨Open from its shortcut menu.

Part IX

The Scary (Or Fun) Stuff

The 5th Wave   By Rich Tennant

"This isn't a quantitative or a qualitative estimate of the job. This is a 'wish-upon-a-star' estimate of the project."

53 Technique

Instant Lists in Excel 2003

Save Time By

- Turning a regular list into an Excel 2003 list
- Toggling totals on and off in the list
- Instantly sorting and filtering the list

The Excel list, a new element in version 2003, is one of the most fun features you're likely to encounter in this latest go-round of the program. It's sometimes described as a spreadsheet within a spreadsheet. By converting a regular list (such as a data list that keeps track of your employees or clients, expense accounts, and so forth) into this new type of list, you not only automate the sorting and filtering of its data but also make calculations super easy, such as totals and averages on its numeric columns (fields) and counts on any type of column. Best yet, if you share the data in conjunction with Microsoft's new SharePoint Services Web site, Excel lists make publishing to the site and synchronizing the online data with the spreadsheet a veritable breeze. (See Technique 54.)

As you find out in this technique, Excel 2003 lists make it easy to manipulate the data in an existing data list as well as enhance the editing process by always giving you room to add a new row of data and by making the insertion and deletion of new rows and columns in the list as painless as can be.

The other great thing about Excel 2003 lists is that you can keep as many lists as you want on the same worksheet without worrying that editing one will affect any of the others. The only thing you do have to be concerned about is the fact that filtering one data list can affect another one if that list shares the same rows — due to the simple fact that filtering the data in one list necessarily involves hiding entire rows in the worksheet that don't meet the filtering criteria. (See Technique 45.) And this, of course, can temporarily remove the display of data items from a list you're not filtering that just happens to share the same rows with a list you are filtering.

Creating an Excel 2003 List

When creating an Excel list, you can either convert an existing data list or create one from scratch. Both processes are really easy. Because you probably already have lots of standard data lists taking up space on spreadsheets that you've created, I start with showing you how to convert a regular data list into an Excel list. Then, on the chance that you fall in love with this new feature and decide that all new lists you start should be of this type, I acquaint you with how to create an Excel list from scratch.

Converting an existing list into an Excel list

The process for turning a standard data list into a dynamic Excel 2003 list couldn't be simpler. Position the cell pointer in a cell of the data list and then choose Data⇨List⇨Create List or press Ctrl+L. Excel automatically selects all the data in the list (assuming that its bounded all around either by a worksheet border or a blank column or row) and then displays the Create List dialog box, as shown in Figure 53-1.

• **Figure 53-1: Converting an existing data list into an Excel 2003 list.**

This dialog box displays the range address for the selected data table in the Where Is the Data for Your List text box and automatically selects the My List Has Headers check box. If Excel somehow selects the wrong range for your data list, select the cell range in the worksheet while the Where Is the Data for Your List text box is selected. (Excel automatically minimizes the Create List dialog box to this text box as you drag through the cell range in the worksheet.) If your list doesn't happen to have a row of field names at top, clear the My List Has Headers check box before clicking OK. (When a list doesn't

have a header row, Excel goes ahead and adds one for you containing generic field names such as Column1, Column2, and so forth.)

When you close the Create List dialog box, Excel automatically adds filter buttons (just like when you choose Data⇨Filter⇨AutoFilter) to each of the cells with the field names in the top row of the list. It also displays the List toolbar whose buttons come in very handy when you need to edit the structure of the new list. (See Figure 53-2.)

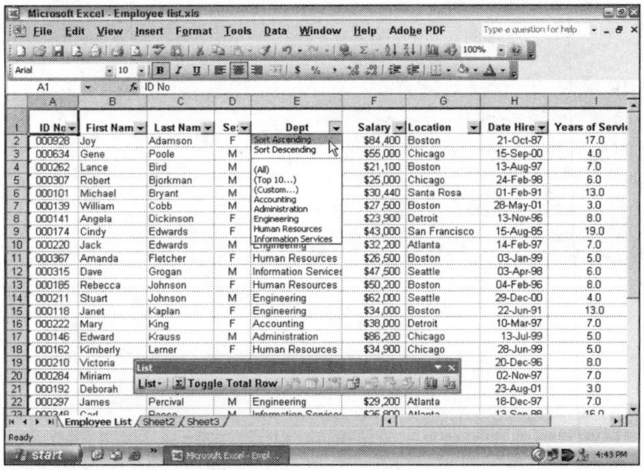

• **Figure 53-2: The Employee data list after converting it into an Excel 2003 list.**

You'll also notice that all the cells of the new list are selected and that Excel draws a dark blue line around its borders. (You may only a see a couple on-screen if your list has more columns and rows than Excel can display at one time.) If you scroll down to the bottom of the list, you'll notice that Excel adds a blank row to the new list marked with a blue asterisk in the first cell. (This asterisk isn't really entered in this cell; it just acts as a marker indicating that this cell is where you enter the new list data.)

You can enter new data for the list directly in this row with the blue asterisk, or you can use the data form to have Excel do it for you. If you choose to enter the data directly into the blank row, Excel adds a new blank row (with the blue asterisk) as soon as you make a data entry in the first cell. You can also use the same keystrokes to enter the data and navigate the list as you do when entering data into a preselected data range. (See Technique 12.)

If you want to use the data form to make new entries, display the form for your list by clicking the List button on the List toolbar and then select the Form item on the pop-up menu. After the list's Data Form displays, you can use it to add the new row (record) to the end of the list or even use it to find and edit existing data. (See Technique 43.)

When you select any cell outside of the Excel list, the program not only deselects all the cells in the list but also removes the blank row at the bottom with the blue asterisk and hides the List toolbar. You'll also notice that the heavy blue line around the perimeter of the list turns light blue. As soon as you select any cell in the list, the blue line turns heavy again, and the blank row for new data entry and the List toolbar both reappear.

 If, as you add rows to the list, Excel encounters a row that contains existing data that could be overwritten, the program displays an alert dialog box indicating that the list is inserting rows that could cause data in cells below to shift down. You then have to click OK to continue work. To prevent this type of interruption to your data entry in the future, be sure to select the Do Not Display This Dialog Again check box.

Creating an Excel list from scratch

To make a brand-new list into an Excel 2003 list, all you have to do is enter the column headings (field names) in the blank row set to become the top row of the list. (This can be anywhere in the worksheet that has blank rows beneath it.) Then, with the cell pointer in a field name cell, press Ctrl+L (or choose Data⇨List⇨Create List) to open the Create List dialog box.

Excel automatically selects the row of column headings as the data range for the new list. Be sure to select the My List Has Headers check box before you click OK. (Excel usually clears this check box when

the list consists only of column headings without data entries in rows beneath.) Excel then adds the filtering buttons to the cells with your column headings and assigns the bold attribute to their field names. The program also adds a blank row for the first list entries (marked with that distinctive blue asterisk) and encloses the cells in this row — plus the row above with column headings — within a heavy blue outline, as shown in Figure 53-3.

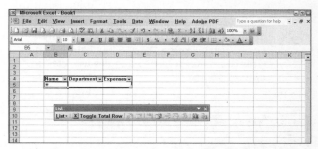

• **Figure 53-3: Starting a brand-new list from column headings alone.**

You can then start adding data to the new list by selecting the cell with the blue asterisk and beginning to type entries in the blank row. You can also do this by opening the data form for the new list (Data⇨Form).

Sorting and Filtering the List

You can use any of the filtering buttons that Excel automatically adds to column headings (or field names) in the top to sort or filter the data in the list just as you use them with a regular data list (See Technique 45.)

If you want to sort the list on the entries in a particular column (field), select either Sort Ascending or Sort Descending from its drop-down menu. Select Sort Ascending to sort text alphabetically from A to Z, numbers from smallest to largest, and dates from least recent to most recent. Select Sort Descending when you want to sort text alphabetically from Z to A, numbers from largest to smallest, and dates from most recent to least recent.

To filter the rows of data in the list so that the list contains records only for a certain entry (such as the Accounting department or the Boston location), select that entry in the particular field's drop-down list. If you need to do more sophisticated filtering of the list, you can use the column's Top 10 or Custom options to do so. (Refer to Technique 45 for details.) To remove the filtering and redisplay all the records in the list, choose Data⇨Filter⇨Show All.

 If you want to remove the filtering buttons from your Excel 2003 list, you can do so by once again choosing Data⇨Filter⇨AutoFilter. (This command sequence toggles the filtering buttons on and off.)

Toggling the List's Total Row On and Off

The coolest feature of an Excel 2003 list just has to be its ability to instantly add a Total row at the bottom of the list (under the blank row with the blue asterisk where you can enter a new row of data). To do this, click the Toggle Total Row button on the List toolbar after you select one of the cells in the Excel list. The moment you click this button, Excel adds a Total row at the bottom of the list. You can then use this row to total columns with numeric entries by following these steps:

1. Click the cell in the Total row of the column you want summed.

A drop-down button appears to the right of the cell.

2. Click Sum on the column's drop-down list, which you can open by clicking its drop-down button.

If you don't want to sum the items in a particular column, you can have the program perform another type of computation, such as averaging the numbers in the column or counting the items (something you can have Excel do even in columns that contain text entries). All you do is select the appropriate type of calculation — Average, Count, or any of the other available computations — from the Total cell's drop-down list.

Figure 53-4 shows the new Excel 2003 Employee list after adding the Total row. Cell F35 now contains the total for the Salary field. I then manually set up the other two calculations in the Total row: cell I35, which calculates the average years of service for the Years of Service field, and C35, which tallies the number of employees in the list by counting the entries in the Last Name field.

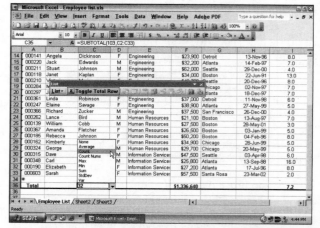

• **Figure 53-4:** The Excel list after adding a Total row with the Toggle Total Row button on the List toolbar.

 To remove the Total row and all its calculations from the Excel list, simply click the Toggle Total Row button on the List toolbar. Excel then removes the row with all its calculations. To redisplay the Total row, just click the Toggle Total Row button again. Note also that as you add rows to the list, Excel automatically updates the calculations in the Total row to reflect the new entries.

Easy List Editing

Excel lists are not only easy to sort, filter, and total, they're also easy to edit. You can insert new columns and rows as quickly as you can delete them. And if, for some reason, the cell range in your list doesn't include all the data you want, you can resize the list (provided that column headings remain in the same row as the original list and the new range overlaps the old one).

Inserting or deleting rows and columns

Sometimes you create a new list only to discover after the fact that you left out a column of data that you need. No problem at all: All you have to do is position the cell pointer in a cell somewhere in the column in front of where you want the missing column to appear. Click the List button on the List toolbar and choose Insert⇨Column from its menu. Excel then inserts a new column, scooting all the other list columns to the right over one to make room for it. The new column is automatically given a generic column heading (such as Column1, Column2, and the like). All you have to do is replace this generic name with one of your own. (See Figure 53-5.)

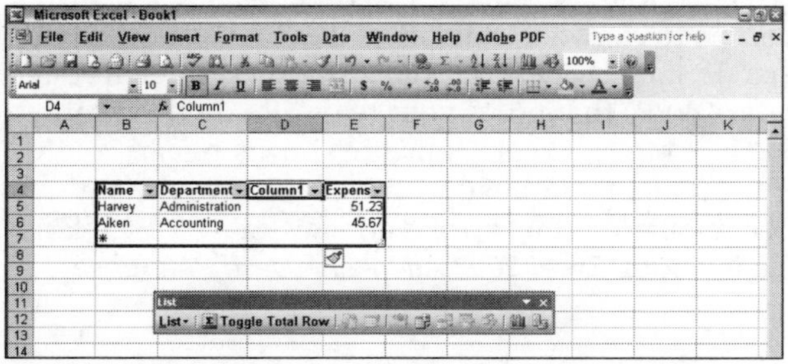

• **Figure 53-5: The Excel list after inserting a new column.**

To delete an unneeded column from your list, position the cell pointer in one of its cells, click the List button on the List toolbar, and then choose Delete⇨ Column from its menu. Excel immediately deletes the column (and all the data it contains), pulling all the existing list columns on the right to fill the gap. Note that when deleting a column from a list, Excel does not warn you when you're about to delete data with the column's removal. If you do this in error, you have to rely on the Edit⇨Undo Delete Column command (Ctrl+Z) to bring the column with the data back.

You can insert and delete rows in the list the same way you insert and delete columns. Position the cell pointer in a cell somewhere in the row where you want to insert a new one, click the List button on the List toolbar, and then choose Insert⇨Row from its menu. To remove a row (and all its data), choose Delete⇨Row from the menu instead.

> The great thing about inserting and deleting rows and columns within an Excel list is that you don't have to worry about adversely affecting existing data in the same rows and columns. Keep in mind that editing the structure is always limited to the boundaries of that list.

Converting a list back into a regular cell range

Excel saves all lists that you define for your spreadsheet. If you decide that you no longer need a particular list, you can convert it to a regular range of cells by clicking the List button on the List toolbar and then selecting the Convert to Range item from its menu (or choose Data⇨List⇨Convert to Range). The program then displays an alert dialog box asking you to confirm the conversion, whereupon you click the Yes button.

Deleting a list

Excel lists in many ways act like self-contained units (thus the moniker, spreadsheet within a spreadsheet). This means that if you decide that you want to get rid of a list in its entirety (not just some of its cell entries or even rows and columns), you first need to select all the cells in the list, including the blank row at the bottom (in other words, every cell that lies within the heavy blue border).

After you select the cells, press Delete to remove the list, headings, data, blue border, and all. Note, however, that Excel does not actually delete the cells containing the list, so existing data in the same columns and rows do not shift their position in the worksheet to fill in the gaps.

54 Technique

Sharing Excel Workbooks and Lists with a SharePoint Web Site

Save Time By

✔ Adding workbooks to your SharePoint site

✔ Adding lists to your SharePoint site

✔ Linking lists with the SharePoint site

Microsoft's SharePoint Services represents a new technology for creating and maintaining collaborative Web sites where team members can easily share information. This information can take the form of shared documents (including Excel spreadsheets, charts, and lists), calendars, to-do lists, event announcements, and other similar notices. Such a team Web site not only serves as a central repository of all information pertinent to the team but also enables team members to enter into online discussions, respond to online surveys, and review and approve documents.

You can run SharePoint Services on an internal server, on which your team site functions as a corporate intranet. If you don't have the manpower, money, or expertise to run SharePoint Services on your own Web server, you can get SharePoint Services as a subscription service through a Web Presence Provider (WPP) that hosts your team site on the Internet. For example, the Mind Over Media Excel Team Site shown in many of the figures in this chapter is hosted by Adhost, with which I have a monthly subscription. (For information on setting up and administering a SharePoint Services Team site, see my book *Excel 2003 All-In-One Desk Reference For Dummies* [Wiley].)

This technique covers how to add Excel workbooks to a SharePoint Web site for review by team members. You also find out how to publish Excel 2003 lists (see Technique 53) to a SharePoint site and link the data so that changes you make to the original list can be quickly and easily synchronized with the copy of the list residing on the SharePoint server.

Adding Excel Spreadsheets to the SharePoint Site

After you've set up your SharePoint Web site, you can easily add to the site the worksheets you want to make available to other team members. Just log on to the home page of your SharePoint Services team site and then follow these steps:

1. Click the Documents link on the home page of your SharePoint site, as shown in Figure 54-1, to open its Documents and Lists page.

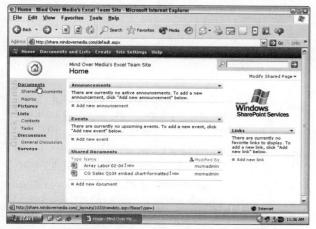

• **Figure 54-1:** Clicking the Documents link on the home page of SharePoint site.

2. If you want to create a new document library for housing the spreadsheets, click the Create Document Library link. Then on the Create Page that appears, click the Document Library link. Finally, fill in the information about the new document library on the New Document Library page and click the Create button.

When you create a new document library, you're creating a new folder on the Web site into which you can upload the related documents to which team members need access. If you don't have many documents to share on the site, you can just put the spreadsheets in the predefined Shared Documents library.

3. Click the Documents and Lists button on the toolbar and then, on the Documents and Lists page, click the name of the document library into which you want to upload the spreadsheets, as shown in Figure 54-2.

To upload Excel spreadsheets into the generic Shared Documents library, click its hyperlink.

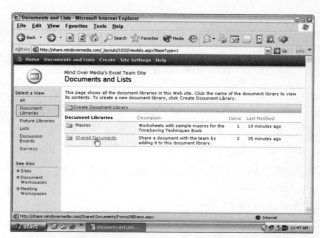

• **Figure 54-2:** Selecting the document library you want to use for uploading the Excel spreadsheets.

4. On the document library's page, click the Upload Document button on the toolbar, as shown in Figure 54-3, to open the Upload Document page for the document folder you selected.

5. Upload a single document or multiple documents:

▶ **Single document:** Click the Browse button on the Upload Document page, select the Excel workbook file in the Choose File dialog box that appears, and then click the Open button.

▶ **Multiple workbooks:** Click the Upload Multiple Documents link on the Upload Document page, and then in the new window that appears, select the drive and folder containing the files. Finally, click the check boxes in front of their filenames, as shown in Figure 54-4.

6. Click the Save and Close button on the Upload Document page.

7. Click the Yes button in the Internet Explorer alert dialog box asking you if you want to continue.

When Windows finishes uploading the files you specified, you're automatically returned to the Document Library page where the workbook file names appear.

8. **Click the Home button on the SharePoint site's toolbar to redisplay the home page.**

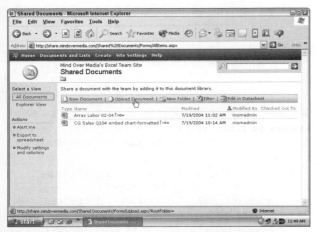

• **Figure 54-3:** Clicking the Upload Document button to start the uploading procedure.

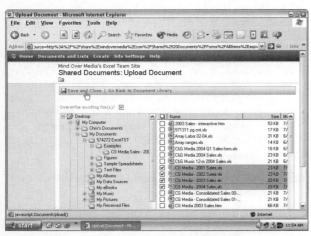

• **Figure 54-4:** Selecting the Excel workbook files to upload to the SharePoint site.

Opening the spreadsheets on the SharePoint site

After uploading spreadsheets to the SharePoint site, other team members who have access to the site can open and view them. Be sure to e-mail all the team members ahead of time and let them know which document library contains what spreadsheets. Team members can then follow these steps to access the spreadsheets:

1. **Log on to the home page of the site and click the link for the document library that contains the uploaded workbooks.**

2. **After the Document Library page opens, click the link attached to the workbook file's name.**

3. **When Internet Explorer displays an alert dialog box warning that if you don't trust the source of the file you shouldn't open it, click OK.**

Internet Explorer downloads the spreadsheet to your local computer, opening it as a read-only file in Excel. When the workbook opens in your copy of Excel, the Shared Workspace task pane is also automatically displayed, as shown in Figure 54-5.

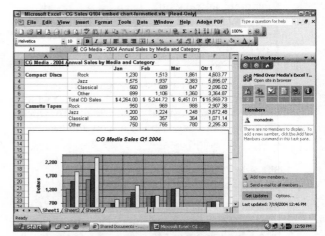

• **Figure 54-5:** Opening a worksheet saved on the SharePoint site in Excel.

The user can then review and print the worksheet opened in Excel. If the user wants to make changes to the spreadsheet and save them, he or she must rename the workbook or save it locally in order to do so. (The read-only status prevents changes to the original document saved on the SharePoint site.)

Adding a list of your spreadsheets to the SharePoint site home page

To make it as easy as possible for users to access the spreadsheets, you can customize the home page of the SharePoint site by adding the document library to the main content area. When you do this, all the spreadsheets saved in a particular document library are listed in this area. A team member can open any of the workbooks listed on the home page simply by clicking the link attached to the workbook's filename.

To add a document library to the main contents area of the home page, follow these steps:

1. **Log on to the home page of your SharePoint site.**

2. **Click the Site Settings button on the home page toolbar.**

3. **Click the Customize Home Page link in the Customization section.**

Internet Explorer returns you to the home page, which now contains an Add Web Parts task pane on the right side. (In the SharePoint world, document libraries are considered Web parts.)

4. **In the Add Web Parts task pane, find the name of the document library you want to add and then drag it to the place in the main contents area where you want it to appear, as shown in Figure 54-6.**

5. **After placing the document library — along with its list of spreadsheet files — where you want it on the home page, click the Close button in the Add Web Parts task pane to get rid of it.**

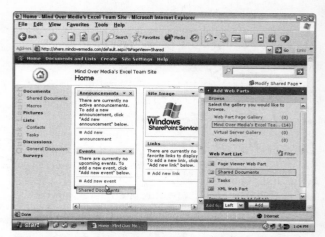

• **Figure 54-6: Dragging the Share Documents document library to the main contents area of the home page.**

Figure 54-7 shows the home page of the Mind Over Media's Excel Team Site after adding the list of spreadsheets uploaded to its Shared Documents document library to the bottom of the main contents area. Now, any team member can open one of these spreadsheets simply by logging on to the home page and then clicking the spreadsheet's hyperlink in the list.

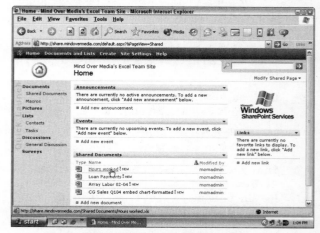

• **Figure 54-7: Home page after adding the list of spreadsheets uploaded to the Shared Documents document library.**

After adding a document library to the home page, you as the administrator can upload new spreadsheets to it by clicking its Add New Document link at the bottom of the list of its documents.

Publishing Lists to the SharePoint Site

In Technique 53, I go on and on about the virtues of Excel 2003's new list feature. In this technique, I show you how slick these lists are when used in a SharePoint Web site. Excel makes it ridiculously easy to publish lists of data to a SharePoint site as well as to make changes in the original worksheet in Excel and then synchronize the data in the lists on the SharePoint site. Excel 2003 can even deal with conflicts that arise in the rare event that a team member makes changes to the same entry in the list on the SharePoint site that you modify in the list in the original Excel worksheet.

Publishing an Excel list on a SharePoint site

The steps for publishing an Excel list (see Technique 53 for information on how to create such a list) to your SharePoint site are exceedingly straightforward:

1. **Click any cell in the Excel list to display the List toolbar.**

2. **Click the List button on the List toolbar and then select Publish List on its pop-up menu.**

The Publish List to SharePoint Site - Step 1 of 2 dialog box opens, as shown in Figure 54-8.

3. **Enter the URL of the SharePoint site in the Address combobox or, if you've published to the site previously, select the URL in the drop-down list.**

4. **Select the Link to the New SharePoint List check box.**

If you don't select this check box when you publish the list, you won't be able to synchronize the data in the list on the Web site with the list in your worksheet.

5. **Enter the name for the list in the Name text box.**

6. **Enter a description of the list in the Description text box and then click Next.**

7. **In the Connect to Share dialog box, enter your user name and password in the appropriate boxes.**

You must be able to enter both your user ID and password to gain entrance to the SharePoint site. Also, in order to publish to the site, your user ID must have Administrator, Advanced Author, or Author status.

8. **Click OK in the Connect to Share dialog box.**

The Publish List to SharePoint Site - 2 of 2 dialog box appears, as shown in Figure 54-9.

When publishing a list to a SharePoint site, each column (field) of data must use one of the recognized data types: text, number, currency, or date. Prior to uploading the list to the Web site, Excel converts the data in your list into one of these types.

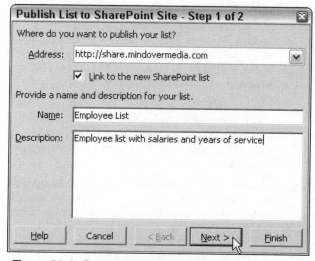

• **Figure 54-8:** Getting ready to publish an Excel list to my SharePoint Web site.

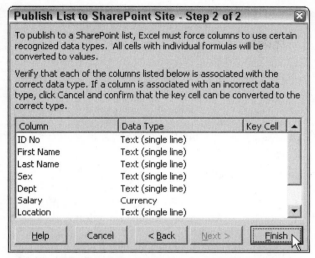

• **Figure 54-9:** Verifying the field types before publishing the list.

9. Verify that the fields in your list are being converted into the correct types. If the information is correct, click the Finish button to publish the list. If not, click Cancel and then make any necessary changes to the data entries in the incorrectly converted fields so that they will be correctly converted the next time you try to publish the list.

Excel closes the Publish List to SharePoint Site - 2 of 2 dialog box, connects to the SharePoint site, and uploads each row (record) of data in the list. When the program finishes uploading the data, a Windows SharePoint Services alert dialog box appears, indicating that the list was successfully published, as shown in Figure 54-10.

10. If you want to view the list now, click the handy link to the page in the Windows SharePoint Services alert dialog box. If you want to view the list at a later time, click OK instead.

After you enter your ID and password again to gain entrance to the SharePoint site, the page with the published list appears in Internet Explorer, as shown

in Figure 54-11. When you first view the list on the Web site, it appears in Datasheet view, a view that mimics the Excel worksheet by showing gridlines for the columns and rows. The column headings (field names) in this view contain filtering drop-down buttons, which you can use to sort and filter the published list just as you would any data list in Excel. (See Technique 45.) If you want to view the published list as a straight list without gridlines and filtering buttons, click the Show in Standard View button on the toolbar located above the list.

• **Figure 54-10:** Opening the Excel list on the SharePoint site from the SharePoint Services alert dialog box.

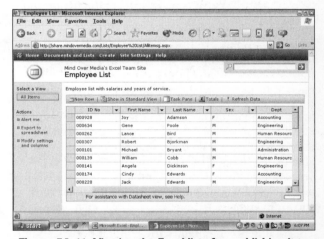

• **Figure 54-11:** Viewing the Excel list after publishing it to the SharePoint site.

To return to the original worksheet in Excel, click the Microsoft Excel button on the Windows taskbar or press Alt+Tab. When you're finished comparing the lists, close the Internet Explorer window by clicking its Close button to return to Excel.

You can view the published list on the SharePoint site at any time after publishing it simply by selecting a cell in the list, clicking the List button on the List toolbar, and then selecting View List on Server on the pop-up menu.

Synchronizing list data

After you've published a list that you've linked to your SharePoint site, it's easy to update the changes that you make to the list in the original worksheet in Excel to the copy of the list on the Web site. All you have to do is choose Data⇨List⇨Synchronize List. Excel then connects to the SharePoint site and updates the list published there with all the changes that you've made. That's all there is to it.

To verify your updates in the list on the SharePoint site, choose Data⇨List⇨View List on Server, or click the List button on the List toolbar and then choose View List on Server on its pop-up menu. If the list is already open in Internet Explorer at the time you make the updates to the original list in Excel, switch to the Internet Explorer window and click the Refresh Data button in the list's toolbar on the Web page in order to see the modifications in the list.

If, when updating the data to the list on the Web site, Excel encounters a conflict in which one of the entries you've changed in the worksheet in Excel has also been changed by a team member on the SharePoint site, a Resolve Conflicts and Errors dialog box appears when you synchronize the lists, as shown in Figure 54-12.

This dialog box highlights the conflict between your change and another team member's change and gives you the opportunity to decide which changes to use:

✔ To use your change and override the other team member's change, click the Retry My Changes button.

✔ To go with the other team member's change instead of yours, click the Discard My Changes button.

✔ If you want to leave the other team member's change on the list on the Web site and keep your changes in the local worksheet, click the Cancel button.

✔ If you need to sever the tie between the local and Web version of the list, click the Unlink My List button. Just be aware that if you select this option (which you can also do by choosing Data⇨List⇨Unlink List), you can no longer have Excel automatically update your changes to the list in the local worksheet on the SharePoint site.

 To remove a list that you've unlinked from the SharePoint site, go to its Web page on the site, click the Modify Settings and Columns link in the task pane on the left, and then click the Delete This List link on the Customize page for the list.

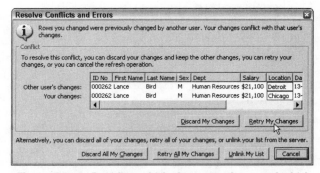

• **Figure 54-12: Deciding which changes to keep and which to discard in the case of a conflict.**

Technique
55

Entering Data and Issuing Commands by Voice

Save Time By

✔ Using the Speech feature to make data entries in the worksheet

✔ Using the Speech feature to issue Excel commands

I don't know about you, but there are days when I dream about not having to "pound the keys" to get my work entered. Even though I have the carpal-tunnel-syndrome worries pretty much under control, at the end of a good day at the old keyboard, I end up with backaches that I swear not even a pretty Geisha girl walking up and down my spine barefoot (nice as that would be) could fix.

Hands-free data entry, the cure to all this tsuris (Yiddish for troubles and distress) for the body, is here today in the form of Office's Speech Recognition feature. In this technique, you find out how you can speak your spreadsheet data entries as well as voice your Excel commands (and believe me, it feels really good to tell a computer where to go!). The only problem with this speech technology is that it requires a good headset microphone, a really quiet office environment, lots of voice training, and loads and loads of patience (because sometimes computers think you've said the darndest things), all of which I'm still lacking, so, if you know any good Geishas, please send them my way.

Hands-Free Data Entry

Excel versions 2002 and 2003 support Speech Recognition, which enables you to do hands-free data entry by dictating the text or numbers that you want entered in the current cell and to issue voice commands that allow you to choose menu items, dialog box options, or even toolbar buttons by simply saying their names.

According to Microsoft, to be able to use Speech Recognition in Excel, your computer must be at least a Pentium II running at a minimum speed of 300 MHz with a minimum of 128MB of RAM. You also need a top-quality microphone, preferably one that's attached to a headset (like the kind used by office receptionists). The giveaway microphones that come with PCs are just not sensitive enough for speech recognition because they tend to pick up stray sounds, which frankly make it impossible to have your voice commands correctly processed.

When using Speech Recognition to dictate data entries, you need to keep the microphone close to your mouth and in the same position as you dictate. Speak normally and in a low but not monotone voice (use the same voice and intonation that you used when training Speech Recognition), pausing only when you come to the end of a thought or the data entry for that cell. Keep in mind that it takes time for your computer to process your speech, and therefore, depending upon the speed of your processor, it may take some time before your words appear on the Formula bar and in the current cell.

Be prepared to turn off your microphone as soon as Speech Recognition has recognized the cell entry (accurately or not) so that you can complete the entry by pressing the Enter key or an arrow key, clicking the Enter button, or clicking another cell. If your mike doesn't have a physical off/on switch, you can turn it off by clicking the Microphone button on the Language bar (see Figure 55-1), shown minimized on the Windows XP taskbar. Note that you can also complete a data entry by clicking the Voice Command button on the Language bar and then saying something like "down arrow" or "enter."

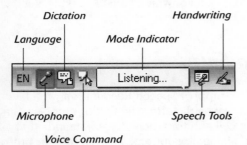

• **Figure 55-1: Putting the Language toolbar in Dictation mode to enter data by voice.**

When dictating cell entries, you can include punctuation and special symbols in your entries by calling the symbol by the word that Speech Recognition understands. Table 55-1 gives you a list of these symbols and what you should say when dictating them as part of the cell entry.

TABLE 55-1: DICTATING PUNCTUATION AND SPECIAL SYMBOLS

To Enter	You Dictate
,	"Comma"
.	"Period" or "dot"
...	"Ellipsis"
:	"Colon"
;	"Semicolon"
?	"Question mark"
/	"Slash"
'	"Single quote"
'	"End quote"
"	"Quote" or "open quote"
"	"Close quote" or "end quote"
~	"Tilde"
!	"Exclamation point"
@	"At sign" or "at"
#	"Pound sign"
$	"Dollar sign"
%	"Percent sign"
^	"Caret"
&	"Ampersand"
*	"Asterisk"
(	"Paren"
)	"Close paren"
-	"Hyphen" or "dash"
—	"Underscore"
=	"Equals"
+	"Plus sign" or "plus"
[	"Open bracket"
]	"Right bracket"
\	"Backslash"

To Enter	You Dictate
|	"Vertical bar"
>	"Greater than"
<	"Less than"
Enter	"New line"

When dictating numeric entries in your cells, keep the following idiosyncrasies in mind:

✔ Speech Recognition spells out all numbers below 20 so that when you say "seven," the program inputs seven and not 7 in the cell.

✔ Speech Recognition enters all numbers 21 and higher as digits so that when you say "thirty-five," the program inputs 35 in the cell.

✔ To have Speech Recognition enter the fraction ½ in the cell, you say "one-half."

✔ To have Speech Recognition enter other fractions, you say the number of the numerator, "slash," followed by the number of the denominator as in "one slash four" to insert ¼ into the cell.

✔ When you say ordinal numbers ("first," "second," and so on), Speech Recognition inputs 1st, 2nd, and the like in the cell.

Just Tell Me What to Do

After you've completed basic voice training as part of installing Speech Recognition, you can start using the feature to issue your menu, toolbar, and dialog box selections verbally. To issue voice commands, you need to display the Language bar and then put Speech Recognition into Voice Command mode. When you engage Speech Recognition (Tools⇨Speech⇨ Speech Recognition) Excel automatically displays the Language bar, which remains a floating toolbar on the Excel window at all times unless you minimize the bar.

If you do minimize the Language bar, Excel adds the buttons on the Language bar to the Windows XP taskbar (immediately to the left of the Notifications area that contains the clock and icons for other items that are running). By minimizing the Language bar on the Windows taskbar, you ensure that its buttons are out the way of the Excel screen so that you don't ever have to interrupt your speaking to move the floating Language bar out of the way.

To open the Language bar, minimize it on the Windows XP taskbar, and then get it into Voice Command mode, follow these steps:

1. **Choose Tools⇨Speech⇨Speech Recognition to engage Speech Recognition and display the Language bar.**

Excel opens the floating Language bar in the middle of the Excel window.

2. **Click the Minimize button (the one with the minus sign icon) at the right end of the floating Language bar.**

Excel adds all the buttons currently displayed on the Language toolbar to the right side of the Windows taskbar.

3. **Click the Voice Command button on the Language bar that now appears on the Windows XP taskbar. (Refer to Figure 55-1.)**

Note that you can also say "voice command" to select this button. You can tell that the Language bar is in Voice Command mode because the words Voice Command replace Starting Speech or Listening in the Language bar's Mode Indicator (the button with the balloon almost midway in the bar).

After Speech Recognition is initiated, you're really ready to tell Excel what to do.

Choosing menu items, dialog box options, and toolbar buttons

To choose pull-down menus or select buttons on an open toolbar (such as the Standard or Formatting toolbar), say the menu and item name or the toolbar's button name. For example, to choose File➪Save on the pull-down menus to save changes to the current workbook, you say "file," and then when Excel opens the File menu, you say "save" to choose the Save menu item. Alternately, you can just say the word "save" to have Excel perform the same action — this time by clicking the Save button on the Standard toolbar.

If you say a menu command that opens a dialog box, you can select its tabs or options by saying their names. For example, if you say "format" and then say "cells," the Format Cells dialog box opens. You can select the Font tab in this dialog box by saying "font," and then you can select the Strikethrough check box by saying "strikethrough." To then close the Format Cells dialog box and apply the strikethrough attribute to the entry in the currently selected cell(s), say "okay." To close a dialog box without putting into effect any of the options that you changed, say "cancel" instead. (You can also say "escape" to close a dialog box without making changes.)

Keep in mind that you can use Voice Command to select the dialog box option that you want to change. Say the word "tab" to have Excel advance through each option displayed on the current tab of a dialog box, selecting each option as it goes. When the dialog box option that you want to change is selected (indicated by highlighting in the case of text boxes and combo boxes, and dotted outlining in the case of option buttons and check boxes), you can then say the new value or suspend Voice Command and enter the new value manually.

If you need to enter a new value in one of the text boxes in a dialog box (or select a value in a drop-down list when you don't already know its name), you must first turn off Voice Command temporarily and then enter or select the new value with the keyboard or mouse. To turn off Voice Command, simply click the Microphone button on the Language bar, thus causing the bar to hide the Dictation and Voice Recognition buttons. To resume giving voice commands after you have entered or selected the new value, click the Microphone button a second time.

Don't forget to turn off Voice Command before you start clicking objects in the Excel window with the mouse or typing something from the keyboard. If you don't, you stand a good chance of having Voice Command decide that your mouse clicks or typing actually sounds like you're speaking some Excel menu command or toolbar button. Having Excel choose a harmless command that you're not expecting can be bad enough, but having the program choose one that alters your worksheet can be devastating. (Usually when I forget to first turn Voice Command off, it responds by having Excel open up a new, blank worksheet, which totally throws me off because the worksheet with all my data is suddenly no longer on-screen!)

Note that the effects of many Excel commands that you choose (whether you do this by voice, keyboard, or mouse) are reversible by immediately using the program's Undo command. (Some commands, such as saving changes in a document, are not reversible, however.) If Speech Recognition ever messes up and chooses the wrong menu command, toolbar button, or dialog box option, immediately say the word "undo." Because Excel supports multiple levels of undo, you may have to repeat the word several times to get your worksheet back to the desired state.

Telling the cell pointer "where to go"

You can use Speech Recognition's Voice Command mode to move the cell pointer to new cells in the worksheet. Here's a list of the words you can say to move the cell pointer in the worksheet:

- "Right" or "right arrow" to move the cell pointer one column to the right

- "Left" or "left arrow" to move the cell pointer one column to the left

- "Up" or "up arrow" to move the cell pointer one row up

- "Down" or "down arrow" to move the cell pointer one row down

- "Home" to move the cell pointer to the beginning of the line

- "End" and then pause and say the name of an arrow key ("up," "down," "left," or "right") to move the cell pointer to the edge of the next data region or worksheet boundary in that direction

 You have a much better chance of having the Speech Recognition feature understand your meaning if you say a phrase such as "left arrow" and "up arrow" instead of just saying solitary words such as "left" and "up."

56

Technique

Sprucing Up Your Spreadsheets with Graphics

Usually when one thinks of spreadsheets, art is the last thing that comes to mind. However, I'm here to tell you that — when used with some self-restraint — graphic images can not only add interest to your otherwise mundane tables and list of numbers but also make their data read better. Here, I'm particularly thinking of hand-drawn graphic shapes that you add to the worksheet to call attention to exceptional aspects of the data (either really good or surprisingly bad).

Excel supports three types of graphic objects that you can use to spruce up your spreadsheets and charts: clip art images supplied by Microsoft, graphics files that can contain drawn images or digital photographs, and hand-drawn graphics that can include simple shapes and lines, text in boxes, and even predefined WordArt and organization-type charts.

Jazz It Up with Clip Art

Most users are familiar with the cutesy, comic-strip-like graphic images collectively referred to as *clip art* that the Microsoft folks let Office users use for free. (They couldn't get away with charging for that stuff, could they?) Along with these cartoon images, clip art collections also include some really fine stock photo images that I like to use. Although I'm definitely not what you'd call a really big fan of comic-strip clip art, Office's stock photo images aren't bad, and I think that you can even sometimes use the cartoon-like images (in moderation, please) to advantage to give an otherwise dull-as-dirt table of data some interest.

Microsoft has provided Excel with its own Clip Art task pane that you can use to search for just the right clip art image and insert it right into your worksheet. To open the Clip Art task pane, first display the task pane in the workbook window (if one's not already open) by pressing Ctrl+F1 and then click the task pane's drop-down button and select Clip Art on the pop-up menu.

The Clip Art task pane contains three text boxes: Search For, Search In, and Results Should Be, as shown in Figure 56-1:

Rotation handle

Sizing handle

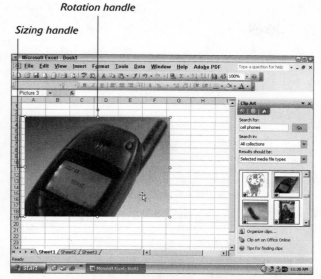

• **Figure 56-1: Selecting a cell phone image in the Clip Art task pane to add to a new worksheet.**

✔ **Search For:** Enter the type of image to use. I entered *cell phones* in this text box to find images of mobile phones.

✔ **Search In:** Select what type of Clip Art collections to search. By default, Excel selects the All Collections option, which includes

▶ The Office Collections that contain the images that come with Microsoft Office

▶ The Web Collections containing images that you pull down from the Internet using the Clip Art on Office Online link at the bottom of the Clip Art task pane

▶ Any personal collections you may have put together

✔ **Results Should Be:** Select the types of media files to include in the search. By default, Excel includes all types of media files (clip art, photographs, movies, and sounds) that are listed in your Microsoft Clip Organizer.

(To have Excel go through all the media files on your computer and organize them into collections with the Organizer, click the Organize Clips link in the Clip Art task pane and then click the Now button in the Add Clips to Organizer dialog box.)

 If you want to see only the cartoonish Clip Art images, clear all check boxes except Clip Art in the Selected Media File Types drop-down list box. To see only stock photographic images (my preference), clear all the check boxes in this list box except for Photographs.

After you do a search, the Clip Art task pane shows you thumbnail images of art that meets your specifications. To insert one of these clip art images into your spreadsheet, click its thumbnail in the Clip Art task pane.

After you insert a clip art image in the worksheet, you can manipulate it in the following ways:

✔ To resize it, drag its sizing handles (the white circles around the perimeter).

✔ To move it, position the mouse pointer somewhere in the image and then drag it to its new position.

✔ To rotate it, position the mouse pointer on the rotation handle and then drag the mouse right (to rotate clockwise) or left (to rotate counterclockwise).

When you've got the image oriented, sized, and positioned the way you want it, click a cell outside the clip art to deselect it.

Adding Images from Graphics Files

In this day and age of digital photography, it's not all that unusual to have photographic files whose images should be made part of the worksheet. Excel makes it easy to insert photos or other types of pictures stored in graphics files on your computer.

To insert a picture into the worksheet, follow these steps:

1. **Choose Insert⇨Picture⇨From File (or click the Insert Picture from File button on the Drawing toolbar, if it's open).**

The Insert Picture dialog box opens. This dialog box works just like the Open dialog box except that it's set to display only the graphics files that Excel can import and it automatically looks in the My Pictures folder on your hard disk. (You can change where Excel looks by selecting another folder in the Look In drop-down list box.)

2. **Locate the graphics file with the image that you want to add to your worksheet, click its thumbnail in the Insert Picture dialog box and then click the Insert button to import the file into the current worksheet.**

Excel then displays the image from the file you selected, along with the Picture toolbar (see Figure 56-2) in the current worksheet.

As with the other graphic objects that you work with, Excel places sizing handles around the perimeter with a rotation handle connected to the sizing handle in the middle at the top of the image. You can then reposition, resize, or rotate the image as needed.

You can also use the tools on the Picture toolbar to edit the photo. Among other things, these tools make it possible to heighten or lessen the brightness or contrast of the image, crop out unwanted areas around the edges, and compress the image so that it doesn't bulk up the size of your workbook (as only high-resolution images can).

 If you have a scanner or digital camera connected to your computer, you can use the Insert⇨Picture⇨From Scanner or Camera command to bring a scanned image or digital photo that you've taken directly into your worksheet.

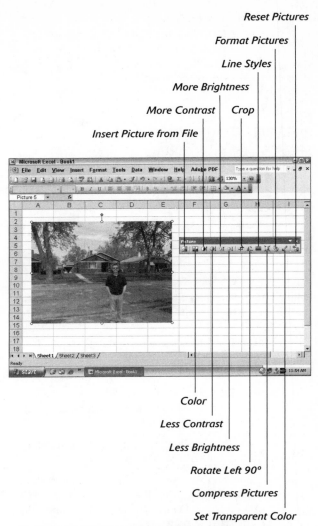

• **Figure 56-2: Inserting a graphics file into the current worksheet.**

Drawing Objects for the Spreadsheet

The Drawing toolbar is jam-packed with great tools for creating and adding all types of graphic objects. About the only graphic that you can't bring in from this toolbar is one that you create on a scanner or import from a digital camera that's attached to your computer. (For that you need to use the Insert⇨ Picture⇨From Scanner or Camera command.) For all the rest of your graphic needs, the Drawing toolbar is your ticket.

Figure 56-3 shows the Drawing toolbar and identifies the buttons that use only symbols. When you first open the Drawing toolbar (by choosing View⇨ Toolbar⇨Drawing), Excel automatically docks it at the bottom of the Excel window immediately above the status bar. You can then move the Drawing toolbar to another side of the Excel window or even float it if you want.

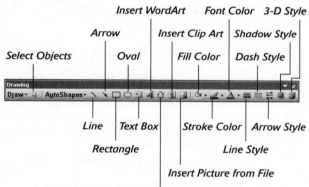

• **Figure 56-3: The Drawing toolbar is full of great tools for drawing almost any graphic object.**

The Draw and AutoShapes buttons are attached to pop-up menus that open when you click their buttons. The Fill Color, Line Color, Font Color, Shadow Style, and 3-D Style buttons are all attached to pop-up palettes that open when you click their buttons and from which you can select new fill, line, and font colors as well as shading and 3-D effects for selected graphic objects.

Drawing various shapes

You can use the various drawing tools on the Drawing toolbar to manually draw straight lines, lines with

arrowheads (simply referred to as *arrows*), rectangular and square shapes, and oval and circular shapes. To draw any of these shapes, click the appropriate button and then drag the thin, black cross pointer to draw its outline. When drawing a line or arrow, Excel draws the line from the place where you originally click the mouse button to the place where you release it.

When drawing a rectangle or an oval, you can constrain the tool to draw a square or circle by holding down the Shift key as you drag the mouse. Note that when drawing a two-dimensional shape — such as a rectangle, a square, an oval, or a circle — Excel automatically draws the shape with a white fill that obscures any data or graphics objects that are beneath the shape on layers below.

After you've drawn the basic shape, you can then use the Fill Color, Line Color, Line Style, Dash Style, Shadow Style, and 3-D Style buttons on the Drawing toolbar to enhance the basic shape.

In addition to drawing your own shapes, you can insert any number of ready-made shapes (including lines, arrows, flow chart symbols, banners, and callouts) by selecting them from the AutoShapes pop-up menu and then sizing them in the worksheet. Figure 56-4 shows this pop-up menu with the cascading palette of shapes to choose from when you select Basic Shapes.

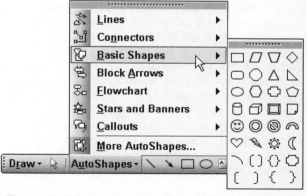

• **Figure 56-4: Selecting a basic shape to draw from the AutoShapes pop-up menu.**

Using text boxes as callouts

Text boxes are graphics that combine text with a rectangular graphic object. (The only other object that does this are the callouts that you insert from the AutoShapes Callout pop-up menu.) They're great for calling attention to significant trends or special features in the charts that you create.

To create a text box, click the Text Box button on the Drawing toolbar and then drag the mouse pointer to draw the outline of the box. When you release the mouse button, Excel places the insertion point in the upper-left corner of the box.

You can then start typing the text that you want displayed in the text box. When the text that you type reaches the right edge of the text box, Excel automatically starts a new line. If you reach the end of the text box and keep typing, Excel scrolls the text up, and you then have to resize the text box to display all the text that you've entered. If you want to break a line before it reaches the right edge of the text box, press the Enter key. When you finish entering the text, click anywhere on the screen outside of the text box to deselect it.

 Although text boxes are similar to cell comments with text-within-a-box display, they differ from comments in that text boxes are *not* attached to particular cells and *are* always displayed in the worksheet. (Comments show only when you position the mouse pointer over the cell or select the comment with the Reviewing toolbar.)

Text boxes differ somewhat from other graphic objects that you add to the worksheet. Unlike the other Excel graphic objects, when you select a text box, it displays sizing handles but no rotation handle (because Excel can't display text at just any angle you may select). Also, unlike other graphic objects, text boxes display two different border patterns when you select them:

✔ A single crosshatched pattern is displayed when you click inside the text box, thus enabling you to format and edit the text.

✔ A double crosshatched pattern (that just looks like a bunch of fuzzy dots on my monitor) is displayed when you click the border of the text box or start dragging the box to reposition it, thus indicating that you can format and edit the box itself.

Making a statement with WordArt

The WordArt button on the Drawing toolbar enables you to insert super fancy headings for your spreadsheets (often a little *too* fancy for my tastes). Keep the following points in mind when using the WordArt feature:

✔ The WordArt text is really a graphic object that happens to have some text associated with it (meaning that you can't edit it directly as you can edit the text that you enter in a text box).

✔ The WordArt styles are intended for really large font sizes (36 points being the default), and many don't work well with regular text font sizes (for example, those below about 24 points in size).

To insert a WordArt graphic object in your worksheet, follow these steps:

1. **Click the WordArt button on the Drawing toolbar.**

The WordArt Gallery dialog box appears, as shown in Figure 56-5. Here, you select the text style that you want to use. As this figure shows, the WordArt Gallery contains a wide variety of styles at different angles with some styles that even run the text down in a vertical line.

2. **Select a WordArt style by clicking its picture in the WordArt Gallery dialog box and then click OK.**

Excel opens the Edit WordArt Text dialog box, shown in Figure 56-6.

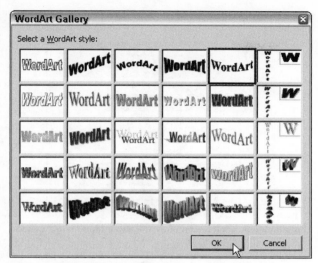

• **Figure 56-5:** Select a WordArt style in the WordArt Gallery dialog box.

3. Replace the dummy text Your Text Here with the words or phrase that you want presented in the WordArt style that you just selected in the Gallery dialog box.

4. If you want to change the font and font size of the text that you enter, use the Font and Size drop-down list boxes. You can also use the Bold and Italic buttons to enhance the text that you enter by making it bold and/or italic.

• **Figure 56-6:** Entering the text to be displayed in the selected WordArt style.

5. After you finish entering and enhancing your text in the Edit WordArt Text dialog box, click OK.

Excel inserts your WordArt graphic object in the worksheet and, at the same time, displays the WordArt toolbar that you can use to further format or make changes to your WordArt masterpiece, as shown in Figure 56-7.

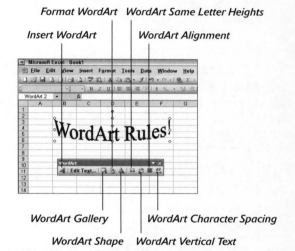

• **Figure 56-7:** Sample WordArt text in a worksheet.

Drawing diagrams and organization charts

You can use the Insert Diagram or Organization Chart button on the Drawing toolbar to quickly add an organization chart or diagram to your worksheet (one place where a graphic object actually conveys the information instead of just embellishing the worksheet data or embedded chart already there). Here's how:

1. Click the Insert Diagram or Organization Chart button to open the Diagram Gallery dialog box, shown in Figure 56-8.

2. Select the style of diagram or the organization chart you want and click OK.

The Diagram Gallery dialog box offers you a choice between an organization chart (the first picture) and five different types of diagrams (Cycle, Radial, Pyramid, Venn, and Target).

After you click OK, Excel inserts a blank chart or diagram into the worksheet as a new graphic object, as shown in Figure 56-9.

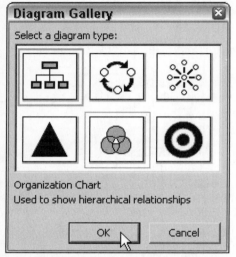

• **Figure 56-8: Selecting an organization chart type in the Diagram Gallery dialog box.**

You can then click the different parts of the chart or diagram and replace its dummy text with text of your own. (Organization charts or diagrams created with the Insert Diagram or Organization Chart button act like big text boxes with a bunch of graphics with little text boxes inside them.)

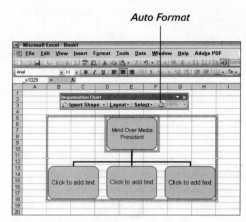

• **Figure 56-9: Worksheet after adding a blank organization chart to it.**

When you create a new organization chart, Excel opens an Organization Chart toolbar containing buttons for editing the shape and layout of the chart as well as for adding new levels and branches. When you create a new diagram (in any of the five available styles), the program opens a Diagram toolbar that contains its own tools for formatting and editing the diagram.

You can use the options on the Insert Shape drop-down list to add new text boxes at the subordinate and assistant levels of the chart. You can use the options on the Layout drop-down list to select a new style for the different levels in the org chart. Finally, you can use the options on the Select drop-down list box to select all the text boxes at a particular level in the org chart.

57

Technique

Doing Automated Table Lookups

I still remember the first time my spreadsheet teacher showed me how to automate lookups in a worksheet table. The magic of being able to retrieve values from long boring schedules of numbers for use in other formulas *without* having to actually find the cell reference myself was quite thrilling. (It doesn't take much to get geeks like me happy.) The only problem is that that the lookup functions that do this magic are considered to be "advanced" functions and therefore a bit scary to new users.

Nevertheless, I think that after you get the hang of using these beauties through this technique, you'll be hooked and as happy as I am about them. (Well, maybe not that happy.) In addition to covering the use of both the VLOOKUP (vertical lookup) and HLOOKUP (horizontal lookup) functions — each of which can retrieve a single value from a table of data — I also introduce the Lookup Wizard, one of the add-in programs that comes with Excel that you can use to look up two values in the table.

Looking Up a Single Table Value

Before talking about how the two particular lookup functions that return a single value from a table work, it's important to note that lookup tables are standard data tables in every way except that the following guidelines must be observed:

✔ The values you want *looked up* in the table (that is, matched against values entered elsewhere in the worksheet) must be in the first column (in a vertical lookup) or row (in a horizontal lookup) of the data table.

✔ The values in this first column or row must be sorted in ascending order, by rows from top to bottom in a vertical lookup and by columns from left to right in a horizontal lookup.

✔ The values in the first column or row must be unique (no duplicate entries allowed here).

Assuming that you set up your lookup table following these three guidelines, you'll have absolutely no trouble getting your lookup formulas to take the correct information out of the table and return it to the appropriate place in your spreadsheet each and every time.

Performing a vertical table lookup

Excel supports two types of lookup functions, vertical and horizontal. The vertical lookup function is called VLOOKUP. The VLOOKUP function searches vertically (top to bottom) the first (leftmost) column of a lookup table until the program locates a value that matches or exceeds the one you're looking up.

The VLOOKUP function uses the following syntax:

```
VLOOKUP(lookup_value,table_array,
    colindex_num,[range_lookup])
```

Here's a closer look at the arguments that make up this function:

- ✔ *lookup_value:* The value that you want to look up and match in the first column of the lookup table.

- ✔ *table_array:* The cell range or name of the lookup table itself.

- ✔ *col_index_num:* The column containing the values that you want returned to the cell containing the VLOOKUP formula when a match is made between the *lookup_value* and an entry in the first column of the table. When entering this argument, you must enter a value greater than zero that doesn't exceed the total number of columns in the lookup table.

- ✔ *range_lookup:* (Optional) The logical TRUE or FALSE value that specifies whether you want Excel to find an exact or approximate match for the *lookup_value* in the *table_array*. When you specify TRUE or omit the *range_lookup*, Excel finds an approximate match. When you specify FALSE as the *range_lookup* argument, Excel finds only exact matches.

Finding approximate matches pertains only when you're looking up numeric entries (rather than text) in the first column or row of the vertical or horizontal lookup table. When Excel doesn't find an exact match in this lookup column or row, it locates the next highest value that doesn't exceed the *lookup_value* argument and then returns the value in the column or row designated by the *col_index_num* or *row_index_num* arguments.

To see how you can use this lookup function, consider the example shown in Figure 57-1. This worksheet contains a tip table that calculates the tip amount at 15% and 20% for total pretax check amounts up to $150.00 in the cell range A1:C152.

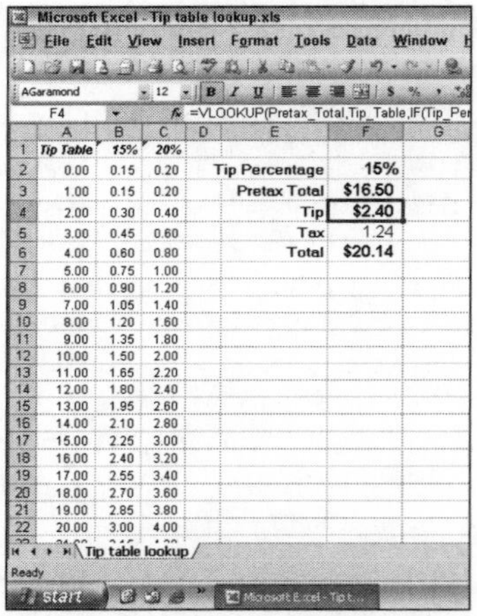

• **Figure 57-1: Tip table using a VLOOKUP function to calculate the amount of tip to add to the bill.**

To use this tip table, you enter the percentage of the tip (either 15% or 20%) in cell F2 (named Tip_Percentage) and the amount of the check before tax in cell F3 (named Pretax_Total). Excel then looks up the value that you enter in the Pretax_Total cell in the first column of the lookup table (A2:C152), named aptly enough, Tip_Table.

Excel then moves down the values in the first column of Tip_Table until it finds a match, whereupon the program uses the `col_index_num` argument in the VLOOKUP function to determine which tip amount from that row of the table to return to cell F4. If Excel finds that the value entered in the Pretax_Total cell ($16.50 in this example) doesn't exactly match one of the values in the first column of Tip_Table, the program continues to search down the comparison range until it encounters the first value that exceeds the pretax total (17.00 in cell A19 in this example). Excel then moves back up to the previous row in the table and returns the value in the column that matches the `col_index_num` argument of the VLOOKUP function. (This is because the optional `range_lookup` argument has been omitted from the function.)

Note that the VLOOKUP function in the tip table example in Figure 57-1 uses an IF function to determine the `col_index_num` argument for the VLOOKUP function in cell F4. The IF function determines the number of the column to be used in the tip table by matching the percentage entered in Tip_Percentage (cell F2) with 0.15. If they match, the function returns 2 as the `col_index_num` argument, and the VLOOKUP function returns a value from the second column (the 15% column B) in the Tip_Table range. Otherwise, the IF function returns 3 as the `col_index_num` argument, and the VLOOKUP function returns a value from the third column (the 20% column C) in the Tip_Table range.

Performing a horizontal lookup

The horizontal lookup function is called HLOOKUP. The HLOOKUP function searches horizontally (left to right) the topmost row of a lookup table until it locates a value that matches or exceeds the one that you're looking up. The HLOOKUP function not only works very much like the VLOOKUP but also follows a nearly identical syntax:

```
HLOOKUP(lookup_value,table_array,rowindex_
    num,[range_lookup])
```

The `row_index_num` argument in the HLOOKUP function is the number of the row whose values

are compared to the `lookup_value` in a horizontal table. This argument must also be greater than zero and not exceed the total number of rows in the table.

Figure 57-2 shows an example that uses the HLOOKUP function to look up the price of each bakery item stored in a separate price lookup table and then return that price to the Price/Doz column of the Daily Sales list.

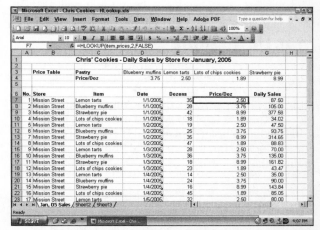

• **Figure 57-2: Using the HLOOKUP function to return the price of each bakery item from a lookup table.**

Cell F7 contains the original formula with the HLOOKUP function that is then copied down column F:

```
=HLOOKUP(item,prices,2,FALSE)
```

In this HLOOKUP function, the range name Item, given to the Item column in the range C7:C66, is defined as the `lookup_value` argument, and the cell range name Prices, given to the cell range D3:G4, is the `table_array` argument. The `row_index_num` argument is 2 because you want Excel to return the prices in the second row of the Prices lookup table, and the optional `range_lookup` argument is FALSE because the item name in the Daily Sales list must match exactly the item name in the Prices lookup table.

By having the HLOOKUP function input the price per dozen for each bakery item in the Daily Sales list, it's easy to update any of the sales in the list. All you do is change its Price/ Doz cost in the Prices lookup table, and the HLOOKUP function immediately updates the new price in the Daily Sales list wherever the item is sold.

Doing a Two-Way Lookup in a Data Table

You can use the Lookup Wizard add-in to build the necessary formulas to do a two-way lookup in a data table. After you activate the Lookup Wizard add-in by selecting the Lookup Wizard check box in the Add-Ins dialog box (Tools⇨Add-Ins), the program adds a Lookup menu item to the Tools menu on the menu bar.

To better understand how the Lookup Wizard works, consider the example shown in Figure 57-3. Here, you want to create a formula that will look up and return the number produced for a particular part in a particular month. To do this, you must fashion a formula that combines the abilities of both the VLOOKUP function, which can look up the correct row based on the part number you give, and the HLOOKUP function, which can look up the correct column based on the month you enter.

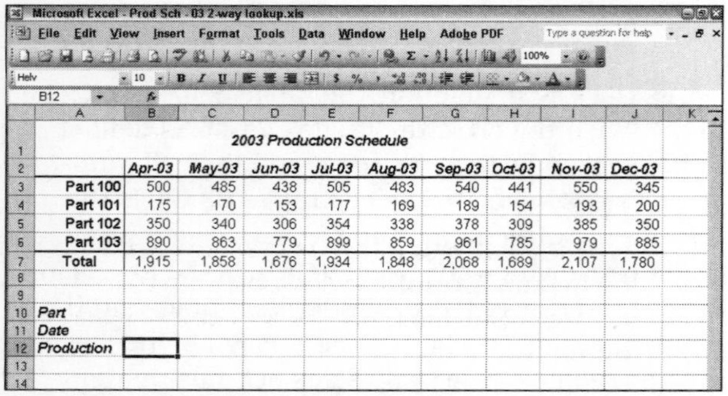

• **Figure 57-3: Production Schedule table that enables you to look up the number produced by the month and part number.**

This is exactly what the Lookup Wizard can do for you. To see how, follow along with these steps:

1. Choose Tools⇨Lookup to open the Lookup Wizard - Step 1 of 4 dialog box, shown in Figure 57-4.

2. Select the cell range containing the data table in which the lookup is to be performed.

For the example shown in Figure 57-3, I select the cell range A2:J6 as this range. (Because this range is named table_data, I could have entered this name instead of selecting the cell range.)

3. When you're finished selecting the cell range, click the Next button to open the Lookup Wizard - Step 2 of 4 dialog box, shown in Figure 57-5.

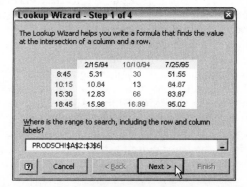

• **Figure 57-4: Designating the cell range of the data table to be searched.**

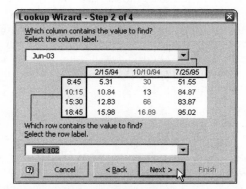

• **Figure 57-5: Designating the column and row in the table that contains the value to be looked up.**

This dialog box is where you select the column and then the row containing the value you want looked up in the data table.

4. **In the Which Column Contains the Value to Find drop-down list, click the name of the column containing the value you want to look up.**

In this particular example, I want to look up the number produced in the column with the heading Jun-03, so I select this heading in the column label.

5. **In the Which Row Contains the Value to Find drop-down list, click the name of the row containing the value you want to look up.**

In this example, I want to look up the number produced in the row with the heading Part 102, so I select this heading in the row label.

6. **When you're finished selecting the row and column, click the Next button to open the Lookup Wizard - Step 3 of 4 dialog box, shown in Figure 57-6.**

7. **Choose how you want the wizard to display the result:**

▶ **Copy Just the Formula to a Single Cell:** Select this option button to have only the formula inserted into a cell.

▶ **Copy the Formula and Lookup Parameters:** Select this option button to have the column and row information copied along with the formula.

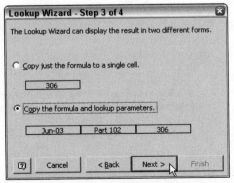

• **Figure 57-6: Selecting the way the Lookup Wizard displays the result of the two-way lookup.**

For this example, I selected the Copy the Formula and Lookup Parameters option button to have Excel copy both the date and the part number into the worksheet above the lookup formula that it creates.

8. **Click the Next button to open the Lookup Wizard - Step 4 of 4 or Step 4 of 6 dialog box (depending upon which option you selected in Step 7).**

If you selected the Copy Just the Formula to a Single Cell option button in Step 8, Excel displays the Lookup Wizard - Step 4 of 4 dialog box where you indicate the cell where the formula is to be copied. In this case, skip ahead to Step 11.

If you selected the Copy the Formula and Lookup Parameters option button in Step 8, the Lookup Wizard - Step 4 of 6 dialog box appears. In this case, continue to Step 9.

9. **Type the address of the cell where you want the column parameter copied or click the cell directly in the spreadsheet and then click the Next button.**

For this example, I select cell B11 to have Jun-03 column label copied there.

When you click Next, Excel displays the Lookup Wizard - Step 5 of 6 dialog box.

10. **Type the address of the cell where you want the row parameter copied or click the cell directly in the spreadsheet and then click the Next button.**

For this example, I select cell B10 to have the Part 102 row label copied there.

When you click Next, Excel displays the Lookup Wizard - Step 6 of 6 dialog box, shown in Figure 57-7.

11. **Type the address of the cell where you want the lookup formula or click the cell directly in the spreadsheet and then click the Finish button.**

Lookup Wizard - Step 6 of 6
Where do you want to copy the lookup formula?
Type or select a cell and then click Finish.
PRODSCH!$B$12
Cancel
< Back
Next >
Finish

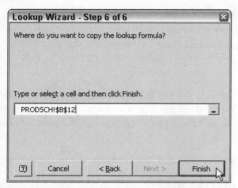

• **Figure 57-7: Designating the cell to contain the formula that performs the two-way lookup.**

Figure 57-8 shows what happened when I clicked the Finish button in the Lookup Wizard - Step 6 of 6 dialog box. The Lookup Wizard copied `Part 102` into cell B10 (which I named part_lookup) and the date `Jun-03` into cell B11 (which I named date_lookup).

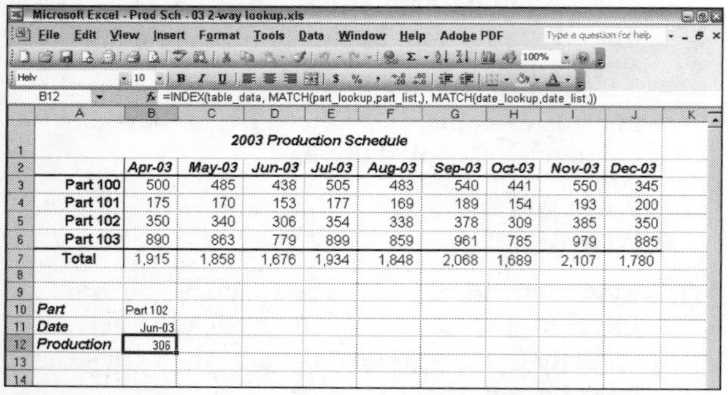
Microsoft Excel - Prod Sch - 03 2-way lookup.xls
B12
=INDEX(table_data, MATCH(part_lookup,part_list,), MATCH(date_lookup,date_list,))
2003 Production Schedule
Apr-03 May-03 Jun-03 Jul-03 Aug-03 Sep-03 Oct-03 Nov-03 Dec-03
Part 100 500 485 438 505 483 540 441 550 345
Part 101 175 170 153 177 169 189 154 193 200
Part 102 350 340 306 354 338 378 309 385 350
Part 103 890 863 779 899 859 961 785 979 885
Total 1,915 1,858 1,676 1,934 1,848 2,068 1,689 2,107 1,780
Part Part 102
Date Jun-03
Production 306

• **Figure 57-8: Worksheet after adding the formula that looks up the number produced based on the part and date given.**

The wizard also created the following formula in cell C12 that actually performs the two-way lookup using the INDEX function to look up the column and row in the Production Schedule returned by the following two MATCH functions:

```
=INDEX(table_data,MATCH(part_lookup,
  part_list,),MATCH(date_lookup,
  date_list,))
```

The MATCH functions return the number of the row and the column in the data table based on the values entered into the cells B10 (named part_lookup) and B11 (named date_lookup), respectively. The INDEX function then uses the row number returned by the first MATCH function and the column number returned by the second MATCH function as its *`row_num`* and *`col_num`* arguments. The INDEX function then returns the value in the cell in the data table that is at the intersection of the row number and column number returned by the two MATCH functions.

To have this INDEX formula look up the number produced for another part number and date, all you have to do is alter the values in the part_lookup cell (B10) and the date_lookup cell (B11), respectively. Figure 57-9 shows the worksheet after changing the part number to `Part 101` in cell B10 and the date to `Sep-03` in cell B11. As you can see, the INDEX function correctly returns `189` from the Production Schedule to cell B12 as soon as these two parameters are input into their respective cells.

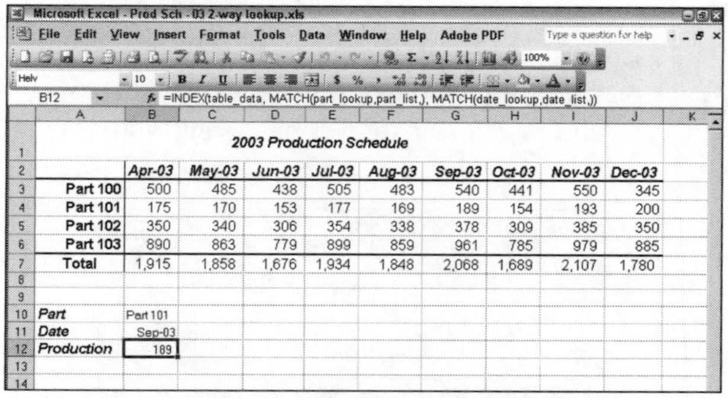
Microsoft Excel - Prod Sch - 03 2-way lookup.xls
B12
=INDEX(table_data, MATCH(part_lookup,part_list,), MATCH(date_lookup,date_list,))
2003 Production Schedule
Apr-03 May-03 Jun-03 Jul-03 Aug-03 Sep-03 Oct-03 Nov-03 Dec-03
Part 100 500 485 438 505 483 540 441 550 345
Part 101 175 170 153 177 169 189 154 193 200
Part 102 350 340 306 354 338 378 309 385 350
Part 103 890 863 779 899 859 961 785 979 885
Total 1,915 1,858 1,676 1,934 1,848 2,068 1,689 2,107 1,780
Part Part 101
Date Sep-03
Production 189

• **Figure 57-9: Worksheet after altering the part number and date in cells B10 and B11, respectively.**

Using Text Formulas
for Fun and Profit

Technique 58

Save Time By

- ✔ Converting all text entries to the correct case
- ✔ Joining text together by formula
- ✔ Replacing text formulas with their results

I definitely put this technique in the fun column. Using Excel's Text functions to convert text entries in your spreadsheet to the proper case is delightfully easy and, more importantly, a real timesaver, especially when you're importing long lists of names and addresses into worksheets with all the letters in an improper case (more often than not, all in uppercase letters).

I also consider knowing how to construct formulas that combine text entries made in separate cells of the worksheet a potentially great timesaver. I've personally had more than a few situations in which I needed to combine first and last name information originally entered in separate columns of a spreadsheet into a single column, and being able to use a text formula rather than having to manually enter the information has saved literally hours of what I consider to be completely wasted effort.

Getting Right on the Case

Excel offers three case-related text functions: UPPER, LOWER, and PROPER. All these functions take a single *text* argument that indicates the source of the text whose case is to be converted. As you'd expect, the UPPER function converts all letters in the *text* argument to uppercase. The LOWER function converts all letters in the *text* argument to lowercase. The PROPER function capitalizes the first letter of each word as well as any other letters in the *text* argument that don't follow another letter, and all other letters in the *text* argument are changed to lowercase.

Figure 58-1 illustrates a situation in which you would use the PROPER function. Here, both last and first name text entries were imported into the worksheet from a text file where the names were all entered in uppercase letters. You need to use the PROPER function to get these names into the proper capitalization, that is, an initial capital letter followed by all lowercase letters.

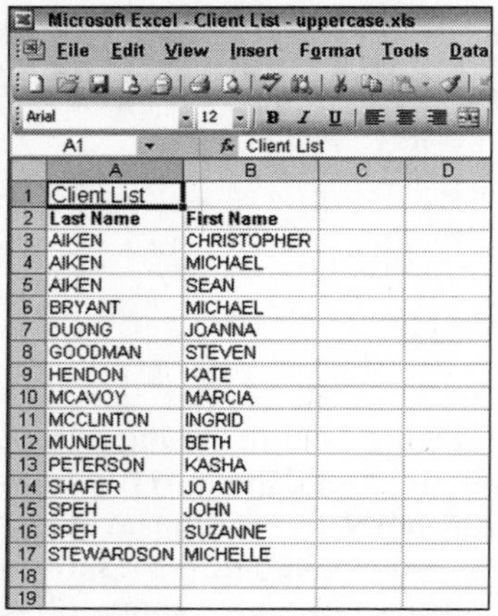

• **Figure 58-1: Sample worksheet with all first and last names entered in all caps.**

Follow along with these steps for using the PROPER function to convert text entries to the proper capitalization:

1. **Position the cell pointer in a blank cell where the first formula with the PROPER function is to go and then click the Insert Function button on the Formula bar to open the Insert Function dialog box.**

For this example, I select cell C3 as the cell in which to enter the first PROPER function.

2. **Select Text in the Category drop-down list box, and then double-click PROPER in the Select a Function list box to open the Function Arguments dialog box.**

3. **Click the first cell in the worksheet whose text needs converting to put its address into the Text box and then click OK to insert the PROPER function into the cell.**

For this example, I select cell A3 for the argument of the first PROPER function. Excel then closes the Insert Function dialog box and inserts the formula =PROPER(A3) in cell C3, which now contains the proper capitalization of the last name Aiken.

4. **Copy the formula with the original PROPER function as needed in the worksheet to convert the rest of the cells whose cases needs fixing.**

For this example, I drag the Fill handle down to cell C17 and then drag it over to D17 to convert all the uppercase entries in both the last and first name columns. Figure 58-2 shows the worksheet after copying this formula. Everything looks fine in columns C and D with the exception of the two last names, Mcavoy and Mcclinton. I still have to fix those names by capitalizing the *A* in McAvoy and the second *C* in McClinton.

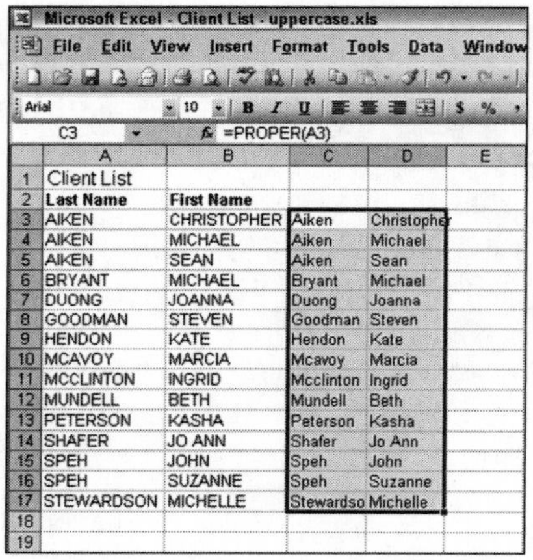

• **Figure 58-2: Worksheet after using the PROPER function in columns C and D.**

Joining Separate Text Entries Together

You can use the ampersand (&) as an operator in an Excel formula to join separate text entries together in a single cell. This procedure is known technically as *concatenating* (joining) text strings. For example, in the sample Client List spreadsheet shown in Figure 58-1, you can use this concatenation operator to join together — and change the order of — the last and first names currently entered in all uppercase letters in the first two columns of the worksheet.

To join the first name entry in cell B3 with the last name entry in cell A3, you would enter the following formula:

```
=B3&" "&A3
```

Notice the use of the double quotes in this formula. They enclose a blank space that is placed between the first and last name you want to join together with the two concatenation operators. If you don't include this space in the formula and just joined the first and last name together with this formula like this

```
=B3&A3
```

Excel would return a fused entry like `Christopher Aiken` in the cell where you enter the formula.

To have Excel convert the name entries in columns A and B to proper capitalization while at the same time reordering and concatenating them, you would enclose the original concatenation formula in the PROPER function as its argument, as in

```
=PROPER(B3&" "&A3)
```

That's all there is to it. Figure 58-3 illustrates the use of this formula to concatenate, reorder, and convert the original last and first name entries in column F.

*• **Figure 58-3:** Worksheet after concatenating the first and last names in column G.*

Replacing Text Formulas with Their Results

There's only one big problem with using Text functions like the PROPER function to get the right case

and the ampersand (&) operator to join text entries together: Although they mostly deliver the results you want, they deliver them as formulas in their cells and not text. And how in the world would you be able to edit the formula results as needed (as in the case of the Mcavoy that should be McAvoy and the Mcclinton that should be McClinton) or sort them in a different order?

The fact is that you have to take the extra step of converting the formulas into their calculated values. Then you can edit and sort the resulting values (actually, text in this case) just as though you'd taken time to type into the spreadsheet yourself.

You use the Paste Special feature to convert the formulas in a selection of cells to their calculated values. In the case of the sample worksheet, which now contains text formulas that need converting in two ranges, C3:D17 and F3:F17, you would take these steps:

1. **Select the first cell range.**

   In this case, C3:D17.

2. **Choose Edit⇨Copy or press Ctrl+C.**

3. **Choose Edit⇨Paste Special to open the Paste Special dialog box.**

4. **Click the Values option button and then click OK.**

   In this step, you're actually replacing the text formulas with the text entries they compute by pasting the names on top of the formulas. This replaces the original formulas with the calculated results so that this cell range now contains text that you can directly edit and sort.

5. **Select the second cell range and repeat Steps 2 through 4.**

 Note that you can't do this formula-to-value conversion in one operation because the Paste Special command works only with single cell ranges.

To convert a single formula to its calculated value, simply select the cell and then press F2 (Edit), F9 (Calculate), and Enter.

Technique 59

Creating Queries to Import Data from an External Database

It's not at all strange that most competent spreadsheet users are at a complete loss when it comes to using full-blown database programs, even relatively simple ones such as Microsoft's own Access. After all, although databases often track the same information as spreadsheets, they do it in a much more elaborate and often customized fashion. (Access, for example, is more of a program for creating database applications than an application program itself.) The answer is not to waste time on learning how to use your company's DBMS (Database Management System) program but to figure out how to use Excel to go in and get the data you need from your company's database and bring it into Excel where you know what you're doing.

Excel makes it easy to query other external databases to which you have access to search for the data that you're interested in and then bring that data back into the comfortable Excel worksheet environment for further manipulation and analysis. To create a query that acquires data from an external database, you must complete two procedures. In the first procedure, you define the *data source* — that is, the external database that contains the data that you want to query. In the second procedure, you specify the query itself, including all the columns of data that you want extracted along with the criteria for selecting them.

Setting Up the Data Source Definition

The first step in doing external database queries is to set up a definition for the data source that you'll be using. This procedure is really straightforward:

1. **Choose Data⇨Import External Data⇨New Database Query to open the Data Source dialog box, shown in Figure 59-1.**

If the External Data Query feature is not already installed on your computer, Excel displays an alert dialog box stating that the Microsoft Query feature is not currently installed and asking if you want to install this feature now. Click Yes to have Excel install this feature. (Remember that you must have your Office 11 CD handy or be able to specify the path on your company's network where the necessary files are stored in order to do this.) After Microsoft Query is installed on your system, the Choose Data Source dialog box appears with the New Data Source item selected on the Databases tab.

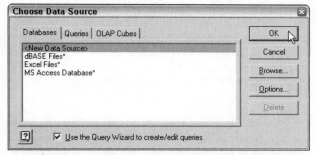

• **Figure 59-1: Creating a new data source for an external database query.**

2. Click OK to accept the default settings and to open the Create New Source Data dialog box, shown in Figure 59-2.

3. Enter a descriptive name for the database query in the What Name Do You Want to Give Your Data Source text box.

By naming the data source definition, you can reuse it without having to go through all these tedious steps for defining it.

4. Click the name of the driver to be used for your data source in the Select a Driver for the Type of Database You Want to Access drop-down list box.

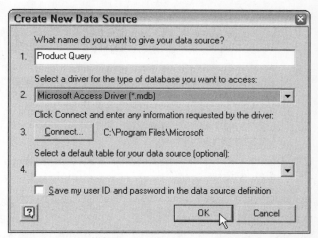

• **Figure 59-2: Creating a new data source for an external database query.**

This drop-down list box contains drivers for all the most popular PC databases, such as Access, dBASE, Paradox, and FoxPro, as well as an SQL driver for sophisticated Database Management Systems, such as dB2, and an OBDC Oracle driver for querying an Oracle database (to name a few).

5. Click the Connect button to open a dialog box for the driver you select. (See Figure 59-3.)

This action opens a dialog box for the driver you selected and in which you can choose the database to be used. For example, if you select Microsoft Access Driver (*.mdb) as the driver in the Create New Data Source dialog box, Excel opens an ODBC Microsoft Access Setup dialog box.

6. Click the Select button, and then in the Select Database dialog box that appears, locate the folder that contains the database file that you want to query and click OK.

Excel returns you to the Create New Data Source dialog box, which now displays the name of the database that you selected.

7. If you want, you can select a default table for use in the database in the Select a Default Table for Your Data Source (Optional) drop-down list box.

8. Also, if you had to specify a user name and password to gain access to the database, you can have this information saved as part of the data source definition by selecting the Save My User ID and Password in the Data Source Definition check box.

9. Click OK to close the Create a New Data Source dialog box.

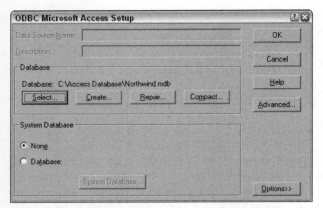

• **Figure 59-3:** Selecting the Access database to use in the ODBC Microsoft Access Setup dialog box.

Excel closes the Create a New Data Source dialog box and immediately opens the Query Wizard - Choose Columns dialog box. If you don't want to create the query to your newly defined data source right away, click the Cancel button and then click No in the alert dialog box asking you if you want to continue editing the query.

Creating the Database Query

The next step in the process of querying an external database is to set up the query that tells Excel which fields you're interested in and what kind of filtering,

if any, you want applied to the records before you extract them. To define your query, you take these steps:

1. Choose Data⇨Import External Data⇨New Database Query. Then select the name of the data source to use and click OK to open the Query Wizard - Choose Columns dialog box showing a list of available tables and fields (see Figure 59-4).

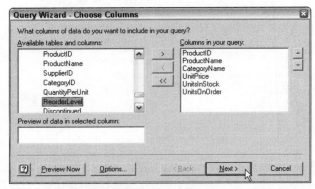

• **Figure 59-4:** Selecting the fields to include in the new query.

If the Query Wizard - Choose Columns dialog box showing the tables and fields in the data source you just defined is already open (from the previous procedure), ignore Step 1 and go right on to Step 2.

2. In the Available Tables and Columns list box on the left, select the fields that you want to use and then copy them to the Columns in Your Query list box on the right.

To select the fields that you want to use, click the Expand button (+) in front of the name of each table in the external database that contains fields that you want. Then click the name of the field followed by the > button to copy the field name to the Columns in Your Query list box. To preview the data in that field, click the Preview Now button when the field name is selected in the Columns in Your Query list box.

Note that the order in which you add the fields determines their column order in your Excel worksheet. To change the order after copying the fields to the Columns in Your Query list box, click the field and then click the up-arrow button to the right to promote the field in the list or click the down-arrow button to demote the field in the list.

3. **Click the Next button to open the Query Wizard - Filter Data dialog box, shown in Figure 59-5.**

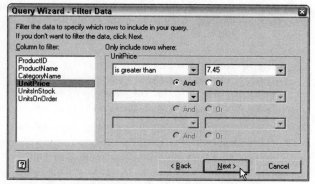

• **Figure 59-5:** Filtering the fields included in the new query.

4. **For each field that should be filtered in the Column to Filter list box, specify the filtering criteria, including any AND and OR conditions, in the criteria and evaluation drop-down list boxes.**

To set up the criteria by which records are selected, select the field for which you want to set criteria and then click the criteria to use and the value to be evaluated in the left and right drop-down list boxes, respectively.

The criteria available in the drop-down list boxes on the left are the same as those used with the Custom AutoFilter (see Technique 45) with the exception of the Like, Not Like, Is Null, and Is Not Null operators, which are not available when setting criteria for the Custom AutoFilter. (The Like criteria refers to entries that sound like one that

you enter in the associated drop-down list box on the right, and Null refers to empty entries in the field.)

When entering the values to be evaluated in the associated drop-down list boxes on the right, you can use the question mark (?), asterisk (*), and wildcard characters (question marks for single characters and the asterisk for multiple characters) in the text that you enter in these boxes. You can also select data entries in a field from which to compare to by clicking them in the drop-down list.

To set up a logical AND condition, make sure that the AND option button is selected when you specify the second and even third set of filtering criteria. (Remember in an AND condition, records are selected only when all sets of criteria are TRUE.) To set up a logical OR condition, click the Or option button before you specify the second or even third set of criteria. (Remember in an OR condition, records are selected when any one of the sets of criteria are TRUE.)

Note that if you want to acquire all data in a selected field, don't specify any filtering criteria for that field in the Filter Data dialog box.

5. **When you're finished entering filtering criteria, click the Next button to open the Query Wizard - Sort Order dialog box, shown in Figure 59-6.**

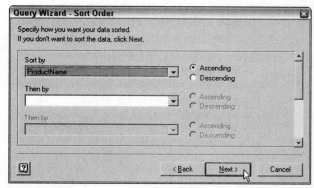

• **Figure 59-6:** Specifying how the fields included in the new query are to be sorted.

6. **Specify the field or fields on which the external data is to be sorted.**

To sort the data that you acquire in the external database query, select the name of the field in the Sort By drop-down list box and then select either the Ascending (default) or Descending option button. To sort any duplicates in the field that you specify as the primary sorting key, select the tie-breaking field for the secondary key in the Then By drop-down list box and then click its Ascending (default) or Descending option button.

Repeat this procedure to sort the incoming data on up to three fields total (just as you can sort a standard Excel data list — see Technique 44). If you don't want the data sorted, click the Next button without selecting any fields as sorting keys.

7. **When you're finished specifying the field or fields on which the external data is to be sorted, click the Next button to open the Query Wizard - Finish dialog box, shown in Figure 59-7.**

This dialog box contains several options that you can choose from in completing the query.

▶ **Return Data to Microsoft Office Excel:** Leave this option button selected if you want to return the data to the current or a new worksheet.

▶ **View Data or Edit Query in Microsoft Query:** Click this option button if you want to view the data and/or edit the query in the Microsoft Query window.

▶ **Create an OLAP Cube from This Query:** Click this option button if you want to create an OLAP (Online Analytic Processing) cube that summarizes the data being acquired. (This is useful when querying huge databases that contain so many records that they need to be summarized before importing them into Excel.)

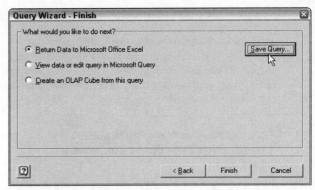

• **Figure 59-7:** Getting ready to save the query file for future use.

8. **If you want to save the query to reuse at a later time, click the Save Query button and then enter the filename for the new query file in the Save As dialog box and click Save.**

Excel saves your query as a separate query file (indicated by the `.dqy` file extension) so that you can reuse it from any workbook file. Note that Excel automatically saves the data source definition as a separate file (indicated by the `.dsn`) when you next save the current workbook but does automatically save the query.

9. **To see the data and review your query before you bring it into your Excel worksheet, select the View Data or Edit Query in Microsoft Query option button and then click OK.**

When you do this, Excel opens a Microsoft Query window similar to the one shown in Figure 59-8, where you can preview the way the acquired data will appear when you bring it into Excel. You can also edit the database query in this window.

10. **After you review the data to be queried, click the Close button in the Microsoft Query window to open the Import Data dialog box, shown in Figure 59-9.**

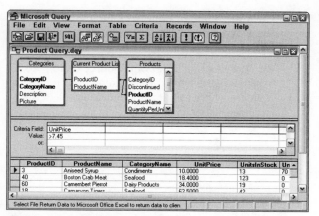

• **Figure 59-8:** Previewing the data to be extracted when executing the external database query.

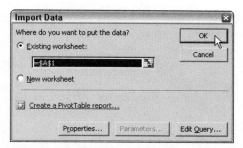

• **Figure 59-9:** Indicating where to put the data extracted from the external database by the query.

11. Either click the Existing Worksheet option button and choose where you want the data imported on the active sheet in the drop-down list or select the New Worksheet option button. Then click OK to start importing the data.

By default, the Existing Worksheet option button is selected, and cell A1 is designated as the start of the range. To change the starting cell, click it in the worksheet. To import the data into a new worksheet in the current workbook, click the New Worksheet option button instead.

When you click OK, Excel executes the database query and acquires the data from the external database. After the program finishes importing all the records that match your filtering criteria, it also displays the External Data toolbar. (See Figure 59-10.) You can use the buttons on this toolbar to update the acquired data or edit the query.

By saving a data query, you can reuse it at any time to connect to an external database and to acquire its data according to the query's parameters. To do this, follow these steps:

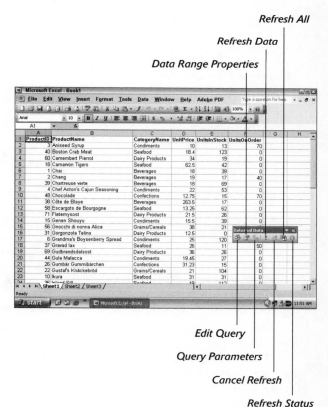

• **Figure 59-10:** Worksheet after executing the query and extracting the information from the external database.

1. **Choose Data⇨Import External Data⇨Import Data From to open the Select Data Source dialog box.**

This dialog box displays the names of all the query files that you create and save (as outlined in the preceding steps).

2. **Click the name of the query file (with the .dqy file extension) to use and then click the Open button.**

Excel closes the Select Data Source dialog box and opens the Import Data dialog box, where you indicate where to put the imported data in the Excel worksheet.

Technique 60

Automating Repetitive Tasks with Macros

By now, even if you haven't started putting them to good use in your Excel spreadsheets, you've undoubtedly heard of *macros,* those wonderful containers for recording almost any sequence of Excel commands and then playing them back in a flash at the touch of a key. By using Excel's macro feature to record tasks that you perform routinely, not only can you speed up the procedure considerably (because Excel can play back your keystrokes and mouse actions a heck of lot faster than you can perform them manually), but you're also assured that each step in the task is carried out the same way every time you perform the task.

Excel's macro feature records all the commands and keystrokes that you make in a language called Visual Basic for Applications (VBA), which is a special version of the BASIC programming language developed by the good folks at Microsoft for use with all the Office application programs. After recording basic macros, I'll show you how you can even play programmer by using Excel's Visual Basic Editor to display and make changes to the macro's basic VBA code.

Recording and Playing Back Macros

The macro recorder built into Excel enables you to capture command sequences from the time you turn on the recorder until the moment you turn it off. When you turn on the macro recorder, it records all your actions in the active worksheet or chart sheet as you make them.

Note that the macro recorder doesn't record the actual keystrokes or mouse actions that you take to accomplish an action, only the VBA code required to perform the action itself. This means that, if you make mistakes while following a command sequence, all the actions you take to rectify them won't be recorded as part of the macro. For example, if you make a typing error and then edit it while the macro recorder is on, only the corrected entry is recorded as part of the macro's VBA instructions.

Whenever you record a macro, Excel adds a special module sheet to the current Excel workbook that contains the VBA code for playing back the sequence. To open the module sheet in Visual Basic Editor to review or edit the macro's VBA commands, choose Tools⇨Macro⇨Visual Basic Editor or simply press Alt+F11.

You can store the macros you record as part of the current workbook, in a new workbook, or in a special, globally available Personal Macro Workbook named personal.xls. When you record a macro in your Personal Macro Workbook, you can run that macro from any workbook that you have open. (That's because the personal.xls workbook is secretly opened whenever you launch Excel, and although it's immediately hidden, the macros it contains are always available.) When you record macros as part of the current workbook or a new workbook, you can run those macros only when the workbook in which they were recorded is open in Excel.

When you create a macro with the macro recorder, you decide not only the workbook in which to store the macro but also what name and shortcut keystrokes to assign it. When creating a name for your macro, use the same guidelines as when you assign a standard range name to a cell range in your worksheet. (See Technique 26.) When assigning a shortcut keystroke to run the macro, you can assign the Ctrl key plus a lowercase letter, as in Ctrl+Q, or the Ctrl key plus an uppercase letter (the equivalent of Ctrl+Shift), as in Ctrl+Shift+Q. You can't, however, assign the Ctrl key plus a punctuation or number key (such as Ctrl+1 or Ctrl+/) to your macro.

Recording the macro

To see how easy it is to create a macro by recording your actions in Excel, follow along with these steps for creating a macro that enters the company name

in a worksheet in 12-point, bold type and centers the company name across rows A through E with the Merge and Center feature:

1. **Open the Excel workbook that contains the worksheet data or chart you want your macro to work with.**

If you're building a macro that adds new data to a worksheet (as in this example), open a worksheet with plenty of blank cells in which to add the data. If you're building a macro that needs to be in a particular cell when its steps are played back, put the cell pointer in that cell.

2. **Choose Tools⇨Macro⇨Record New Macro to open the Record Macro box, shown in Figure 60-1.**

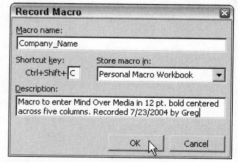

• **Figure 60-1: Getting ready to record the Company_Name macro.**

3. **Replace the Macro1 temporary macro name by entering your name for the macro in the Macro Name text box.**

Remember that when naming a macro, you can't use spaces in the macro name, and it must begin with a letter and not a number or punctuation symbol. For this example macro, replace Macro1 in the Macro Name text box with the name Company_Name.

4. **If you want to be able to play back the macro by pressing a keystroke shortcut, select the Shortcut Key text box and then enter the letter of the alphabet that you want to assign to the macro.**

In the Shortcut Key text box, you can enter a lowercase or uppercase letter between A and Z that acts like a shortcut key for running the macro when you press Ctrl followed by that letter key.

Just remember that Excel has already assigned a number of Ctrl+letter keystroke shortcuts for doing common tasks, such as Ctrl+C for copying an item to the Clipboard and Ctrl+V for pasting an item from the Clipboard into the worksheet. (Look up Keyboard Shortcuts in the Assistant task pane opened by pressing F1 for a complete list.) If you assign the same keystrokes to the macro that you're building, your macro's shortcut keys override and, therefore, disable Excel's ready-made shortcut keystrokes.

For this example macro, enter C (uppercase) to assign Ctrl+Shift+C as the shortcut keystroke (so as not to disable the ready-made Ctrl+C shortcut).

5. **On the Store Macro In drop-down list, select one of the following options for storing the new macro:**

▶ **Personal Macro Workbook:** Select this option to be able to run the macro anytime you like.

▶ **This Workbook (the default):** Select this option when you need to run the macro only when the current workbook is open.

▶ **New Workbook:** Select this option if you want to open a new workbook in which to record and save the new macro.

For this example macro, select the Personal Macro Workbook so that you can use it to enter the company name in any Excel workbook that you create or edit.

6. **Select the Description list box and then insert a brief description of the macro's purpose in front of the information indicating the date and who recorded the macro.**

In the Description list box, you should document the purpose and functioning of your macro. Although this step is optional, it's a good idea to get in the habit of recording this information every time you build a new macro so that you and your coworkers can always know what to expect from the macro when running it.

7. **Click OK to close the Record Macro dialog box and automatically open the Stop Recording toolbar, shown in Figure 60-2.**

Stop Recording

Relative Recording

• **Figure 60-2: The floating Stop Recording toolbar appears whenever you turn on the macro recorder.**

The floating Stop Recording toolbar appears as soon as you turn the macro recorder on (although all you can see is St and the first part of the o in the title bar because this toolbar is so short). Also, the message Recording now appears on the status bar to remind you that the results of all the actions you take (including selecting cells, entering data, and choosing commands) will now be recorded as part of your macro.

The Stop Recording toolbar contains a Stop Recording button that you can click to turn off the macro recorder and a Relative Reference button that you click when you want the macro recorder to record the macro relative to the position of the current cell.

8. **Click the Relative Reference button if you want to be able to play back the macro anywhere in the worksheet.**

For the example macro that enters the company name and formats it in the worksheet, you definitely need to click the Relative Reference button before you start recording commands. Otherwise, you can use the macro only to enter the company name starting in cell A1 of a worksheet.

9. **Select the cells, enter the data, and choose the Excel commands required to perform the tasks that you want recorded just as you normally would in creating or editing the current worksheet. You can use the keyboard or the mouse or a combination of the two.**

For the example macro, all you do is type the company name and click the Enter button on the Formula bar to complete the entry in the current cell. Next, click the Bold button and then select 12 on the Font Size drop-down list on the Formatting toolbar. Finally, drag through cells A1:E1 to select this range and then click the Merge and Center button, again on the Formatting toolbar.

When you finish taking all the actions in Excel that you want recorded, you're ready to shut off the macro recorder.

10. **Click the Stop Recording button on the floating Stop Recording toolbar (or you can choose Tools⇨Macro⇨Stop Recording).**

When you shut off the macro recorder, the Recording message on the status bar immediately disappears, letting you know that no further actions will be recorded.

Playing back the macro

To play back a macro you've recorded, press Alt+F8 or choose Tools⇨Macro⇨Macros to open the Macro dialog box, shown in Figure 60-3. This dialog box lists all the macros in the current workbook as well as

those in your Personal Macro Workbook (provided you've created one). Click the name of the macro that you want to play and then click the Run button or press Enter.

If you assigned a shortcut keystroke to the macro, you don't have to bother opening the Macro dialog box to play the macro: Simply press Ctrl plus the letter key or Ctrl+Shift plus the letter key you assigned, and Excel immediately plays back all the commands that you recorded.

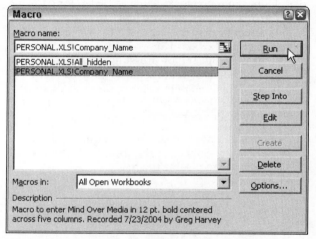

• **Figure 60-3: Selecting the macro to run in the Macro dialog box.**

 You can assign the macros that you create to buttons or menu items on custom toolbars or menus that you create (see Technique 2) and then play them back by clicking the custom button or selecting the custom menu item to which the macro is assigned.

Before testing a new macro, you may need to select a new worksheet or, at least, a new cell range within the active worksheet. When recording cell references in a macro, the macro recorder always inserts absolute references in the macro sheet unless you click the Relative Reference button on the Stop Recording toolbar before you start choosing the commands and taking the actions in the spreadsheet that you want recorded as part of the macro. This means that your macro enters its data entries or performs its formatting in the same area of the active worksheet (unless the code in the macro itself causes the macro to first select a new area or select a new sheet in the workbook active).

Excel automatically sets the level of macro security to the highest level — a level that prevents macros that aren't digitally signed from running. To enable Excel to run macros that aren't signed but that you know come from trustworthy sources (such as Fred in Accounting), reset the macro security level to Medium on the Security Level tab of the Security dialog box (Tools⇨Macro⇨Security). Excel thereafter prompts you to enable such macros in the worksheet.

Editing Macros in the Visual Basic Editor

After you've created a macro, you don't necessarily have to rerecord it to change the way it behaves. In many cases, you may find it more efficient to change its behavior by simply editing its contents in Visual Basic Editor (also known as the VBA — as in Visual Basic for Applications — Editor for short).

Before you can use VBA Editor to edit a macro that you saved in your Personal Macro Workbook, you must first unhide this workbook by selecting PERSONAL.XLS in the Unhide dialog box (Window⇨Unhide).

To open a macro for editing in Visual Basic Editor, follow these general steps:

1. **Press Alt+F8 or choose Tools⇨Macros⇨Macro to open the Macro dialog box.**

2. **Select the name of the macro that you want to edit in the Macro Name list box and then click the Edit button to open the module sheet containing the macro in VBA Editor, as shown in Figure 60-4.**

• **Figure 60-4: VBA Editor after maximizing the Code window.**

Excel opens Visual Basic Editor with the code for your macro displayed in the Code window — unless you select the name of a macro saved in the Personal Macro Workbook and this workbook is still hidden. In that case, Excel displays an alert dialog box telling you that you can't edit a hidden macro and informing you that you need to use the Window⇨Unhide command. You then need to click OK in the alert dialog box, press Esc to close the Macro dialog box, and then unhide the Personal Macro Workbook before you repeat these first two macro editing steps.

After you have the lines of code for the macro displayed in the Code window in Visual Basic Editor, you can edit any of its statements as needed. If you want to obtain a printout of the lines of code in your macro before you begin making changes, choose File⇨Print or press Ctrl+P. This action opens a Print dialog box with the Current Module option button selected in the Range section and the Code check box selected in the Print What section so that you just click OK to have Excel print all the statements in the macro.

3. **Edit the statements in the Code window of Visual Basic Editor as needed.**

When editing the macro's commands, remember that you can use the Edit⇨Undo (Ctrl+Z) command to undo any deletion that you make by mistake. You can also find out what a particular statement or property does in the macro by selecting it with the I-beam mouse pointer and pressing F1 or by clicking the Help button on the Standard toolbar.

After you finish editing the macro, you're ready to return to your spreadsheet where you can test out the modified macro and make sure that you haven't added some wacky, unwanted command to the macro or, even worse, crippled it so that it no longer runs at all.

4. **Click the View Microsoft Excel button at the beginning of the Standard toolbar or click the workbook's minimized button on the Windows taskbar to return to the worksheet.**

Select an appropriate or safe place in which to test your modified macro and then run it, either by pressing its shortcut keys or by pressing Alt+F8, clicking it in the Macro list box, and then clicking the Run button.

If something doesn't work as intended or if the macro doesn't work at all, return to the Visual Basic Editor and find and correct your error(s). Click the minimized Microsoft Visual Basic button on the Windows taskbar to return to the Visual Basic Editor and have a try at editing the code one more time.

If everything checks out and runs as planned, save your changes as outlined in Step 5.

5. **Press Ctrl+S or choose File⇨Save to save the changes to the modified macro if it's stored as part of the current workbook.**

 If you modified a macro saved in the Personal Macro Workbook, you have to exit Excel in order to save your changes to the macro. When you exit the program (Alt+F4 or File⇨Exit), Excel displays an alert dialog box asking if you want to save the changes you made to the `personal.xls` file. Be sure to click the Yes button to save the changes to your global macro before you close Excel.

Modifying the settings for VBA properties

Even when you don't know anything about programming in VBA (and aim to keep it that way), you can get the gist of the more obvious properties in a macro that change certain settings, such as number format or font attribute, by experimenting with assigning them new values.

For example, in the code of the Company_Name macro (refer to Figure 60-4), you can probably identify the section of VBA commands that begins with the line `With Selection.Font` and ends with the line `End With` as containing the procedure for assigning various font attributes for the current cell selection.

Going a step further, you probably can figure out that most of these attributes are being reset by making the attribute equal to a new entry or value, such as

```
.Name = "Arial"
```

which sets the text font to Arial, followed by

```
.Size = 12
```

which sets the text size to 12 point. You can also see in this section that particular attributes are being turned on by setting them equal to True or False, such as

```
Selection.Font.Bold = True
```

which makes the text in the current cell selection bold.

You can make your macro behave differently just by doing some careful editing of these settings. For example, if you want the final font size to be 24 points instead of 12, all you have to do is edit the Size property by changing its value from 12 to 24 as follows:

```
.Size = 24
```

Likewise, you can have the macro apply single underlining to the cell selection by editing the xlUnderlineStyle property from none to single as follows:

```
.Underline = xlUnderlineStyleSingle
```

 When the allowable settings for a particular property are not obvious (such as in the case of the Underline property), select the property in the Code window without selecting its current setting and then Press F1 to open the VBA Help window with information on that property. Usually the Example section at the bottom of this Help window gives you an idea of the different types of values that the property can take.

Getting user input by adding a custom dialog box

One of the biggest problems with recording macros is that any text or values that you have the macro enter for you can never vary thereafter. If you create a macro that enters the heading Mind Over Media in the current cell of your worksheet, this is the only heading you'll ever get out of that macro. However, you can get around this inflexibility by using the InputBox function. When you run the macro, this Visual Basic function causes Excel to display an input dialog box where you can enter whatever title makes sense for the new worksheet. The macro then puts that text into the current cell and formats this text, if that's what you've trained your macro to do next.

To see how easy it is to use the InputBox function to add interactivity to an otherwise staid macro, follow along with the steps for converting the Company_Name macro that currently inputs the text Mind Over Media to one that prompts you for the name that you want entered. The InputBox function uses the following syntax:

```
InputBox(prompt[,title][,default][,xpos]
    [,ypos][,helpfile,context])
```

In this function, only the *prompt* argument is required; the rest of the arguments are optional. The *prompt* argument specifies the message that appears inside the input dialog box, prompting the user to enter a new value (or in this case, a new company name). The *prompt* argument can be up to a maximum of 1,024 characters. If you want the prompt message to appear on different lines inside the dialog box, enter the functions Chr(13) and Chr(10) in the text (to insert a carriage return and a linefeed in the message).

The optional *title* argument specifies what text to display in the title bar of the input dialog box. If you don't specify a *title* argument, Excel displays the application name on the title bar.

The optional *default* argument specifies the default response that automatically appears in the text box at the bottom of the input dialog box. If you don't specify a *default* argument, the text box is empty in the input dialog box.

The *xpos* and *ypos* optional arguments specify the horizontal distance from the left edge of the screen to the left edge of the dialog box and the vertical distance from the top edge of the screen to the top edge of the dialog box. If you don't specify these arguments, Excel centers the input dialog box horizontally and positions it approximately one-third of the way down the screen vertically.

The *helpfile* and *context* optional arguments specify the name of the custom Help file that you make available to the user to explain the workings of the input dialog box as well as the type of data that it accepts. As part of the process of creating a custom Help file for use in the Excel Help system, you assign the topic a context number appropriate to its content, which is then specified as the *context* argument for the InputBox function. When you specify a Help file and *context* argument for this function, Excel adds a Help button to the custom input dialog box that users can click to access the custom Help file in the Help window.

Before you can add the line of code to the macro with the InputBox function, you need to find the place in the Visual Basic commands where the line should go. To enter the `Mind Over Media` text into the active cell, the Company_Name macro uses the following Visual Basic command:

```
ActiveCell.FormulaR1C1 = "Mind Over Media"
```

To add interactivity to the macro, you need to insert the InputBox function on a line in the Code window right above this `ActiveCell.FormulaR1C1` statement. To supply the first three arguments of the InputBox function (*prompt*, *title*, and *default*), you create variables whose declared values are used. Finally, you create a variable that contains the entire InputBox function and sets it equal to the `ActiveCell` statement that begins the macro instructions.

To make these editing changes to the basic recorded macro, follow these steps:

1. Position the insertion point in the Code window at the beginning of the `ActiveCell.FormulaR1C1` statement and press Enter to insert a new line.

2. Press the ↑ key to position the insertion point at the beginning of the new line.

3. Type the following code to create the InputMsg variable on line 8 and then press the Enter key to start a new line 9:

```
InputMsg = "Enter the title for this
    worksheet in the text box below and
    then click OK:"
```

On this line, you want to create a variable that supplies the *prompt* argument to the InputBox function. To do this, state the name of the variable (InputMsg in this case) followed by its current entry. Be sure to enclose the message text on the right side of the equal sign in a closed pair of double quotation marks.

4. Type the following code to create the InputTitle variable on line 9 and then press Enter to insert a new line 10:

```
InputTitle = "Company Name"
```

Create a variable named InputTitle that supplies the optional *title* argument for the InputBox function. This variable makes the text `Company Name` appear as the title of the input dialog box. Again, be sure to enclose the name for the dialog box title bar in quotation marks.

5. Type the following code to create the DefaultText variable on line 10 and then press Enter to insert a new line 11:

```
DefaultText = "Mind Over Media"
```

Create a variable named DefaultText that supplies the optional *default* argument to the InputBox function. This variable makes the text `Mind Over Media` appear as the default entry on the text box at the bottom of the custom Company Name input dialog box.

6. Type the following code to create the CompanyName variable that uses the InputBox function on line 11:

```
CompanyName = InputBox(InputMsg,
    InputTitle, DefaultText)
```

Create a final variable named CompanyName that specifies the InputBox function as its entry (using the InputMsg, InputTitle, and DefaultText variables that you just created) and stores the results of this function.

7. **Select** `"Mind Over Media"` **on line 12 and replace it with** `CompanyName` **(with *no* quotation marks).**

Replace the value `"Mind Over Media"` in the ActiveCell.FormulaR1C1 property with the CompanyName variable (whose value is determined by whatever is input into the Company Name input dialog box), thus effectively replacing this constant in the macro with the means for making this input truly interactive.

Figure 60-5 shows the Code window with the edited Company_Name macro after adding the statements that make it interactive. All you have to do at this point is to test the macro to make sure that the input dialog box performs the way you want it to and then save the changes in the VBA Editor.

Figure 60-6 shows the Company Name input dialog box in action in the worksheet when you execute the edited Company_Name macro. This Company Name dialog box automatically appears and prompts you for input whenever you run the edited and now fully interactive version of the Company_Name macro.

To enter the default name of Mind Over Media into the current cell and then have the macro format this text by using the rest of the macro commands, just click the OK button in this custom dialog box. To

enter and format the name of another company, simply type the name of the company (which automatically replaces Mind Over Media in the text box) before you click OK.

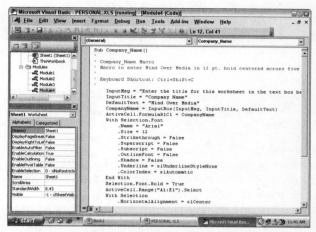

• **Figure 60-5: VBA Editor after adding the statements to Company_Name macro to create the input dialog box.**

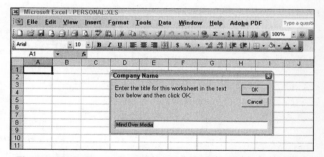

• **Figure 60-6: Executing the edited macro that uses the custom Company Name dialog box.**

Technique 61

Creating Custom Functions to Use in Your Worksheets

Save Time By

✔ Defining custom functions for Excel

✔ Saving custom functions in add-in files

Let's face it: Although Excel comes stocked with a wide variety of built-in functions, some of which are pretty specialized, they don't begin to cover all the types of specific computations you need to perform. Wouldn't it be great if you could extend the body of built-in Excel functions to include ones that your business uses? Well, you can do this, and this technique is dedicated to showing you how. Here, you find out how to turn your most precise and exacting calculations into functions available to any spreadsheet user through Excel's thoroughly familiar Insert Function feature.

All it takes for you to begin creating your own custom functions (known technically as user-defined functions or UDFs for short) is the briefest familarity with Excel's VBA (Visual Basic for Applications) language and Visual Basic Editor and the information you find in this technique.

Creating Custom Functions

To create a user-defined function, you must do four things:

✔ Create a new module sheet where the custom function is to be defined in Visual Basic Editor. To do this, select its project in the Project Explorer window and then choose Insert⇨Module on the Visual Basic Editor menu bar.

✔ On the first line in the Code window, enter the name of the custom function and specify the names of the arguments that this function takes. Note that you can't duplicate any built-in function names, such as SUM or AVERAGE functions, and so on, and you must list argument names in the order in which they are processed and enclosed in parentheses.

✔ Enter the formula or set of formulas that tells Excel how to calculate the custom function's result. You do this by entering the argument names listed in the Function command with whatever arithmetic operators or built-in functions are required to get the calculation made on the line or lines below.

✔ Indicate that you've finished defining the user-defined function by entering the End Function command on the last line.

To see how this procedure works in action, consider the following scenario. You need a custom function for your spreadsheets that calculates the sales commissions for your salespeople based on the number of sales they make in a month as well as the total amount of their monthly sales (they sell big-ticket items, such as RVs). The custom Commission function you want to create requires two arguments: *TotalSales* and *ItemsSold* so that the first line of code on the module sheet in the Code window would have to be this:

```
Function Commission(TotalSales,ItemsSold)
```

In determining how the commissions are actually calculated, suppose that you base the commission percentage on the number of sales made during the month. For five sales or fewer in a month, you pay a commission rate of 4.5 percent of the salesperson's total monthly sales; for sales of six or more, you pay a commission rate of 5 percent.

To define the formula section of the Commission custom function, you need to set up an IF construction. This IF construction is similar to the IF function that you enter into a worksheet cell except that you use different lines in the macro code for the construction in the custom function. An ELSE command separates the command that is performed if the expression is True from the command that is performed if the expression is False. The macro code is terminated by an END IF command.

To set the custom function so that your salespeople get 4.5 percent of total sales for five or fewer items sold and 5 percent of total sales for more than five items sold, you enter the following lines of code underneath the line with the Function command:

```
If ItemsSold <= 5 Then
    Commission = TotalSales * 0.045
Else
    Commission = TotalSales * 0.05
End If
```

Figure 61-1 shows you how the code for this user-defined function appears in the Code window for its

module sheets. Note that I have added a comment line (prefaced by an apostrophe that prevents Excel from trying to execute the text that follows on that line) directly beneath the Function statement that documents the purpose of the custom function. The indents that you see for the IF...END IF statements in the code are made with the Tab key to make it easy to differentiate the parts of the IF construction. The first formula, Commission = TotalSales * 0.045, is used when the IF expression ItemsSold <= 5 is found to be True. Otherwise, the second formula underneath the Else command, Commission = TotalSales * 0.05, is used.

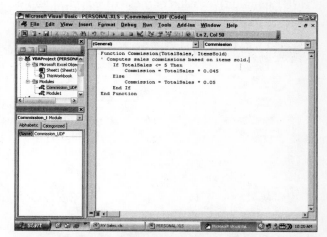

• **Figure 61-1: Entering the code for the Commission function the Personal Macro Workbook.**

After entering the definition for your user-defined function, save it by choosing File⇨Save on the Visual Basic Editor menu bar or by pressing Ctrl+S. Then click the View Microsoft Excel button on the Editor's Standard toolbar to return to the worksheet where you can try out your new custom function.

 If you want to be able to use your user-defined function in any spreadsheet you create, be sure that you select VBAProject(personal.xls) in the Project Explorer window before you open a new module and define the custom function there.

The really nice thing about custom functions is that you can use Excel's Insert Function button on the Formula bar to use them in your spreadsheets. Figures 61-2 and 61-3 illustrate how easy it is to enter the custom Commission function in a worksheet with the Insert Function feature.

Figure 61-2 shows a worksheet that contains a table with the April 2004 RV sales for three salespeople: Fred, Holly, and Jack. For this sample worksheet, I used the Automatic Subtotals feature (Technique 35) to compute both the monthly total sales (with the SUM function) and the number of sales (with the COUNT function) for each of these three salespeople.

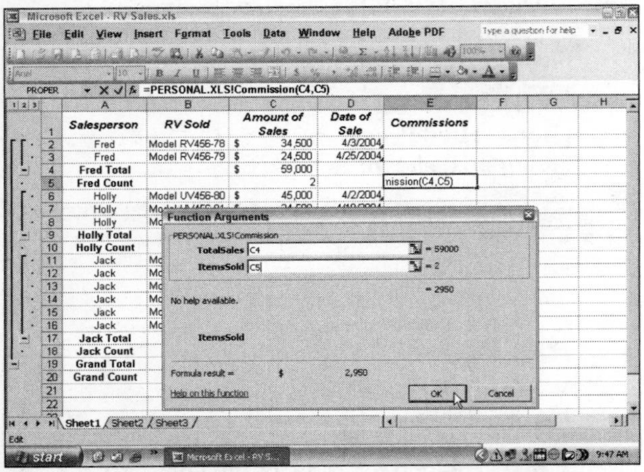

• **Figure 61-2:** Entering the arguments for the custom Commission function.

To use the custom Commission function to compute the sales commissions for all the salespeople, I click the Insert Function button on the Formula bar to open the Insert Function dialog box, where I select the User Defined category and then select PERSONAL. XLS!Commission function from the Select a Function list. Excel then opens the Function Arguments dialog box (shown in Figure 61-2), where I supply the necessary arguments for this custom function.

Figure 61-3 shows the sample RV Sales worksheet after using the custom Commission function to calculate the sales commissions for all three salespeople.

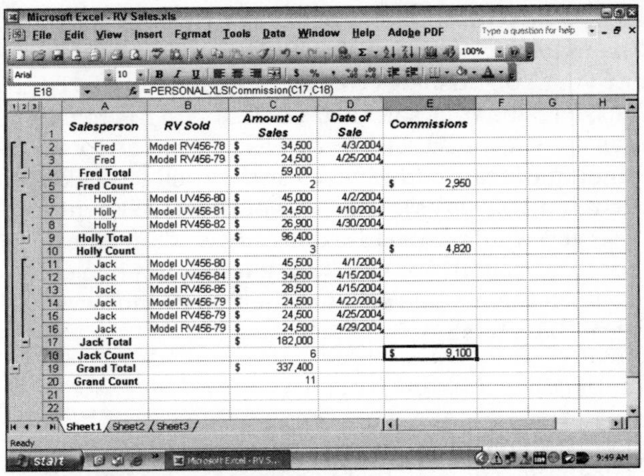

• **Figure 61-3:** Sample worksheet after using the custom function to calculate the sales commissions.

Saving Custom Functions in an Excel Add-in

The only limitation to user-defined functions is that when you enter them directly into a cell (without the use of the Insert Function dialog box), you must preface their function names with their filenames. For example, if you want to type in the custom Commission function that's saved in the Personal Macro Workbook and you enter the following formula:

```
=Commission(C9,C10)
```

(assuming that cell C9 contains the total sales and cell C10 contains the number of items sold), Excel returns the #NAME? error value to the cell. If you then edit the function to include the Personal Macro Workbook's filename as follows:

```
=Personal.xls!Commission(C9,C10)
```

Excel then calculates the sales commission based on the *TotalSales* in C9 and the *ItemsSold* in C10, returning this calculated value to the cell containing this user-defined function.

To be able to omit the filenames from custom functions when you enter them directly into a cell, you need to save the workbook file that contains them as a special add-in file. (See Technique 8.) Then, after saving the workbook with your user-defined functions as an add-in file, you can start entering the functions into any worksheet sans their filename qualifiers by activating the new add-in file in the Add-Ins dialog box (Tools⇨Add-Ins).

To convert a workbook containing the user-defined functions that you want to be able to enter into worksheets without their filenames, follow these steps:

1. **Open the workbook in which you've saved your user-defined functions in Excel.**

   Make sure that each custom function works properly.

2. **Press Alt+F11 or choose Tools⇨Macro⇨Visual Basic Editor to open Visual Basic Editor.**

3. **Choose Tools⇨VBAProject Properties from Visual Basic Editor's menu bar to open the VBAProject - Project Properties dialog box, shown in Figure 61-4.**

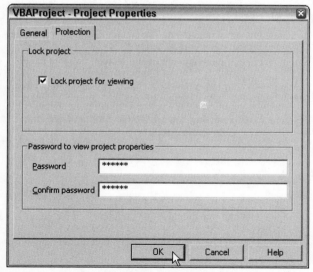

• **Figure 61-4: Password-protecting the custom functions from further changes.**

4. **Select the Protection tab and then select the Lock Project for Viewing check box.**

   Selecting this check box prevents other users from viewing the custom functions so that they can't make any changes to them.

5. **Select the Password text box, enter the password there, and then select the Confirm Password text box and re-enter the password exactly as you entered it in the text box above. Then click OK.**

   This password prevents users from removing the view-protection status.

6. **Click the View Microsoft Excel button at the beginning of the Standard toolbar in the Visual Basic Editor window to return to the Excel worksheet.**

7. **Choose File⇨Properties to open the Properties dialog box, shown in Figure 61-5.**

PERSONAL.XLS Properties

| General | Summary | Statistics | Contents | Custom |

Title: Custom Function for Determing Sales Commisson

Subject:

Author: Greg Harvey

Manager:

Company: Mind Over Media, Inc.

Category:

Keywords:

Comments: Commissons,user-defined functions

Hyperlink base:

Template:

☐ Save preview picture

OK   Cancel

• **Figure 61-5: Entering a title for the new add-in file.**

8. Enter a descriptive title for the add-in in the Title text box, enter a description of its contents in the Comments text box, and then click OK.

Before saving the workbook as an add-in, you should add a title and description of the user-defined functions that it contains. (This information then appears in the Add-Ins dialog box whenever you select the add-in file.)

After you click OK, you're ready to save the workbook file as a special add-in file.

9. Choose File⇨Save As to open the Save As dialog box.

10. From the Save as Type drop-down list, select Microsoft Excel Add-In (*.xla).

This action selects the Add-Ins folder in the Save In drop-down list box showing the names of any add-in files that you've saved there.

11. Select the File Name drop-down list box and replace the current filename with one of your own (without changing the .xla filename extension) and then click the Save button.

After saving your workbook as an add-in file, you need to follow the remaining steps to activate it so that you can enter its user-defined functions in any worksheet.

12. Choose Tools⇨Add-Ins to open the Add-Ins dialog box, shown in Figure 61-6.

13. Click the Browse button in the Add-Ins dialog box to open the Browse dialog box.

14. Select the name of your new add-in file in the Browse list box and then click OK.

The Browse dialog box closes, and you return to the Add-Ins dialog box.

15. Select the check box in front of the name of the new add-in and then click OK to close the Add-Ins dialog box.

This action activates the add-in so that you can enter its user-defined functions in any worksheet.

After you close the Add-Ins dialog box, you can start entering the custom functions that this add-in file contains directly into the cells of any spreadsheet without having to open the Insert Function dialog box.

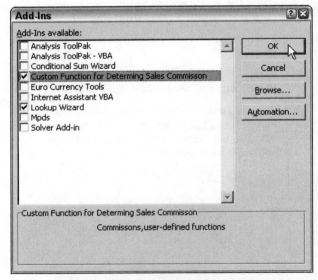

• **Figure 61-6:** Selecting the add-in file that contains the custom functions.

Index

A

absolute cell references, 131–133

accept changes, sharing workbooks on network, 244–245

Accept Labels in Formulas check box, 152

Access, 358, 360

add-ins
  about, 40
  built-in, 41
  deactivating, 41
  free, 42
  installing, 40–41
  online, 42–43
  saving custom functions, 376–378

Add-Ins dialog box, 40, 378

Add Words To, Spell Check feature, 202

adding
  custom words to dictionary, 203
  Excel to Quick Launch toolbar, 37–38
  headings to report printing, 225–227
  images, 343–344
  list of spreadsheets, SharePoint, 333–334
  macros and links to toolbars and menus, 17–18
  spreadsheets to SharePoint, 330–334
  vertical separator bar, 15

Advanced File Search task pane, File Search task pane, 174–175

Advanced Filter feature
  about, 272
  calculated filtering criteria, 276–277
  AND criteria, 274–275
  filtering criteria, 274
  OR criteria, 274–275

Advanced Text Import Settings dialog box, 234

Alert before Overwriting Cells options, 33

alignment
  about, 111
  centering heading across columns, 116

indenting data entries, 112–113
  nonstandard vertical, 113
  Orientation, 112
  Right-to-Left, 112
  rotating text entries, 113–114
  shrinking text to fit in cells, 115–116
  styles, 92
  Text Alignment, 111
  Text Control, 112
  text wrap within cells, 114–115

Alignment tab, Format Cells dialog box, 112

All Hidden button, 109

All Programs menu, 39

Allow Cell Drag and Drop option, 33

Always Show Full Menus check box, 14

ampersand, 18, 356

Analysis ToolPak, 41

Analysis ToolPak VBA, 41

AND criteria, Advanced Filter feature, 274–275

Apply Names feature, 146

applying predefined styles, 93

arranged workspace, 19

array formulas
  about, 137–140
  editing, 140

Assign Hyperlink dialog box, 18

Assign Macro dialog box, 18

assigning
  hot keys, 17
  passwords for spreadsheets, 207–209
  range names to constants, 144

auto-hiding Windows taskbar, 9

AutoComplete, Edit settings, 32

AutoCorrect
  about, 58
  hyperlinks, 59–60
  settings, 58–59
  Smart Tags, 60–61
  Spell Check feature, 203

AutoFill
    about, 67
    copying entries, 69–70
    custom lists, 71
    data entry, 67–71
    incremental entries, 70
    numbered series, 69
    series, 68
AutoFill Options button, 69
AutoFilter
    about, 267–268
    customizing settings, 270–271
    saving subsets, 269
    top 10 list, 268–269
AutoFormat As You Type, 58
AutoFormat range formatting, 87–89
automated lookups
    about, 349
    single table value, 349–352
    two-way in data table, 352–354
automatic hyperlinks setting, 59–60
AutoRecover settings, changing, 25–26
AutoSelect, 54–55
AutoShapes button, 345
AVERAGE function, 193, 195

B

Basic File Search, File Search task pane, 172–173
BASIC programming language, 365
blank worksheets, 8
Boolean logic filtering, 274–275
Border styles, 92
built-in add-in programs, 41
buttons
    All Hidden button, 109
    AutoFill Options button, 69
    AutoShapes button, 345
    Column Level button, 192
    Criteria button, 258
    Custom Button, 17
    Decrease Decimal button, 93
    deleting from toolbar, 15
    Draw button, 345
    Import button, 71
    Insert Diagram button, 347
    Insert Function button,150–152
    Insert Hyperlink button, 318
    Last Tab button, 50
    Merge and Center button, 116
    Next Comment button, 251
    Next Group button, 50
    Organization Chart button, 347
    Previous Comment button, 251
    Print Preview button, 30
    repositioning, 16
    ScreenTip button, 318
    Speak Cells button, 83
    Trace Error button, 162
    Trace Precedents button, 160

C

calculated fields
    about, 255
    pivot tables, 297–298
calculated filtering criteria, Advanced Filter, 276–277
Calculation tab, 163
capturing information, Web Query, 310–313
case-related text functions, 355–356
Category fields, summary data, 24
cell pointer
    direction, 32
    Edit settings, 32
    Speech Recognition feature, 340–341
cell selections
    about, 53–54
    AutoSelect, 54–55
    big, 56–57
    columns, 56
    complete columns, 56
    Go To feature, 55–56
    multiple worksheets, 57
    rows, 56
    sequential data, 54
    worksheets, 56
Cell Value Is, conditional formatting, 98
cells
    copying formatting, 89
    deleting, 187–188
    existing range, 187–188
    inserting, 187–188
    reference destination, 318
centering heading across columns, 116

changes from different users, sharing workbooks on network, 243–245
changing
    AutoRecover settings, worksheets, 25–26
    passwords, 210–211
    scale printing, 224–225
    tracking, sharing workbooks on network, 241–243
Character Map program, 104
Chart Options dialog box, 127
Chart Wizard, 119–122
Chart Wizard dialog box, 120–121
charts
    about, 117
    Chart Wizard, 119–122
    embedded charts, 121–122
    formatting axes, 125–127
    headings, 119, 123–125
    instant, 117–119
    plotted data, 127–128
    printing in reports, 228–229
    repositioning, 122
    resizing, 122
    scaling axes, 125–127
    titles, 119, 123–125
check boxes
    Accept Labels in Formulas, 152
    Always Show Full Menus, 14
    Enable Background Error Checking, 29
    Merge Cells, 116
    Move Selection After Enter, 32
    Prompt for Workbook Properties, 24
    Show Quick Launch, 37
Circle Invalid Data, Formula Auditing toolbar, 159
circular references, 163
Clear Validation Circles, Formula Auditing toolbar, 159
Clip Art task pane, 342–343
Clipboard, copying to, 34
Close Side by Side, Compare Side by Side feature, 185
Clustered Bar charts, 123
Clustered Column charts, 125
clustered column charts, 118
codes
    headers and footers, 226
    number formats, 103–104
Column Level button, 192

columns
    about, 8
    copying widths, 90
    headings names, 142–143
    Inserting, 49
    sorting in data list, 266
    widths, 221
comma, 234
Comma (0) style, 93
Comma style, 93
Commands tab, 14, 15
comments, workbook
    deleting, 249–250
    editing, 248–249
    formatting, 248–249
    showing, 248
Compare Side by Side feature
    about, 184
    Close Side by Side, 185
    Reset Window Position, 185
    Synchronous Scrolling, 185
comparing
    sheets in same workbook, 184–185
    sheets in separate workbooks, 185–186
concatenating, 356
Condition, Search For, 175
conditional formatting
    about, 97
    Cell Value Is, 98
    criteria, 98
    finding cells, 100
    Formula Is, 98
    number formats, 105–106
    outstanding errors, 100–101
    two conditions, 99–100
Conditional Formatting dialog box, 98
Conditional Formatting features, 29–30
Conditional Sum Wizard, 41
conflict resolution worksheet style, 243–244
Connect to Share dialog box, 334
consolidated data linking, 197–198
Consolidation feature
    about, 195
    data by category, 197
    data by position, 195–197
    linking consolidated data, 197–198
constants, assigning range names, 144

converting existing list, 329
Copy To range, 275
copying
    absolute cell references, 131–133
    cell formatting, 89
    to Clipboard, 34
    column widths, 90
    with Ctrl key, 33
    data validation settings, 74–75
    dimensions, 133–135
    entries, AutoFill, 69–70
    formulas, 131–136
    range formatting, 90–91
    relative cell references, 131–133
COUNT function, 193, 195
COUNTA function, 195
crashes, computer, 26
Create List dialog box, 326
Create Names dialog box, 142
criteria
    conditional formatting, 98
    data validation, 75
Criteria button, 258
Criteria data form, 260
Ctrl key
    copying with, 33
    moving cell pointer with, 48–49
Currency (0) style, 93
Currency style, 93
Custom AutoFilter, 270–271
Custom Button, 17
custom dialog box macros, 371–373
custom display settings saving, 11–12
custom functions
    about, 374
    creating, 374–376
    saving in add-ins, 376–378
custom lists, AutoFill, 71
custom menus
    creating, 16–17
    hyperlinks, 321–322
custom number formats, 102–106
Custom Settings tab, 73
custom toolbars
    creating, 16–17
    hyperlinks, 321–322
Custom View feature, 180–181

CUSTOM.DIC, 203
Customize dialog box, 14
customizing
    menus, 13–18
    predefined styles, 94
    settings, AutoFilter, 270–271
    Spell Check feature, 202–203
    toolbars, 13–18, 14–16
    worksheet gridlines, 11

D

data
    by category, Consolidation feature, 197
    on different worksheets, 182
    by position, Consolidation feature, 195–197
data entry
    about, 58, 62
    AutoCorrect, 58–61
    AutoFill, 67–71
    Group mode, 65–66
    hands-free, 337–339
    preselect ranges, 63–65
    same entry in many places, 62–63
data forms
    adding new records, 257–258
    creating, 255–260
    editing records, 259
    finding records, 258–259
    navigating, 256–257
    removing records, 260
data lists
    about, 255
    adding new records, 257–258
    creating, 255–260
    editing records, 259
    filtering, 267–271
    finding records, 258–259
    removing records, 260
    statistics, 277–279
data sharing
    about, 230
    embedding Excel data in Office documents, 235–237
    importing text files, 232–235
    swapping data via Clipboard, 230–232
data source definition, 358–360

Data Table feature
  about, 280
  one-variable, 280–282
  two-variable, 282–283
  two-way automated lookup, 352–354
data validation
  about, 72
  copying data validation settings, 74–75
  criteria, 75
  drop-down list, 73–74
  error alert message, 76–77
  finding cells, 75
  input message, 75–76
  Settings tab, 72–73
database queries, import data from external
    database, 360–364
Date, Settings tab, 73
dates
  AutoFill, 68
  errors, 28
  formulas, 164–166
DAVERAGE function, 277–279
days, AutoFill, 68
DCOUNT function, 277–279
deactivating add-ins, 41
decimal places, numerical entry, 79–80
decimal Settings tab, 72
Decrease Decimal button, 93
Default File Location, 23–24
deleting
  buttons from toolbar, 15
  cells in existing range, 187–188
  columns, Excel 2003 lists, 329
  comments, workbook, 249–250
  lists, 329
  passwords, 210–211
  rows, Excel 2003 lists, 329
  rows and columns, 188–189
  vertical separator bar, 15
  worksheet protection, 213–214
  worksheets, 190
deletion editing
  about, 187
  deleting cells in existing range, 187–188
  deleting rows and columns, 188–189
  deleting worksheets, 190
delimited files, 232

dependents, 158
desktop shortcut, program startup, 36–37
destinations, hyperlinks, 318
Diagram Gallery dialog box, 348
diagrams, drawing, 347–348
dialog boxes
  Add-Ins dialog box, 40, 378
  Advanced Text Import Settings, 234
  Assign Hyperlink, 18
  Assign Macro, 18
  Chart Options, 127
  Chart Wizard, 120–121
  Conditional Formatting, 98
  Connect to Share, 334
  Create List, 326
  Create Names, 142
  custom, 371–373
  Customize, 14
  Diagram Gallery, 348
  Edit WordArt Text, 347
  Error Checking, 163
  File Properties, 24
  Filter Data, 361
  Format Cells, 30, 102, 112
  Go To, 51
  Go To Special, 100
  Hyperlink, 38
  ODBC Microsoft Access Setup, 360
  Open, 175–176
  Options, 21, 25
  Paste Special, 91
  Protect Sheet, 212
  Protect Workbook, 217
  Rearrange Commands, 15–16
  Save Workspace, 21
  Scenario Summary, 287
  Search Results, 37
  Sort, 262–264
  Speech Properties, 84
  Speech Recognition, 340
  Start Menu Properties, 37
  Style, 107
Dictionary Language, Spell Check, 202
dimensions, copying formulas, 133–135
direct cell editing, 34–35
direct precedents, 158
Disable AutoRecover check box, 26

distributing copies, sharing workbooks, 245–246

#DIV/0! error, 154

Document Recovery task pane, 26

dqy files, 364

drag-and-drop

   Edit settings, 33–34

   failure, 33–34

drag-and-drop editing, 33–34

Draw button, 345

drawing

   diagrams, 347–348

   objects, 344–348

   organization charts, 347–348

   shapes, 345

Drawing toolbar, 345

drop-down lists, data validation, 73–74

DSUM function, 277

E

e-mail address destination, 318

Edit settings

   about, 31

   AutoComplete, 32

   cell pointer, 32

   direct cell editing, 34–35

   drag-and-drop, 33–34

Edit WordArt Text dialog box, 347

editing

   array formulas, 140

   changes, sharing workbooks, 239

   comments, workbook, 248–249

   drag-and-drop, 33–34

   Excel 2003 lists, 328–329

   hyperlinks in worksheet, 321

   long formulas, 34–35

   macros, 369–373

embedded charts, 121–122

embedding data in Office documents

   about, 235

   embedded worksheet data, 235–236

   linking worksheet data, 237

Enable AutoComplete for Cell Values option, 32

Enable Background Error Checking box, 29

enabling cell range editing, 214–216

Equal to, Criteria button, 258

error checking

   about, 27–28

hiding error values on-screen and in print, 29–30

   modifying settings, 28–29

   suppressing all error indicators, 29

Error Checking dialog box, 163

Error Checking tab, Options dialog box, 28, 29

Error Indicator Color pop-up palette, 29

error messages, data validation, 76–77

error tracing

   about, 158

   finding original error and fixing formula, 162–163

   Formula Auditing toolbar, 158–160

   formula precedents, 160–161

   tracing formula dependents, 161–162

error values

   about, 27

   hiding on-screen and in print, 29–30

errors

   about, 154

   Evaluates to Error Value, 28, 29

   formula, 27

   logical functions, 154–155

   suppressing indicators, 29

   trapping all types of error values, 156–157

   trapping division by zero errors, 155–156

Euro conversion ISO codes, 110

Euro Currency formats, 109–110

Euro Currency Tools, 41

EUROCONVERT function, 41

EuroValue toolbar, 109–110

Evaluate Formula, Formula Auditing toolbar, 159

Evaluates to Error Value error, 28, 29

Excel 2003 lists

   about, 325

   converting existing list, 326–327, 329

   creating, 325–327

   deleting columns, 329

   deleting lists, 329

   deleting rows, 329

   editing, 328–329

   filtering, 327–328

   inserting columns, 329

   inserting rows, 329

   new list, 327

   sorting, 327–328

   total row, 328

EXCEL.EXE, 36

EXT mode, 54

F

F2 key, 34
F5 key, 51
FALSE condition, 98
field argument, 277
fields, 255
File Properties dialog box, 24
File Search task pane
    about, 172
    Advanced File Search task pane, 174–175
    Basic File Search, 172–173
    Search Results task pane, 173–174
filenames
    destination, 318
    extensions, 19
files
    default file location, 23–24
    delimited, 232
    dqy, 364
    File Properties dialog box, 24
    HTML, 303–309
    importing text, 232–235
    modifying default file location, 23–24
    protecting structure of workbook, 216–217
    saving with summary information, 24–25
    tab-delimited, 232
    turn off file sharing, 245
    XLA, 40, 41
    xls, 235
    xlw, 19
    XML, 309
    XML Data, 313
    XML Schema, 313
    XML Transform, 313
    xsd, 313
    xsl, 313
Fill handle, 68
Fill Series, 69
Filter Data dialog box, 361
filtering
    advanced, 272–277
    criteria, Advanced Filter, 274
    data lists, 267–271
    Excel 2003 lists, 327–328

Find and Replace feature
    about, 199–201
    Formulas and Values Look In option, 201
finding
    cells, conditional formatting, 100
    cells, data validation, 75
    original error and fixing formula, 162–163
FIX, 79
Fixed Decimal setting, 79–80
folders, designating alternate startup, 20
Font styles, 92
footers
    codes, 226
    printing, 225–226
Format Cells dialog box
    about, 30, 102
    Alignment tab, 112
Format Painter, 89–90
Format tab, 308
Formats option, Paste Special dialog box, 91
formatting
    axes on charts, 125–127
    comments, workbook, 248–249
    copying, 90–91
    values, pivot tables, 295–296
Formatting toolbar styles, 93–94
Formula Auditing toolbar
    about, 158, 228
    Circle Invalid Data, 159
    Clear Validation Circles, 159
    Evaluate Formula, 159
    New Comment, 159
    Remove All Arrows, 159
    Remove Dependent Arrows, 159
    Remove Precedent Arrows, 159
    Slow Watch Window, 159
    Trace Dependents, 159
    Trace Error, 159
    Trace Precedents, 158
formula errors, 27
Formula Is, conditional formatting, 98
Formula Omits Cells in Region error, 28
Formula tab, 308
Formula toolbar, 8

formulas
  about, 148
  copying, 131–136
  dates, 164–166
  editing long, 34–35
  IF, 155–156
  Insert Function button, 150–152
  labels instead of cell references, 152–153
  pointing out cell references, 148–150
  precedents, 160–161
  printing in reports, 227–228
  range names, 144–147
  replacing with results, 357
  SUM formulas, 132–133
  time, 164, 166–167
Formulas and Values Look In option, Find and
    Replace feature, 201
Formulas Referring to Empty Cells error, 28
Fraction category, 105
free add-ins, 42–43
Freeze Panes feature, 179–180
freezing computer, 26
Frozen Panes feature, 179–180
Full Screen view, 8
functions
  AVERAGE function, 193, 195
  COUNT function, 193, 195
  COUNTA function, 195
  custom, 374–378
  DAVERAGE function, 277–279
  DCOUNT function, 277–279
  DSUM function, 277
  EUROCONVERT, 41
  INDEX functions, 354
  ISERROR function, 29, 156
  ISNUMBER function, 80–81
  logical functions errors, 154–155
  LOWER function, 355–356
  MATCH functions, 354
  MAX function, 195
  MAXIMUM function, 193
  MIN function, 195
  MINIMUM function, 193
  NOT function, 277
  PMT function, 136
  PRODUCT function, 193, 195
  PROPER function, 355–356

  STDEV function, 195
  STDEVP function, 195
  SUM function, 193
  summary, 296–297
  TABLE function, 282
  UPPER function, 355–356
  VAR function, 195
  VARP function, 195

G

General tab, Options dialog box, 24
Go To dialog box, 51
Go To feature
  cell selections, 55–56
  navigating worksheets, 51
Go To Special dialog box, 100
Goal Seek feature
  graph style, 289–290
  what-if analysis, 288–290
graph style, Goal Seek feature, 289–290
graphics
  about, 342
  adding images, 343–344
  Clip Art task pane, 342–343
  drawing diagrams, 347–348
  drawing objects, 344–348
  drawing organization charts, 347–348
  drawing shapes, 345
  text boxes as callouts, 346
  WordArt, 346–347
Greater than, Criteria button, 258
Greater than or equal to, Criteria button, 258–259
gridlines, 8
Gridlines tab, 127
Group mode, data entry, 65–66

H

hands-free data entry, 337–339
headings
  centering across columns, 116
  charts, 119, 123–125
  codes, 226
  printing, 225–226

hiding
    error values on-screen and in print, 29–30
    formulas shortcuts, 228
    number format entries, 106
    sensitive data, spreadsheet, 217–218
HLOOKUP (horizontal table lookup), 349, 351–352
horizontal I-beam pointer, 33
horizontal split bar, 183
horizontal table lookup (HLOOKUP), 349, 351–352
hot keys, assigning, 17
HTML files, 303–309
Hyperlink dialog box, 38
hyperlinks
    about, 317
    adding to worksheets, 317–320
    AutoCorrect, 59–60
    custom menus and toolbars, 321–322
    editing links in worksheet, 321
    following in worksheets, 320–321

I

I-beam pointer
    horizontal, 33
    vertical, 33
IF construction, 155
IF formula, 155–156
Ignore Internet and File Addresses, Spell Check
    feature, 202
Ignore Words in UPPERCASE, Spell Check feature,
    202
Ignore Words with Numbers, Spell Check feature, 202
Import button, 71
importing
    data from external database queries, 358–364
    text files, data sharing, 232–235
    Web data into worksheets, 310–316
    XML data into worksheets, 313–316
Inconsistent Formula in Region error, 28
inconsistent formulas, 28
incremental entries, AutoFill, 70
indenting data entries, 112–113
INDEX functions, 354
information capture, Web Query, 310–313
input message, data validation, 75–76
Insert Diagram button, 347

Insert Function button, 150–152
Insert Hyperlink button, 318
inserting
    cells in existing range, 187–188
    columns, 49
    columns, Excel 2003 lists, 329
    rows, 49
    rows, Excel 2003 lists, 329
    rows and columns, 188–189
    worksheets, 190
insertion editing
    about, 187
    inserting cells in existing range, 187–188
    inserting rows and columns, 188–189
    inserting worksheets, 190
installing
    add-in programs, 40–41
    Text to Speech, 82
instant charts, 117–119
interactive Web page worksheets, 307–309
Internet Assistant VBA, 41
ISERROR function, 29, 156
ISNUMBER function, 80–81

J

joining separate text entries, 356–357

K

keystroke macros, recording, 108–109
keystrokes, moving within cell ranges, 64

L

Label Data with Smart Tags, 60
labels instead of cell references, 152–153
Language toolbar, 338–339
last cell, navigating worksheets, 49–50
Last Tab button, 50
launching Excel on Windows startup, 39
left cell pointer, 32
Less than, Criteria button, 259
Less than or equal to, Criteria button, 259
Library folder, 40

linking
    about, 235
    consolidated data, 197–198
    to toolbars and menus, 17–18
    worksheet data, 237
List, Settings tab, 73
List Data Validation Error, 28
lists
    about, 325
    converting existing, 326–327, 329
    creating, 325–327
    deleting, 329
    deleting columns, 329
    deleting rows, 329
    editing, 328–329
    filtering, 327–328
    inserting columns, 329
    inserting rows, 329
    new list, 327
    sorting, 327–328
    total row, 328
logical FALSE, 154
logical functions errors, 154–155
logical TRUE, 154
long formulas, editing, 34–35
Lookup Wizard, 41, 352–354
LOWER function, 355–356

M

Macro Systems, 42–43
macros
    about, 365
    adding, 17–18
    custom dialog box, 371–373
    editing, 369–373
    modifying settings, 370–371
    playing back, 368–369
    recording, 365–368
    recording keystrokes, 108–109
magnification, 52
margins widths, 221
MATCH functions, 354
MAX function, 195
MAXIMUM function, 193
memory, add-ins and, 41

menus
    All Programs menu, 39
    custom menus, 16–17
    custom menus hyperlinks, 321–322
    Microsoft Office submenu, 39
    pull-down menus, 13
    Speech Recognition feature, 340
Merge and Center button, 116
Merge Cells check box, 116
merging
    different copies, workbooks on network, 245–246
    styles, 95–96
merging changes
    sharing workbooks on network, 246
    workbook review, 250–251
Microsoft Access, 358, 360
Microsoft Office submenu, 39
Microsoft SharePoint Services, 330–336
MIN function, 195
MINIMUM function, 193
modifying
    default file location, 23–24
    number of workbook sheets, 10–11
modifying settings
    error checking, 28–29
    macros, 370–371
    Text to Speech, 84
monitor size, 14
months, AutoFill, 68
Move Selection After Enter check box, 32
moving
    cell pointer with Ctrl key, 48–50
    within cell ranges keystrokes, 64
multiple worksheets, selecting, 57

N

#NA error, 154
#NAME, 156
names
    column headings, 142–143
    ranges, 141–144
    row headings, 142–143
navigating worksheets
    about, 47
    blanks, 48–49
    data ranges, 48

Go To feature, 51
last cell, 49–50
saving cell pointer's position, 47
Zoom feature, 52
negative numbers, 79
network, sharing workbooks on
about, 238
accept or reject changes, 244–245
change tracking, 241–243
changes from different users, 243–245
conflict resolution worksheet style, 243–244
distributing copies, 245–246
editing changes, 239
merging changes, 246
merging different copies, 245–246
setting sharing options, 240–241
Share Workbook, 238–239
turn off file sharing, 245
New Comment, Formula Auditing toolbar, 159
new document destination, 318
new files with summary information, 24–25
New Menu item, 16
Next Comment button, 251
Next Group button, 50
None table format, 88
nonstandard vertical alignment, 113
Normal style, 93
Not equal to, Criteria button, 259
NOT function, 277
NUM indicator, 79
Number of Programs on Start Menu option, 38
Number Stored as Text error, 28
Number styles, 92
Number tab, Format Cells dialog box, 105
numbers
about, 78, 102
codes, 103–104
conditionally format entries, 105–106
custom, 102–106
decimal places, 79–80
Euro Currency formats, 109–110
hide entries, 106
ISNUMBER function, 80–81
stored as text, 28
to styles, 107–109
to toolbars, 107–109
numeric keypad, 78–79

O

objects drawing, 344–348
ODBC Microsoft Access Setup dialog box, 360
Office Web Components, 307
on-screen error values hiding, 29–30
one-dimensional array ranges, 138
one-variable Data Table, 280–282
Open dialog box Search, 175–176
opening
panes, worksheet windows, 182–184
password-protected workbook, 209–210
spreadsheet workspace on launch, 20–21
spreadsheets, SharePoint Web sites, 332–333
Options dialog box, 21, 25
OR criteria, Advanced Filter feature, 274–275
Organization Chart button, 347
organization charts, drawing, 347–348
Orientation alignment, 112
Outline feature
about, 191
adding levels to table or list, 191–193
Subtotal feature, 193–194
Outlook e-mail, 251
outstanding errors, 100–101

P

Page Break Preview feature, 223–224
page breaks, 222–224
page settings, 221–222
Page Setup dialog box, 30, 229
palettes, Error Indicator Color pop-up, 29
parsed data, 234
Password text box, 377
passwords
assigning for spreadsheets, 207–209
changing, 210–211
deleting, 210–211
opening password-protected workbook, 209–210
spreadsheet security, 207–211
Paste Link option, 237
Paste Special dialog box, 91
pathnames
about, 23
installing add-in programs, 40

Patterns styles, 92
Percent style, 93
period, 234
Personal Macro Workbook, 370
pinning Excel to Start menu, 38–39
pivot charts, 298–299
pivot tables
    about, 291
    calculated fields, 297–298
    creating, 291–298
    formatting values, 295–296
    pivoting fields, 294–295
    summary functions, 296–297
pivoting fields, 294–295
Places text box, 79
playing back macros, 368–369
plotted data charts, 127–128
PMT function, 136
pointing out cell references, 148–150
preselect ranges, 63–65
Previous Comment button, 251
Print Preview, 219–222
Print Preview button, 30
printing
    about, 219
    adding headings to report, 225–227
    changing scale, 224–225
    charts in reports, 228–229
    error values hiding, 29–30
    formulas in reports, 227–228
    headers and footers, 225–226
    margins and column widths, 221
    page breaks, 222–224
    page settings, 221–222
    Print Preview, 219–222
    titles on every page, 226–227
PRODUCT function, 193, 195
Production styles, 92
program startup
    about, 36
    adding Excel to Quick Launch toolbar, 37–38
    desktop shortcut, 36–37
    launching Excel on Windows startup, 39
    pinning Excel to Start menu, 38–39
    streamlining, 36–39
Prompt for Workbook Properties check box, 24
PROPER function, 355–356

Property Search For, 175
Protect Sheet dialog box, 212
Protect Workbook dialog box, 217
protecting structure of workbook file, 216–217
Protection tab, 377
publishing Excel lists to SharePoint Web sites, 334–336
pull-down menus, 13

Q

queries
    creating database query, 360–364
    data source definition, 358–360
    import data from external database, 358–364, 360–364
Query Wizard, 360–364
Quick Launch toolbar, adding Excel to, 37–38

R

range formatting
    about, 87
    AutoFormat, 87–89
    copying formatting, 90–91
    Format Painter, 89–90
range names
    about, 141
    assigning to constants, 144
    destination, 318
    formulas, 144–147
    spanning sheets, 143–144
rearrange buttons from toolbar, 15
Rearrange Commands dialog box, 15–16
Recently Used file list, 171–172
recently used workbooks, 171–172
recognizers, 60
recording
    keystroke macros, 108–109
    macros, 365–368
Recovered version of software, 26
#REF, 156
references
    absolute cell references, 131–133
    3-D references, 143

reject changes, sharing workbooks on network, 244–245

relative cell references, 131–133

Remove All Arrows, Formula Auditing toolbar, 159

Remove Dependent Arrows, Formula Auditing toolbar, 159

Remove Precedent Arrows, Formula Auditing toolbar, 159

Replace Contents alert box, 33

replacing formulas with results, 357

reply with changes, workbook review, 250

repositioning
    buttons, 16
    charts, 122

Reset Window Position, Compare Side by Side feature, 185

resizing charts, 122

Results Should Be, 173

right cell pointer, 32

Right-to-Left alignment, 112

rotating text entries, 113–114

rows
    about, 8
    deleting, 188–189
    inserting, 49, 188–189
    name headings, 142–143

S

Save tab, Options dialog box, 25

Save Workspace dialog box, 21

saving
    about, 22
    changing AutoRecover settings, 25–26
    custom display settings, 11–12
    custom functions in add-ins, 376–378
    modifying default file location, 23–24
    new files with summary information, 24–25
    saving new files with summary information, 24–25
    spreadsheet workspace, 19–20
    worksheets, 22–26

scaling axes charts, 125–127

Scenario Name text box, 285

Scenario Summary dialog box, 287

scenarios, what-if analysis, 284–287

screen display
    about, 7

customizing worksheet display, 9–11
    saving custom display settings, 11–12
    standard display settings, 8
    switching to full screen, 8–9

ScreenTip button, 318

Search, Open dialog box, 175–176

Search For
    Condition, 175
    Property, 175
    Value, 175

Search In combo box, 173

Search Results dialog box, 37

Search Results task pane, 173–174

Search Text box, 172

sending out workbook review, 250–251

sequential data cell selections, 54

setting
    sharing options, 240–241
    standard column width, 9–10
    standard row height, 9

settings, AutoCorrect, 58–59

Settings tab
    Custom, 73
    Date, 73
    Decimal, 72
    List, 73
    Text Length, 73
    Time, 73
    Whole Number, 72

shapes drawing, 345

Share Workbook, 238–239

SharePoint Services, 330–336

SharePoint Services Team site, 330

SharePoint Services Web sites
    about, 325, 330
    adding list of spreadsheets, 333–334
    adding spreadsheets to, 330–334
    opening spreadsheets, 332–333
    publishing Excel lists to, 334–336
    publishing lists to, 334–336
    synchronizing list data, 336

sharing workbooks on network
    about, 238
    accept or reject changes, 244–245
    change tracking, 241–243
    changes from different users, 243–245
    conflict resolution worksheet style, 243–244

sharing workbooks on network *(continued)*
  distributing copies, 245–246
  editing changes, 239
  merging changes, 246
  merging different copies, 245–246
  setting sharing options, 240–241
  Share Workbook, 238–239
  turn off file sharing, 245
Sheet Name text box, 309
Sheet tab, 50, 309
shortcut icon, 37
shortcuts
  hiding formulas, 228
  program startup, 36–37
Show Quick Launch check box, 37
showing
  comments, workbook, 248
  toolbars and menus, 13–14
shrinking text to fit in cells, 115–116
single table value, automated lookups, 349–352
single worksheets window, 182
Slow Watch Window, Formula Auditing toolbar, 159
Smart Tab, 27
Smart Tags
  about, 58
  AutoCorrect, 60–61
Solver Add-In, 41
Sort Ascending, 268
Sort Descending, 268
Sort dialog box, 262–264
Sort feature
  about, 261
  sorting field names in data list, 265–266
  sorting list with three key fields, 264–265
  sorting on record number, 264
  sorting records in data list, 262–264
Sort Order dialog box, 361
sorting
  columns in data list, 266
  Excel 2003 lists, 327–328
  field names in data list, 265–266
  list with three key fields, 264–265
  on record number, 264
  records in data list, 262–264
  worksheet data, 261–266
spanning sheets, range names, 143–144
Speak Cells button, Text to Speech, 83
Speak on Enter mode, Text to Speech, 83

Speech Properties dialog box, 84
Speech Recognition feature
  about, 337–339
  cell pointer, 340–341
  dialog boxes, 340
  menu items, 340
  punctuation and special symbols, 338–339
  toolbar buttons, 340
  Voice Command mode, 339
Spell Check feature
  about, 201–202
  Add Words To, 202
  adding custom words to dictionary, 203
  AutoCorrect Options, 203
  customizing, 202–203
  Dictionary Language, 202
  Ignore Internet and File Addresses, 202
  Ignore Words in UPPERCASE, 202
  Ignore Words with Numbers, 202
  Suggest from Main Dictionary Only, 202
spreadsheet security
  about, 207
  enabling cell range editing, 214–216
  hiding sensitive data, 217–218
  passwords, 207–211
  protecting structure of workbook file, 216–217
  removing worksheet protection, 213–214
  turn on worksheet protection, 212–213
  unlocking cells for data entry, 211–212
spreadsheet workspace
  about, 19
  opening on Excel launch, 20–21
  saving, 19–20
standard column width, 9–10
standard row height, 9
Start menu, pinning Excel to, 38–39
Start Menu Properties dialog box, 37
statistics, data lists, 277–279
STDEV function, 195
STDEVP function, 195
Stop Recording toolbar, 367
streamlining program startup, 36–39
strings, 199–201
Style dialog box, 107
styles
  about, 92
  Alignment, 92

applying predefined styles, 93
Border, 92
Comma (0) style, 93
Comma style, 93
creating your own, 94–95
Currency (0) style, 93
Currency style, 93
customizing predefined styles, 94
Font, 92
from Formatting toolbar, 93–94
merging styles, 95–96
Normal style, 93
number formats, 107–109
Patterns, 92
Percent style, 93
Production, 92
Subject fields, summary data, 24
Subtotal feature
    about, 191
    Outline feature, 193–194
Suggest from Main Dictionary Only, Spell Check
        feature, 202
SUM formulas, 132–133
SUM function, 193
summary functions, pivot tables, 296–297
summary information, saving new files with, 24–25
Summary tab
    File Properties dialog box, 24
    Options dialog box, 25
suppressing error indicators, 29
swapping data via Clipboard, 230–232
synchronizing list data, SharePoint, 336
Synchronous Scrolling, Compare Side by Side
        feature, 185

T

tab-delimited files, 232
TABLE function, 282
Tablet PC, 247
task panes
    Advanced File Search task pane, 174–175
    Clip Art task pane, 342–343
    Document Recovery task pane, 26
    File Search task pane, 172–175
    Search Results task pane, 173–174

templates
    creating, 11–12
    using, 12
Text Alignment, 111
text boxes as callouts, 346
Text Control alignment, 112
Text Date with 2 Digit Years error, 28
text entries rotating, 113–114
text functions
    about, 355
    case-related, 355–356
    joining separate text entries, 356–357
    replacing formulas with results, 357
Text Import Wizard, 232–233
Text Length, Settings tab, 73
Text to Speech
    about, 82
    installing, 82
    modifying settings, 84
    Speak Cells button, 83
    Speak on Enter mode, 83
text wrap within cells, 114–115
3-D references, 143
tilde, 228
time
    AutoFill, 68
    formulas, 164, 166–167
Time Saving Microsoft Excel Solutions, 42
Time Settings tab, 73
titles
    charts, 119, 123–125
    on every page, 226–227
toolbars
    custom, 16–17, 321–322
    customizing, 14–16
    Drawing, 345
    Formula, 8
    Formula Auditing, 158–160, 228
    number formats, 107–109
    Quick Launch, 37–38
    showing, 13–14
    Speech Recognition feature, 340
    Stop Recording, 367
ToolTips
    about, 27–28
    AutoFill, 68
top 10 list, AutoFilter, 268–269

total row, Excel 2003 lists, 328
Trace Dependents, Formula Auditing toolbar, 159
Trace Error, Formula Auditing toolbar, 159
Trace Error button, 162
Trace Precedents button, 160
tracing formula dependents, 161–162
trapping
    all types of error values, 156–157
    division by zero errors, 155–156
TRUE condition, 98
turn off file sharing, 245
two-dimensional array ranges, 138
two-variable Data Table, 282–283
two-way in data table, automated lookups, 352–354

U

Ungroup Sheets, 66
Unlocked Cells Containing Formulas error, 28
up cell pointer, 32
UPPER function, 355–356
URL destination, 318

V

Value, Search For, 175
values
    Cell Value Is, 98
    error, 27
    Evaluates to Error Value, 28, 29
    formatting, pivot tables, 295–296
    hiding error values on-screen and in print, 29–30
    single table value, 349–352
    trapping, 156–157
VAR function, 195
VARP function, 195
VBA Editor, 369–373
vertical I-beam pointer, 33
vertical split bar, 183
vertical table lookup (VLOOKUP), 349–352
Visual Basic for Applications (VBA)
    about, 365
    editing macros in, 369–373
VLOOKUP (vertical table lookup), 349–352
Voice Command mode, 339
Voice Selection drop-down list, 84

W

Web data into worksheets importing, 310–316
Web page worksheets
    about, 303
    adding data to, 306–307
    interactive, 307–309
    opening, 305
    saving as, 303–307
    saving part of worksheet, 306
Web Presence Provider (WPP), 330
Web Query feature
    about, 310
    capturing information, 310–313
    importing XML data into worksheets, 313–316
Web sites add-ins, 42
what-if analysis
    about, 280
    Goal Seek feature, 288–290
    one-variable Data Table, 280–282
    scenarios, 284–287
    two-variable Data Table, 282–283
Whole Number, Settings tab, 72
wildcards, 172
Windows startup, launching Excel on, 39
wizards
    Chart Wizard, 119–122
    Conditional Sum Wizard, 41
    Lookup Wizard, 41, 352–354
    Query Wizard, 360–364
    Text Import Wizard, 232–233
WordArt, 346–347
workbook review
    about, 247
    comments, 248–250
    getting workbook ready for, 247–250
    merging changes, 250–251
    reply with changes, 250
    sending out, 250–251
workbook sheets, modifying number of, 10–11
Workbook tab, 309
workbooks finding
    File Search task pane, 172–175
        recently used, 171–172
worksheet data sorting, 261–266
worksheet gridlines customizing, 11

worksheet windows
    about, 177, 182
    comparing sheets in same workbook, 184–185
    comparing sheets in separate workbooks, 185–186
    Custom View feature, 180–181
    data on different worksheets, 182
    Freeze Panes feature, 179–180
    Frozen Panes feature, 179–180
    opening panes, 182–184
    single worksheets, 182
    Zoom In feature, 177–179
    Zoom Out feature, 177–179
worksheets
    deleting, 190
    following hyperlinks, 320–321
    Group mode, 65–66
    importing Web data into, 310–316
    inserting, 190
    navigating, 47–52
    saving, 22–26
    as Web pages, 303–309

X

X axis, 127
XLA files, 40, 41
xls files, 235
XLSTART folder, 20
xlw files, 19
XML Data files, 313
XML data into worksheets importing, 313–316
XML files, 309
XML Lists, 314
XML Schema files, 313
XML Transform files, 313
xsd files, 313
xsl files, 313

Y

Y axis, 125–126
years, AutoFill, 68

Z

Zoom feature, 52
Zoom In feature, 177–179
Zoom Out feature, 177–179